C000179354

THE ESSENTIAL BOSWELL

Also by Peter Martin

Pursuing Innocent Pleasures: The Gardening World of
Alexander Pope

British and American Gardens in the
Eighteenth Century (editor)

From Jamestown to Jefferson: The Pleasure Gardens
of Virginia

Edmond Malone, Shakespearean Scholar: A Literary Biography

A Life of James Boswell

A Dog Called Perth

THE ESSENTIAL BOSWELL

Selections from the Writings of James Boswell

Selected and Introduced by
Peter Martin

Weidenfeld & Nicolson
LONDON

For my own Cindy,
The heart of me,
A precious gift of
Love without end.

First published in Great Britain in 2003
By Weidenfeld & Nicolson

© 2003 Peter Martin

All rights reserved. No part of this publication may be
reproduced, stored in a retrieval system, or transmitted,
in any form or by any means, electronic, mechanical,
photocopying, recording or otherwise, without the prior
permission of both the copyright owner and the above publisher.

The right of Peter Martin to be identified as the
author of this work has been asserted by him in accordance
with the Copyright, Designs and Patents Act 1988.

A CIP catalogue record for this book
is available from the British Library.

ISBN 0 297 60718 9

Typeset by Selwood Systems, Midsomer Norton

Printed in Great Britain by Butler & Tanner Ltd
Frome and London

Weidenfeld & Nicolson

The Orion Publishing Group Ltd
Orion House
5 Upper Saint Martin's Lane
London, WC2H 9EA

Contents

Introduction

Who was the real James Boswell? It is a mere beginning to identify him as the author of the monumental Life of Samuel Johnson, still regarded by many as the greatest biography ever written; or as the scribbling sidekick of the Great Cham of the age, the clubbable Londoner who had a knack for remembering conversations; or as the man whose name has become a byword in the English language for people who attach themselves to others in order to record and write up their lives. 'I am a composition of an infinite variety of ingredients,' Boswell once wrote of himself. Elsewhere, in an entry in his journal that is one of a thousand of its kind, he compared himself to an actor on stage, an expressive ego surrounded by many mirrors, each reflecting back at him a multitude of delightfully gratifying, agonising, distorting, warring and apparently irreconcilable reflections. He had an endless appetite for studying them, hungry to stabilise his wild, oscillating, ranging thoughts and emotions by trying to come to terms with what he was and why. He failed most of the time, as we would fail, too, if we felt complacent enough and were impelled to reduce him to quantifiable dimensions. But his introspection, and the compulsive need to write about it, is our literary good fortune. Because he was his own most interesting subject in a remarkable literary outpouring, chiefly in his journals but also in his biographical writing, we have inherited a huge literary harvest. In his journals, all thirteen volumes of them in the modern edition, he has given us one of the most completely described, complex personalities in literary history.

Society has taken a long time to love Boswell. The reasons for this have less to do with what he wrote, however, and more with his behaviour. In addition to the Life of Johnson, he published an international bestseller, An Account of Corsica, about his audacious visit to Corsica to meet the fabled rebel leader, Pasquale Paoli, and the Tour to the Hebrides, his journal of the celebrated journey he and Johnson took through the wilds of the Scottish Highlands. But in spite of the literary fame he won and a galaxy of eminent literary, political and artistic friends, he died with something of a gaudy reputation as a womaniser, prowler of the streets, drunk, neurotic, buffoon, vain exhibitionist, gambler, reckless social climber and irresponsible husband. As his journal abundantly illustrates, much of this gossip about Boswell during his lifetime was deserved. But the Victorians took it from there. Thomas Babington Macaulay, for example, with a ruthless, lengthy denunciation in which he left few stones unturned in Boswell's personality, cuttingly judged that if Boswell 'had not been a great fool, he would never have been a great writer'. For the rest of the century and into the early years of the next, Boswell's reputation was thrashed, even as more than forty editions of the Life of Johnson were published. The publication in 1856 of many of his letters to his best friend William Temple, revealing undreamed of nuance and angst in his mind and character, did not appear to make much of an impact on the hardening public attitude against him. This is not to say that eminent voices were not on occasion raised in his defence. Of the Life of Johnson, Thomas Carlyle wrote, 'Boswell has given more pleasure than any other man of this time, and perhaps, two or three excepted, has done the world greater services.' And Robert Louis Stevenson even raised him to a sacred level, 'I am taking a little of Boswell daily by way of a Bible. I mean to read him now until the day I die.' But they were voices crying in Boswell's posthumous wilderness.

Then, beginning in the 1920s, Boswell's gradual restoration was launched with sensational discoveries in Ireland and Scotland of masses of his manuscripts. In the process he has become the best example in English literary history of how the discovery of personal papers can overhaul a writer's status as both artist and individual, although even today his name conjures up images of immorality, amorality, exhibitionism and vanity. He is still the butt of jokes and the object of disdainful finger-pointing. Many simply do not like him. But the mountains of discovered manuscripts, which include almost all his journals and thousands of letters, reveal a literary artistry of the first order. They also present a man who, although he had an intricate and confused personality, had also a genius for making people like him, a charm that endeared him to or at least enabled him to get the ear of many of the intellectual, political and literary giants of the age.

Boswell was born in 1740 in Edinburgh and died in 1795 in London, only four vacillating, idle years after the publication of his great biography. He was the eldest of three boys. The son of a strict

Presbyterian mother, early on he conceived a fear (especially on Sundays) of what awaited him after death, a morbidity aggravated by gloomy Edinburgh Old Town streets, fears of ghosts and recurring nightmares. 'What a world of chimeras had I when young!' he wrote at forty, 'It is impossible to give a notion of this to others.' From his father, the eminent Lord Auchinleck, one of the fifteen distinguished Lords of the Justiciary and the Laird of Auchinleck, the family seat near Ayr, he scarcely ever received the warmth and encouragement that would have started him on his course through life with confidence and stability. Neither did his father ever encourage Boswell's literary inclinations when they began to show themselves in his late teens. Meaningful exchanges between them would always be few and far between, on literature or any other subject. His father and boyhood tutors bred in him a social inferiority complex that he never was able to exorcise, even in the heady glow of later literary fame. He yearned for approval from his father, for recognition of what he was, but what he received was cold (and often mocking) hostility and distrust. He never really had a proper father and had to find substitutes wherever he could.

Underpinning this recipe for unhappiness and unhealthy intro-spection was a constitutional melancholy or hypochondria, as it was called at the time, that he felt he inherited from his family. 'I was born with a melancholy temperament. It is the temperament of our family,' he wrote to Jean-Jacques Rousseau at the age of twenty-four. For his entire life hypochondria, the 'black dog' or fiend, was his recurring companion, never leaving him alone for very long, deter-mining the pattern of his existence, affecting his behaviour. Many of the most powerful entries in his journal describe movingly, in anguish, this oppressive, suffocating disease. In his late thirties and early forties he even wrote analytical, autobiographical essays about it for the London Magazine, which he hoped would help both himself and the public. He tried everything to get rid of it, at times imagining himself successful in doing so, but it would always return, sometimes with a vengeance, for weeks and months at a time.

This hypochondria marred Boswell's life. It produced a permanent restlessness and volatility. His depression and erratic behaviour mani-fested itself in a psychosomatic illness at the age of twelve. His parents sent him to a spa to be healed – he was happy to get out of the house – and it was here that he appears to have had his sexual initiation. 'Melancholy temperaments are given to love,' he confessed to Rousseau, 'I swear to you that before the age of twelve I felt all that the soul can know of this passion. Carnal desires had not yet their full strength. They would develop in the most singular fashion.'

From the beginning of his journalising, with which he first experimented briefly at eighteen, the 'hypo' produced highly vivid, colourful journal entries. It also produced dark outbursts of guilt and gloom, desperation, self-doubt and failure that still make for painful reading more than two centuries later.

The extremes in his behaviour also became a source of wonder to him. He believed that his melancholia was partly the unique product of his highly-strung imagination, a sign of genius in fact. This became a conviction that he never outgrew. It generated a nervous energy, craving for novelty, audacity, spontaneity and unpredictability, even a brilliance, for which he became known. In the years to come, in London especially, it led him into places and situations, meetings and interviews, that confirmed this notion of himself – 'I hugged myself' was a recurring phrase of his to describe his unbounded pleasure with what he had done, whom he had met, what he was. On the other hand, frantic to escape melancholic 'flatness', one of his favourite words to describe his periods of depression and despondency, he pursued liaisons with women of all the social classes and fell into the arms of prostitutes. He talked to criminals about to be executed, attended multiple executions, drank excessively, gambled and threw himself into a whirlwind of dinner parties, theatre and lingering social calls. All of this could lift him temporarily out of his gloom, but often it only made things worse and he would fall back into the black dog's clutches.

At thirteen, the conventional age for university entrance, he entered Edinburgh University – where he made a lifelong friend, William Temple, his extensive correspondence with whom affords one of the richest insights into his mind – but university convinced him that the legal profession was not for him. He feared that its dullness would bring on hypochondria, and that to practise it in gloomy and (to him) unexciting Edinburgh would be his undoing. So, in exchange for agreeing to study Civil Law with his father for two years and for passing a private examination in the subject, which he did in the summer of 1762, his father agreed to allow him a year in London, with an allowance of £200, to see if he could obtain a commission in the Horse Guards instead of having to take up law. His obsessive need was to get to the metropolis and taste its intellectual and physical pleasures. Two and a half years earlier he had tasted them briefly when in the dead of night he fled from Glasgow University – to which his father had peremptorily removed him because he had consorted with actors and actresses at the Edinburgh Theatre – and raced to London on horseback. Now, in November 1762, coming upon London with a clear head and hopeful heart, he looked down on it from Highgate Hill, shouted three huzzahs and triumphantly entered the Promised Land. Thus began his lifelong love-affair with the city.

He failed to obtain a commission in the Guards – his father secretly guaranteed this by sending a word here and there that he should be discouraged – though he did thrill himself with an affair with an actress named Anne Lewis, who by way of a code name he called Louisa, from whom he contracted a bad attack of gonorrhoea. He had had an affair already with an actress in Edinburgh. Then on 16 May 1763 occurred one of the most famous meetings in the history of English literature, his introduction to Samuel Johnson in Thomas Davies's bookshop at No. 8, Russell Street, Covent Garden. Those few moments while he was drinking tea in Davies's back parlour changed his life forever. For Boswell, Johnson was already a hero, whose *Rambler* moral essays had several times lifted him out of youthful despondency. Shaking off Johnson's famous initial snubs, which were amusing yet brutal, Boswell quickly won Johnson's affection with his boyish forwardness. All of this and much more, including several remarkably detailed conversations with Johnson and Oliver Goldsmith, Boswell vividly recorded in his journal.

Rather than return to Edinburgh with his tail between his legs to practise law, having failed to get into the Guards, that summer he agreed with his father to study law at Utrecht for a year. He embarked from Harwich, to where Johnson accompanied him, a remarkable gesture by the great man that we can too easily take for granted. 'My dear Boswell!' Johnson told him, 'I should be very unhappy at parting, did I think we were not to meet again.' In Utrecht Boswell immediately fell into a desperately severe attack of the 'black dog', one that was sustained for many weeks by his dull, self-imposed regimen of study. He found time to fall in love, however, with Belle de Zuylen (Zélide), a potential dream woman – extremely intelligent, attractive, wealthy and outspokenly unconventional. But his nerve, or his double standard, failed him. He decided he could not endorse her kind of independent thought in a woman, and he backed off. The lingering question, perhaps a romantically deluded one, is whether if he had married this energetic and lively woman, which it seems he could have done, her stimulation and his contentment would have rescued him from the miseries that life had in store for him. Probably not.

After the year in Utrecht Boswell again prevailed on his father to permit him to make his way successfully through the petty German royal courts. From there it was on to Switzerland, and briefly to France, in pursuit of Rousseau and Voltaire. He met and conquered Rousseau and even succeeded in having two or three candid interviews with Voltaire – two literary scalps which further heightened his growing belief in his emergence as a man of 'singular merit' whom nobody could resist, though he failed to win an interview with Frederick the Great and Horace Walpole in Paris scarcely gave him the time of day. His carefully recorded, dramatic and amusing interviews with Rousseau and Voltaire are the pride of this section of his journals, handled with a sure hand worthy of a novelist.

His father was set against any further travels after that, especially to Italy, but Boswell had his way there, too, and before long he was on his way to this land of classical enchantment. His father told him to spend only a few short weeks there; he stayed nine months. 'O Italy! Land of felicity! True seat of all elegant delight!' he wrote. Although all along the way he drooled over the classical Italy he saw, and was inspired especially by the Catholic sublimity of Mass in music and spectacle, at least as much as anything else he wanted to make his Italian tour a sexual pilgrimage. He both failed and succeeded with the allegedly loose Italian women. His great success was in Siena with the thirty-five-year-old wife of the town's mayor. She fell in love with him and he surrendered himself to five intense weeks of 'delicious enjoyment'. In Naples he ran into and hit it off with the notorious firebrand politician John Wilkes, and in Rome he had a full-length oil portrait done of himself, decked out in the vivid colours of his 'greatcoat of green camlet lined with fox-skin fur'. He looks insufferably smug and complacent in it, but this is deceptive. The 'black dog' was for much of the time in Italy nipping at his heels and he was full of ineradicable self-doubt.

One way to outdistance hypochondria was to keep moving, so without his father's permission but with Rousseau's encouragement, he darted for Corsica to meet General Pasquale de Paoli, the island's great patriot leader and rebel in the fight for independence against the Genoese and French. He trekked across the rugged mountainous and dangerous length of the island, burst upon Paoli, and after a few awkward moments while Paoli tried to decide who this strange young man was who had blown in from nowhere, was welcomed in and treated royally. Intoxicated with this breeding-ground of freedom he had discovered in the primitivistic wilds of Corsica, Boswell fancied he had finally forged an emotional communion in his travels. He and Paoli became friends for life. His decision to descend into Corsica was vindicated in 1768 with his *Account of Corsica*, the climax of a growing Corsican enthusiasm, which made him famous as 'Corsica Boswell' and a champion of Romantic libertarianism. He said it elevated his soul to write it. Within six weeks of publication, all 3,500 copies printed were sold.

All heady stuff. He had been abroad for three and a half years, but by March 1766 he was back in Edinburgh. It was a sad return because his mother had died while he was on his way home. He passed his examination in Scots law in July and was admitted as a Scots advocate that month. Rolling up his sleeves and getting down to work, he wrote in his commonplace book, *Boswelliana,* that he told his fellow advocates, 'Gentlemen, I am pressed into the service here; but I have observed that a pressed man, either by sea or land, after a little time does just as well as a volunteer.' Predictably, he immediately fell under a melancholic 'cloud'. 'I am a weaker man than can well be imagined,' he wrote. 'My brilliant qualities are like embroidery upon gauze.' It was a pattern that would repeat itself year after year as he returned to Edinburgh to pick up his practice after exhilarating escapes to London and elsewhere. For all his efforts and imagination, he felt it was as if he were trying to write in the sand, only to have the surf erase all traces of his genius. Nonetheless, as he was an excellent courtroom speaker and did his homework, he was off to a flying start and quickly won the esteem of his peers and superiors. He also earned some good money. 'What, Bozzy! Two hundred pounds! A great deal,' Johnson crowed when Boswell told him how much he had earned in a year.

The other major business at hand was to find a wife. His father hoped he would have the good sense to marry a wealthy wife so as to improve the fortunes of Auchinleck. After a series of comic false starts, and some good reporting in his journal, however, Boswell finally decided on his poor cousin, Margaret Montgomerie, the only woman he discovered he truly loved. With typical Boswellian eccentricity or unpredictability, he decided this on a journey to Ireland with Margaret to visit a wealthy sixteen-year-old Irish heiress whom it seems he could have had for his wife. As a result, when he announced his engagement on his return home he incurred once more the hostility of his father. Defiantly, Boswell decided to marry on the very day his father chose for his remarriage. He labelled his stepmother the 'noverca' (Italian for stepmother) and for the rest of his father's life suspected her of feathering her own nest and widening the gulf between him and his father. His father never invited Margaret to Auchinleck. It was a perpetually dismal family situation that caused the son great misery, not least because there is little he wished for more than a loving and warm father who would embrace his wife and the several children born to him and Margaret in the next few years.

To be the wife of a man like Boswell was never going to be easy. Margaret knew this when they married. The first two or three years were happy and stable enough, but then he lapsed again into 'concubinage', as he called it, gaming, excessive drinking and a generally indiscreet behaviour that gradually shook his standing in the Edinburgh legal world and placed great strains on his marriage. There were violent scenes at home, which afterwards tormented him with guilt and remorse. Margaret was always there, nursing his mental and physical wounds and feeding him broth in the wee hours of the morning. He even took to leaving his journal on tables, deliberately opened to explicit accounts of extraordinary dissipation and immorality as a type of confession. She took it as well as she could, occasionally exploding, sometimes denying him her bed, but in the end always forgiving him.

Hypochondria, moreover, would not leave him alone. Nor would introspection and metaphysical speculation on the afterlife which was guaranteed to bring on depression. He could not wait to escape to London for two to three months every spring during the Court of Session recess, where he could take up with Johnson, other members of The Club, including Goldsmith (until he died in 1774), David Garrick, Sir Joshua Reynolds, Burke, Bennet Langton and his own circle of literary and political acquaintances. And of course there were the endless dinners, prostitutes and executions. It was as if he was launched into another orbit when he arrived in London, released like a coiled spring from a box. Except for the admonitions of Johnson, Paoli (who was in exile in London) and others, there was no check on him there. Numerous attacks of gonorrhoea followed. It was a recipe for more hypochondria, a vicious cycle.

This was on the whole a period of gathering gloom, except notably for the autumn of 1773, when after years of talking about it Johnson courageously travelled to Edinburgh to meet Boswell and embark on their (now legendary) strenuous three-month tour of the Highlands and Hebrides. 'I was elated by the thought of having been enabled to entice such a man to this remote part of the world,' he wrote in his journal. 'I compared myself to a dog who had got hold of a large piece of meat, and runs away with it to a corner, where he may devour it in peace, without any fear of others taking it from him.' His journal for that period is as complete, comic, dramatic and vivid as anything he ever wrote, repeatedly encouraged by Johnson, who loved reading it as they sailed, hiked and rode westward. 'You improve. It grows better and better,' Johnson told him at Dunvegan Castle. But after the trip, for whatever reason, Johnson emphatically disapproved of his publishing the journal and went ahead himself to publish his own *Journey to the Western Islands of Scotland* (1775). Not until 1785, after Johnson's death, did Boswell feel able to publish his own journal of the journey. It was gratifying to him that several of Johnson's circle confessed to him quietly that they preferred his to Johnson's account, largely because it was more about people, chiefly Johnson of course, than places. And, as in the *Account of Corsica*, he used himself as co-protagonist, opening up his character with a kind of abandon. The critics gave him a mixed response, most applauding the personal energy of his writing and the feast of Johnson's conversation but several also disapproving that he featured himself so indiscriminately and, as they thought, foolishly and vainly. But Boswell was following the promise of *Corsica* in refining a new approach to biography and travel literature, one in which personal, intimate detail, rather than decorum and formal restraint, provided the guiding impetus. It was a style that came naturally to him.

During the summer following the Hebridean tour Boswell represented a sheep-stealer in a cause that highlighted his impulses as an advocate toward flamboyant and emotional sensationalism, the same impulses that accounted for his compulsive attendance at executions. Everybody knew Boswell was this kind of advocate; this time, though, he rather went off the rails. Several years earlier he had won an acquittal for John Reid from the same charge with a colourful defence that deeply alienated a few of the justices. They thought he had overstepped the bounds of legal propriety. Now Boswell was up to his same tricks and this time they were not about to be denied their quarry. He knew this and was convinced that Reid was therefore likely to be the victim of a biased verdict, although he had little doubt that Reid had in fact stolen the nineteen sheep in question. Sheep-stealing was a hanging offence, so the stakes were high.

The problem was that Boswell allowed himself to become so emotionally involved in the cause that he permanently damaged his legal reputation. When the Court of Session found Reid guilty and he was sentenced to death, Boswell did everything except tear down the gallows in an effort to save his client, writing to his friend the Earl of Pembroke and even the King in an effort to have the sentence commuted. As the days passed and they waited, almost daily he visited Reid in the Tolbooth, trying to persuade him to confess, interviewing him and his wife, arranging for his portrait to be painted and observing how a condemned man behaved in the eleventh hour. When all else failed, he pursued a crackbrained scheme to have Reid's body resuscitated once it was taken from the gallows. Only at the last moment did he give the idea up. He even went so far as to publish a letter in the London Chronicle attacking the brutality of Britain's penal laws and the bias of Thomas Miller, the Lord Justice-Clerk, who had insisted that no royal mercy should be shown to Reid. For this, Miller's nineteen-year-old son, William, was later poised to challenge Boswell to a duel. 'It vexed me to think that I had a boy for my antagonist,' Boswell moaned, as he took duelling lessons from friends and Margaret wrung her hands with worry. 'What! And make me and your poor children quite miserable?' she cried. It was one of several duels from which Boswell backed down. At home, after Reid's hanging, he almost suffocated in gloom as the 'foul fiend' sat with him. Margaret was no comfort. He noted in his journal, 'I was so affrighted that I started every now and then and durst hardly rise from my chair at the fireside.'

The Reid episode was a turning point in his life and career in another way. It dramatised his distaste for practice as a Scots lawyer and dramatised his deeper interests in biography. It illustrated his capacity to enter imaginatively into the life of another person, even (or in some ways especially) if the character was a failed human being, someone who was either a member of the underworld or hovered on its fringes. 'I had by sympathy sucked the dismal ideas of John Reid's situation, and as spirits or strong substance of any kind, when transferred to another body of a more delicate nature, will have much more influence than on the body from which it is transferred, so I suffered much more than John did.' Boswell's restlessness in the rational Enlightenment world into which he was born is never more evident than in his behaviour in the Reid trial. His rebelliousness against his father, the legal and religious establishments and general social rigidity all seemed to come to a head. His sense of his own inadequacies, his failures, his moral turpitude, his hypochondria, his temper and guilt, and his profound dissatisfaction with the life he was leading all translates into an accelerating rebelliousness that delineates his own life even as he becomes more interested in biography[1].

Beset by the fearful monotony of his life, and the prospect of much more of it except for the anticipated excursions to London, in 1775 Boswell took stock of his life and in a representative piece of despondent introspection wrote 'A Review of My Life During the Summer Session 1775'. 'I do not remember any portion of my existence flatter than these two months,' he wrote. 'I was indolent in body and in mind ... My father's coldness to me, the unsettled state of our family affairs, and the poor opinion which I had of the profession of a lawyer in Scotland, which consumed my life in the mean time, sunk my spirits woefully ... Gloomy doubts of a future existence harassed me. I thought myself disordered in mind. Yet I was able to discharge my duty as a lawyer, wrote sixty papers, though none of them were very long indeed, and got one hundred and eighteen guineas and one pound in fees.' Life continued pretty much in this vein in Edinburgh, together with his diet of debauchery, prostitutes, drink and gaming. On one occasion he drank five bottles of claret, then raged through the streets, hunting for women, stumbling down dangerous steps in some wynd or other and injuring himself. Then he would be filled with remorse and attend church. His temper and conversation deteriorated. Once, in a rage at Margaret's badgering over the increasing coarseness of his talk, he threw a five-guinea note (more than £300 today) into the fire, then quickly plucked it out, hoping that the bank would redeem it.

In London, however, it was a different story, except for the debauchery, and as the years passed, the journals fill up with fertile, sparkling conversations with Johnson and other sharply drawn personalities in vividly recreated scenes in fashionable houses, taverns and the domiciles of the famous and great. There were also opportunities to be with Johnson outside London, such as in Oxford when more than once they were together with Dr William Adams, now Master of Pembroke College and one of Johnson's friends from his student days there; or when in 1777 they journeyed together up to Ashbourne, Derbyshire, to visit Dr John Taylor, Johnson's old school chum. They passed through Lichfield, Johnson's birthplace, where Boswell was able to see his friend, for the first time, in the environment of his youth, as well as interview Lucy Porter, Johnson's stepdaughter, and David Garrick's brother.

By November 1775, with Johnson's endorsement, he had settled on his plan to write the great man's biography. All their friends knew this and that his journal was becoming a stockpile of precious recordings. But he had a rival, Hester Thrale, the wife of a wealthy brewer who had befriended Johnson in his loneliness. The Thrales welcomed him into their house to the extent of giving him the regular use of a room, feeding him and making him the frequent centrepiece of social occasions in their homes at Streatham Park and in Southwark. When Boswell learned to his dismay that Mrs Thrale was herself keeping a journal of Johnsoniana, he knew he had competition, not least because Johnson at times seemed more intimate with her than with him. 'I must try to get this Thralian Miscellany, to assist me in writing Mr Johnson's Life,' he wrote, but she knew what she was about and resisted all requests. During the Hebridean tour, jealously he was struck by how often Johnson wrote to her and how he would not allow any jokes at her expense or idle toasts in her name. After Johnson's death, when she published her correspondence with him, Boswell was acutely (though briefly) depressed at the extent of his idol's dependence on her, which seemed to him to exceed his dependence on him. In any case, the race was on, and in the last few years of Johnson's life Boswell's relations with Mrs Thrale, though previously more cordial than warm – the Thrales often invited him to dinner when Johnson was going to be there – turned cool and suspicious. There were other potential biographers, like Sir John Hawkins, but only Mrs Thrale weighed on his mind.

And so the years passed, with dramatic ups and downs of mood, during which Boswell increasingly seems to have been running in place, waiting for some major, unexpected change in his social fortunes.

His chief hopes were pinned on political office, but one by one vacancies he thought were perfect for him came and went and he was passed by, notwithstanding the efforts of the great and powerful whom he cajoled to help him. These disappointments became the conduits of hypochondria. Self-pity and self-doubt flowed in, with their usual consequences of contradictory behaviour: an excellent and terrible husband, fond father of an increasing family and rampaging womaniser. While affectionately embraced by his famous friends and the London literati, he was nonetheless spurned by his father. He hoped that interviews with the great sceptic David Hume, who was on his deathbed, would yield some last-minute metaphysical acceptance of the afterlife from the philosopher. He craved the lift such an admission would give him. He recorded the interviews at length, dramatically and poignantly, but they yielded no such admission. Instead, the melancholic effect on him for weeks was devastating. On top of all that, in the late 1770s, Margaret showed signs of consumption and began to spit blood even as she continued to have children. His father grew seriously ill, too. There was the suppressed hope of a last resort: when his father died, he would inherit Auchinleck and he could take on the mantle of lairdship and bathe in all the self-worth he was sure would follow. Perhaps political position would follow. His wife and children could move into his paternal acres and the usurping 'noverca' would be banished. The problem with this scenario was that he loved his father and longed for some love from him.

The day finally arrived in August 1782. He haltingly recorded his father's final moments in the room with his stepmother: 'I wished to go near. She said, "It will confuse his head. Don't torture him in his last moments." I was benumbed and stood off. Wept; for, alas! there was not affection between us ... Lady Auchinleck, [when I asked to] see if he could speak, [said,] "There's all that remains of him." Wished to stay all night ... Went home to bed.' He was now Laird of Auchinleck. They all moved into the Palladian mansion on Johnson's birthday, which Boswell assured Johnson was purely a coincidence, 'no conceit of my superstitious mind'. Nonetheless, it was fitting. Life immediately would have improved had he not discovered that his father had settled large portions of his estate on the 'noverca' and had Margaret not continued to cough up blood. He thought he might have a go at learning estate management, and he actually tried to learn something about it, but the thought of staying in the country for weeks and months on end engaged in rural and horticultural pursuits soon enough welcomed in the 'black dog' again. He eventually elected to manage the estate in *absentia* with the help of his overseer and others. That freed him to keep to his pattern of London visits even as he remained closely and emotionally involved in estate business.

This was also the period of the 'Hypochondriack' essays that he wrote for the *London Magazine*, in which he owned a partnership interest. Between 1777 and 1783 he wrote seventy such essays on a wide variety of subjects, including hypochondria, marriage, love, diaries, drinking, suicide, executions, religion, living in the country, penuriousness and wealth, and youth and age. Not especially erudite, they are distinguished by their autobiographical urgency, and while on the whole they lack philosophical depth, many are powerful because their common touchstone is the hard edge of reality, his reality. Like his journal and biographical writing, they reveal character under pressure. Johnson liked them, probably for this reason, and offered to help him revise a group of them for publication. But before that could happen Johnson died in 1784. He wrote on the day he received the news, 'I was stunned, and in a kind of maze ... My feeling was just one large expanse of stupor.' Nothing ever came of the idea of a 'Hypochondriack' volume.

For some time Boswell had been playing with what he called his London Bar scheme, qualifying to practise law in England. His favourite pastime became asking people whether they thought he should or could do it. Did he have the ability to succeed? Would he earn enough to be able to afford living in London? Johnson's death forced him to make a decision. It altered his and his family's lives dramatically because it soon became evident that the time had come for him to write and publish about the sage. The Johnsonian circle expected it. Others like Hawkins and Mrs Thrale would cash in on the Johnsonian sweepstakes soon enough, and his publisher and friend Charles Dilly urged him to produce a 400-page volume in just a few months. He knew he had to take much longer than that, however, years in fact, and would not be rushed. The thought of the effort involved overwhelmed him. 'I was now uneasy to think that there would be considerable expectations from me of memoirs of my illustrious friend,' he noted in his journal, 'but that habits of indolence and dejection of spirit would probably hinder me from laudable exertion. I wished I could write now as when I wrote my *Account of Corsica*.' He knew he would have to be relatively

free from legal duties to take on a mammoth task like the Life of Johnson;
he also suspected he could not write it anywhere but in London.
Encouraged and urged on constantly by his dear new friend Edmond
Malone, the great Shakespearean, who spent hours with him revising,
he decided to prepare his Hebridean journal for publication as a type
of warm-up for the Life. He ended up doing all the work on it entirely
in London, and quickly. But it was painful to be away from his family
for even that amount of time. It was clear that he would have to move
his family to the metropolis.

So in 1786, on the dubious strength of his Auchinleck rents, at the
age of forty-five he abandoned his practice at the Scottish Bar and
moved his whole family, which by then included three daughters and
two sons. This London experiment was by any measure a drastic and
dangerous step that Margaret hated from the outset and that had a
lasting and not entirely positive effect on the children. It was made
even more miserable for her by his philanderings and neglect of her.
She stayed home while he went off to dinner parties in his essentially
masculine London world. London life had always been a bachelor's
life for him, and now he discovered that he could not adapt it to
accommodate family life. His guilt over his behaviour, which he
seemed unable to control, was boundless. He felt himself woefully
unworthy of Margaret and feared he was hastening the end of her life.

Malone was Boswell's literary saviour, keeping him to the Life of
Johnson, making suggestions and helping with revisions. He also admon-
ished him against wine and urged him to stop whining and be grateful
for the positive things in his life, which were considerable. He
succeeded in making him realise that the Life, not political and legal
diversions, not social status, would be his shining achievement, his
claim to fame. They spent hundreds of hours together in Malone's
rooms. The task was so daunting, with such an enormous amount of
sorting, arranging and contacting people for information, in addition
to the writing, that it is fair to say Boswell could never have done it
without Malone. He got on with it, and in spite of a legion of
interruptions and an abundance of mental turmoil brought on by his
wife's illness and disappointed political hopes, made steady progress.
By the beginning of 1789 he had almost finished the first draft. 'You
cannot imagine what labour, what perplexity, what vexation I have
endured in arranging a prodigious multiplicity of materials, in supplying omissions, in searching for papers buried in different masses,'

he wrote to Temple near the end of the year, 'and all this besides the exertion of composing and polishing. Many a time have I thought of giving it up ... Would that it were in the booksellers shops. Methinks if I had this magnum opus launched, the public has not farther claim upon me; for I have promised no more, and I may die in peace, or retire into dull obscurity.'

Alarmingly ill, spitting blood regularly, Margaret could not stay the course. She implored him to move back to Auchinleck and resume his work in the Court of Session. His heart went out to her, he wanted to, but he could not bear the thought of giving up the London Bar or leaving Malone before finishing the Life. Finally, knowing she was dying, in the spring of 1788 he took her and the children (except for Veronica, the eldest, who remained in a London school) back to Auchinleck. After five weeks he returned to London alone. At this point his journal tells a very tragic tale of painful indecision, torn as he was between being with his wife in her last hours and remaining in London where his literary, legal and political hopes lay. When news of her imminent end came to him in London in the spring of the following year, he was in the obsequious service of the ruthless Earl of Lonsdale, who destructively exploited his vain hopes of ultimately getting into Parliament. He rushed home with his youngest son James but arrived too late. As he rode up the house, his second daughter Euphemia rushed out towards them, crying, with the news that her mother was dead.

Gloomy months of false starts followed, until finally in the new year he started in on the massive revisions of his first draft of the Life, only half of which he did with Malone since, in the summer, the latter left for six months in Ireland. It was a cruel blow. Boswell's children were at times more than he could deal with, and he idly contemplated remarriage. He kept up with prostitutes, from one of whom he contracted another gonorrhoeal infection. Perhaps worst of all, Lord Lonsdale was still luring him away from his work with cruel bland-ishments and pipe-dream promises of political appointment. His journal is a witness to his misery at Lonsdale's hands. In Carlisle, where he was wasting time for Lonsdale – against whom he almost fought a duel – he scribbled, 'What a wretched register is this! "A lazar-house it seemed." It is the journal of a diseased mind.' There were lighter moments, such as one in November when he was present at the Lord Mayor's banquet at the Guildhall, attended also by William Pitt, for whom (in a slightly drunken state) he sang, 'William Pitt: The Grocer of London'. Pitt seems not to have been amused and may have walked out.

The old demons of hypochondria did not desert him, however. 'The *possibility of a disturbed imagination* reducing me to the mode of existence in my youth frightens me,' he moaned in a letter to Temple. Suddenly, after years of 'sickly-minded' incarceration by his *magnum opus*, in the spring of 1791 he was finished. The *Life of Johnson* finally made its entrance into the world on 16 May in two quarto volumes.

The book immediately sold well and he became the toast of the town, in spite of a good bit of cavilling from critics and political enemies offended by this ground-breaking autobiographical, intimately detailed, anecdotal biography. Several accused him of intruding into the narrative and of casting himself in the role of a naïve stooge, as in the *Tour to the Hebrides*, to get Johnson to talk. There was a vein of criticism suggesting that his reconstruction of conversation was frivolous. Others thought he was too critical of his subject, too insistent on portraying Johnson's alleged brutality. But the praise easily overwhelmed the blame. He made some good money from it, too, which enabled him to pay off a number of debts.

The *Life* celebrates not only Johnson's mental powers but also Boswell's zest for living, his delight in spinning out stories, energetic and agitated. It is indeed an autobiography within a biography. It should come as no surprise to anyone who has read Boswell's journals that he should himself play such a part in the book. As a boy, what drew him to Johnson was his *Rambler* essays, their attempts to 'manage' his mind with its 'diseased imagination' or morbid melancholy. This now provided a major link between them in the biography. As he put it, the *Life* is a history of 'the progress of his [Johnson's] mind', but it is also a record of Boswell's efforts to be 'healed' by Johnson, to attach himself to his philosophy and humanity in order to manage his own mind. Writing the biography may be seen as Boswell's painful journey through the metaphoric hell of hypochondria.

If Boswell thought he would now be able to live happily among his children, secure in the fame he had won, he was tragically mistaken. The four years he had left were as bleak as any. The anticlimax was excruciating. He could not bring himself at this late hour to take up permanent residence in his Auchinleck demesne, so there he was in London, his children enrolled in several schools across the city, and he making a feeble effort to practise law, still re-enacting those golden days of the Johnsonian circle when the great man was among them. His life in London was again the life of a bachelor, as in years past, but now he was tired and dispirited. In spite of his literary triumph, he felt he was a failure. None of his grand schemes except the biography had ever come to anything. He dragged himself around to 'jovial scenes', and while in them he was a charming guest, but there came a time when he had to go out on to the streets and return to a lonely house. Temple, who visited him in London, was shocked by his lack of purpose and shameful behaviour, with 'no pleasure in existence except the mere gratification of the senses'.

On 14 April 1795 he suddenly took ill at a meeting of The Club, seized with a fever. After a month of acute suffering, he was dead. His friends were completely taken by surprise, as if a bright and warming light had suddenly been turned off. Malone put it best, 'I shall miss him more and more every day. He was in the constant habit of calling upon me almost daily, and I used to grumble sometimes at his turbulence, but now miss and regret his noise and his hilarity and his perpetual good humour, which had no bounds. Poor fellow, he has somehow stolen away from us, without any notice, and without my being at all prepared for it.'

Boswell took with him to the grave the conviction that he had written the greatest book about one of the greatest literary figures in English literature, a monumental gift to posterity – it is, indeed, a work that many still believe is the greatest biography ever written. We should add that he also died unaware that he had written the most remarkable journal in English literature, a work that taken as a whole must be seen as the great English epic of autobiography. Curiously, he emerges from it strikingly modern, a contemporary figure, a man for our own age with its preoccupation with personality. Its journalistic (tabloid) taste for the unsavoury, realistic and sensational; its union of hedonism and anxiety – these are recipes for success with millennium man. As one newspaper commentator put it, if Boswell were living today he would be on television interviewing the famous and great – an eighteenth-century David Frost or Michael Parkinson – an agreeable and brash presence in our media-induced voyeurism. It seems impossible that we would ever tire of him.

A Note on the Text

Most of Boswell's surviving journals, which represent well over 90 per cent of his journalising, have been published in a 'trade' edition of thirteen volumes – begun in 1950 and concluded in 1989 – as part of the Yale Editions of the Private Papers of James Boswell. The mountain of Boswell manuscripts, including the journals, letters and much more, purchased in 1949 by Yale University, resides in the Beinecke Rare Book and Manuscript Library at Yale. In order to make these journals and the appropriate letters that have been interspersed with them as widely appealing and accessible as possible to modern audiences, the editorial policy of the 'trade' editions has always been to bring spelling, punctuation and capitalisation in line with modern practice. My selections from journals and letters have followed the same practice, except where I have felt that Boswell's idiosyncrasies as an author would have been obscured by this practice. The correspondence continues to be edited in the splendid Research Series volumes of the Yale Editions. The Research Series is also producing the journals in scholarly editions. No modern edition of the complete *Account of Corsica* exists, so I have used the 1768 edition of that work. I have used the G. B. Hill and L. F. Powell edition of *Boswell's Life of Johnson* (Oxford, 6 vols., 1934–64) for my selections from both the *Tour to the Hebrides* (vol. V) and *The Life of Johnson* (vols. I–IV). The 'Hypochondriack' essays have been taken from the edition, *Boswell's Column*, edited by Margery Bailey (1951).

I have followed the lead of the 'trade' editions in also using the journals and letters in concert so as to establish a continuity of Boswell's life and a clear context for the selections. Even this method, however, would often have left the reader wondering what was happening, so at the start of each chapter, and at regular intervals throughout it, I have provided short introductions and connecting biographical links that I hope help to illuminate the text. There are a few notes, tucked at the end of this book, that identify people, places and events not explained in the text. If further background is needed or desired, I encourage readers to pick up the 'Trade' editions of the journals and the Research Editions of the letters, as well as the Hill-Powell edition of the *Life*, where they may feast on eighteenth-century riches to their hearts' content. That, after all, is one of the purposes of this selection: to interest readers enough so that they will turn to the complete works for the entire picture of Boswell's life and art.

Finally, constraints of space have made decisions about what to include extremely difficult. Since I have wished to include certain of Boswell's interviews or mini-dramas in their entirety, I have had to be sparing elsewhere. One of the options to this end that I have reluctantly used is often to include only part of a journal entry, or part of a letter. The reader, I dare say, will come to hate those ubiquitous ellipses at the beginning, in the middle and at the end of enticing entries, indicating omissions, and curse the editor for using them. For these omissions I do apologise and hope that the reader will find that what is here will still prove to be an enjoyable selection.

Acknowledgements

For the privilege of quoting from Boswell's journals and letters I am very grateful to Yale University, with considerable thanks due to the Editorial Committee of the Yale Editions of *The Private Papers of James Boswell* and to Gordon Turnbull, General Editor, for his timely help, and for his assistance in scouring the manuscript for errors. I am also indebted to Edinburgh University Press for kind permission to quote from the Temple-Boswell correspondence. Oxford University Press has allowed me to quote from the six-volume Hill-Powell edition of *Boswell's Life of Johnson* for selections from the *Life* and the *Tour to the Hebrides*. Many thanks to Liz Helmer for hours of help reading the proofs, and also to Peggy Ouderkirk and Karen Winder. Finally, my thanks also to Ion Trewin of Weidenfeld & Nicolson, who took on the editing himself and helped me through last-minute problems.

I dedicate this book to Cindy, my wife, my heart and soul, and the forty years of love, hope and adventure we spent together. My cup runneth over.

Peter Martin

2003

PART ONE

ONE

Beginning the Journal
1762–1763

Boswell's journals, which he kept over a period of thirty-three years, are the great British autobiographical epic in prose, a unique and astonishing achievement in English literature. They represent and capture the core of his character. With some rare exceptions, he is totally honest in them, so they can be relied upon for sincere and genuine responses, feelings and ideas at any given moment. Their complexity embraces his endless complexity. This is important to keep in mind as we read them because although all Boswell's surviving journals have now been published and may today be read in their entirety, the abundance of misapprehension in popular conceptions of him may interfere in our using them properly, in our coming to terms with who he was and why. We will not always like him – at times, he will disgust us – but if we suspend hasty moral judgements at least we will be responding to him, not reacting to the popular myths. With these journals to read, there is no excuse for misrepresentation.

We need also to bear in mind that in these journals we have a man who has more completely portrayed himself than probably any human being who has ever lived. Not many of us would stand up to this sort of infinitesimal self-revelation and self-scrutiny, either in our own or others' eyes. Would we not be mocked? Would others not be disillusioned in us? How many of our friends would we lose? What would posterity think of us, if posterity were interested? Boswell's compulsion to get his thoughts down almost always prevailed over such thoughts of self-protection. Most of us develop thick skins to protect ourselves from society. He was too fascinated by his own mind and imagination to bother with it. It was a form of artistic integrity with him to allow his journal to be a transparency, or a mirror, for his overactive, introspective, restless thought.

Beyond that, he felt that his life and imagination were not real unless he recorded them. He occasionally remarked that if his journals were to be destroyed, he would in a sense cease to exist. He feared that this could easily happen, which is why he took such inordinate and at times bizarre steps to protect them. They comprised in large measure the substance of his life, the mirrored reflection of his being with more reality for him than his actual existence.

Journal of My Jaunt, Harvest 1762

After a period of intense cramming in the spring of 1762, Boswell passed his law exams and was qualified to practise in Edinburgh as a Scottish advocate. As his father and he had agreed, he was now free to fly to London with an allowance of £100 per year to try his chances in obtaining a commission in the Guards. He had no intention of practising law. But it was too early for London since the fashionable season did not begin until late October. First, he would take a farewell 'jaunt' in September through the Scottish Lowlands. It was a propitious decision because it was during these peregrinations that he first tried his hand at keeping a fully written journal. He struggles with how and whether to do it, beginning first with a short exposition on why a journal is important to him.

PROLOGUE

I think it is proper to say something by way of introduction to this journal; not at all by way of ceremonious formality in order to give it dignity and éclat, as is the case when ladies of quality on a tour of visits are ushered into a drawing-room. But as it is a certain truth that what comes unexpected appears greater than it really is, and as I am seriously afraid that my journal will rather be bad than otherwise, I would not choose to have it considered with a microscopic eye, which, although Nature has denied it literally to man, yet may belong to him at times metaphorically. Indeed I would retract my expression of being seriously afraid, for as it is only intended for the perusal of Dr McQuhae and Johnston[1], I shall be quite easy and unconcerned. Let us then consider the Introduction in another light, which I am positive is a just one. For I would not choose again to be unsaying what I had a little ago gravely affirmed. It has an awkward and ridiculous look; and, not to wander far out of this plain road which I am now pursuing, it may be observed that a man who is found out to be changeable in his opinions, and especially in his schemes of life, is looked upon by the generality of mankind as a weak and often a silly fellow. For with the multitude, obstinate perseverance, even in dullness, meets with more quarter than the most sprightly fickleness. The light in which I would now consider it is, as when a man wants to bring his friend acquainted with a man of genius and finds it proper to explain his character a little, in order to make him relish the sooner. The character of my journal is a very mixed one. As it is written for amusement and in a careless, dissipated way, it cannot fail to be very incorrect both in the arrangement of the subjects and in the expression. It must therefore meet with much indulgence; and, although it should appear sometimes trifling and insipid and sometimes stupidly sententious, it must not be allowed to disgrace its writer. As it is written at different times and in different humours, it will have great variety. Sometimes I would hope it will not be deficient in good sense, and sometimes please with the brilliancy of its thoughts and the elegant ease of its language. Now and then it will surprise with an oddity and peculiar turn of humour or a vivacious wildness of fancy. I have divided it into days from the love of regularity; but these days will be of a very unequal length, according as I find myself disposed for indolence or activity. If it shall give any pleasure to those whom I regard, I shall think myself fortunate. At any rate, I have an immediate satisfaction in writing it.

1762

Saturday 18 September 1762 [Kirroughtrie, the home of Patrick Heron][2]

I was in very high glee and talked away and sung with uncommon life. Here ... is room for a little philosophical consideration. I have felt myself within these few weeks dull, uneasy, and really distressed. Now I am cheerful, easy, and serene; and yet I am neither more sensible, more esteemed, nor more virtuous than I was then. What is this owing to? How powerful is the imagination! What a great proportion does it bear in this wonderful frame, man! Happiness and misery can be alternately the portion of a human being according as the imagination is affected, without the intervention of any external cause, or any workings of reason. Of what infinite consequence is it for us to preserve it clear and bright, unpolluted with the dregs of black melancholy! I am aware that the imagination's having so great an influence is not general. But, at the same time, I am convinced of that's being the case with the finer souls, of which I have vanity enough to think myself one. The discovery of that has not been made without pain, but pain and pleasure are finely proportioned by an all-wise Providence, and I desire to be thankful for my liberal share of the latter. Such an imagination as mine must be gently soothed and tenderly indulged; though at the same time care should be taken that reason remain its superior. It is more agreeable, as well as proper, to have it under direction...

Wednesday 13 October 1762 [Brampton, at a village entertainment]

Little did I think when I entered this scene of rude amusement that the gentle Goddess of Love was laying snares for me. However, that was the case. On the bench behind me sat a young lady in a red cloak and black hat very like, but younger and handsomer, than Lady Dunmore. I instantly addressed myself to her in the most engaging manner that I could, and found her tender enough; and during the hubbub, I obtained from her the sweetest kiss that virgin ever gave. She told me that she was maid to an innkeeper in the town, and that she could not have opportunity of seeing me. However, she agreed that she would go to London with me if I would take her. Dear little creature! How fond was I of her. Punch and the other puppets next appeared, who diverted me much, but my girl went to another seat and when I followed her, was excessively prudish. Whether she observed some acquaintance that she stood in awe of, or for what other reason, I could not imagine; but while my mind was occupied with mingled concern and merriment, I was sent for by my fellow-travellers to supper and was obliged to leave my charmer. This adventure, though, pleased me at the time and does well for my journal.

At supper I fell much in love with the chambermaid who served us, who was a handsome girl with an insinuating wantonness of look. I made her light me to my room, and when I had her there, she indulged me in many endearments, but would by no means consent to the main object of my ardent desires, and seemed afraid of the people in the house hearing us make noise. So I was obliged to sleep by myself. However, I discovered that sleep has prevented me from felicity, for Lord Kames's servant joked me next morning and told me seriously that he saw her go into my room and shut the door after I was gone to bed. This was going pretty far; but I suppose she had not assurance enough to wake me.

Thursday 14 October 1762

We breakfasted at Glenwhelt, a very handsome inn. This forenoon my Lord [Kames][3] and I walked about four miles and had a great deal of conversation. He told me that my greatest disadvantage was a too great avidity of pleasure, by which he understood elevation of spirits and high relish of company, which rendered me idle and made me unhappy in a calm situation. Just as a man who is accustomed to fine-seasoned dishes has no taste of plain and wholesome food ... 'Now,' said he, 'Boswell, take care of splitting upon the same rock. You are going to London. You are very agreeable; your company will be much sought after. Be upon your guard in time. Be your own master. Keep the reins in your own hand. Resolve to be able to live at times by yourself.' In reality it is a matter of infinite consequence to be able to support retirement with satisfaction. I am resolved to be in earnest to attain this, while in London. I shall see how my resolution is performed.

We talked upon books and the inclination which many people, especially when young, have to be authors; which to be sure is an agreeable wish, and if one succeeds must be very pleasing. It is making another self, which can be present in many places and is not subject to the inconstancies of passion which the man himself is. I told him that I should like much to be distinguished in that way; that I was sure that I had genius, and was not deficient in easiness of expression, but was at a loss for something to say; and, when I set myself seriously to think of writing, that I wanted a subject. He said that he thought me well calculated for writing lively periodical papers, and insisted that I should begin at Kames to do something in that way; and said he should assist me and put me upon a method of improving ...

Wednesday 10 *November* 1762 [*Edinburgh*]

I breakfasted with my father, and passed all the forenoon in the house, and was serenely blest. I felt myself easy and content, and considered the many scenes I had run through as conducive to my felicity by furnishing ideas to amuse my mind. I have often found a day passed at home in a careless nightgown way as pleasant as any. About noon my mother and Davy[4] came. I dined with them. I now resolved to set out for London on Monday.

The London Journal 1762–1763

INTRODUCTION

The ancient philosopher certainly gave a wise counsel when he said, 'Know thyself.' For surely this knowledge is of all the most important. I might enlarge upon this. But grave and serious declamation is not what I intend at present. A man cannot know himself better than by attending to the feelings of his heart and to his external actions, from which he may with tolerable certainty judge 'what manner of person he is'. I have therefore determined to keep a daily journal in which I shall set down my various sentiments and my various conduct, which will be not only useful but very agreeable. It will give me a habit of application and improve me in expression; and knowing that I am to record my transactions will make me more careful to do well. Or if I should go wrong, it will assist me in resolutions of doing better. I shall here put down my thoughts on different subjects at different times, the whims that may seize me and the sallies of my luxuriant imagination. I shall mark the anecdotes and the stories that I hear, the instructive or amusing conversations that I am present at, and the various adventures that I may have.

I was observing to my friend Erskine[5] that a plan of this kind was dangerous, as a man might in the openness of his heart say many things and discover many facts that might do him great harm if the journal should fall into the hands of my [his] enemies. Against which there is no perfect security. 'Indeed,' said he, 'I hope there is no danger at all; for I fancy you will not set down your robberies on the highway, or the murders that you commit. As to other things there can be no harm.' I laughed heartily at my friend's observation, which was so far true. I shall be upon my guard to mention nothing that can do harm. Truth shall ever be observed, and these things (if there should be any such) that require the gloss of falsehood shall be passed by in silence. At the same time I may relate things under borrowed names with safety that would do much mischief if particularly known.

In this way I shall preserve many things that would otherwise be lost in oblivion. I shall find daily employment for myself, which will save me from indolence and help to keep off the spleen, and I shall lay up a store of entertainment for my afterlife. Very often we have more pleasure in reflection on agreeable scenes that we have been in than we had from the scenes themselves. I shall regularly record the business or rather the pleasure of everyday. I shall not study much correctness, lest the labour of it should make me lay it aside altogether. I hope it will be of use to my worthy friend Johnston, and that while he laments my personal absence, this journal may in some measure supply that defect and make him happy.

Monday 15 November 1762

Elated with the thoughts of my journey to London, I got up. I called upon my friend Johnston [Grange], but found he was not come from the country, which vexed me a little, as I wished to bid him cordially adieu ... I ... had a long serious conversation with my father and mother.[6] They were very kind to me. I felt parental affection was very strong towards me; and I felt a very warm filial regard for them. The scene of being a son setting out from home for the wide world and the idea of being my own master, pleased me much. I parted with my brother Davy, leaving him my best advices to be diligent at his business as a banker and to make [himself] rich and be happy.

At ten I got into my chaise, and away I went. As I passed the Cross, the caddies and the chairman bowed and seemed to say, 'GOD prosper long our noble Boswell.' I rattled down the High Street in high elevation of spirits, bowed and smiled to acquaintances, and took up my partner at Boyd's Close ... I made the chaise stop at the foot of the Canongate ... I walked to the Abbey of Holyroodhouse, went

round the Piazzas, bowed thrice: once to the Palace itself, once to the
crown of Scotland above the gate in front, and once to the venerable
old Chapel. I next stood in the court before the Palace, and bowed
thrice to Arthur Seat, that lofty romantic on which I have so often
strayed in my days of youth, indulged meditation and felt the raptures
of a soul filled with ideas of the magnificence of GOD and his creation.
Having thus gratified my agreeable whim and superstitious humour, I
felt a warm glow of satisfaction. Indeed, I have a strong turn to what
the cool part of mankind have named superstition. But this proceeds
from my genius for poetry, which ascribes many fanciful properties
to everything. This I have great pleasure from; as I have now by
experience and reflection gained the command of it so far that I can
keep it within just bounds by the power of reason, without losing the
agreeable feeling and play to the imagination which it bestows. I am
surely much happier in this way than if I just considered Holyroodhouse
as so much stone and lime which has been put together in a certain
way, and Arthur Seat as so much earth and rock raised above the
neighbouring plains.

Friday 19 November 1762

When we came upon Highgate hill and had a view of London, I
was all life and joy ... I sung all manner of songs, and began to make
one about an amorous meeting with a pretty girl, the burthen of
which was as follows:

> She gave me this, I gave her that;
> And tell me, had she not tit for tat?

I gave three huzzas, and we went briskly in.
    I got from Digges[7] a list of the best houses on the road, and also a
direction to a good inn at London. I therefore made the boy drive me
to Mr Hayward's, at the Black Lion, Water Lane, Fleet Street. The noise,
the crowd, the glare of shops and signs agreeably confused me. I was
rather more wildly struck than when I first came to London ... I then
had a bit of dinner, got myself shaved and cleaned, and had my
landlord, a civil jolly man, to take a glass of wine with me. I was all
in a flutter at having at last got to the place which I was so madly

fond of, and being restrained, had for so many wild schemes to get back to.

Sunday 21 November 1762

I got up well and enjoyed my good situation. I had a handsome dining-room and bed-chamber, just in Pall Mall, the finest part of the town; I was in pursuit of my [military] commission, which I was vastly fond of; and I had money enough to live like a gentleman...

Since I came up [the preceding year], I have begun to acquire a composed genteel character very different from a rattling uncultivated one which for some time past I have been fond of. I have discovered that we may be in some degree whatever character we choose. Besides, practice forms a man to anything. I was now happy to find myself cool, easy, and serene.

Saturday 27 November 1762

Lord Eglinton[8] and I talked a little privately. He imagined me much in the style that I was three years ago: raw, curious, volatile, credulous. He little knew the experience I had got and the notions and the composure that I had obtained by reflection. 'My Lord,' said I, 'I am now a little wiser.' 'Not so much as you think,' said he. 'For, as a boy who has just learned the alphabet when he begins to make out words thinks himself a great master of reading, so the little advance you have made in prudence appears very great, as it is so much before what you was formerly.' I owned that there was some justice in what he said. And I hoped that a little diffidence would help to keep me safe. I told him I was sorry that my dedication without leave to the Duke of York had been ill-taken[9], and I insisted that he should make it up and bring us together, which he half-assented to.

Sunday 28 November 1762

I went to St James's Church and heard service and a good sermon on 'By what means shall a young man learn to order his ways', in which the advantages of early piety were well displayed. What a curious, inconsistent thing is the mind of man! In the midst of divine service I was laying plans for having women, and yet I had the most

sincere feelings of religion. I imagine that my want of belief is the
occasion of this, so that I can have all the feelings. I would try to make
out a little consistency this way. I have a warm heart and a vivacious
fancy. I am therefore given to love, and also to piety or gratitude to
GOD, and to the most brilliant and showy method of public worship . . .

Friday 3 December 1762

I began now to be much at home in my lodgings and to get into a
regular method. I resolved to want a servant for my first year and in
every respect to be frugal, that I might learn the value of money, see
what I could afford to do with my allowance, and rather live within
than exceed my income. I am really surprised at the coolness and
moderation with which I am proceeding. GOD grant I may continue
to do well, which will make me happy and all my friends satisfied. (I
have all along been speaking in the perfect tense, as if I was writing
the history of some distant period. I shall after this use the present
often, as most proper. Indeed, I will not confine myself, but take
whichever is most agreeable at the time.) I never had a fire in my
bedroom, but one in my parlour in the morning and one in my living-
room in the evening. I had my own tea and sugar, and got in bread
and butter and milk as I wanted it. In short I regulate everything in
the most prudent way. At the end of the year I shall subjoin a succinct
account of my expenses. Sure no minister of state could talk with more
formality.

I had called once or twice and left my name at Northumberland
House.[10] But hearing nothing from it, I began to think that they
neglected me. However, I now received a card of invitation to the rout
on Tuesday the 7. This raised my spirits, gave me notions of my
consequence, and filled me with grandeur. Fain would I have got rich
laced clothes, but I commanded my inclination and got just a plain
suit of a pink colour, with a gold button.

Monday 6 December 1762

I waited on General Douglas, who told me that the Duke told him
that he thought it would not be in his power to get me a commission.[11]
This was a discouraging piece of information. I left him in bad humour,

cursed a state of waiting for anything from great men, and in short despaired a good deal of getting it...

At one I went to the Duke's, and being in a kind of despair, I talked freely and boldly to him. He was gently informing me that the thing was very difficult. To show him that this did not affect me, 'My Lord,' said I, 'it is as difficult as can be imagined, yet I should think your Grace's interest might do it.' (I should have mentioned that I wrote a letter to him, some days ago, very fully.) 'My Lord,' said I now, and looked him in the face, 'a state of suspense and hanging on is a most disagreeable thing. I have heard people talk of it, and I have read in the poets of it, but now I feel it. I have got an independent spirit, and I can assure your Grace that if I had not a good opinion of you as a man, upon my soul, I would not ask such a thing of you. It just comes to this; if your Grace is so generous as to make a push for me (which indeed I can scarcely ask), I believe the thing may do.' I could see that the good old man was pleased with my spirit. He told me that he would do what he could with Lord Ligonier.[12]

Tuesday 7 December 1762

In the evening I went to Northumberland House, to the rout, which was indeed magnificent. Three large rooms and the gallery (a prodigious one) were full of the best company, between three and four hundred of them. The gallery is like one of the rooms in Holyroodhouse for size and richly adorned on the walls and ceiling with landscapes and gilding. The King and Lady Northumberland are exhibited in full-length portraits, in their robes. As I was standing in pleasing reverie in the gallery musing on the splendid scene around me and joining with that the ancient ideas of the family of Percy, my Lady came up to me with the greatest complacency and kindness: 'Mr Boswell, I am very happy to see you. How do you do? I hope you are come to settle among us. I was very sorry that I was not at home when you called. I gave positive orders that you should be admitted whenever you called.' This put me into the finest humour. I thanked her sincerely. I chatted easily. She then carried me to my Lord, who was very glad to see me and very civil to me. This is indeed a noble family in every respect. They live in a most princely manner, perfectly suitable to their high rank. Yet they are easy and affable. They keep up the true figure of old English nobility.

I felt a little awkward this night, as I scarcely knew anybody in the room. I told my Lady so. She said that would go off by degrees. I could observe people looking at me with envy, as a man of some distinction and a favourite of my Lady's. Bravo! thought I. I am sure I deserve to be a favourite. It was curious to find of how little consequence each individual was in such a crowd. I could imagine how an officer in a great army may be killed without being observed. I came home quiet, laid by my clothes, and went coolly to bed. There's conduct for you.

Wednesday 8 December 1762

I sat in writing till one. I then strolled through the streets. I was somewhat dull and thought myself a poor sort of a being. At night I went to Covent Garden and saw Love in a Village [by Isaac Bickerstaffe], a new comic opera, for the first night. I liked it much. I saw it from the gallery, but I was first in the pit. Just before the overture began to be played, two Highland officers came in. The mob in the upper gallery roared out, 'No Scots! No Scots! Out with them!' hissed and pelted them with apples. My heart warmed to my countrymen, my Scotch blood boiled with indignation. I jumped up on the benches, roared out, 'Damn you, you Rascals,' hissed and was in the greatest rage. I am very sure at that time I should have been the most distinguished of heroes. I hated the English; I wished from my soul that the Union was broke and that we might give them another battle of Bannockburn. I went close to the officers and asked them what regiment they were of. They told me Lord John Murray's, and that they were just come from the Havana. 'And this,' said they, 'is the thanks that we get – to be hissed when we come home. If it was French, what could they do worse?' 'But,' said one, 'if I had a grup o yin or twa o the tamd rascals I sud let them ken what they're about.' The rudeness of the English vulgar is terrible. This indeed is the liberty which they have: the liberty of bullying and being abusive with their blackguard tongues. They soon gave over. I then went to the gallery and was really well entertained with the opera.

Sunday 12 December 1762

My landlord is a jolly, civil man. His wife a quiet, well-behaved woman, and his sister a neat-handed, clever girl. They do everything to serve me. Mr Terrie [the landlord] is in a public office, so that he supplies me with paper and all materials for writing in great abundance, for nothing. Mrs Terrie gets all things that I want bought for me, and Miss sews the laced ruffles on my shirts, and does anything of that kind. They have always a good plain dinner. I have the art to be easy and chatty and yet maintain a proper distance. In short, I live very comfortably. I order any little alterations that I wish. For instance, there was no communication between my dining-room and bedchamber. I ordered a door to be struck out, which was instantly done. I ordered some large breakfast cups and a carpet to my bedchamber and a bureau to my dining-room. It is inconceivable with what attention and spirit I manage all my concerns. I sat in all this evening calm and indulgent. I had a fire in both my rooms above-stairs. I drank tea by myself for a long time. I had my feet washed with milk-warm water, I had my bed warmed, and went to sleep soft and contented.

Tuesday 14 December 1762

It is very curious to think that I have now been in London several weeks without ever enjoying the delightful sex, although I am surrounded with numbers of free-hearted ladies of all kinds: from the splendid Madam at fifty guineas a night, down to the civil nymph with white-thread stockings who tramps along the Strand and will resign her engaging person to your honour for a pint of wine and a shilling. Manifold are the reasons for this my present wonderful continence. I am upon a plan of economy, and therefore cannot be at the expense of first-rate dames. I have suffered severely from the loathsome distemper [gonorrhoea], and therefore shudder at the thoughts of running any risk of having it again. Besides, the surgeons' fees in this city come very high. But the greatest reason of all is that fortune, or rather benignant Venus, has smiled upon me and favoured me so far that I have had the most delicious intrigues with women of beauty, sentiment, and spirit, perfectly suited to my romantic genius.

Indeed, in my mind, there cannot be higher felicity on earth enjoyed by man than the participation of genuine reciprocal amorous affection with an amiable woman. There he has a full indulgence of all the delicate feelings and pleasures both of body and mind, while at the same time in this enchanting union he exults with a consciousness that he is the superior person. The dignity of his sex is kept up. These paradisial scenes of gallantry have exalted my ideas and refined my taste, so that I really cannot think of stooping so far as to make a most intimate companion of a grovelling-minded, ill-bred, worthless creature, nor can my delicacy be pleased with the gross voluptuousness of the stews. I am therefore walking about with a healthful stout body and a cheerful mind, in search of a woman worthy of my love, and who thinks me worthy of hers, without any interested views, which is the only sure way to find out if a woman really loves a man. If I should be a single man for the whole winter, I will be satisfied. I have had as much elegant pleasure as I could have expected would come to my share in many years.

However, I hope to be more successful. In this view, I had now called several times for a handsome actress of Covent Garden Theatre, whom I was a little acquainted with, and whom I shall distinguish in this my journal by the name of LOUISA[13]. This lady had been indisposed and saw no company, but today I was admitted. She was in a pleasing undress and looked very pretty. She received me with great politeness. We chatted on the common topics. We were not easy – there was a constraint upon us – we did not sit right on our chairs, and we were unwilling to look at one another. I talked to her on the advantage of having an agreeable acquaintance, and hoped I might see her now and then. She desired me to call in whenever I came that way, without ceremony. 'And pray,' said she, 'when shall I have the pleasure of your company at tea?' I fixed Thursday, and left her, very well satisfied with my first visit.

Wednesday 15 December 1762

A beefsteak-house is a most excellent place to dine at. You come in there to a warm, comfortable, large room, where a number of people are sitting at table. You take whatever place you find empty; call for what you like, which you get well and cleverly dressed. You may either chat or not as you like. Nobody minds you, and you pay very reasonably. My dinner (beef, bread and beer and water) was only a shilling. The waiters make a great deal of money by these pennies.

Indeed, I admire the English for attending to small sums, as many smalls make a great, according to the proverb.

At five I filled my pockets with gingerbread and apples (quite the method), put on my old clothes and laced hat, laid by my watch, purse, and pocket-book, and with oaken stick in my hand sallied to the pit. I was too soon there. So I went into a low inn, sat down amongst a parcel of arrant blackguards, and drank some beer...

I then went to the Cockpit, which is a circular room in the middle of which the cocks fight. It is seated round with rows gradually rising. The pit and the seats are all covered with mat. The cocks, nicely cut and dressed and armed with silver heels, are set down and fight with amazing bitterness and resolution. Some of them were quickly dispatched. One pair fought three quarters of an hour. The uproar and noise of betting is prodigious. A great deal of money made a very quick circulation from hand to hand. There was a number of professed gamblers there. An old cunning dog whose face I had seen at Newmarket sat by me a while. I told him I knew nothing of the matter. 'Sir,' said he, 'you have as good a chance as anybody.' He thought I would be a good subject for him. I was young-like. But he found himself balked. I was shocked to see the distraction and anxiety of the betters. I was sorry for the poor cocks. I looked round to see if any of the spectators pitied them when mangled and torn in a most cruel manner, but I could not observe the smallest relenting sign in any countenance. I was therefore not ill pleased to see them endure mental torment. Thus did I complete my true English day, and came home pretty much fatigued and pretty much confounded at the strange turn of this people.

Thursday 16 December 1762

In the afternoon I went to Louisa's. A little black young fellow, her brother, came in. I could have wished him at the Bay of Honduras. However, I found him a good quiet obliging being who gave us no disturbance. She talked on a man's liking a woman's company, and of the injustice people treated them with in suspecting anything bad. This was a fine artful pretty speech...

We chatted pretty easily. We talked of love as a thing that could not be controlled by reason, as a fine passion. I could not clearly discern how she meant to behave to me. She told me that a gentleman had

come to her and offered her £50, but that her brother knocked at the
door and the man run out of the house without saying a word. I said
I wished he had left his money. We joked much about the £50. I said
I expected some night to be surprised with such an offer from some
decent elderly gentlewoman. I made just a comic parody to her story.
I sat till past eight. She said she hoped it would not be long before
she had the pleasure of seeing me again.

This night I made no visible progress in my amour, but I in reality
was doing a great deal. I was getting well acquainted with her. I was
appearing an agreeable companion to her; I was informing her by my
looks of my passion for her.

Friday 17 December 1762

I engaged in this amour just with a view of convenient pleasure but
the god of pleasing anguish now seriously seized my breast. I felt the
fine delirium of love. I waited on Louisa at one, found her alone, told
her that her goodness in hoping to see me soon had brought me back:
that it appeared long to me since I saw her. I was a little bashful.
However, I took a good heart and talked with ease and dignity. 'I
hope, Madam, you are at present a single woman.' 'Yes, sir.' 'And
your affections are not engaged?' 'They are not, Sir.' 'But this is leading
me into a strange confession. I assure you, Madam, my affections are
engaged.' 'Are they, Sir?' 'Yes, Madam, they are engaged to you.' (She
looked soft and beautiful.) 'I hope we shall be better acquainted and
like one another better.' 'Come, Sir, let us talk no more of that now.'
'No, Madam, I will not. It is like giving the book in the preface.' 'Just
so, Sir, telling in the preface what should be in the middle of the
book.' (I think such conversations are best written in the dialogue
way.) 'Madam, I was very happy to find you. From the first time that
I saw you, I admired you.' 'O, Sir.' 'I did, indeed. What I like beyond
everything is an agreeable female companion, where I can be at home
and have tea and genteel conversation. I was quite happy to be here.'
'Sir, you are welcome here as often as you please. Every evening, if
you please.' 'Madam I am infinitely obliged to you.'

This is just what I wanted. I left her, in good spirits...

Saturday 18 December 1762

I then went to Louisa's. I was really in love. I felt a warmth at my heart which glowed in my face...

I talked on love very freely. 'Madam,' said I, 'I can never think of having a connection with women that I don't love.' 'That, Sir,' said she, 'is only having a satisfaction in common with the brutes. But when there is a union of minds, that is indeed estimable. But don't think, Sir, that I am a Platonist. I am not indeed.' (This hint gave me courage.) 'To be sure, Madam, when there is such a connection as you mention, it is the finest thing in the world. I beg you may just show me civility according as you find me deserve it.' 'Such a connection, Sir, requires time to establish it.' (I thought it honest and proper to let her know that she must not depend on me for giving her much money.) 'Madam,' said I, 'don't think too highly of me. Nor give me the respect which men of great fortune get by custom. I am here upon a very moderate allowance. I am upon honour to make it serve me, and I am obliged to live with great economy.' She received this very well.

At night I went to Mr Thomas Davies's shop and sat awhile. I told him that I wanted much to see Johnson. 'Sir,' said he, 'if you'll dine with me on Christmas day, you shall see him. He and some more men of letters are to be with me.' I very readily accepted this invitation.

Monday 20 December 1762

I went to Louisa's after breakfast. 'Indeed,' said I, 'it was hard upon me to leave you so soon yesterday. I am quite happy in your company.' 'Sir,' said she, 'you are very obliging. But,' said she, 'I am in bad humour this morning. There was a person who professed the greatest friendship for me; I now applied for their assistance, but was shifted. It was such a trifle that I am sure they could have granted it. So I have been railing against my fellow-creatures.' 'Nay, dear Madam, don't abuse them all on account of an individual. But pray what was this favour? Might I know?' (She blushed.) 'Why, Sir, there is a person has sent to me for a trifling debt. I sent back word that it was not convenient for me to let them have it just now, but in six weeks I should pay it.'

I was a little confounded and embarrassed here. I dreaded bringing myself into a scrape. I did not know what she might call a trifling sum. I half-resolved to say no more. However, I thought that she might now be trying my generosity and regard for her, and truly this was the real test. I thought I would see if it was in my power to assist her.

'Pray, Madam, what was the sum?' 'Only two guineas, Sir.' Amazed and pleased, I pulled out my purse. 'Madam,' said I, 'if I can do you any service, you may command me. Two guineas is at present all that I have, but a trifle more. There they are for you. I told you that I had very little, but yet I hope to live. Let us just be honest with one another. Tell me when you are in any little distress, and I will tell you what I can do.' She took the guineas. 'Sir, I am infinitely obliged to you. As soon as it is in my power, I shall return them. Indeed I could not have expected this from you.' Her gratitude warmed my heart. 'Madam! though I have little, yet as far as ten guineas, you may apply to me. I would live upon nothing to serve one that I regarded.'

I did not well know what to think of this scene. Sometimes I thought it artifice, and that I was taken in. And then again, I viewed it just as a circumstance that might very easily happen. Her mentioning returning the money looked well. My naming the sum of ten guineas was rash; however, I considered that it cost me as much to be cured of what I contracted from a whore, and that ten guineas was but a moderate expense for women during the winter.

I had all along treated her with a distant politeness. On Saturday I just kissed her hand. She now sung to me. I got up in raptures and kissed her with great warmth. She received this very genteelly. I had a delicacy in presuming too far, lest it should look like demanding goods for my money. I resumed the subject of love and gallantry. She said, 'I pay no regard to the opinion in the world so far as contradicts my own sentiments.' 'No, Madam, we are not to mind the arbitrary rules imposed by the multitude.' 'Yet, Sir, there is a decency to be kept with the public and I must do so, whose bread depends upon them.' 'Certainly, Madam. But when may I wait upon you? Tomorrow evening?' 'Sir, I am obliged to be all day with a lady who is not well.' 'Then next day, Madam.' 'What? to drink a dish of tea, Sir?' 'No, no, not to drink a dish of tea.' (Here I looked sheepish.) 'What time may I wait upon you?' 'Whenever you please, Sir.' I kissed her again, and went away highly pleased with the thoughts of the affair being settled.

Wednesday 22 December 1762

This forenoon I went to Louisa's in full expectation of consummate bliss. I was in a strange flutter of feeling. I was ravished at the prospect of joy, and yet I had such an anxiety upon me that I was afraid that my powers would be enervated. I almost wished to be free of this assignation. I entered her apartment in a sort of confusion. She was elegantly dressed in the morning fashion, and looked delightfully well. I felt the tormenting anxiety of serious love. I sat down and I talked with the distance of a new acquaintance and not with the ease and ardour of a lover, or rather a gallant. I talked of her lodgings being neat, opened the door of her bedchamber, looked into it. Then sat down by her in a most melancholy plight. I would have given a good deal to be out of the room.

... 'Madam,' said I, 'I would ask you to do nothing that you should be sorry to confess. Indeed I have a great deal of principle in matters of gallantry, and never yet led any woman to do what might afterwards make her uneasy. If she thinks it wrong, I never insist.' She asked me some questions about my intrigues, which I nicely eluded. I then sat near her and began to talk softly, but finding myself quite dejected with love, I really cried out and told her that I was miserable; and as I was stupid, would go away. I rose, but saluting her with warmth, my powers were excited, I felt myself vigorous. I sat down again. I beseeched her, 'You know, Madam, you said you were not a Platonist. I beg it of you to be so kind. You said you are above the finesse of your sex.' (Be sure always to make a woman better than her sex.) 'I adore you.' 'Nay, dear Sir,' (I pressing her to me and kissing her now and then) 'pray be quiet. Such a thing requires time to consider of.' 'Madam, I own this would be necessary for any man but me. But you must take my character from myself. I am very good-tempered, very honest, and have little money. I should have some reward for my particular honesty.' 'But, Sir, give me time to recollect myself.' 'Well then, Madam, when shall I see you?' 'On Friday, Sir.' 'A thousand thanks.' I left her and came home and took my bread and cheese[14] with great contentment ...

Sunday 26 December 1762

I this day received a letter from the Duke of Queensberry, in answer to one that I had wrote him, telling me that a commission in the Guards was a fruitless pursuit, and advising me to take to a civil rather than a military life. I was quite stupefied and enraged at this. I imagined my father was at the bottom of it. I had multitudes of wild schemes. I thought of enlisting for five years as a soldier in India, of being a private man either in the Horse or Foot-guards, &c. At last good sense prevailed, and I resolved to be cheerful and to wait and to ask it of Lady Northumberland.

1763

Saturday 1 January 1763

I received for a suit of old clothes 11s., which came to me in good time. I went to Louisa at once. 'Madam, I have been thinking seriously.' 'Well, Sir, I hope you are of my way of thinking.' 'I hope, Madam, you are of mine. I have considered this matter most seriously. The week is now elapsed[15], and I hope you will not be so cruel as to keep me in misery.' (I then began to take some liberties.) 'Nay, Sir-now-but do consider-' 'Ah, Madam!' 'Nay, but you are an encroaching creature!' (Upon this I advanced to the greatest freedom by a sweet elevation of the charming petticoat.) 'Good heaven, Sir!' 'Madam, I cannot help it. I adore you. Do you like me?' (She answered me with a warm kiss, and pressing me to her bosom, sighed, 'O Mr Boswell!') 'But, my dear Madam! Permit me, I beseech you.' 'Lord, Sir, the people may come in.' 'How then can I be happy? What time? Do tell me.' 'Why, Sir, on Sunday afternoon my landlady, of whom I am most afraid, goes to church, so you may come here a little after three.' 'Madam, I thank you a thousand times.' 'Now, Sir, I have but one favour to ask of you. Whenever you cease to regard me, pray don't use me ill, nor treat me coldly. But inform me by a letter or any other way that it is over.' 'Pray, Madam, don't talk of such a thing. Indeed, we cannot answer for our affections. But you may depend on my behaving with civility and politeness.'

Here a little speculation on the human mind may well come in. For here was I, a young man full of vigour and vivacity, the favourite lover of a handsome actress and going to enjoy the full possession of my warmest wishes. And yet melancholy threw a cloud over my mind. I could relish nothing. I felt dispirited and languid. I approached Louisa with a kind of an uneasy tremor. I sat down. I toyed with her. Yet I was not inspired by Venus. I felt rather a delicate sensation of love than a violent amorous inclination for her. I was very miserable. I thought myself feeble as a gallant, although I had experienced the reverse many a time. Louisa knew not my powers. She might imagine me impotent. I sweated almost with anxiety, which made me worse. She behaved extremely well; did not seem to remember the occasion of our meeting at all. I told her I was very dull. Said she, 'People cannot always command their spirits.' The time of church was almost elapsed when I began to feel that I was still a man. I fanned the flame by pressing her alabaster breasts and kissing her delicious lips. I then barred the door of her dining-room, led her all fluttering into her bedchamber, and I was just making a triumphal entry when we heard her landlady coming up. 'O Fortune why did it happen thus?' would have been the exclamation of a Roman bard. We were stopped most suddenly and cruelly from the fruition of each other. She ran out and stopped the landlady from coming up. Then returned to me in the dining-room. We fell into each other's arms, sighing and panting, 'O dear, how hard this is.' 'O Madam, see what you can contrive for me.' 'Lord, Sir, I am so frightened.'

Her brother then came in . . .

Monday 3 January 1763

I begged Louisa to invent some method by which we might meet in security. I insisted that she should go and pass the night with me somewhere. She begged time to think of it.

Tuesday 4 January 1763

Louisa told me that she would go with me to pass the night when she was sure that she would not be wanted at the playhouse next day; and she mentioned Saturday as most convenient, being followed by Sunday, on which nothing is done. 'But, Sir,' said she, 'may not this be attended with expense? I hope you'll excuse me.' There was something so kind and so delicate in this hint that it charmed me. 'No, Madam, it cannot be a great expense, and I can save on other articles to have money for this.' . . .

I then bethought me of a place to which Louisa and I might safely go. I went to my good friend Hayward's at the Black Lion, told him that I had married, and that I and my wife, who was to be in town on Saturday, would sleep in his house till I got a lodging for her. The King of Prussia says in one of his poems that gallantry comprises every vice. That of lying it certainly does, without which intrigue can never be carried on. But as the proverb says, in love and war all is fair. I who am a lover and hope to be a soldier think so. In this instance we could not be admitted to any decent house except as man and wife. Indeed, we are so if union of hearts be the principal requisite. We are so, at least for a time. How cleverly this can be done here. In Scotland it is impossible. We should be married with a vengeance. I went home and dined. I thought my slender diet weakened me. I resolved to live hearty and be stout. This afternoon I became very low-spirited. I sat in close. I hated all things. I almost hated London. O miserable absurdity! I could see nothing in a good light. I just submitted and hoped to get the better of this[16].

Sunday 9 January 1763

After church I went in sober yet gay humour to Louisa and got her to fix Wednesday without fail as the happy night . . . I dined at home and drank tea with my brother. We were very merry talking over the days when we were boys . . .

[Disappointed by Queensberry, Boswell now pinned his hopes on the Duchess of Northumberland. By this time, however, he had lowered his sights to the cavalry, the Royal Horse Guards, called the 'Blues' possibly because they wore blue tunics, distinct from the red tunics that Boswell had had his heart set on in the Life-Guards. It is a measure of his desperation that he was willing to give up a red uniform and, given his poor horsemanship, ready to grasp at a place in the cavalry. The 'Blues', moreover, were not as desirable in his mind as the Guards because they were based outside London.]

Monday 10 January 1763

I waited on Lady Northumberland ... 'I hope, Madam,' said I, 'you will not forget me.' 'No, Sir,' said she, 'you may be sure I will not.' As I hope to have the honour of a forenoon's conversation with her Ladyship every week, I shall enrich my journal with it in the form of the original dialogue.

LADY NORTHUMBERLAND. There was a gentleman presented yesterday on his getting a commission in the Guards. I thought of you, Mr Boswell.

BOSWELL. Ay, the Guards, Madam; that is the thing. Really, I have been thinking on the subject since I saw you, and must tell your Ladyship that the Guards is the particular thing that I have always been fond of, just like the woman that a man is in love with. At the same time I mentioned the Blues, as to be sure I should rather choose to serve there than not at all. But I beg leave to speak plain and let your Ladyship know exactly what my views are, that in case you did me the honour to put me into the Blues, you might not be surprised or think me an odd changeable fellow if after half a year I should beg to have it changed for a commission in the Guards.

LADY NORTHUMBERLAND. Why, Sir, I wish we may get you into the Guards.

BOSWELL. Indeed, Madam, I should be sorry that you had to say, 'This man does not know what he would be at. I got him into the Blues, which he was very desirous of, and now he is discontent and wants to change.' The thing is this, that I am anxious to live in London, and besides the exercise of the Horse would be disagreeable to me; whereas in the Guards my duty would be quite a pleasure to me.

LADY NORTHUMBERLAND. Indeed, Sir, that is of a good deal of consequence. I shall therefore present you to the Marquis as a friend of mine who is very desirous to serve in the Guards, and next to that in his own corps. He is a good-natured man and is therefore ready to give his promise.

BOSWELL. I hope, Madam, we will keep him in mind of it. I wish I was introduced to him.

LADY NORTHUMBERLAND. Why, to be sure, Sir, I will very naturally say, 'My Lord, you will give me leave to present Mr Boswell to you'; and then you can keep him in mind of it.

BOSWELL. I am extremely obliged to your Ladyship. Indeed, I set a higher value on the countenance you show me than anybody could do. For, Madam, I have the old notions about families. I think of

> The Percy out of Northumberland
> And a vow to GOD made he.

Indeed, Madam, these notions are much out now.

LADY NORTHUMBERLAND (well pleased). Really, Sir, they are too much out, as people show by the strange connections that they make.

BOSWELL. I wish I had this commission of mine.

LADY NORTHUMBERLAND. I wish you had. Could not you have the thing mentioned to your countryman, Lord Rothes?

BOSWELL. I was yesterday, Madam, with a Scotch Member, a brother of General Craufurd's, who is very intimate with Lord Rothes and promised to introduce me. But you know, Madam, there is a delicacy in talking to a colonel when a man is not to purchase, as he gets the profits of the commissions that are sold.

LADY NORTHUMBERLAND. Indeed, Sir, it would be the best thing for you to purchase if you could.

BOSWELL. But then, Madam, my father is rather averse to the scheme and would not advance the money; and by borrowing it, I should bring myself into difficulties. Indeed, I am determined to purchase if I cannot get in without it. But I think it is worth while to wait a twelvemonth.

LADY NORTHUMBERLAND. It is so, Sir.

BOSWELL. I did not know whether or not to apply to Lord Rothes. It is not everybody one would be obliged to. And I reckon myself very happy in depending on your Ladyship, whom I am very happy to be obliged to.

LADY NORTHUMBERLAND. O Sir!

BOSWELL. I did not know but your Ladyship might be displeased at my speaking to anybody else.

LADY NORTHUMBERLAND. Not at all, Sir.

BOSWELL. Pray, Madam, could you do anything with Mr Ellis, the Secretary of War?

LADY NORTHUMBERLAND. Sir, I tell you honestly what I can do and what I cannot. I have asked a favour from Mr Ellis and have not yet got it, so that I have not much to say with him. I assure you,

Sir, I have all the inclination in the world to serve you. I beg you may not judge of my inclination by my success.

BOSWELL. Madam, I will not if it be bad. But I will if it be good.

LADY NORTHUMBERLAND. It was a bad night for you, Mr Boswell, last Friday, as you was the only person that did not play [at cards]. I hope we shall have more company for you next Friday.

BOSWELL. Indeed, it was a little dull for me.

LADY NORTHUMBERLAND. Why don't you go to Court, Mr Boswell? I'm sure that's a cheap diversion; it costs you nothing, and you see all the best company, and chat away. It is the best coffee-house in town.

BOSWELL. But ought I not, Madam, to be introduced first?

LADY NORTHUMBERLAND. You should, Sir. To be sure, some people do go and stand there without being presented. But that would not be right for a man of your rank.

BOSWELL. I shall pay my respects to my Lord Northumberland and be obliged to him to take me there.

LADY NORTHUMBERLAND. He will present you to the Queen. But one of the Lords of the Bedchamber must do it to the King. Your friend Lord Eglinton will do that.

BOSWELL. I shall certainly go there.

LADY NORTHUMBERLAND. You should.

BOSWELL. Do you know, Madam, that Lord Eglinton really used me ill? He encouraged me much in my scheme of the Guards; and when I applied to him, put me off in a most shameful manner. Now, Madam, I would upon no account ask his interest.

LADY NORTHUMBERLAND. To be sure, Sir. Pray is your house in the country finished[17]?

BOSWELL. It is, Madam.

LADY NORTHUMBERLAND. It is a very good house; and then the Old Castle is very fine.

BOSWELL. Indeed, Madam, there are more romantic beauties there than at any place I know. (Rising.) Your Ladyship's most obedient. You are very good to me. I hope you won't give the porter orders to deny you my company.

LADY NORTHUMBERLAND. Sir, I gave him particular orders to let you in.

BOSWELL. Madam, your most obedient. (Shutting the door.) You won't forget me?

LADY NORTHUMBERLAND. No, Sir.

This is the substance of our conversation today, I dare say I was half an hour with her. Her kindness made me very happy. I dined at home.

Tuesday 11 January 1763

I am amazed how I have neglected last Friday to mention a circumstance so very material to me as the payment of my allowance, which indeed elevated me to a most extraordinary pitch. Many a time did I lay the lovely shining pieces upon my table, count them over, put them in rank and file like the Guards, and place them in many different sorts of figures. In short, a boy at school could not be more childishly fond of sugar plums than I was of golden guineas.

This day I had some agreeable conversation with my dear Louisa. All was now agreed upon. I had been at Hayward's on Saturday morning and told that we could not be there that night, as my wife was not come to town. But that we would be there next week and take our chance for a bed. And here a hint or two of Louisa's history may well come in. She was born of very creditable parents in London. But being too strictly confined, she ran off and married heedlessly. She was obliged for subsistence to go upon the stage, and travelled in different companies. Her husband proved a harsh, disagreeable creature, with whom she led a terrible life; at last, as it was discovered that they were illegally married, they parted by consent, and she got into Covent Garden Theatre.

Wednesday 12 January 1763

Louisa and I agreed that at eight at night she would meet me in the Piazzas of Covent Garden. I was quite elevated, and felt myself able and undaunted to engage in the wars of the Paphian Queen.

At the appointed hour of eight I went to the Piazzas, where I sauntered up and down for a while in a sort of trembling suspense, I knew not why. At last my charming companion appeared, and I immediately conducted her to a hackney-coach which I had ready waiting, pulled up the blinds, and away we drove to the destined scene of delight. We contrived to seem as if we had come off a journey, and carried in a bundle our night-clothes, handkerchiefs, and other little things. We also had with us some almond biscuits, or as they call them in London, macaroons, which looked like provision on the road. On our arrival at Hayward's we were shown into the parlour, in the same manner that any decent couple would be. I here thought proper to conceal my own name (which the people of the house had never heard), and assumed the name of Mr Digges. We were shown up to the very room where he slept. I said my cousin, as I called him, was very well. That Ceres and Bacchus might in moderation lend their assistance to Venus, I ordered a genteel supper and some wine...

I asked her if we did not just look like man and wife. 'No,' said she, 'we are too fond for married people.' No wonder that she may have a bad idea of that union, considering how bad it was for her. She has contrived a pretty device for a seal. A heart is gently warmed by Cupid's flame, and Hymen comes with his rude torch and extinguishes it. She said she found herself quite in a flutter. 'Why, really,' said I, 'reason sometimes has no power. We have no occasion to be frightened, and yet we are both a little so. Indeed, I preserve a tolerable presence of mind.' I rose and kissed her, and conscious that I had no occasion to doubt my qualifications as a gallant, I joked about it: 'How curious would it be if I should be so frightened that we should rise as we lay down.' She reproved my wanton language by a look of modesty. The bells of St Bride's church rung their merry chimes hard by. I said that the bells in Cupid's court would be this night set a-ringing for joy at our union.

We supped cheerfully and agreeably and drank a few glasses, and then the maid came and put the sheets, well aired, upon the bed. I now contemplated my fair prize. Louisa is just twenty-four, of a tall rather than short figure, comely made in person, with a handsome face and an enchanting languish in her eyes. She dresses with taste. She has sense, good humour, and vivacity, and looks quite a woman in genteel life. As I mused on this elevating subject, I could not help being somehow pleasingly confounded to think that so fine a woman was at this moment in my possession, that without any motives of interest she had come with me to an inn, agreed to be my intimate companion, as to be my bedfellow all night, and to permit me the full enjoyment of her person.

When the servant left the room, I embraced her warmly and begged that she would not now delay my felicity. She declined to undress before me, and begged I would retire and send her one of the maids. I did so, gravely desiring the girl to go up to Mrs Digges. I then took a candle in my hand and walked out to the yard. The night was very dark and very cold. I experienced for some minutes the rigours of the season, and called into my mind many terrible ideas of hardships, that I might make a transition from such dreary thoughts to the most gay and delicious feelings. I then caused make a bowl of negus, very rich of the fruit, which I caused be set in the room as a reviving cordial.

I came softly into the room, and in a sweet delirium slipped into bed and was immediately clasped in her snowy arms and pressed to her milk-white bosom. Good heavens, what a loose did we give to amorous dalliance! The friendly curtain of darkness concealed our blushes. In a moment I felt myself animated with the strongest powers of love, and, from my dearest creature's kindness, had a most luscious feast. Proud of my godlike vigour, I soon resumed the noble game. I was in full glow of health. Sobriety had preserved me from effeminacy and weakness, and my bounding blood beat quick and high alarms. A more voluptuous night I never enjoyed. Five times was I fairly lost in supreme rapture. Louisa was madly fond of me; she declared I was a prodigy, and asked me if this was not extraordinary for human nature. I said twice as much might be, but this was not, although in my own mind I was somewhat proud of my performance. She said it was what there was no just reason to be proud of. But I told her I could not help it. She said it was what we had in common with the beasts. I said no. For we had it highly improved by the pleasures of sentiment. I asked her what she thought enough. She gently chid me for asking such questions, but said two times. I mentioned the Sunday's assignation, when I was in such bad spirits, told her in what agony of mind I was, and asked her if she would not have despised me for my imbecility. She declared she would not, as it was what people had not in their own power.

She often insisted that we should compose ourselves to sleep before I would consent to it. At last I sunk to rest in her arms and she in mine. I found the negus, which had a fine flavour, very refreshing to me. Louisa had an exquisite mixture of delicacy and wantonness that made me enjoy her with more relish. Indeed I could not help roving in fancy to the embraces of some other ladies which my lively imagination strongly pictured. I don't know if that was altogether fair. However, Louisa had all the advantage. She said she was quite fatigued and could neither stir leg nor arm. She begged I would not despise her, and hoped my love would not be altogether transient. I have painted this night as well as I could. The description is faint; but I surely may be styled a Man of Pleasure.

Thursday 13 January 1763

We awaked from sweet repose after the luscious fatigues of the night. I got up between nine and ten and walked out till Louisa should rise. I patrolled up and down Fleet Street, thinking on London, the seat of Parliament and the seat of pleasure, and seeming to myself as one of the wits in King Charles the Second's time. I then came in and we had an agreeable breakfast, after which we left Hayward's, who said he was sorry he had not more of our company, and calling a hackney-coach, drove to Soho Square, where Louisa had some visits to pay. So we parted. Thus was this conquest completed to my highest satisfaction. I can with pleasure trace the progress of this intrigue to its completion. I am now at ease on that head, having my fair one fixed as my own. As Captain Plume [in George Farquhar's *The Recruiting Officer*] says, the best security for a woman's mind is her body. I really conducted this affair with a manliness and prudence that pleased me very much. The whole expense was just eighteen shillings.

Friday 14 January 1763

I drank tea with Louisa . . . At night I went to Lady Northumberland's. There was a very full meeting, and many people of my acquaintance, so that I was at my ease and had plenty of conversation. I strutted up and down, considering myself as a valiant man who could gratify a lady's loving desires five times in a night; and I satisfied my pride by considering that if this and all my other great qualities were known, all the women almost in the room would be making love to me.

Sunday 16 January 1763

I then went to Louisa and was permitted the rites of love with great complacency; yet I felt my passion for Louisa much gone. I felt a degree of coldness for her and I observed an affectation about her which disgusted me. I had a strong proof of my own inconstancy of disposition, and I considered that any woman who married me must be miserable. Here I argued wrong. For as a licentious love is merely the child of passion, it has no sure ground to hope for a long continuance, as passion may be extinguished with the most sudden and trifling breath of wind; but rational esteem founded on just motives must in all probability endure, especially when the opinion of the world and many other considerations contribute to strengthen and preserve it.

Tuesday 18 January 1763

I this day began to feel an unaccountable alarm of unexpected evil: a little heat in the members of my body sacred to Cupid, very like a symptom of that distemper with which Venus, when cross, takes it into her head to plague her votaries. But then I had run no risks. I had been with no woman but Louisa; and sure she could not have such a thing. Away then with such idle fears, such groundless, uneasy apprehensions! When I came to Louisa's, I felt myself stout and well, and most courageously did I plunge into the fount of love, and had vast pleasure as I enjoyed her as an actress who had played many a fine lady's part. She was remarkably fond of me today, and sighing said, 'What will become of me if I lose you now?'

Wednesday 19 January 1763

This was a day eagerly expected by Dempster[18], Erskine, and I, as it was fixed as the period of our gratifying a whim proposed by me: which was that on the first day of the new tragedy called Elvira's being acted, we three should walk from the one end of London to the other, dine at Dolly's, and be in the theatre at night; and as the play would probably be bad, and as Mr David Malloch, the author, who has changed his name to David Mallet Esq., was an arrant puppy, we determined to exert ourselves in damning it. I this morning felt stronger symptoms of the sad distemper, yet I was unwilling to imagine such a thing. However, the severe exercise of today, joined with hearty eating and drinking, I was sure would confirm or remove my suspicions.

We walked up to Hyde Park Corner, from whence we set out at ten. Our spirits were high with the notion of the adventure, and the variety that we met with as we went along is amazing. As the Spectator observes, one end of London is like a different country from the other in look and in manners. We eat an excellent breakfast at the Somerset Coffee-house. We turned down Gracechurch Street and went upon the top of London Bridge, from whence we viewed with a pleasing horror the rude and terrible appearance of the river, partly froze up, partly covered with enormous shoals of floating ice which often crashed against each other. Dempster said of this excursion from the road that our Epic Poem would be somewhat dull if it were not enlivened by such episodes. As we went along, I felt the symptoms increase, which was very confounding and very distressing to me. I thought the best thing I could do was not to keep it secret, which would be difficult and troublesome, but fairly to own it to Dempster and Erskine and ask their advice and sympathy. They really sympathised, and yet they could not help smiling a little at my catching a tartar so very unexpectedly, when I imagined myself quite safe, and had been vaunting most heroically of my felicity in having the possession of a fine woman, to whom I ascribed so many endearing qualities that they really doubted of her existence, and used to call her my ideal lady. We went half a mile beyond the turnpike at Whitechapel, which completed our course, and went into a little public house and drank some warm white wine with aromatic spices, pepper and cinnamon. We were pleased with the neat houses upon the road...

When I got home, though, then came sorrow. Too, too plain was Signor Gonorrhoea. Yet I could scarce believe it, and determined to go to friend Douglas [a physician] next day.

Thursday 20 January 1763

I rose very disconsolate, having rested very ill by the poisonous infection raging in my veins and anxiety and vexation boiling in my breast. I could scarcely credit my own senses. What! thought I, can this beautiful, this sensible, and this agreeable woman be so sadly defiled? Can corruption lodge beneath so fair a form? Can she who professed delicacy of sentiment and sincere regard for me, use me so very basely and so very cruelly? No, it is impossible. I have just got a gleet by irritating the parts too much with excessive venery. And yet these damned twinges, that scalding heat, and that deep-tinged loathsome matter are the strongest proofs of an infection. But she certainly must think that I would soon discover her falsehood. But perhaps she was ignorant of her being ill. A pretty conjecture indeed! No, she

could not be ignorant. Yes, yes, she intended to make the most of me.
And now I recollect that the day we went to Hayward's, she showed
me a bill of thirty shillings about which she was in some uneasiness,
and no doubt expected that I would pay it. But I was too cautious,
and she had not effrontery enough to try my generosity in direct terms
so soon after my letting her have two guineas. And am I then taken
in? Am I, who have had safe and elegant intrigues with fine women,
become the dupe of a strumpet? Am I now to be laid up for many
weeks to suffer extreme pain and full confinement, and to be debarred
all the comforts and pleasures of life? And then must I have my poor
pocket drained by the unavoidable expense of it? And shall I no more
(for a long time at least) take my walk, healthful and spirited, round
the Park before breakfast, view the brilliant Guards on the Parade, and
enjoy my pleasing amusements? And then am I prevented from making
love to Lady Mirabel, or any other woman of fashion? O dear, O dear!
What a cursed thing this is! What a miserable creature am I!

In this woeful manner did I melancholy ruminate. I thought of
applying to a quack who would cure me quickly and cheaply. But then
the horrors of being imperfectly cured and having the distemper
thrown into my blood terrified me exceedingly. I therefore pursued
my resolution of last night to go to my friend Douglas, whom I knew
to be skillful and careful; and although it should cost me more, yet to
get sound health, was a matter of great importance, and I might save
upon other articles. I accordingly went and breakfasted with him . . .

After breakfast Mrs Douglas withdrew, and I opened my sad case to
Douglas, who upon examining the parts, declared I had got an evident
infection and that the woman who gave it me could not but know of
it. I joked with my friend about the expense, asked him if he would
take a draught on my arrears, and bid him visit me seldom that I
might have the less to pay. To these jokes he seemed to give little
heed, but talked seriously in the way of his business . . .

Enraged at the perfidy of Louisa, I resolved to go and upbraid her
most severely; but this I thought was not acting with dignity enough.
So I would talk to her coolly and make her feel her own unworthiness . . .

I then went to Louisa. With excellent address did I carry on this
interview, as the following scene, I trust, will make appear.

LOUISA. My dear Sir! I hope you are well today.

BOSWELL. Excessively well, I thank you. I hope I find you so.

LOUISA. No, really, Sir. I am distressed with a thousand things.

(Cunning jade, her circumstances!) I really don't know what to do.

BOSWELL. Do you know that I have been very unhappy since I saw you?

LOUISA. How so, Sir?

BOSWELL. Why, I am afraid that you don't love me so well, nor have not such a regard for me, as I thought you had.

LOUISA. Nay, dear Sir! (Seeming unconcerned.)

BOSWELL. Pray, Madam, have I no reason?

LOUISA. No, indeed, Sir, you have not.

BOSWELL. Have I no reason, Madam? Pray think.

LOUISA. Sir!

BOSWELL. Pray, Madam, in what state of health have you been in for some time?

LOUISA. Sir, you amaze me.

BOSWELL. I have but too strong, too plain reason to doubt of your regard. I have for some days observed the symptoms of disease, but was unwilling to believe you so very ungenerous. But now, Madam, I am thoroughly convinced.

LOUISA. Sir, you have terrified me. I protest I know nothing of the matter.

BOSWELL. Madam, I have had no connection with any woman but you these two months. I was with my surgeon this morning, who declared I had got a strong infection, and that she from whom I had it could not be ignorant of it. Madam, such a thing in this case is worse than from a woman of the town, as from her you may expect it. You have used me very ill. I did not deserve it. You know you said where there was no confidence, there was no breach of trust. But surely I placed some confidence in you. I am sorry that I was mistaken.

LOUISA. Sir, I will confess to you that about three years ago I was very bad. But for these fifteen months I have been quite well. I appeal to GOD Almighty that I am speaking true; and for these six months I have had to do with no man but yourself.

BOSWELL. But by G-D, Madam, I have been with none but you, and here am I very bad.

LOUISA. Well, Sir, by the same solemn oath I protest that I was ignorant of it.

BOSWELL. Madam, I wish much to believe you. But I own I cannot upon this occasion believe a miracle.

LOUISA. Sir, I cannot say more to you. But you will leave me in the greatest misery. I shall lose your esteem. I shall be hurt in the opinion of everybody, and in my circumstances.

BOSWELL (to himself). What the devil does the confounded jilt mean by being hurt in her circumstances? This is the grossest cunning. But I won't take notice of that at all. Madam, as to the opinion of everybody, you need not be afraid. I was going to joke and say that I never boast of a lady's favours. But I give you my word of honour that you shall not be discovered.

LOUISA. Sir, this is being more generous than I could expect.

BOSWELL. I hope, Madam, you will own that since I have been with you I have always behaved like a man of honour.

LOUISA. You have indeed, Sir.

BOSWELL (rising). Madam, your most obedient servant...

... She is in all probability a most consummate dissembling whore.

Thus ended my intrigue with the fair Louisa, which I flattered myself so much with, and from which I expected at least a winter's safe copulation. It is indeed very hard. I cannot say, like young fellows who get themselves clapped in a bawdy-house, that I will take better care again. For I really did take care. However, since I am fairly trapped, let me make the best of it. I have not got it from imprudence. It is merely the chance of war.

I then called at Drury Lane for Mr Garrick[19]. He was vastly good to me. 'Sir,' said he, 'you will be a very great man. And when you are so, remember the year 1763. I want to contribute my part towards saving you. And pray, will you fix a day when I shall have the pleasure of treating you with tea?' I fixed next day. 'Then, Sir,' said he, the cups shall dance and the saucers skip.'

What he meant by my being a great man I can understand. For really, to speak seriously, I think there is a blossom about me of something more distinguished than the generality of mankind. But I am much afraid that this blossom will never swell into fruit, but will be nipped and destroyed by many a blighting heat and chilling frost. Indeed, I sometimes indulge noble reveries of having a regiment, of getting into Parliament, making a figure, and becoming a man of consequence in the state. But these are checked by dispiriting reflections on my melancholy temper and imbecility of mind. Yet I may probably become sounder and stronger as I grow up. Heaven knows. I am resigned. I trust to Providence. I was quite in raptures with Garrick's kindness – the man whom from a boy I used to adore and look upon as a heathen god – to find him paying me so much respect! ... I was this day with him what the French call un étourdi. I gave free vent to my feelings. Love was by, to whom I cried, 'This, Sir, is the real scene.' And taking Mr Garrick cordially by the hand, 'Thou greatest of men,' said I, 'I cannot express how happy you make me.' This, upon my soul, was no flattery. He saw it was not. And the dear great man was truly pleased with it. This scene gave me a charming flutter of spirits and dispelled my former gloom.

Friday 21 January 1763

Between nine and ten I went to Mr Garrick's. He received me with particular kindness. Mrs Garrick[20] made breakfast for us. She is an Italian lady, was a famous dancer on the stage, and when she married Mr Garrick, Lord Burlington gave her £10,000. She is a genteel, agreeable, unaffected creature...

I quite forgot my distemper. It was a fine morning. We had a genteel breakfast, which I think the most agreeable meal, in ease and plenty. I was sitting with the great Roscius of the age ... In short, this was a period of felicity. I was happy, could not tell how. We walked into Mr Garrick's library, which is a handsome room with a pretty large collection of good books and some busts and pictures. As he was obliged to attend rehearsal in the forenoon, we were too soon deprived of his company. He asked me to come whenever I could. I rejoiced. This is really establishing myself in a charming place. I shall there see all the men of genius of the age. Let me indulge the pleasing prospect of the many happy hours which I shall pass there when I again am blessed with health.

Saturday 22 January 1763

Calmly and considerately did I sit down in my arm-chair this morning and endeavour to call up all the philosophy that I could. A distemper of this kind is more dreadful to me than most people. I am of a warm constitution: a complexion, as physicians say, exceedingly amorous, and therefore suck in the poison more deeply. I have had two visitations of this calamity. The first lasted ten weeks. The second four months. How severe a reflection is it! And, O, how severe a prospect! Yet let me take courage. Perhaps this is not a very bad

infection, and as I shall be scrupulously careful of myself, I may get rid
of it in a short time. Then ... a time of indisposition is not altogether
a time of misery. There is a softness of disposition and an absence of
care which attend upon its indolent confinement. Then, I have often
lamented my ignorance of English history. Now I may make up that
want. I may read all Hume's six volumes [History of England]. I may also
be amused with novels and books of a slighter nature. I gave orders to
say at the door that I was gone to the country, except to a few friends.

Tuesday 25 January 1763

Lord Eglinton came to me this forenoon ... I could not help
beginning upon my difference with him, as I felt my old love for him.
Our dialogue was as follows:
BOSWELL. Upon my word, my Lord, you and I ought to be upon
a good footing. But we are not.
EGLINTON. I am sorry for it, Jamie. But it is not my fault. I am
sure I forgive you all your little follies.
BOSWELL. But, my Lord, I don't forgive you.
EGLINTON. How so now? Let me hear your complaints. Tell your
story.
BOSWELL. Why then, my Lord, to begin and go regularly through.
You know I left Scotland abruptly and came up to London two years
ago in an odd enough way. Your Lordship was kind enough to take
particular notice of me. You took me into your own house. And you
brought me right: You pulled me out of the mire, washed me and
cleaned me and made me fit to be seen. I was told by some friends
that the cause of all this was the election in Ayrshire being then in
dependence. But I was convinced not. No, no. I was a fine fellow. It
was all on my own account. Well, my Lord, you then pointed out to
me a most agreeable way of life, which was to be an officer of the
Guards; indeed, the only real employment that I ever liked; and you
promised to use all your interest for me. My father then came up and
I was hurried down to Scotland, confined to live in my father's family,
and pressed to study law, so that my situation was very unhappy. Your
Lordship in the mean time continued to profess a regard for me and
promised me your assistance. Nay, my Lord, you went so far as to say
to me, 'Jamie, to be sure, I cannot do so much for you as your father;
but if you and he cannot agree, come to me, and I will do all I can

for you.' Now, my Lord, this was saying the strongest thing you could say. It was making me more indifferent as to breaking with my father. At last I got my father's consent. I immediately applied to you. And you know, my Lord, how you used me, how you put me off. It was very hard.

EGLINTON. Now, Jamie, I acknowledge all this true that you have said. Have not I heard you patiently? I hope you will hear me in the same way. When you was first in London, I found that you had been much hurt by being forced to studies contrary to the natural bent of your genius, and been obliged to live with your parents, who, though very good people, had a strictness and confined way of thinking which a man of your strength of imagination and natural freedom of sentiment could not put up with. I pointed out the Guards to you, as I thought the gaiety of a military life was the best thing in the world to keep off that melancholy to which you was a little subject. Upon my going down to Scotland, I found your father much averse to it, and I need not tell you that he did all he could to thwart and oppose it. Now, you must allow that it would have been very disagreeable for me just directly to oppose him.

BOSWELL. I grant you this, my Lord. But then —

EGLINTON. Allow me to go on. You wrote to me in May last that you had got your father's consent, and therefore you hoped I would now get you into the Guards. But then you desired expressly that your commission might be in one of the battalions at home. Now, will you consider what sort of a demand this was? No doubt, it would have been the utmost difficulty for me to get such a thing at any rate; and I would have required every argument, and among the rest, that the young man was anxious to go upon service. But how could I possibly ask for one at home? And you know, Jamie, I wrote you this very strongly.

BOSWELL. You did so, my Lord. But you should have done it more gently.

EGLINTON. I confess to you that my letter was too harsh from a man to his friend. But then you must consider that I was really in a passion for your having brought me into a sad scrape by publishing your Cub[21] and dedicating it to the Duke of York without his leave. I can assure you he was very angry.

BOSWELL. I think, my Lord, he was wrong there. For in my opinion I paid him a compliment.

EGLINTON. So I think indeed.

BOSWELL. Well, but, my Lord, you know I answered your letter and told you that I was willing to go abroad.

EGLINTON. You did so. But it was in such a way that I could not imagine it anything else than a genteel evasion, and what I should have expected from a man of your sense and genius if you did not want flatly to refuse going upon service, but yet chose to shun it. I have your letters yet to show you. I put that point very home to you. I expected an explicit answer. And you only said that no doubt you would be very willing to go if your regiment went. But this was what no man could refuse to do except he would declare himself an arrant poltroon. He would rather go and take the chance of not coming to action.

BOSWELL. Well, I assure you, my Lord, that my meaning was this: that my great plan in getting into the Guards was not so much to be a soldier as to be in the genteel character of a gentleman; and therefore I would have rather chose that my commission should have been in one of the battalions at home. But I should certainly have rather gone abroad than not get in.

EGLINTON. Indeed, Jamie, I did not understand you so. You wrote me two letters. The first treated the thing slightly. In the second you seemed very angry. I assure you, I took it in this light, that I thought you would not accept a commission in a battalion in Germany.

BOSWELL. Then, my Lord, all this has just been a mistake. But I think my taking your behaviour so ill is a proof that I really meant as I say, to go abroad if that should be necessary.

EGLINTON. It is so. But I hope I have explained my conduct to you. No doubt, as you took it, you had great reason to blame me and think I had broke my promise to you. But you see how it was. (Here my heart melted with tenderness, genuine candour, and joy.)

BOSWELL. My Lord, I did not intend to have spoken on the subject at all to you. I was quite convinced of your bad usage. I intended just to be off with you. But, my Lord, I am happy we have had this conversation. I see you was not to blame. (Taking him by the hand.) I suffered very much in thinking myself so deceived.

EGLINTON. Well, I hope all is over now, and we're just where we were.

BOSWELL (almost weeping). We are indeed, my Lord. I rejoice at my being ill at present, as it has given us this opportunity. Even when

I was most angry, I could not help now and then having returns of fondness for you as strong as ever.

EGLINTON. Like what one feels for a mistress, was it not?

BOSWELL. Just so, my Lord.

EGLINTON. I assure you, Jamie, I have the same regard for you I ever had. I have made allowance for you all this time, writing me such cards and never coming near me was enough to make me break with you. But I made allowance for your mistakes. Had you been a man of as much prudence and discernment as you take yourself to be, I would not have forgiven it. Though I believe you now know your own character pretty well. I will own to you that I have too much resentment in my disposition, more than a man of noble mind ought to have. Your liveliness of fancy and warmth of heart, Jamie, are the qualities most ready to lead a man wrong.

BOSWELL. I believe that is very true.

EGLINTON. Believe me, I was always ready to serve you, and I will help you at this time.

BOSWELL. Will you, my Lord?

EGLINTON. Indeed will I.

I then told him all my different expectations about my commission: the Duke of Queensberry, Lady Northumberland, the Marquis of Granby. He said he would take me to Lord Bute's levée, and I should push at all hands. All would help. We went on:

BOSWELL. Do you think, my Lord, it is worth my while to please myself with the idea of having a regiment by the time I am sixty?

EGLINTON. Ay, by the time you're forty. It is agreeable to have a prospect before one.

BOSWELL. Yes, my Lord, but what will you say to a man who is philosopher enough to know that a man, even before he gets the first step, can enjoy his bottle, his girl, and his friend just as well as when he comes to be a general? That is my case.

EGLINTON. I'll tell you what I would do. When things go well, I would encourage the ideas of rising; and when they go ill, I would be the philosopher.

BOSWELL. Your Lordship is right.

EGLINTON. Well, Jamie, I must go. Now think seriously on what I have said to you, and I am sure you will see it stronger and stronger.

We embraced each other cordially, and he left me. Here now is a very material period in my journal. I was deeply offended with the behaviour of this nobleman. I had resolved to give up all regard for him; and now, by our coming to an explanation, I am perfectly convinced that he was not to blame ... We shall be intimate companions.

Thursday 3 February 1763

I was not so well as yesterday. I was somewhat morose. I thought the treacherous Louisa deserved to suffer for her depravity. I therefore wrote her the following letter.

MADAM. My surgeon will soon have a demand upon me of five guineas for curing the disease which you have given me. I must therefore remind you of the little sum which you had of me some time ago. You cannot have forgot upon what footing I let you have it. I neither paid it for prostitution nor gave it in charity. It was fairly borrowed, and you promised to return it. I give you notice that I expect to have it before Saturday sennight. I have been very bad, but I scorn to upbraid you. I think it below me. If you are not rendered callous by a long course of disguised wickedness, I should think the consideration of your deceit and baseness, your corruption both of body and mind, would be a very severe punishment. Call not that a misfortune which is the consequence of your own unworthiness. I desire no mean evasions. I want no letters. Send the money sealed up. I have nothing more to say to you. JAMES BOSWELL.

This, I thought, might be a pretty bitter potion to her. Yet I thought to mention the money was not so genteel. However, if I get it (which is not probable), it will be of real service to me; and to such a creature as her a pecuniary punishment will give most pain. Am not I too vindictive? It appears so; but upon better consideration I am only sacrificing at the shrine of Justice; and sure I have chosen a victim that deserves it ...

At three I swallowed an apple-tart, then wrapped myself well up in two pair of stockings, two shirts, and a greatcoat; and thus fortified against the weather, I got into a snug chair [sedan chair] and was carried to Drury Lane. I took up my associates at the Rose Tavern, and we went into the pit at four, where, as they had not dined, they laid down their hats, one on each side of me, and there did I sit to keep their places. I was amused to find myself transported from my room of indisposition to the gay, gilded theatre. I put myself as much as possible into proper humour for seeing the play. Luckily, Dr Goldsmith came into the seat behind me. I renewed my acquaintance with him, and he agreed to keep the same place for the night. His conversation revived in my mind the true ideas of London authors, which are to me something curious, and, as it were, mystical.

Wednesday 9 February 1763

Upon my word my journal goes charmingly on at present. I was very apprehensive that there would be a dreary vacancy in it for some weeks, but by various happy circumstances I have been agreeably disappointed. I think, too, that I am making a good use of the hint which Captain Erskine gave me, and am taking more pains upon it, and consequently writing it in a more correct style. Style is to sentiment what dress is to the person. The effects of both are very great, and both are acquired and improved by habit. When once we are used to it, it is as easy to dress neatly as like a sloven; in the same way, custom makes us write in a correct style as easily as in a careless, inaccurate one...

How easily and cleverly do I write just now! I am really pleased with myself; words come skipping to me like lambs upon Moffat Hill; and I turn my periods smoothly and imperceptibly like a skillful wheelwright turning tops in a turning-loom. There's fancy! There's simile! In short, I am at present a genius: in that does my opulence consist, and not in base metal.

Thursday 10 February 1763

This forenoon a maid from Louisa left a packet for me. It was most carefully sealed up, 'by the hands of attention', but was not addressed to me. I opened it up and found my two guineas returned, without a single word written. I felt a strange kind of mixed confusion. My tender heart relented. I thought I had acted too harshly to her. I imagined she might perhaps have been ignorant of her situation. I was so foolish as to think of returning her the money and writing her a letter of atonement. I have too much of what Shakespeare calls 'the milk of human kindness'. I mentioned the thing to Dempster. He said it was just a piece of deep artifice in her. I resolved to think no more on the matter, and was glad that I had come off two guineas better than I expected.

Sunday 27 February 1763

I had now kept the house five complete weeks ... My disorder was now over. Nothing but a gleet remained, which gave me no pain and which could be removed in three days. But I chose to give it a little longer time, that I might get clear of the least tincture of infection. I thought, since I had been so much in earnest hitherto to have a complete cure, I would undoubtedly complete it. Douglas gave it as his opinion that I should confine myself no longer. There was now no danger; and he thought a little air, exercise, and amusement would be of great use both to my health and spirits. This day the sun shone prettily, yet I doubted as to going abroad. However, a battalion of the Guards from Germany were this day to march into town; and when I heard the beat of their drums, I could not restrain my ardour, and thought this the happiest occasion for me to emerge from obscurity and confinement, to light and to life.

... I wrapped myself up in my great-coat, and taking my staff in my hand ... walked out to the Park. The Battalion was not drawn up on the Parade, as I expected, but was marched up to Lincoln's Inn Fields, so I lost that show. However, I was much obliged to my soldiers for bringing me fairly out. I might really have got a habit of laziness and become mopish altogether. The sweet elevation of spirits which I now felt is scarcely to be conceived. I was quite in an ecstasy. O how I admired all the objects around me! How I valued ease and health! To see the variety of people in the Park again put me all in a flutter. The sight of the Parade and the splendid Guards brought back my love to that profession with redoubled force. I was convinced that it was indeed the genuine object of my inclinations, and the only station in real life which (at least for some years) I could fill with pleasure.

And now I swear that this is the true language of my heart ... I now see the sickly suggestions of inconsistent fancy with regard to the Scotch bar in their proper colours[22]. Good heaven! I should by pursuing that plan have deprived myself of felicity when I had it fairly in my power, and brought myself to a worse state than ever. I shudder when I think of it. I am vexed at such a distempered suggestion's being inserted in my journal ... Let me consider that the hero of a romance or novel must not go uniformly along in bliss, but the story must be chequered with bad fortune. Aeneas met with many disasters in his voyage to Italy, and must not Boswell have his rubs?

Monday 21 March 1763

When I went home in the evening, I felt myself quite dissipated by running about so much. I was indolent and careless and could not fix to anything. Even this my journal was in danger of being neglected. Near a whole week had elapsed without my writing a single page of it. By way therefore of penance for my idleness, and by way of making up for the time lost and bringing up my business, I determined to sit up all this night; which I accordingly did, and wrote a great deal. About two o'clock in the morning I inadvertently snuffed out my candle, and as my fire was long before that black and cold, I was in a great dilemma how to proceed. Downstairs did I softly and silently step to the kitchen. But, alas, there was as little fire there as upon the icy mountains of Greenland. With a tinderbox is a light struck every morning to kindle the fire, which is put out at night. But this tinderbox I could not see, nor knew where to find. I was now filled with gloomy ideas of the terrors of the night. I was also apprehensive that my landlord, who always keeps a pair of loaded pistols by him, might fire at me as a thief. I went up to my room, sat quietly till I heard the watchman calling, 'Past three o'clock.' I then called to him to knock at the door of the house where I lodged. He did so, and I opened it to him and got my candle relumed without danger. Thus was I relieved and continued busy till eight next day.

Friday 25 March 1763

As I was coming home this night, I felt carnal inclinations raging through my frame. I determined to gratify them. I went to St James's Park, and, like Sir John Brute, picked up a whore. For the first time did I engage in armour [wear a condom], which I found but a dull satisfaction. She who submitted to my lusty embraces was a young Shropshire girl, only seventeen, very well-looked, her name Elizabeth Parker. Poor being, she has a sad time of it! I supped at Lord Eglinton's.

Thursday 31 March 1763

I sauntered about all the day. I did not dine and was somewhat lowish. At night I strolled into the Park and took the first whore I met, whom I without many words copulated with free from danger, being safely sheathed. She was ugly and lean and her breath smelt of spirits. I never asked her name. When it was done, she slunk off. I had a low opinion of this gross practice and resolved to do it no more.

Saturday 2 April 1763

I have often and often made inquiry for my friend Temple[23]. On Sunday last I heard of him and wrote to him immediately. I breakfasted this day at Dempster's. Erskine ... and other jolly Scots were there. I then set out for the City. Just at St Paul's Churchyard whom should I meet but Temple. We met with a kind of confused joy at our unexpected interview. I engaged to breakfast with him next day. I was a little afraid that he and I might not find ourselves so happy together as we formerly were. We have not met for these five years, except one day at Cambridge. In so long a time we may have acquired new habits of thinking and living. When we were together, we were both very studious and scrupulously moral. Now I am pretty idly disposed. I have not the same high opinion of learning that I had when at college. I am more fond of conversation and amusement. I am also much more of a libertine.

Tuesday 3 May 1763

I walked up to the Tower in order to see Mr Wilkes[24] come out. But he was gone. I then thought I should see the prisoners of one kind or other, so went to Newgate. I stepped into a sort of Court before the cells. They are surely most dismal places. There are three rows of 'em, four in a row, all above each other. They have double iron windows, and within these, strong iron rails; and in these dark mansions are the unhappy criminals confined. I did not go in, but stood in the court, where were a number of strange blackguard beings with sad countenances, most of them being friends and acquaintances of those under sentence of death. Mr Rice the broker [convicted of the capital offence of forgery] was confined in another part of the house. In the cells were Paul Lewis for robbery and Hannah Diego for theft. I saw them pass by to chapel. The woman was a big unconcerned being. Paul, who had been in the sea-service and was called Captain, was a genteel, spirited young fellow. He was just a Macheath[25]. He was dressed in a white coat and blue silk vest and silver, with his hair neatly queued and a silver-laced hat, smartly cocked.

Wednesday 4 May 1763

My curiosity to see the melancholy spectacle of the executions was so strong that I could not resist it, although I was sensible that I would suffer much from it. In my younger years I had read in the Lives of the Convicts so much about Tyburn that I had a sort of horrid eagerness to be there. I also wished to see the last behaviour of Paul Lewis, the handsome fellow whom I had seen the day before. Accordingly I took Captain Temple with me, and he and I got upon a scaffold very near the fatal tree, so that we could clearly see all the dismal scene. There was a most prodigious crowd of spectators. I was most terribly shocked, and thrown into a very deep melancholy.

I went to Lord Eglinton and begged he would try to relieve me. He made me dress and dine with him, and said he would take me at night to Ranelagh and introduce me to some pretty women. Dress and dinner gave me spirits...

I went home and changed my clothes. But gloomy terrors came upon me so much as night approached that I durst not stay by myself; so I went and had a bed (or rather half a one) from honest Erskine, which he most kindly gave me.

Tuesday 10 May 1763

At the bottom of the Haymarket I picked up a strong, jolly young damsel, and taking her under the arm I conducted her to Westminster Bridge, and then in armour complete did I engage her upon this noble edifice. The whim of doing it there with the Thames rolling below us amused me much. Yet after the brutish appetite was sated, I could not but despise myself for being so closely united with such a low wretch.

[On 16 May Boswell met Samuel Johnson. It was the most important meeting in his life and one of the most important in English literary history. With this single incident in Thomas Davies's bookshop his life was permanently transformed.]

Monday 16 May 1763

I drank tea at Davies's in Russell Street, and about seven came in the great Mr Samuel Johnson, whom I have so long wished to see. Mr Davies introduced me to him. As I knew his mortal antipathy at the Scotch, I cried to Davies, 'Don't tell where I come from.' However, he said, 'From Scotland.' 'Mr Johnson,' said I, 'indeed I come from Scotland, but I cannot help it.' 'Sir,' replied he, 'that, I find, is what a very great many of your countrymen cannot help.' Mr Johnson is a man of a most dreadful appearance. He is a very big man, is troubled with sore eyes, the palsy, and the king's evil [scars from scrofula]. He is very slovenly in his dress and speaks with a most uncouth voice. Yet his great knowledge and strength of expression command vast respect and render him very excellent company. He has great humour and is a worthy man. But his dogmatical roughness of manners is disagreeable ... I was sorry to leave him there at ten.

[The reader is referred to Boswell's elaboration of his first meeting with Johnson in the entry for this date from The Life of Johnson included on pages 376–7.]

Thursday 19 May 1763

I ... sallied forth to the Piazzas in rich flow of animal spirits and burning with fierce desire. I met two very pretty little girls who asked me to take them with me. 'My dear girls,' said I, 'I am a poor fellow. I can give you no money. But if you choose to have a glass of wine and my company and let us be gay and obliging to each other without money, I am your man.' They agreed with great good humour. So back to the Shakespeare I went. 'Waiter,' said I, 'I have got here a couple of human beings; I don't know how they'll do.' 'I'll look, your Honour,' cried he, and with inimitable effrontery stared them in the face and then cried, 'They'll do very well.' 'What,' said I, 'are they good fellow-creatures? Bring them up, then.' We were shown into a good room and had a bottle of sherry before us in a minute. I surveyed my seraglio and found them both good subjects for amorous play. I toyed with them and drank about and sung Youth's the Season[26] and thought myself Captain Macheath; and then I solaced my existence with them, one after the other, according to their seniority. I was quite raised, as the phrase is: thought I was in a London tavern, the Shakespeare's Head, enjoying high debauchery after my sober winter. I parted with my ladies politely and came home in a glow of spirits.

Tuesday 24 May 1763

I went and waited upon Mr Samuel Johnson, who received me very courteously. He has chambers in the Inner Temple, where he lives in literary state, very solemn and very slovenly. He had some people with him, and when they left him, I rose too. But he cried, 'No, don't go away.' 'Sir,' said I, 'I am afraid that I intrude upon you. It is benevolent to allow me to sit and hear you.' He was pleased with this compliment, which I sincerely paid him, and he said he was obliged to any man who visited him. I was proud to sit in such company.

He said that mankind had a great aversion at intellectual employment. But even supposing knowledge easily attained, most people were equally content to be ignorant.

'Moral good depends on the motive from which we act. If I fling half a crown at a beggar with intention to break his head, and he picks it up and buys victuals with it, the physical effect is good; but with respect to me, the action is very wrong. In the same way, religious services, if not performed with an intention to please GOD, avail us nothing. As our Saviour saith of people who perform them from other motives, "Verily they have their reward." ' . . .

I listened to this great oracle with much satisfaction; and as I feel myself uneasy by reason of scepticism, I had great comfort in hearing so able an advocate for Revelation; and I resolved to read the books he mentioned. He pressed me to stay a second time, which I did. He said he went out at four in the afternoon and did not come home, for most part, till two in the morning. I asked him if he did not think it wrong to live so and not make use of his talents. He said it was a bad idea.

Wednesday 8 June 1763

At night I received a very kind letter from my father, in which he told me that he would allow me to follow any profession that I please, but at the same time said that the Army was but a poor scheme, and that if I would pursue the law, though moderately, and be in the style of his eldest son, that he would give me all encouragement. It was a most sensible and indulgent letter. It made me think seriously, and I considered that I had now experienced how little I could depend on the favour of the great, which, when only founded on personal liking, is very slight. I considered too that I could have no prospect of rising in the Army. That my being in that way contrary to my parents' advice was uphill work, and that I could not long be fond of it. I considered that by getting into the plan of civil life, I should have all things smooth and easy, be on a respectful footing and of consequence in my own country, and please my worthy father, who, though somewhat narrow in his notions, is one of the best men in the world.

Saturday 25 June 1763

At nine in the evening Mr Johnson and I went to the Mitre Tavern in Fleet Street. He was vastly obliging to favour me with his company. I was quite proud to think on whom I was with...

I then told my history to Mr Johnson, which he listened to with attention. I told him how I was a very strict Christian, and was turned from that to infidelity. But that now I had got back to a very agreeable way of thinking. That I believed the Christian religion; though I might not be clear in many particulars. He was much pleased with my ingenuous open way, and he cried, 'Give me your hand. I have taken a liking to you.'...

I told him all my story. 'Sir,' said he, 'your father has been wanting to make the man of you at twenty which you will be at thirty. Sir, let me tell you that to be a Scotch landlord, where you have a number of families dependent upon and attached to you, is perhaps as high a situation as humanity can arrive at...

'Sir, I think your breaking off idle connections by going abroad is a matter of importance. I would go where there are courts and learned men.'

I then complained to him how little I knew, and mentioned study. 'Sir,' said he, 'don't talk of study just now. I will put you upon a plan. It will require some time to talk of that.' I put out my hand. 'Will you really take a charge of me? It is very good in you, Mr Johnson, to allow me to sit with you thus. Had I but thought some years ago that I should pass an evening with the Author of *The Rambler*!' These expressions were all from the heart and he perceived that they were;

and he was very complacent and said, 'Sir, I am glad we have met. I hope we shall pass many evenings and mornings too together.'

Wednesday 6 July 1763

I had engaged Mr Johnson and some more company to sup at my lodgings, and as my having the parlour of an evening was a favour from my landlord, I would by no means think of it. I went to Mr Johnson and told him my distress. He laughed and bid me consider how little a distress it would appear a twelvemonth hence. He said that if my landlord insisted that the bargain should stand and the lodgings be mine for a year, that I could certainly use them as I pleased. 'So, Sir,' said he, 'you may quarter two Life Guard men upon him; or you may get the greatest scoundrel you can find and send into his house; or you may say that you want to make some experiments in natural philosophy and may burn a large quantity of asafoetida in his house.' Such ludicrous fertility can this great man throw out!

What amazing universality of genius has Mr Johnson, who has written The English Dictionary, a work of infinite labour and knowledge; The Rambler, which contains a rich store of morality and knowledge of human life, embellished with great imagination; Rasselas, where we find a humane preceptor delighting the fancy and mending the heart; The Life of Savage, which is distinguished for perspicuity of narration, and abounds with excellent reflection; The Translations of the Third and Tenth Satires of Juvenal, and The Prologue spoken at Mr Garrick's Opening Drury-Lane Theatre, which display strong poetical genius, strength of sentiment, keenness of satire, vivaciousness of wit and humour, and manly power of versification. His conversation, too, is as great as his writing. He throws out all his powers with force of expression; and he mixes inimitable strokes of vivacity with solid good-sense and knowledge, so that he is highly instructive and highly entertaining...

In recollecting Mr Johnson's conversation, I labour under much difficulty. It requires more parts than I am master of even to retain that strength of sentiment and perspicuity of expression for which he is remarkable. I shall just do my best and relate as much as I can[27].

Saturday 16 July 1763

Since my being honoured with the friendship of Mr Johnson, I have more seriously considered the duties of morality and religion and the dignity of human nature. I have considered that promiscuous concubinage is certainly wrong. It is contributing one's share towards bringing confusion and misery into society; and it is a transgression of the laws of the Almighty Creator, who has ordained marriage for the mutual comfort of the sexes and the procreation and right educating of children. Sure it is that if all the men and women in Britain were merely to consult animal gratification, society would be a most shocking scene. Nay, it would soon cease altogether. Notwithstanding of these reflections, I have stooped to mean profligacy even yesterday. However, I am now resolved to guard against it . . .

He advised me to keep a journal of my life, fair and undisguised. He said it would be a very good exercise, and would yield me infinite satisfaction when the ideas were faded from my remembrance. I told him that I had done so ever since I left Scotland. He said he was very happy that I pursued so good a plan. And now, O my journal! art thou not highly dignified? Shalt thou not flourish tenfold? No former solicitations or censures could tempt me to lay thee aside; and now is there any argument which can outweigh the sanction of Mr Samuel Johnson? He said indeed that I should keep it private, and that I might surely have a friend who would burn it in case of my death. For my own part, I have at present such an affection for this my journal that it shocks me to think of burning it. I rather encourage the idea of having it carefully laid up among the archives of Auchinleck. However, I cannot judge fairly of it now. Some years hence I may. I told Mr Johnson that I put down all sorts of little incidents in it. 'Sir,' said he, 'there is nothing too little for so little a creature as man. It is by studying little things that we attain the great knowledge of having as little misery and as much happiness as possible.'

Monday 18 July 1763

Mr Johnson has a curious-looking little man called [Robert] Levett[28] who stays with him. I asked Goldsmith what this man was. 'Sir,' said he, 'he is poor and honest, which is enough to Johnson.' Levett went up with me to Mr Johnson's library, which is four pair of stairs up, in two garrets where Lintot (son to the famous Lintot) had his printing-house. I was much pleased to be in the library of this great man, where I saw a number of good books, but very dusty and confusedly placed. I saw too an apparatus for chemical experiments, of which it seems Mr Johnson was fond. And I saw manuscript leaves scattered up and down which I looked upon with a degree of veneration, as they perhaps might be pieces of The Rambler, or of Rasselas. Mr Johnson goes up to his library when he wants to study, as he will not allow his servant to say he is not at home when he is. I don't know but I may have mentioned before in my journal that he thinks that a servant's notions of truth would be hurt by such a practice. A philosopher may know that it is a mere form of denial, but few servants are such nice distinguishers. No place can be more favourable for meditation than such a retirement as this garret. I could not help indulging a scheme of making it for myself many years hence, when its present great possessor will in all probability be gone to a more exalted situation. This was in a strong sense of 'building my castles in the air'.

Friday 22 July 1763

At night, Mr Johnson and I had a room at the Turk's Head Coffee-house...

Mr Johnson said he loved the acquaintance of young people, 'because,' said he, 'in the first place, I don't like to think myself turning old. In the next place, young acquaintances must last longest, if they do last; and in the next place, young men have more virtue than old men. They have more generous sentiments in every respect. I love the young dogs of this age: they have more wit and humour and knowledge of life than we had. But then the dogs are not so good scholars. Sir, in my early years I read very hard. It is a hard enough reflection, but a true one, that I knew almost as much at eighteen as I do now. My judgment, to be sure, was not so good, but I had all the facts. I remember very well when I was about five and twenty an old gentleman at Oxford said to me, "Young man, ply your book diligently now and acquire a stock of knowledge; for when years come upon you, you will find that poring upon books will be but an irksome task."'

I complained to Mr Johnson that I was much afflicted with melancholy, which was hereditary in our family. He said that he himself

had been greatly distressed with it, and for that reason had been
obliged to fly from study and meditation to the dissipating variety of
life. He advised me to have constant occupation of mind, to take a
great deal of exercise, and to live moderately; especially to shun
drinking at night. 'Melancholy people,' said he, 'are apt to fly to
intemperance, which gives a momentary relief but sinks the soul much
lower in misery.' He observed that labouring men who work much
and live sparingly are seldom or never troubled with low spirits. It
gave me great relief to talk of my disorder with Mr Johnson; and when
I discovered that he himself was subject to it, I felt that strange
satisfaction which human nature feels at the idea of participating
distress with others; and the greater person our fellow sufferer is, so
much the more good does it do us...

He said he wished to visit the Western Isles of Scotland, and would
go thither with me when I returned from abroad, unless some very
good companion should offer when I was absent, which he did not
think probable.

He said, 'There are few people whom I take so much to as you';
and when I talked of leaving England[29], he said (with an affection that
almost made me cry), 'My dear Boswell! I should be very unhappy at
parting, did I think we were not to meet again.'

Thursday 28 July 1763

At night, Mr Johnson and I had a room at the Turk's Head...

I begged Mr Johnson's advice as to my method of study at Utrecht.
'Come,' said he, 'let us make a day of it. Let us go down to Greenwich
and dine.' Accordingly Saturday was fixed for that jaunt, if a sail on
the river may be so expressed. It must be something curious for the
people in the Turk's Head Coffee-house to see this great man and poor
Me so often together by ourselves. My vanity is much flattered.

As we walked along the Strand tonight, arm in arm, a woman of
the town came enticingly near us. 'No,' said Mr Johnson, 'no, my girl,
it won't do.' We then talked of the unhappy situation of these wretches,
and how much more misery than happiness, upon the whole, is
produced by irregular love. He parted from me at the Temple Gate, as
he always does.

And here I must record perhaps the most curious singularity that
ever a man had. When Mr Johnson's wife was alive, she brought into

the house as a companion Miss [Anna] Williams, an amiable, ingenious woman who had attained a remarkable knowledge of the modern languages. This lady's eyes were tender. The disorder increased and ended at last in a *gutta serena*, so that she became stone-blind. Mrs Johnson died, and while Mr Johnson continued to keep house, Miss Williams remained with him. When he took to chambers in the Temple, Miss Williams then went to a lodging of her own. But Mr Johnson is never a night without seeing her. Let him be never so late in company, Miss Williams sits up till he comes and drinks tea with her. I believe Miss Williams is supported chiefly by Mr Johnson's generosity, and I believe nobody has ever had the folly or the malice to suspect anything criminal between them.

Saturday 30 July 1763

Mr Johnson and I took a boat and sailed down the silver Thames...

We landed at the Old Swan and walked to Billingsgate, where we took oars and moved smoothly along the river. We were entertained with the immense number and variety of ships that were lying at anchor. It was a pleasant day, and when we got clear out into the country, we were charmed with the beautiful fields on each side of the river...

When we got to Greenwich, I felt great pleasure in being at the place which Johnson celebrates in his *London: a Poem*. I had the poem in my pocket, and read the passage on the banks of the Thames, and literally 'kissed the consecrated earth'.

We walked about and then had a good dinner (which he likes very well), after which he run over the grand scale of human knowledge ... We then came up by water. I was a little discomposed [cold and tired] even by this small excursion, and felt warm comfort at being again in London.

We supped at the Turk's Head. Mr Johnson said, 'I must see thee go; I will go down with you to Harwich.' This prodigious mark of his affection filled me with gratitude and vanity. I gave him an account of the family of Auchinleck, and of the Place [Auchinleck House and its landscape]. He said, 'I must be there, and we will live in the Old Castle; and if there is no room remaining, we will build one.' This was the most pleasing idea that I could possibly have: to think of

seeing this great man at the venerable seat of my ancestors. I had been
up all last night yet was not sleepy.

Thursday 4 August 1763

   This is now my last day in London before I set out upon my travels,
and makes a very important period in my journal. Let me recollect my
life since this journal began. Has it not passed like a dream? Yes, but
I have been attaining a knowledge of the world. I came to town to go
into the Guards. How different is my scheme now! I am now upon a
less pleasurable but a more rational and lasting plan. Let me pursue it
with steadiness and I may be a man of dignity. My mind is strangely
agitated. I am happy to think of going upon my travels and seeing the
diversity of foreign parts; and yet my feeble mind shrinks somewhat
at the idea of leaving Britain in so very short a time from the moment
in which I now make this remark. How strange must I feel myself in
foreign parts. My mind too is gloomy and dejected at the thoughts of
leaving London, where I am so comfortably situated and where I have
enjoyed most happiness. However, I shall be the happier for being
abroad, as long as I live. Let me be manly. Let me commit myself to
the care of my merciful Creator.

THE END OF MY JOURNAL BEFORE MY TRAVELS

TWO

Travels
1763–1766

Holland 1763–1764

The record of Boswell's year in Holland begins on 5 August 1763 as Johnson accompanies him by stagecoach from London to Harwich for his embarkation, a remarkable development in the developing friendship between this young, unlearned and inexperienced Scot and the great moralist of The Rambler essays, author of the majestic English Dictionary, and greatest English man of letters of the day. It was fodder for Boswell's growing conviction that he was a person of 'singular merit' with a uniquely engaging character.

Boswell for some time had worried about being in Utrecht because of its alleged dullness and the legal studies he was being sentenced to at the university. He feared that his hypochondria might worsen in the gloom there, and he was right. It became his constant companion. Partly because of the monotony of Utrecht for him, partly because he subjected himself to (for him) an unnaturally rigorous regimen of study and 'retenu' – his word for discreet and controlled behaviour – that oppressed him, during his months in Holland he endured some of the darkest depression of his entire life. Without Grange and Temple's letters, and Johnson's Rambler essays, he might not have lasted the course in Utrecht. Utrecht society, however, eventually opened up to him and he became a great favourite. His chief compensation was Belle du Zuylen, or Zélide, with whom it may be said he fell in love. Zélide, who belonged to one of the oldest families in Holland (Tuyll) and is when Boswell meets her already a published author, was the most intelligent, sprightly, witty and independent woman with whom he ever became intimate. The story of their relationship over the next four to five years was, on Boswell's part, one of prevarication and indecision, but there was a great deal of charm in it. She represents the road not taken, a bud of promise in his life that never bore fruit.

In Holland Boswell copiously kept an elaborate journal of almost 600 manuscript pages. Tragically, however, it was mysteriously lost even before he returned to Britain. What we have to go on instead as a record of these months is a collage of stray pieces of the journal, letters, memoranda (from which he intended later to write up his journal in even more detail), essay exercises including French 'Themes', and ten-line verses (mostly doggerel). The French 'Themes' were efforts to learn the language, at which since he was a good linguist he was fairly successful.

1763

Boswell to Grange, 23 September 1763 [Utrecht]

I set out upon my travels with a kind of gloom upon my mind. My enthusiastic love of London made me leave it with a heavy heart. It might not have been the case had I been setting out on an immediate tour through the gay regions of Italy and France. But to comply with my father's inclinations I had agreed to pass my first winter at Utrecht, a Dutch university town of which I had received the most disagreeable prepossessions. Mr Samuel Johnson honoured me with his company to Harwich, where he saw me embark and set sail from Britain. I was sick and filled with a crowd of different ideas. But we had a good passage, and landed on Sunday the 7 of August, at twelve noon ... I began to turn low-spirited, and set out for Utrecht. I travelled between Leyden and Utrecht nine hours in a sluggish trek schuit [barge] without any companion, so that I brooded over my own dismal imaginations. I arrived at Utrecht on a Saturday evening. I went to the Nouveau Chateau d'Anyers. I was shown up to a high bedroom with old furniture, where I had to sit and be fed by myself. At every hour the bells of the great tower played a dreary psalm tune. A deep melancholy seized upon me. I groaned with the idea of living all winter in so shocking a place. I thought myself old and wretched and forlorn. I was worse and worse next day. All the horrid ideas that you can imagine, recurred upon me. I was quite unemployed and had not a soul to speak to ... I sunk quite into despair. I thought that at length the time was come that I should grow mad. I actually believed myself so. I went out to the streets, and even in public could not refrain from groaning and weeping bitterly. I said always, 'Poor Boswell! Is it come to this? Miserable wretch that I am! what shall I do?'

[*To see himself through the threatening gloom and depression in Utrecht and keep himself on course, Boswell wrote out an 'Inviolable Plan' calculated to remind him who he was and what he was supposed to be doing. It is a document full of optimism and hope, a quest for self-understanding.*]

INVIOLABLE PLAN, TO BE READ OVER FREQUENTLY

You have got an excellent heart and bright parts. You are born to a respectable station in life. You are bound to do the duties of a Laird of Auchinleck. For some years past you have been idle, dissipated, absurd, and unhappy. Let those years be thought of no more. You are now determined to form yourself into a man. Formerly all your resolutions were overturned by a fit of the spleen. You believed that you had a real distemper. On your first coming to Utrecht you yielded to that idea. You endured severe torment. You was pitiful and wretched. You was in danger of utter ruin. This severe shock has proved of the highest advantage. Your friend Temple showed you that idleness was your sole disease. The Rambler showed you that vacuity, gloom, and fretfulness were the causes of your woe, and that you was only afflicted as others are. He furnished you with principles of philosophy and piety to support the soul at all times. You returned to Utrecht determined. You studied with diligence. You grew quite well. This is a certain fact. You must never forget it. Nor attempt to plead a real incurable distemper; for you cured it, when it was at its very worst, merely by following a proper plan with diligence and activity. This is a great era in your life; for from this time you fairly set out upon solid principles to be a man. Your worthy father has the greatest affection for you and has suffered much from your follies. You are now resolved to make reparation by a rational and prudent conduct. Your dear mother is anxious to see you do well. And your friends and relations expect that you will be an honour to them and will be useful to them as a lawyer, and make them happy as an agreeable private gentleman.

You have been long without a fixed plan and have felt the misery of being unsettled. You are now come abroad at a distance from company with whom you lived as a frivolous and as a ludicrous fellow. You are to attain habits of study, so that you may have constant entertainment by yourself, nor be at the mercy of every company; and to attain propriety of conduct, that you may be respected. You are not to set yourself to work to become stiff and unnatural. You must avoid affectation. You must act as you ought to do in the general tenor of life, and that will establish your character. Lesser things will form of course.

Remember that idleness renders you quite unhappy. That then your imagination broods over dreary ideas of its own forming, and you become contemptible and wretched. Let this be no more. Let your mind be filled with nobler principles. Remember religion and morality. Remember the dignity of human nature. Remember everything may be endured.

Have a sense of piety ever on your mind, and be ever mindful that this is subject to no change, but will last you as long as life and support you at death. Elevate your soul by prayer and by contemplation without mystical enthusiasm. Preserve a just, clear, and agreeable idea of the divine Christian religion. It is very clearly proved. You cannot expect demonstration. There is virtue in faith; in giving a candid assent upon examination. Keep quite clear of gloomy notions which have nothing to do with the mild and elegant religion of Jesus as it is beautifully displayed in the New Testament. Have this faith always firm. Be steady to the Church of England, whose noble worship has always raised your mind to exalted devotion and meditation on the joys of heaven. Be firm to religion, and at all times show your displeasure to profanity, like a decent gentleman. But don't enter into disputes in riotous and ludicrous companies where sacred things cannot be properly weighed.

Without a real plan, life is insipid and uneasy. You have an admirable plan before you. You are to return to Scotland, be one of the Faculty of Advocates, have constant occupation, and a prospect of being in Parliament, or having a gown. You can live quite independent and go to London every year; and you can pass some months at Auchinleck, doing good to your tenants and living hospitably with your neighbours, beautifying your estate, rearing a family, and piously preparing for immortal felicity. To have all these advantages, firmness is necessary. Have constant command of yourself. Restrain ludicrous talents and, by habit, talk always on some useful subject, or enliven conversation with moderate cheerfulness. Keep to study ever to improve. Have your own plan and don't be put out of it. Your friends Temple and Johnston will assist you to do well. Never talk of yourself, nor repeat what you hear in a company. Be firm, and persist like a philosopher.

Now remember what you have resolved. Keep firm to your plan. Life has much uneasiness; that is certain. Always remember that, and it will never surprise you. Remember also life has much happiness. To bear is the noble power of man. This gives true dignity. Trifles are more frequently the causes of our disturbance than great matters. Be prepared therefore for uneasy trifles. You have indulged antipathies to places and persons. That is the sign of a weak and diseased mind. A hysteric lady or a sickly peevish boy may be so swayed. But let not antipathies move a man. It is not sensibility. You can cure it and at all times do so . . .

Sunday 23 October 1763

Yesterday you was still too jocular and talked of yourself, particularly of your whoring, which was shameful; however, you continue your plan of study, and you make no great deviations. Lesser things must come by degrees. Try firmly this week never once to speak of yourself. It will be great. Go to French church. Then home and read Xenophon and bring up journal clear today. You have a good deal to insert. If you can once be silent and have habits of study and manly thought and conduct, you will do well and may marry a woman of the best family in England. Bravo! But be prudent.

Saturday 12 November 1763

Yesterday was an irregular day. You passed three hours at Brown's with Miss de Zuylen[1]. You was too much off guard, and gave way too much to instantaneous fancy, and was too keen about the Highlanders. You was a little light-headed . . .

1764

Boswell to Grange, 20 January 1764 [Utrecht]

I have found Utrecht to be a most excellent place. I have here excellent opportunity to study, and at the same time to see foreign company. There are a number of noble families who reside here in the winter. I have been received into their assemblies, where I pass two or three evenings a week improving in French and in politeness. At Christmas we had a month of vacation. I then went to The Hague, where I passed three weeks in the most brilliant gaiety. The style of living there is much in the manner of Paris. I found my relations there [the Sommelsdyck family] to be people of the first rank, and was treated by them with the utmost civility; I had recommendations to a variety of people. I was presented to the Prince of Orange and the other princes there, to all the foreign ambassadors − in short, to everybody. I passed a couple of days at Leyden, where I supped twice with the young Prince of Strelitz, our Queen's brother, once at his own house ... and now I am returned to this seat of the Dutch muses and have resumed my studious regularity with much satisfaction.

Formerly such a change of life used to unhinge me quite. Now I am firm and keep my post. I shall ever reverence Utrecht, for it was there that I first began to act upon steady and manly principles. I am already not a little altered. But altered for the better. However, I must guard against extremes. No longer ago than last winter I was the ardent votary of pleasure, a gay sceptic who never looked beyond the present hour, a hero and philosopher in dissipation and vice. Now I am all devoted to prudence and to morality. I am full of the dignity of human nature; and so far am I from indulging myself in mimicry and ludicrous jocularity that I must always have some grave or some useful subject. Perhaps I am too much an enthusiast in rectitude. But candour makes me own that rectitude has to me all the charms of novelty. You see then in what situation your friend now is. Are you not happy to be informed of it?

French Theme 22 January 1764[2]

...I am lazy myself. I have a natural disposition to that vice. I am fat, and I have a temperament so constituted that although I have plenty of fire I have also a good deal of sluggishness. It is a rather extraordinary constitution. An officer in the English military service gave a very ingenious illustration of it. He said that I was like a great stone couched on the slope of a mountain, and while I stayed there, I was lumpish and heavy; but when I was once set in motion, I went with amazing velocity, so that it was impossible to stop me until the projectile force being exhausted, I came again to rest. Indeed, it is a very apt illustration, for when I am in company, it is equal odds that you will see me taciturn and sombre, and on the other hand, if I begin to speak, you will hear a brilliant vivacity, a rapidity of thoughts; if I may use that expression, a fire of language of which you have not often heard the like. It is the same in my actions. For example, when I have been some days without studying, I have a shocking disposition to indolence. I am wretched when I am idle, but I have not enough force of mind to return promptly to work, and it is only through the pangs of *ennui* that I am obliged to take a road which I am sure leads me to happiness.

French Theme 27 March 1764

[Indolence] attacks me especially in the morning. I go to bed at night with the most determined resolutions to get up early. François, my faithful servant, wakes me at half-past six. But when I open my eyes and see daylight again, a crowd of disagreeable ideas comes into my mind. I think gloomily of the vanity and misery of human life. I think that it is not worthwhile to do anything. Everything is insipid or everything is dark ... I believe the explanation is some physical disorder. My nerves at that time are relaxed, the vapours have risen to my head. If I get up and move about a little, I am happy and brisk. But it is with the utmost difficulty that I can get up. I have thought of having my bed constructed in a curious fashion. I would have it so that when I pulled a cord, the middle of the bed would be immediately raised and me raised with it and gradually set up on the floor. Thus I should be gently forced into what is good for me.

[From 24 May until he leaves Utrecht on 18 June, Boswell's journal has survived because he wrote it after he left Utrecht. What he wrote before departing he left behind to be carried back to Scotland for him.]

Saturday 26 May 1764 [Amsterdam]

At five I went to a bawdy-house. I was shown up stairs, and had a bottle of claret and a juffrouw. But the girl was much fitter for being wrapped in the blankets of salivation than kissed between the sheets of love. I had no armour, so did not fight. It was truly ludicrous to talk in Dutch to a whore. This scene was to me a rarity as great as peas in February. Yet I was hurt to find myself in the sinks of gross debauchery. This was a proper way to consider the thing. But so sickly was my brain that I had the low scruples of an Edinburgh divine.

Wednesday 13 June 1764

At two I had a chaise and drove ... out to [Castle] Zuylen, where we dined. Zélide and I had a long conversation. She said she did not care for respect. She liked to have everybody free with her, and that they should tell her her faults. I told her that this was very wrong; for she would hardly find a husband of merit who had not some pride, and who would not be hurt at finding people so free with his wife. I owned to her that I was very sorry to leave her. She gave me many a tender look. We took a kind farewell, as I did of all the family. Monsieur de Zuylen and I talked a long time. I am sure he liked me. He has been exceedingly civil to me.

[Boswell grew both more exasperated and in love with Zélide as he journeyed away from her. As he travelled through the Continent, their correspondence became animated and not a little perplexing, to them as well as to us. He talked himself in and out of love many times over. Zélide did all she could to let him know she loved him, that marriage to him was not out of the question, at the same time disparaging his enigmatic northernness; but he would not commit himself, although he, too, made it clear that he was interested in marriage. This went on for a year and a half, and at a much reduced pitch for about three more years even after he returned to Scotland.]

Boswell to Zélide, 9 July 1764 [Berlin]

As you and I, Zélide, are perfectly easy with each other, I must tell you that I am vain enough to read your letters in such a manner as to imagine that you really was in love with me, as much as you can be with any man. I say was, because I am much mistaken if it is not over before now ... You have no command of yourself. You can conceal nothing. You seemed uneasy. You had a forced merriment. The Sunday evening that I left you, I could perceive you touched. But I took no notice of it. From your conversation I saw very well that I had a place in your heart, that you regarded me with a warmth more than friendly. Your letters showed me that you was pleasing yourself with having at last met with the man for whom you could have a strong and a lasting passion. But I am too generous not to undeceive you. You are sensible that I am a man of strict probity. You have told me so ... But there are many stronger reasons against your being my wife; so strong that, as I said to you formerly, I would not be married to you to be a King. I know myself and I know you. And from all probability of reasoning, I am very certain that if we were married together, it would not be long before we should be both very miserable. My wife must be a character directly opposite to my dear Zélide, except in affection, in honesty, and in good humour. You may depend upon me as a friend.

... Tell me that you will make a very good wife. Let me ask you then, Zélide, could you submit your inclinations to the opinion, perhaps the *caprice* of a husband? Could you do this with cheerfulness, without losing any of your sweet good humour, without boasting of it? Could you live quietly in the country six months in the year? Could you make yourself agreeable to plain honest neighbours? Could you talk like any other woman, and have your fancy as much at command as your harpsichord? Could you pass the other six months in a city where there is very good society, though not the high mode? Could you live thus and be content, could you have a great deal of amusement in your own family? Could you give spirits to your husband when he is melancholy? I have known such wives, Zélide. What think you?

... If you love me, own it. I can give you the best advice. If you change, tell me. If you love another, tell me. I don't understand a word of your mystery about a certain gentleman whom you think of three times a day. What do you mean by it? ... I love you more than ever. I would do more than ever to serve you. I would kneel and kiss your hand if I saw you married to the man that could make you happy. Answer me this one question: If I had pretended a passion for you (which I might easily have done, for it is not difficult to make us believe what we are already pleased to imagine) – answer me: would you not have gone with me to the world's end? Supposing even that I had been disinherited by my father, would you not have said, 'Sir, here is my portion. It is yours. We may live genteelly upon it.'

[Zélide writes to him on 27 January 1765 expressing surprise that a man for whom she has felt 'much attachment' should turn out in his letters to have 'the puerile vanity of a fatuous fool', along with 'the arrogant rigidity of an old Cato'. She concludes by assuring him that she will always remain his friend. Boswell promises to return to Utrecht and talk things out on his way back to Britain, but he receives word in France of his mother's death and has to return home immediately. Zélide spent the winter of 1767–1768 in London and never told Boswell she was there, though she still thought they might marry. He then wrote to her endearingly, to which she replied from Utrecht on 26 February 1768, 'Allow me to remark that you certainly take your time for everything. You waited to fall in love with me until you were in the island of Corsica; and to tell me so, you waited until you were in love with another woman and had spoken to her of marriage ... I read your belated endearments with pleasure, with a smile. Well! So you once loved me! ... It seems to me that you interest me and belong to me a little more because of that than if you had always been my cold and philosophic friend ... We have balls where I dance without much pleasure, because I do not have a lover. We have great assemblies: I learn to play cards. One needs a lover if one is to like dancing, one does not need a lover to like gaming.' The game was soon over. Boswell wrote to her, 'My pride and your vanity would never agree' (quoted from Boswell to William Temple, 14 May 1768).]

The Grand Tour: Germany, Switzerland and Italy 1764–1766

Dempster urged Boswell to waste no time getting out of Utrecht once the university term ended. Boswell was now twenty-four. His idea was to tour the

German courts, where he hoped to meet no lesser figure than Frederick the Great and hobnob with German princes and princesses. Then he would make boldly for Switzerland and briefly France to seek out Voltaire and Rousseau, both of whom he hoped to interview. His father would not hear of his continuing on to Italy. As was always the case with Boswell, once he got moving his spirits rose and his hypochondria faded, though without disappearing. These would be among the least troubled days of his entire life. At the end of his travels, he hoped to be a new man, with the sorts of continental experiences, friendships and acquaintances that would give him some 'gravitas' and sophistication, raise him above his provincial friends in Scotland, and fine-tune what he regarded as his exceptional imagination. It would be a journey of reinventing himself. In many of the journal entries he takes stock of how he is faring in this overhaul of his character. And Zélide was very much on his mind the whole way.

As arranged by powerful friends in Scotland, he set off in the company of the great Jacobite military leader, George Keith, the Tenth Earl Marischal of Scotland, Ambassador of Frederick the Great. Marischal was also a friend of Rousseau's. The other traveller was an excruciatingly quiet Turkish girl, Madame de Froment, whom Marischal had adopted. He also had a Swiss servant named Jacob who stayed with him through all his travels and provided some rich comic interludes along the way.

Sunday 24 June 1764

We came at night to an inn in the territory of Hanover. Thus was I laid. In the middle of a great German salle, upon straw spread on the floor, was a sheet laid; here 'great Boswell lay'. I had another sheet and a coverlet. On one side of me were eight or ten horses; on the other, four or five cows. A little way from me sat on high a cock and many hens; and before I went to sleep the cock made my ears ring with his shrill voice, so that I admired the wisdom of the Sybarites, who slew all those noisy birds. What frightened me not a little was an immense mastiff chained pretty near the head of my bed. He growled most horribly, and rattled his chain. I called for a piece of bread and made a friendship with him. Before me were two great folding doors wide open, so that I could see the beauties of the evening sky. In this way, however, did I sleep with much contentment, and much health.

[The following audacious letter to King Frederick the Great of Prussia's 'Reader' may be seen as a warm-up for his overtures to Rousseau and Voltaire.]

Boswell to Henri de Catt, Reader to King Frederick (original in French), 31 July 1764 [Berlin]

I take the liberty, Sir, of writing to you ... Yes, Sir, I am not ashamed to confess my envy of a man who spends his hours in the company of the King of Prussia.

I have already told you of my enthusiastic wish to be presented to your monarch. I am not quite so easy to please as the English knight who made the trip from London to Potsdam solely to see the King, and when he had seen him on the Parade, went quietly home again. I am like the ancient philosopher who said, 'Speak, so that I can see you.' I have already had the honour of seeing His Majesty two or three times. Imagination may do much, but I am sure that he has an aspect of superior guise. Upon my soul, I was struck. He electrified me. Every time I looked at him, I felt a shock of the heroic. You, Sir, whose blood does not circulate so rapidly as mine, may laugh at a stranger. No doubt I seem to you like a child who gazes open-mouthed at a picture of Alexander or Julius Caesar. Well and good. I am willing to keep something of the spirit of childhood...

I am not satisfied with having seen the King. If it is possible, I should like to hear him speak ... It is certain that I am not a great man, but I have an enthusiastic love of great men and I derive a kind of glory from it. I am told that at least I can sometimes conceive an idea of greatness of soul. How many fine things should I not do if I were not hindered by the fear of appearing absurd! How often should I not follow the lively inclinations that come into my mind! Do you know that one evening at Charlottenburg I was very near the King in the garden, and that I felt a powerful impulse to throw myself at his feet and risk telling him how much I had wished to see His Majesty? But I thought a little, and my heated imagination cooled. Yet I am sure that I showed something of unusual agitation, for General Wylich said to me with a serious but cordial air, 'Calm yourself, Sir.' I shall not forget that little anecdote. I am truly the old Scottish baron: I might have said the old feudal baron. I am haughty towards the tenants on my estate. But for a superior like the King of Prussia I have prodigious veneration. Do not reason with me. What I am describing to you is a fixed sentiment. I find that sentiments firmly impressed have much more power than arguments proved up to the hilt; and it is to sentiments that I always return...

Will you have the goodness, Sir, to let me know if you think there is any chance that I may be presented to the King somehow or other before his departure for Silesia? It is perhaps a piece of unreasonable curiosity on my part, and perhaps I might repent of it, for I should probably be so timid that His Majesty would consider me an egregious blockhead. Nevertheless you will afford me a very lively pleasure by giving me your advice in this matter. It will seem exceedingly hard to me to have been in Prussia and not to be able to tell my grandsons that I paid my respects to Frederick the Great.

I hope, Sir, that you will be able to understand my bad French.

[Catt's polite but tentative reply was that perhaps in Berlin it might be possible to arrange a meeting. He said he would mention to the King Boswell's keen desire to meet him. Nothing came of it.]

Monday 13 August 1764

There came into my room this morning the sweetest girl I ever saw, a *blanchisseuse* [laundress], eighteen, fresh, gay. I spoke German to her with unusual ease, and told her that I would not for the world debauch her to give myself a few days' pleasure, but if she would go with me to England and then to Scotland, I would be very kind to her. She was really innocent. Her beauty thrilled my frame. I thought that I might be an old patriarch upon occasions and could not see any harm in taking her with me. She refused to go, but promised to come back from time to time.

Boswell to Grange, 10 September 1764 [Berlin]

To give you my history since I emerged from Holland would be to transcribe or abridge my journal, neither of which would I wish to do. For I hope to have the satisfaction of reading it with you at length ...

As to the course which I am next to steer, I cannot as yet exactly inform you. I would wish to pass four months in Italy, but my father is averse to my going to that intoxicating region. He wishes to have me pass the winter at Geneva, and go to Paris in the spring. I however still beg to be allowed to see Rome. My Lord Marischal and Mr [Sir Andrew] Mitchell have both written in my favour, so that I am not without hopes that my request may be granted. In the mean time, I am to leave this in ten days, make a tour by Dessau, Dresden, Gotha, Mannheim and some more courts to Geneva, where I shall receive my father's final determination, and from whence I have a plain passage into France, or a mountainous one into Italy. If my father is absolutely against my going to Italy, I shall see how I like Geneva. If it is agreeable, I shall stay there till the spring. If otherwise, I shall go to some university town in France. I shall however have an opportunity of seeing Voltaire and Rousseau. I hope to be very well amused in the German courts which I intend to visit. You shall hear from when I get to Geneva.

Friday 21 September 1764 [Potsdam]

The whim struck me to put on a blue bonnet and appear quite a Scots gentleman. I went in this dress to the parade of the Prince of Prussia. The Prince observed me and asked Scott [Captain, of the Prince of Prussia's regiment], 'What is that little cap which that gentleman is wearing?' Scott said, 'It is the kind of cap which Scottish gentlemen wear.' The poor Prince did not like it much, nor could he think that he was a lord's son who wore it. No matter. I was pleased and boldly did I march upon the Parade before the Palace where I again saw the King. But he did not look towards me. However, I was pleased to have shown the first blue bonnet on the Prussian Parade.

[At this point, Lord Marischal stays behind in Potsdam while Boswell moves on to other German courts and then to Switzerland in hopes of seeing Rousseau.]

Sunday 30 September 1764 [Wittenberg]

I was in a true solemn humour, and a most curious and agreeable idea presented itself, which was to write to Mr Samuel Johnson from the tomb of Melanchthon. The woman who showed the church was a good obliging body, and very readily furnished me with pen and ink. That my paper might literally rest upon the monument, or rather the simple epitaph, of this great and good man, I laid myself down and wrote in that posture. The good woman and some more simple beings gathered round and beheld me with wonder. I dare say they supposed me a little mad. Tombs have been always the favourite resort of gloomy, distracted mortals ... I vowed to Mr Johnson an eternal attachment. This letter must surely give him satisfaction. I shall not send it till I see if he gives me a favourable answer to my two last letters. It is really an excellent thought. The letter shall be a valuable remain.

Boswell to Samuel Johnson, 30 September 1764 [Wittenberg]

My ever dear and much respected Sir: You know my solemn enthusiasm of mind. You love me for it, and I respect myself for it, because in so far I resemble Mr Johnson. You will be agreeably surprised when you learn the reason of my writing this letter. I am at Wittenberg in Saxony. I am in the old church where the Reformation was first preached and where some of the Reformers lie interred. I cannot resist the serious pleasure of writing to Mr Johnson from the tomb of Melanchthon. My paper rests upon the gravestone of that great and good man, who was undoubtedly the worthiest of all the Reformers. He wished to reform abuses which had been introduced into the Church, but had no private resentment to gratify. So mild was he that when his aged mother consulted him with anxiety on the perplexing disputes of the times, he advised her to keep to the old religion. At this tomb, then, my ever dear and respected friend, I vow to thee an eternal attachment. It shall be my study to do what I can to render your life happy, and if you die before me, I shall endeavour to do honour to your memory and, elevated by the remembrance of you, persist in noble piety. May God, the Father of all beings, ever bless you! And may you continue to love your most affectionate friend and devoted servant, JAMES BOSWELL.

Monday 8 October 1764 [on the road to Dresden]

After sleeping all night in a thick mist on the post-wagon, I awaked much out of order. My blood was quite stagnated, and my teeth were loose. I was alarmed. When we came to a station, I got down and danced with much vigour, which by degrees brought me to myself. I must really take care on these wagons. I now wrap myself up, head and all, in a great cloak. But even thus the cold gets at me. Besides, when so wrapped up, I am quite an Egyptian mummy and have no use of my arms, so that if the wagon were overturned, I should be quite helpless, and probably be bruised and broken. Let me then take care.

Thursday 25 October 1764 [Kassel]

All the morning I wrote. My method is to make a memorandum every night of what I have seen during the day. By this means I have my materials always secured. Sometimes I am three, four, five days without journalising. When I have time and spirits, I bring up this my journal as well as I can in the hasty manner in which I write it[3]. Some years hence I shall perhaps abridge it in a more elegant style. I take up too much time in writing letters. I am resolved to guard against this. I shall make my correspondence valued by making it scarce. Yet while I am abroad it is pleasant to have a variety of correspondents, and it will also be pleasant when I am settled at home. Well, then, why make grave, proud resolutions of writing little? I was in the wrong, and there's an end on't.

Monday 3 December 1764 [Neuchâtel]

I let Jacob go for a week to see his relations, which made him very happy. One great object which I have ever had in view since I left Britain has been to obtain the acquaintance, and if possible the regard, of Rousseau. I was informed that he lived in a wild valley, five leagues from Neuchâtel. I set out early this morning, mounted on a little horse, with a *Reysesac* [portmanteau] which held some shirts. I was joined by Abraham François, a merchant here. My horse was lazy; he lent me a spur and a whip, and on we jogged very cordially...

...Monsieur Rousseau lives in the village of Môtiers ... I wished that I might not see Rousseau till the moment that I had permission to wait upon him. I perceived a white house with green window-boards. He mentions such a one in Émile. I imagined it might perhaps be his, and turned away my eyes from it. I rode calmly down the street, and put up at the Maison de Village. This inn is kept by Madame Grandpierre, a widow, and her two daughters, fat, motherly maidens...

I asked for Monsieur Rousseau. I found he kept himself very quiet here, as my landlady had little or nothing to chatter concerning him. I had heard all that could be said as to his being difficult of access. My Lord Marischal had given me a card with compliments to him, which I was sure would procure me admission. But my romantic genius, which will never be extinguished, made me eager to put my own merit to the severest trial. I had therefore prepared a letter [see below] to Monsieur Rousseau, in which I informed him that an ancient Scots gentleman of twenty-four was come hither with the hopes of seeing him. I assured him that I deserved his regard, that I was ready to stand the test of his penetration. Towards the end of my letter I showed him that I had a heart and a soul. I have here given no idea of my letter. It can neither be abridged nor transposed, for it is really a masterpiece. I shall ever preserve it as a proof that my soul can be sublime. I dressed and dined and sent my letter *chez* Monsieur Rousseau, ordering the maid to leave it and say she'd return for the answer, so that I might give him time to consider a little, lest perhaps he might be ill and suddenly refuse to see me. I was filled with anxiety. Is not this romantic madness? Was I not sure of admittance by my recommendations? Could I not see him as any other gentleman would do? No: I am above the vulgar crowd. I would have my merit fairly tried by this great judge of human nature. I must have things in my own way. If my bold attempt succeeds, the recollection of it will be grand as long as I live. But perhaps I may appear to him so vain, or so extraordinary, that he may be shocked by such a character and may not admit me. I shall then be in a pretty situation, for I shall be ashamed to present my recommendations. But why all this doubt and uneasiness? It is the effect of my melancholy timidity. What! can the author of *Eloisa* be offended at the enthusiasm of an ingenuous mind? But if he does admit me, I shall have a very difficult character to support; for I have written to him with unusual elevation, and given him an idea of me which I shall hardly come up to.

Boswell to Jean-Jacques Rousseau (original in French), 3 December 1764 [Môtiers] [Boswell wrote three drafts.]

SIR: — I am a Scots gentleman of ancient family. Now you know my rank. I am twenty-four years old. Now you know my age. Sixteen months ago I left Great Britain a completely insular being, knowing hardly a word of French. I have been in Holland and in Germany, but not yet in France. You will therefore excuse my handling of the language. I am travelling with a genuine desire to improve myself. I have come here in the hope of seeing you. I have heard, Sir, that you are very difficult, that you have refused the visits of several people of the first distinction. For that, Sir, I respect you the more. If you admitted all those who from vanity wished to be able to say, 'I have seen him,' your house would no longer be the retreat of exquisite genius or elevated piety, and I should not be striving so eagerly to be received into it. I present myself, Sir, as a man of singular merit, as a man with a feeling heart, a lively but melancholy spirit. Ah, if all that I have suffered does not give me singular merit in the eyes of Monsieur Rousseau, why was I made as I am? Why did he write as he has written?

Do you ask if I have recommendations? Surely you do not need them? In the commerce of the world a recommendation is necessary in order to protect people who lack penetration from imposters. But you, Sir, who have made such deep study of human nature, can you be deceived in a character? I think of you thus: excepting for the incomprehensible essence of the soul, you have a perfect knowledge of all the principles of body and mind, of their movements, their sentiments; in short, of everything they can do, of everything they can acquire which truly affects man as man. And yet, Sir, I dare present myself before you. I dare to put myself to the test. In cities and in courts, where there are numerous companies, one can disguise one's self, one can sometimes dazzle the eyes of the greatest philosophers. But for my part, I put myself to the severest test. It is in the silence and the solitude of your sacred retreat that you shall judge of me, and think you in such circumstances I shall be able to dissimulate?

Your writings, Sir, have melted my heart, have elevated my soul, have fired my imagination. Believe me, you will be glad to have seen me. You know what Scots pride is. Sir, I am coming to see you in order to make myself more worthy of a nation that has produced a Fletcher of Saltoun [a Scots patriot] and a Lord Marischal. Forgive me, Sir, I feel myself moved. I cannot restrain myself. O dear Saint-Preux! [the hero of Nouvelle Héloïse] Enlightened Mentor! Eloquent and amiable Rousseau! I have a presentiment that a truly noble friendship will be born today.

I learn with deep regret, Sir, that you are often indisposed. Perhaps you are so at present. But I beg you not to let that prevent you from receiving me. You will find in me a simplicity that will put you to no trouble, a cordiality that may help you forget your pains.

I have much to tell you. Though I am only a young man, I have experienced a variety of existence that will amaze you. I find myself in serious and delicate circumstances concerning which I eagerly hope to have the counsel of the author of the Nouvelle Héloïse. If you are the charitable man I believe you to be, you cannot hesitate to grant it to me. Open your door, then, Sir, to a man who dares to tell you that he deserves to enter it. Place your confidence in a stranger who is different. You will not regret it. But I beg you, be alone. In spite of all my enthusiasm, after having written to you in this fashion, I know not if I would not prefer never to see you than to see you for the first time in company. I await your reply with impatience. BOSWELL

Monday 3 December 1764 [continued]

To prepare myself for the great interview, I walked out alone. I strolled pensive by the side of the river Reusel in a beautiful wild valley surrounded by immense mountains, some covered with frowning rocks, others with clustering pines, and others with glittering snow. The fresh, healthful air and the romantic prospect around me gave me a vigorous and solemn tone. I recalled all my former ideas of J. J. Rousseau, the admiration with which he is regarded over all Europe, his Héloïse, his Émile: in short, a crowd of great thoughts. This half hour was one of the most remarkable that I ever passed.

I returned to my inn, and the maid delivered to me a card with the following answer from Monsieur Rousseau: 'I am ill, in pain, really in no state to receive visits. Yet I cannot deprive myself of Mr Boswell's, provided that out of consideration for the state of my health, he is willing to make it short.'

My sensibility dreaded the word 'short'. But I took courage, and went immediately. I found at the street door Mademoiselle Le Vasseur waiting for me. She was a little, lively, neat French girl[4] and did not increase my fear. She conducted me up a darkish stair, then opened a door. I expected, 'Now I shall see him' – but it was not so. I entered a room which serves for vestibule and for kitchen. My fancy formed many, many a portrait of the wild philosopher. At length his door opened and I beheld him, a genteel black man in the dress of an Armenian. I entered saying, 'Many, many thanks.' After the first looks and bows were over, he said, 'Will you be seated? Or would you rather take a turn with me in the room?' I chose the last, and happy I was to escape being formally placed upon a chair. I asked him how he was. 'Very ill. But I have given up doctors.' 'Yes, yes; you have no love for them.' As it is impossible for me to relate exactly our conversation, I shall not endeavour at order, but give sentences as I recollect them.

BOSWELL. 'The thought of your books, Sir, is a great source of pleasure to you?'

ROUSSEAU. 'I am fond of them; but when I think of my books, so many misfortunes which they have brought upon me are revived in my memory that really I cannot answer you. And yet my books have saved my life.' He spoke of the Parlement of Paris: 'If any company could be covered with disgrace, that would be. I could plunge them into deep disgrace simply by printing their edict against me on one side, and the law of nations and equity on the side opposite. But I have reasons against doing so at present.'

BOSWELL. 'We shall have it one day, perhaps?'

ROUSSEAU. 'Perhaps.'

I was dressed in a coat and waistcoat, scarlet with gold lace, buckskin breeches, and boots. Above all I wore a greatcoat of green camlet lined with fox-skin fur, with the collar and cuffs of the same fur. I held under my arm a hat with a solid gold lace, at least with the air of being solid. I had it last winter at The Hague. I had a free air and spoke well, and when Monsieur Rousseau said what touched me more than ordinary, I seized his hand, I thumped him on the shoulder. I was without restraint. When I found that I really pleased him, I said, 'Are you aware, Sir, that I am recommended to you by a man you hold in high regard?'

ROUSSEAU. 'Ah! My Lord Marischal?'

BOSWELL. 'Yes, Sir; my Lord furnished me with a note to introduce me to you.'

ROUSSEAU. 'And you were unwilling to take advantage of it?'

BOSWELL. 'Nay, Sir; I wished to have proof of my own merits.'

ROUSSEAU. 'Sir, there would have been no kind of merit in gaining access to me by a note of Lord Marischal's. Whatever he sends will always find a welcome from me. He is my protector, my father; I would venture to say, my friend.' One circumstance embarrassed me a little: I had forgotten to bring with me from Neuchâtel my Lord's billet. But a generous consciousness of innocence and honesty gives a freedom which cannot be counterfeited. I told Monsieur Rousseau, 'To speak truly, I have forgotten to bring his letter with me; but you accept my word for it?'

ROUSSEAU. 'Why, certainly. Numbers of people have shown

themselves ready to serve me in their own fashion; my Lord Marischal has served me in mine. He is the only man on earth to whom I owe an obligation.' He went on, 'When I speak of kings, I do not include the King of Prussia. He is a king quite alone and apart. That force of his! Sir, there's the great matter, to have force – revenge, even. You can always find stuff to make something out of. But when force is lacking, when everything is small and split up, there's no hope. The French, for example, are a contemptible nation.'

BOSWELL. 'But the Spaniards, Sir?'

ROUSSEAU. 'Yes, you will find great souls in Spain.'

BOSWELL. 'And in the mountains of Scotland. But since our cursed Union, ah –'

ROUSSEAU. 'You undid yourselves.'

BOSWELL. 'Truly, yes. But I must tell you a great satisfaction given me by my Lord. He calls you Jean Jacques out of affection. One day he said to me, "Jean Jacques is the most grateful man in the world. He wanted to write my brother's life; but I begged him rather to write the life of Mr Fletcher of Saltoun, and he promised me he would do so." '

ROUSSEAU. 'Yes, Sir; I will write it with the greatest care and pleasure. I shall offend the English, I know. But that is no matter. Will you furnish me with some anecdotes on the characters of those who made your Treaty of Union, and details that cannot be found in the historians?'

BOSWELL. 'Yes, Sir; but with the warmth of an ancient Scot.'

ROUSSEAU. 'By all means'...

ROUSSEAU. 'Sir, you don't see before you the bear you have heard tell of. Sir, I have no liking for the world. I live here in a world of fantasies, and I cannot tolerate the world as it is.'

BOSWELL. 'But when you come across fantastical men, are they not to your liking?'

ROUSSEAU. 'Why, Sir, they have not the same fantasies as myself – Sir, your country is formed for liberty. I like your habits. You and I feel free to stroll here together without talking. That is more than two Frenchmen can do. Mankind disgusts me. And my housekeeper tells me that I am in far better humour on the days when I have been alone than on those when I have been in company.'

BOSWELL. 'There has been a great deal written against you, Sir.'

ROUSSEAU. 'They have not understood me...'

BOSWELL. 'Tell me, Sir, do you not find that I answer to the description I gave you of myself?'

ROUSSEAU. 'Sir, it is too early for me to judge. But all appearances are in your favour.'

BOSWELL. 'I fear I have stayed too long. I shall take the honour of returning tomorrow.'

ROUSSEAU. 'Oh, as to that, I can't tell.'

BOSWELL. 'Sir, I shall stay quietly here in the village. If you are able to see me, I shall be enchanted; if not, I shall make no complaint.'

ROUSSEAU. 'My Lord Marischal has a perfect understanding of man's feelings, in solitude no less than in society. I am overwhelmed with visits from idle people.'

BOSWELL. 'And how do they spend their time?'

ROUSSEAU. 'In paying compliments. Also I get a prodigious quantity of letters. And the writer of each of them believes that he is the only one.'

BOSWELL. 'You must be greatly surprised, Sir, that a man who has not the honour of your acquaintance should take the liberty of writing to you?'

ROUSSEAU. 'No. I am not at all surprised. For I got a letter like it yesterday, and one the day before yesterday, and others many times before that.'

BOSWELL. 'Sir, your very humble servant – What, you are coming further?'

ROUSSEAU. 'I am not coming with you. I am going for a walk in the passage. Good-bye.' . . .

Tuesday 4 December 1764

After taking a walk in the *vallon*, I went to the door of Monsieur Rousseau. Mademoiselle Le Vasseur was abroad, and I could not get in. I met her on the street, and she said, 'Monsieur Rousseau will let you know this afternoon at what hour he can see you.' . . .

At five I went to Monsieur Rousseau, whom I found more gay than he had been yesterday. We joked on Mademoiselle Le Vasseur for keeping him under lock and key. She, to defend herself, said he had another door to get out at. Said he, 'Ah, Mademoiselle, you can keep nothing to yourself.'

He gave me the character of Abbé de Saint-Pierre, 'a man who did good, simply because he chose to do good: a man without enthusiasm. One might say that he was passionately reasonable. He would come to a discussion armed with notes, and he used to say, "I shall be sneered at for this," "I shall get a hissing for that." It was all one to him. He carried his principles into the merest trifles. For example, he used to wear his watch suspended from a button on his coat, because that was more convenient. As he was precluded from marriage, he kept mistresses, and made no secret of it. He had a number of sons. He would allow them to adopt none but the most strictly useful professions; for example, he would not allow any son of his to be a wig-maker. "For," said he, "so long as Nature continues to supply us with hair, the profession of wig-making must always be full of uncertainty." He was completely indifferent to the opinion of men, saying that they were merely overgrown children. After paying a long visit to a certain lady, he said to her, "Madam, I perceive I am wearisome to you, but that is a matter of no moment to me. You amuse me." One of Louis XIV's creatures had him turned out of the Academy for a speech he had made there. Yet he perpetually visited this man. "For," said he, "he acted in his own interests, and I bear him no grudge for that. He amuses me. He has no grounds for being offended with me. I have grounds for offence against him, but I am not offended." In short, he continued to call on this Academician, until the latter put a stop to it because he found it disagreeable to see a man whom he had injured. He had plenty of good sense, but a faulty style: long-winded and diffuse, yet always proving his point. He was a favourite with women; he would go his own way independently, and he won respect. If you become a Member of Parliament, you must resemble the Abbé de Saint-Pierre. You must stick to your principles.'

BOSWELL. 'But, then, one must be very well instructed.'

ROUSSEAU. 'Ah, sure enough. You must have a well-furnished head.'

BOSWELL. 'But Sir, a Member of Parliament who behaves as a strictly honest man is regarded as a crazy fool.'

ROUSSEAU. 'Well then, you must be a crazy fool of a Member; and believe me, such a man will be respected – that is, if he holds consistently by his principles. A man who changes round on every occasion is another affair.'

He talked of his *Plan for Perpetual Peace, taken from the Abbé de Saint-Pierre.* I frankly owned that I had not read it. 'No?' said he – then took one down from his bookcase and gave it me. I asked him smilingly if he would not put his name upon it. He laughed heartily at me. I talked to him of the German album and how I had been forced to take one; but that except what was written by the person who gave it me, there was nothing in it. Said he, 'Then your album is *album*.' There was a sally for you. A precious pearl; a pun made by Rousseau. He said, 'I have seen the Scottish Highlanders in France. I love the Scots; not because my Lord Marischal is one of them but because he praises them. You are irksome to me. It's my nature. I cannot help it.'

BOSWELL. 'Do not stand on ceremony with me.'

ROUSSEAU. 'Go away.'

Mademoiselle always accompanies me to the door. She said, 'I have been twenty-two years with Monsieur Rousseau; I would not give up my place to be Queen of France. I try to profit by the good advice he gives me. If he should die, I shall have to go into a convent.' She is a very good girl, and deserves to be esteemed for her constancy to a man so valuable. His simplicity is beautiful. He consulted Mademoiselle and her mother on the merits of his *Héloïse* and his *Émile*.

Wednesday 5 December 1764

When I waited upon Monsieur Rousseau this morning, he said, 'My dear Sir, I am sorry not to be able to talk with you as I would wish.' I took care to waive such excuses, and immediately set conversation a-going. I told him how I had turned Roman Catholic and had intended to hide myself in a convent in France. He said, 'What folly! I too was Catholic in my youth. I changed, and then I changed back again. I returned to Geneva and was readmitted to the Protestant faith. I went again among Catholics, and used to say to them, "I am no longer one of you"; and I got on with them excellently.' I stopped him in the middle of the room and I said to him, 'But tell me sincerely, are you a Christian?' I looked at him with a searching eye. His countenance was no less animated. Each stood steady and watched the other's looks. He struck his breast, and replied, 'Yes. I pique myself upon being one.'

BOSWELL. 'Sir, the soul can be sustained by nothing save the Gospel.'

ROUSSEAU. 'I feel that. I am unaffected by all the objections. I am weak; there may be things beyond my reach; or perhaps the man who recorded them made a mistake. I say, God the Father, God the Son, God the Holy Ghost.'

BOSWELL. 'But tell me, do you suffer from melancholy?'

ROUSSEAU. 'I was born placid. I have no natural disposition to melancholy. My misfortunes have infected me with it.'

BOSWELL. 'I, for my part, suffer from it severely. And how can I be happy, I, who have done so much evil?'

ROUSSEAU. 'Begin your life anew. God is good, for he is just. Do good. You will cancel all the debt of evil. Say to yourself in the morning, "Come now, I am going to pay off so much evil." Six well-spent years will pay off all the evil you have committed.'

BOSWELL. 'But what do you think of cloisters, penances, and remedies of that sort?'

ROUSSEAU. 'Mummeries, all of them, invented by men. Do not be guided by men's judgments, or you will find yourself tossed to and fro perpetually. Do not base your life on the judgments of others; first, because they are as likely to be mistaken as you are, and further, because you cannot know that they are telling you their true thoughts; they may be impelled by motives of interest or convention to talk to you in a way not corresponding to what they really think.'

BOSWELL. 'Will you, Sir, assume direction of me?'

ROUSSEAU. 'I cannot. I can be responsible only for myself.'

BOSWELL. 'But I shall come back.'

ROUSSEAU. 'I don't promise to see you. I am in pain. I need a chamber-pot every minute.'

BOSWELL. 'Yes, you will see me.'

ROUSSEAU. 'Be off; and a good journey to you.'

[Frustrated that Rousseau was not responding personally enough to his problems, Boswell wrote out for him his 'A Sketch of My Life', a confessional tour through his short existence. He then went away for a few days, returning on 14 December, by which time Rousseau had read it and was prepared to talk about it.]

'SKETCH OF MY LIFE' (original in French), 5 December 1764

...I loved the daughter of a man of the first distinction in Scotland[5]. She married a gentleman of great wealth. She allowed me to see that she loved me more than she did her husband. She made no difficulty of granting me all. She was a subtle philosopher. She said, 'I love my husband as a husband, and you as a lover, each in his own sphere. I perform for him all the duties of a good wife. With you I give myself up to delicious pleasures. We keep our secret. Nature has so made me that I shall never bear children. No one suffers from our loves. My conscience does not reproach me, and I am sure that God cannot be offended by them.' Philosophy of that sort in the mouth of a charming woman seemed very attractive to me. But her father had heaped kindnesses on me. Her husband was one of the most amiable of men ... I was seized with the bitterest regrets. I was sad. I was almost in despair, and often wished to confess everything to Monsieur de —, in order to compel him to deprive me of my wretched life. But that would have been the most fatal of follies. I opened my heart to Madame de —. Although she was affectionate and generous, she was set in her ideas. She reproached me for my weakness. What could I do? I continued my criminal amour, and the pleasures I tasted formed a counterpoise to my remorse. Sometimes even in my transports I imagined that heaven could not but smile on so great a happiness between two mortals. At twenty-two, my father permitted me to go to London. I was glad to escape from Madame de —'s vicinity. I made a resolve never to write to her, and for two years we have had no news of each other, except that we are in good health ... Sir, I have given you in haste a record of all the evil I have done. I have told you of all there is good in me. Tell me, is it possible for me yet to make myself a man? Tell me if I can be a worthy Scots laird. If I can – heavens, how much I fear the contrary! – if I can be virtuous as regards Madame de —. Perhaps she has changed too. O charitable philosopher, I beseech you to help me. My mind is weak but my soul is strong. Kindle that soul, and the sacred fire shall never be extinguished.

Friday 14 December 1764

... I arrived at Môtiers before noon. I alighted at Rousseau's door. Up and I went and found Mademoiselle Le Vasseur, who told me, 'He is very ill.' 'But can I see him for a moment?' 'I will find out. Step in, Sir.' I found him sitting in great pain.

ROUSSEAU. 'I am overcome with ailments, disappointments, and sorrow. I am using a probe. – Everyone thinks it my duty to attend to him.'

BOSWELL. 'That is most natural; and are you not pleased to find you can be of so much help to others?'

ROUSSEAU. 'Why –'

I had left with him when I was last here what I called a 'Sketch of My Life', in which I gave him the important incidents of my history and my melancholy apprehensions, and begged his advice and friendship. It was an interesting piece: He said, 'I have read your Memoir. You have been gulled. You ought never to see a priest.'

BOSWELL. 'But can I yet hope to make something of myself?'

ROUSSEAU. 'Yes. Your great difficulty is that you think it so difficult a matter. Come back in the afternoon. But put your watch on the table.'

BOSWELL. 'For how long?'

ROUSSEAU. 'A quarter of an hour, and no longer.'

BOSWELL. 'Twenty minutes.'

ROUSSEAU. 'Be off with you! Ha! Ha!' Notwithstanding the pain he was in, he was touched with my singular sally and laughed most really. He had a gay look immediately.

I dined in my old room with the two boarders. After dinner I walked out. There had fallen much rain, and the river was all overflowed. Nature looked somewhat different from the time that I was first here. I was sorry that such a scene was subject to any change.

At four I went to Monsieur Rousseau. 'I have but a moment allowed me; I must use it well. – Is it possible to live amongst other men, and to retain singularity?'

ROUSSEAU. 'Yes, I have done it.'

BOSWELL. 'But to remain on good terms with them?'

ROUSSEAU. 'Oh, if you want to be a wolf, you must howl. – I attach very little importance to books.'

BOSWELL. 'Even to your own books?'

ROUSSEAU. 'Oh, they are just rigmarole.'

BOSWELL. 'Now you are howling.'

ROUSSEAU. 'When I put my trust in books, I was tossed about as you are—though it is rather by talking that you have been tossed. I had nothing stable here' (striking his head) 'before I began to meditate.'

BOSWELL. 'But you would not have meditated to such good purpose if you had not read.'

ROUSSEAU. 'No. I should have meditated to better purpose if I had begun sooner.'

BOSWELL. 'But I, for example, would never have had the agreeable ideas I possess of the Christian religion, had I not read "The Savoyard's Creed". Yet, to tell the truth, I can find no certain system. Morals appear to me an uncertain thing. For instance, I should like to have thirty women. Could I not satisfy that desire?'

ROUSSEAU. 'No!'

BOSWELL. 'Why?'

ROUSSEAU. 'Ha! Ha! If Mademoiselle were not here, I would give you a most ample reason why.'

BOSWELL. 'But consider: if I am rich, I can take a number of girls; I get them with child; propagation is thus increased. I give them dowries, and I marry them off to good peasants who are very happy to have them. Thus they become wives at the same age as would have been the case if they had remained virgins, and I, on my side, have had the benefit of enjoying a great variety of women.'

ROUSSEAU. 'Oh, you will be landed in jealousies, betrayals, and treachery.'

BOSWELL. 'But cannot I follow the Oriental usage?'

ROUSSEAU. 'In the Orient the women are kept shut up, and that means keeping slaves. And, mark you, their women do nothing but harm, whereas ours do much good, for they do a great deal of work.'

BOSWELL. 'Still, I should like to follow the example of the old Patriarchs, worthy men whose memory I hold in respect.'

ROUSSEAU. 'But are you not a citizen? You must not pick and choose one law here and another law there; you must take the laws of your own society. Do your duty as a citizen, and if you hold fast, you will win respect. I should not talk about it, but I would do it. – And as for your lady, when you go back to Scotland you will say, "Madam, such conduct is against my conscience, and there shall be no more of it." She will applaud you; if not, she is to be despised.'

BOSWELL. 'Suppose her passion is still lively, and she threatens to tell her husband what has happened unless I agree to continue our intrigue?'

ROUSSEAU. 'In the first place, she will not tell him. In the second, you have no right to do evil for the sake of good.'

BOSWELL. 'True. None the less, I can imagine some very embarrassing situations. And pray tell me how I can expiate the evil I have done?'

ROUSSEAU. 'Oh, Sir, there is no expiation for evil except good.'

A beautiful thought this. Nevertheless, I maintained my doctrine of satisfaction by punishment. Yes, I must ever think that immutable justice requires atonement to be made for transgressions, and this atonement is to be made by suffering. This is the universal idea of all nations, and seems to be a leading principle of Christianity. I gave myself full scope; for since I left England I have not had anybody to whom I could lay open entirely my mind till I found Monsieur Rousseau.

I asked him, 'When I get to France and Italy, may I not indulge in the gallantries usual to those countries, where the husbands do not resent your making love to their wives? Nay, should I not be happier as the citizen of such a nation?'

ROUSSEAU. 'They are corpses. Do you want to be a corpse?' He was right.

BOSWELL. 'But tell me, has a virtuous man any true advantages, is he really better off than a man given up to sensuality?'

ROUSSEAU. 'We cannot doubt that we are spiritual beings; and when the soul escapes from this prison, from this flesh, the virtuous man will find things to his liking. He will enjoy the contemplation of happy souls, nobly employed. He will say, "I have already lived a life like that." Whereas those who experience nothing but the vile passions which have their origin in the body will be dissatisfied by the spectacle of pleasures which they have no means of enjoying.'

BOSWELL. 'Upon my word, I am at a loss how to act in this world; I cannot determine whether or not I should adopt some profession.'

ROUSSEAU. 'One must have a great plan.'

BOSWELL. 'What about those studies on which so much stress is laid? Such as history, for instance?'

ROUSSEAU. 'They are just amusements.'

BOSWELL. 'My father desires me to be called to the Scottish bar; I am certainly doing right in satisfying my father; I have no such certainty if I follow my light inclinations. I must therefore give my mind to the study of the laws of Scotland.'

ROUSSEAU. 'To be sure; they are your tools. If you mean to be a carpenter, you must have a plane.'

BOSWELL. 'I do not get on well with my father. I am not at my ease with him.'

ROUSSEAU. 'To be at ease you need to share some amusement.'

BOSWELL. 'We look after the planting together.'

ROUSSEAU. 'That's too serious a business. You should have some amusement that puts you more on an equal footing: shooting, for example. A shot is missed and a joke is made of it, without any infringement of respect. You enjoy a freedom which you take for granted. – Once you are involved in a profession, you must keep on with it even though another, and apparently better, should present itself. If you keep changing, you can achieve nothing.'

(I should have observed that when I pushed the conversation on women, Mademoiselle went out, and Monsieur Rousseau said, 'See now, you are driving Mademoiselle out of the room.' She was now returned.) He stopped, and looked at me in a singular manner. 'Are you greedy?'

BOSWELL. 'Yes.'

ROUSSEAU. 'I am sorry to hear it.'

BOSWELL. 'Ha! Ha! I was joking, for in your books you write in favour of greed. I know what you are about to say, and it is just what I was hoping to hear. I wanted to get you to invite me to dinner. I had a great desire to share a meal with you.

ROUSSEAU. 'Well, if you are not greedy, will you dine here tomorrow? But I give you fair warning, you will find yourself badly off.'

BOSWELL. 'No, I shall not be badly off; I am above all such considerations.'

ROUSSEAU. 'Come then at noon; it will give us time to talk.'

BOSWELL. 'All my thanks.'

ROUSSEAU. 'Good evening.'

Mademoiselle carried me to the house of a poor woman with a great many children whom Monsieur Rousseau aids with his charity. I contributed my part. I was not pleased to hear Mademoiselle repeat to the poor woman just the common consolatory sayings. She should have said something singular.

Saturday 15 December 1764

I was full of fine spirits. Gods! Am I now then really the friend of Rousseau? What a rich assemblage of ideas! I relish my felicity truly in such a scene as this. Shall I not truly relish it at Auchinleck? I was quite gay, my fancy was youthful, and vented its gladness in sportive sallies. I supposed myself in the rude world. I supposed a parcel of young fellows saying, 'Come, Boswell, you'll dine with us today?' 'No, gentlemen, excuse me; I'm engaged. I dine today with Rousseau.' My tone, my air, my native pride when I pronounced this! Temple! You would have given half a guinea to see me at that moment.

...I then went to Monsieur Rousseau. 'I hope your health is better today.'

ROUSSEAU. 'Oh, don't speak of it.' He seemed unusually gay. Before dinner we are all so, if not made to wait too long. A keen appetite gives a vivacity to the whole frame.

I said, 'You say nothing in regard to a child's duties towards his parents. You tell us nothing of your Émile's father.'

ROUSSEAU. 'Oh, he hadn't any. He didn't exist.' It is, however, a real pity that Monsieur Rousseau has not treated of the duties between parents and children. It is an important and a delicate subject and deserves to be illustrated by a sage of so clear a judgment and so elegant a soul.

He praised the *Spectator*. He said, 'One comes across allegories in it. I have no taste for allegories, though your nation shows a great liking for them.'

I gave him very fully the character of Mr Johnson. He said with force, 'I should like that man. I should respect him. I would not disturb his principles if I could. I should like to see him, but from a distance, for fear he might maul me.' I told him how averse Mr Johnson was to write, and how he had his levee. 'Ah,' said he, 'I understand. He is a man who enjoys holding forth.' I told him Mr Johnson's *bon mot* upon the innovators: that truth is a cow which will yield them no more milk, and so they are gone to milk the bull. He said, 'He would detest me. He would say, "Here is a corrupter: a man who comes here to milk the bull." '

I had diverted myself by pretending to help Mademoiselle Le Vasseur to make the soup. We dined in the kitchen, which was neat and cheerful. There was something singularly agreeable in this scene. Here was Rousseau in all his simplicity, with his Armenian dress, which I have surely mentioned before now. His long coat and nightcap made him look easy and well.

Our dinner was as follows: 1. A dish of excellent soup. 2. A *bouilli* of beef and veal. 3. Cabbage, turnip, and carrot. 4. Cold pork. 5. Pickled trout, which he jestingly called tongue. 6. Some little dish which I forget. The dessert consisted of stoned pears and of chestnuts.

We had red and white wines. It was a simple, good repast. We were quite at our ease. I sometimes forgot myself and became ceremonious. 'May I help you to some of this dish?'

ROUSSEAU. 'No, Sir. I can help myself to it.' Or, 'May I help myself to some more of that?'

ROUSSEAU. 'Is your arm long enough? A man does the honours of his house from a motive of vanity. He does not want it forgotten who is the master. I should like everyone to be his own master, and no one to play the part of host. Let each one ask for what he wants; if it is there to give, let him be given it; otherwise, he must be satisfied without. Here you see true hospitality.'

BOSWELL. 'In England, it is quite another matter. They do not want to be at ease; they are stiff and silent, in order to win respect.'

ROUSSEAU. 'In France, you find no such gloom among people of distinction. There is even an affectation of the utmost liberty, as though they would have you understand, "We stand in no fear of losing our dignity." That is a more refined form of self-esteem.'

BOSWELL. 'Well, and do you not share that yourself?'

ROUSSEAU. 'Yes, I confess that I like to be respected; but only in matters of importance.'

BOSWELL. 'You are so simple. I expected to find you quite different from this: the Great Rousseau. But you do not see yourself in the same light as others do. I expected to find you enthroned and talking with a grave authority.'

ROUSSEAU. 'Uttering oracles? Ha! Ha! Ha!'

BOSWELL. 'Yes, and that I should be much in awe of you. And really your simplicity might lay you open to criticism; it might be said, "Monsieur Rousseau does not make himself sufficiently respected." In Scotland, I assure you, a very different tone must be taken to escape from the shocking familiarity which is prevalent in that country. Upon my word, I cannot put up with it. Should I not be justified in forestalling it by fighting a duel with the first man who should treat me so, and thus live at peace for the rest of my life?'

ROUSSEAU. 'No. That is not allowable. It is not right to stake one's life on such follies. Life is given us for objects of importance. Pay no heed to what such men say. They will get tired of talking to a man who does not answer them.'

BOSWELL. 'If you were in Scotland, they would begin at the very start by calling you Rousseau; they would say, "Jean Jacques, how goes it?" with the utmost familiarity.'

ROUSSEAU. 'That is perhaps a good thing.'

BOSWELL. 'But they would say, "Poh! Jean Jacques, why do you allow yourself all these fantasies? You're a pretty man to put forward such claims. Come, come, settle down in society like other people." And they would say it to you with a sourness which I am quite unable to imitate for you.'

ROUSSEAU. 'Ah, that's bad.'

There he felt the thistle, when it was applied to himself on the tender part. It was just as if I had said, 'Hoot, Johnnie Rousseau man, what for hae ye sae mony figmagairies? Ye're a bonny man indeed to mauk siccan a wark; set ye up. Canna ye just live like ither fowk?' It was the best idea could be given in the polite French language of the rude Scots sarcastical vivacity.

BOSWELL. 'I have leanings towards despotism, let me tell you. On our estate, I am like an ancient laird, and I insist on respect from the tenants.'

ROUSSEAU. 'But when you see an old man with white hair, do you, as a young man, have no feelings at all? Have you not respect for age?'

BOSWELL. 'Yes. I have even on many occasions been very affable. I have talked quite freely with the tenants.'

ROUSSEAU. 'Yes, you forgot yourself, and became a man.'

BOSWELL. 'But I was sorry for it afterwards. I used to think, "I have lowered myself."'

ROUSSEAU. 'Ha! Ha! Ha!'

BOSWELL. 'I have leanings towards despotism, let me tell you. Give me credentials as your ambassador to the Corsicans. Will you make me his Excellency? Are you in need of an ambassador? I offer you my services: Mr Boswell, Ambassador Extraordinary of Monsieur Rousseau to the Isle of Corsica.'

ROUSSEAU. 'Perhaps you would rather be King of Corsica?'

BOSWELL. 'On my word! Ha! Ha! Not I. It exceeds my powers' (with a low bow). 'All the same, I can now say, "I have refused a crown."'

ROUSSEAU. 'Do you like cats?'

BOSWELL. 'No.'

ROUSSEAU. 'I was sure of that. It is my test of character. There you have the despotic instinct of men. They do not like cats because the cat is free and will never consent to become a slave. He will do nothing to your order, as the other animals do.'

BOSWELL. 'Nor a hen, either.'

ROUSSEAU. 'A hen would obey your orders if you could make her understand them. But a cat will understand you perfectly and not obey them.'

BOSWELL. 'But a cat is ungrateful and treacherous.'

ROUSSEAU. 'No. That's all untrue. A cat is an animal that can be very much attached to you; he will do anything you please out of friendship. I have a cat here. He has been brought up with my dog; they play together. The cat will give the dog a blow with his tail, and the dog will offer him his paw.' (He described the playing of his dog and cat with exquisite eloquence, as a fine painter draws a small piece.) He put some victuals on a trencher, and made his dog dance round it. He sung to him a lively air with a sweet voice and great taste. 'You see the ballet. It is not a gala performance, but a pretty one all the same.' I think the dog's name was Sultan. He stroked him and fed him, and with an arch air said, 'He is not much respected, but he gets well looked after.'

BOSWELL. 'Suppose you were to walk in upon a drinking party of young folk, who should treat you with ridicule, would you be above minding it?'

ROUSSEAU. 'It would put me out of countenance. I am shy by nature. I have often, for example, been overcome by the raillery of women. A party such as you describe would be disagreeable to me. I should leave it.' I was comforted to find that my sensibility is not despicable weakness.

BOSWELL. 'The Anglican Church is my choice.'

ROUSSEAU. 'Yes. It is no doubt an excellent religion, but it is not the Gospel, which is all simplicity. It is another kind of religion.'

BOSWELL. 'The Gospel, at the outset, was simple but rigorous too, as when Paul says it is better not to marry than to marry.'

ROUSSEAU. 'Paul? But that is not the Gospel.'

BOSWELL. 'Then you have no liking for Paul?'

ROUSSEAU. 'I respect him, but I think he is partly responsible for muddling your head. He would have been an Anglican clergyman.'

BOSWELL. 'Mr Johnson is a Jacobite, but he has a pension of £300 sterling from the King.'

ROUSSEAU. 'He ought not to have accepted a pension.'

BOSWELL. 'He says that he does not drink the health of King James with the wine given him by King George.'

ROUSSEAU. 'But you should not employ the substance given you by this wine in attacking King George.'

Mademoiselle said, 'Shall you, Sir, see Monsieur de Voltaire?'

BOSWELL. 'Most certainly.' (To Rousseau.) 'Monsieur de Voltaire has no liking for you. That is natural enough.'

ROUSSEAU. 'Yes. One does not like those whom one has greatly injured. His talk is most enjoyable; it is even better than his books.'

BOSWELL. 'Have you looked at the *Philosophical Dictionary?*'

ROUSSEAU. 'Yes.'

BOSWELL. 'And what of it?'

ROUSSEAU. 'I don't like it. I am not intolerant, but he deserves –' (I forget his expression here.) 'It is very well to argue against men's opinions; but to show contempt, and to say, "You are idiots to believe this," is to be personally offensive. – Now go away.'

BOSWELL. 'Not yet. I will leave at three o'clock. I have still five and twenty minutes.'

ROUSSEAU. 'But I can't give you five and twenty minutes.'

BOSWELL. 'I will give you even more than that.'

ROUSSEAU. 'What! Of my own time? All the kings on earth cannot give me my own time.'

BOSWELL. 'But if I had stayed till tomorrow I should have had five and twenty minutes, and next day another five and twenty. I am not taking those minutes. I am making you a present of them.'

ROUSSEAU. 'Oh! You are not stealing my money, you are giving it to me.' He then repeated part of a French satire ending with 'And whatever they leave you, they count as a gift'.

BOSWELL. 'Pray speak for me, Mademoiselle.' (To Rousseau.) 'I have an excellent friend here.'

ROUSSEAU. 'Nay, but this is a league.'

BOSWELL. 'No league at all.' Mademoiselle said, 'Gentlemen, I will tell you the moment the clock strikes.'

ROUSSEAU. 'Come; I need to take the air after eating.'

We walked out to a gallery pendant upon his wall.

BOSWELL. 'In the old days I was a great mimic. I could imitate every one I saw. But I have left it off.'

ROUSSEAU. 'It is a dangerous talent, for it compels one to seize upon all that is small in a character.'

BOSWELL. 'True. But I assure you there was a nobleness about my art, I carried mimicry to such a point of perfection. I was a kind of virtuoso. When I espied any singular character I would say, "It must be added to my collection."' He laughed with all his nerves [from the heart]: 'You are an odd character.'

BOSWELL. 'I am a physiognomist, believe me. I have studied that art very attentively, I assure you, and I can rely on my conclusions.' He seemed to agree to this.

ROUSSEAU. 'Yet I think the features of the face vary between one nation and another, as do accent and tone of voice; and these signify different feelings among different peoples.' This observation struck me as new and most ingenious.

BOSWELL. 'But in time one learns to understand them.'

ROUSSEAU. 'The roads are bad. You will be late.'

BOSWELL. 'I take the bad parts on foot; the last league of the way is good. – Do you think that I shall make a good barrister before a court of justice?'

ROUSSEAU. 'Yes. But I regret that you have the talents necessary for defending a bad case.'

BOSWELL. 'Have you any commands for Italy?'

ROUSSEAU. 'I will send a letter to Geneva for you to carry to Parma.'

BOSWELL. 'Can I send you anything back?'

ROUSSEAU. 'A few pretty tunes from the opera.'

BOSWELL. 'By all means. Oh, I have had so much to say, that I have neglected to beg you to play me a tune.'

ROUSSEAU. 'It's too late.'

MADEMOISELLE. 'Sir, your man is calling for you to start.' Monsieur Rousseau embraced me. He was quite the tender Saint-Preux. He kissed me several times, and held me in his arms with elegant cordiality. Oh, I shall never forget that I have been thus.

ROUSSEAU. 'Good-bye. You are a fine fellow.'

BOSWELL. 'You have shown me great goodness. But I deserved it.'

ROUSSEAU. 'Yes. You are malicious; but 'tis a pleasant malice, a malice I don't dislike. Write and tell me how you are.'

BOSWELL. 'And you will write to me?'

ROUSSEAU. 'I know not how to reach you.'

BOSWELL. 'Yes, you shall write to me in Scotland.'

ROUSSEAU. 'Certainly; and even at Paris.'

BOSWELL. 'Bravo! If I live twenty years, you will write to me for twenty years?'

ROUSSEAU. 'Yes.'

BOSWELL. 'Good-bye. If you live for seven years, I shall return to Switzerland from Scotland to see you.'

ROUSSEAU. 'Do so. We shall be old acquaintances.'

BOSWELL. 'One word more. Can I feel sure that I am held to you by a thread, even if of the finest? By a hair?' (Seizing a hair of my head.)

ROUSSEAU. 'Yes. Remember always that there are points at which our souls are bound.'

BOSWELL. 'It is enough. I, with my melancholy, I, who often look on myself as a despicable being, as a good-for-nothing creature who should make his exit from life, – I shall be upheld for ever by the thought that I am bound to Monsieur Rousseau. Good-bye. Bravo! I shall live to the end of my days.'

ROUSSEAU. 'That is undoubtedly a thing one must do. Good-bye.'

Mademoiselle accompanied me to the outer door. Before dinner she told me, 'Monsieur Rousseau has a high regard for you. The first time you came, I said to him, "That gentleman has an honest face. I am sure you will like him."' I said, 'Mademoiselle is a good judge.' 'Yes,' said she, 'I have seen strangers enough in the twenty-two years that I have been with Monsieur Rousseau, and I assure you that I have sent many of them packing because I did not fancy their way of talking.' I said, 'You have promised to let me have news of you from time to time.' 'Yes, Sir.' 'And tell me what I can send you from Geneva. Make no ceremony.' 'Well, if you will, a garnet necklace.' [Boswell sent this.]

We shook hands cordially, and away I went to my inn. My eldest landlady looked at me and said, 'Sir, I think you are crying.' This I retain as a true elogium of my humanity. I replied, '[No.] Yet I am unhappy to leave Monsieur Rousseau. I will see you again in seven years.' I got a-horseback and rode by the house of Monsieur Rousseau. Mademoiselle waited for me at the door, and cried, 'Bon voyage; write to us.' Good creature.

Monday 24 December 1764 [Geneva]

I took a coach for Ferney, the seat of the illustrious Monsieur de Voltaire. I was in true spirits; the earth was covered with snow; I surveyed wild nature with a noble eye. I called up all the grand ideas which I have ever entertained of Voltaire . . . His château was handsome. I was received by two or three footmen, who showed me into a very elegant room. I sent by one of them a letter to Monsieur de Voltaire which I had from Colonel Constant [Constant d'Hermenches] at The Hague. He returned and told me, 'Monsieur de Voltaire is very much annoyed at being disturbed. He is Abed.' I was afraid that I should not see him. Some ladies and gentlemen entered, and I was entertained for some time. At last Monsieur de Voltaire opened the door of his apartment, and stepped forth. I surveyed him with eager attention, and found him just as his print had made me conceive him. He received me with dignity, and that air of the world which a Frenchman acquires in such perfection. He had a slate-blue, fine frieze greatcoat nightgown and a three-knotted wig. He sat erect upon his chair, and simpered when he spoke. He was not in spirits, nor I neither. All I presented was the 'foolish face of wondering praise'.

We talked of Scotland. He said the Glasgow editions were 'tres belles'. I said, 'An Academy of Painting was also established there, but it did not succeed. Our Scotland is no country for that.' He replied with a keen archness, 'No; to paint well it is necessary to have warm feet. It's hard to paint when your feet are cold.' Another would have given a long dissertation on the coldness of our climate. Monsieur de Voltaire gave the very essence of raillery in half a dozen words.

I mentioned the severe criticism which the Gazette littéraire has given upon Lord Kames's Elements. I imagined it to be done by Voltaire, but would not ask him. He repeated me several of the bons mots in it, with an air that confirmed me in my idea of his having written this criticism. He called my Lord always 'ce Monsieur Kames'.

I told him that Mr Johnson and I intended to make a tour through the Hebrides, the Northern Isles of Scotland. He smiled, and cried, 'Very well; but I shall remain here. You will allow me to stay here?' 'Certainly.' 'Well then, go. I have no objections at all.'

I asked him if he still spoke English. He replied, 'No. To speak English one must place the tongue between the teeth, and I have lost my teeth.' . . .

The gates of Geneva shut at five, so I was obliged to hasten away after dinner without seeing any more of Monsieur de Voltaire.

Tuesday 25 December 1764

Although this was Christmas-day, I fairly fasted, nor stirred out of doors except a moment to the Église de St Pierre, which was formerly a Catholic church and is a handsome building. Worship was over, but I heard a voluntary upon the organ. I was in supreme spirits, and a noble idea arose in my mind. I wrote a very lively letter to Madame Denis, begging to be allowed to sleep a night under the roof of Monsieur de Voltaire. I sent it by an express, and Voltaire wrote the answer in the person of his niece, making me very welcome. My felicity this night was abundant. My letter with the answer to it are most carefully preserved.

Tuesday 27 December 1764

I then went to Ferney, where I was received with complacency and complimented on my letter ... After dinner we returned to the drawing-room ... Some sat snug by the fire, some chatted, some sung, some played the guitar, some played at shuttlecock. All was full. The canvas was covered. My hypochondria began to muse. I was dull to find how much this resembled any other house in the country, and I had heavy ennui...

Between seven and eight we had a message that Voltaire was in the drawing-room. He always appears about this time anight, pulls his bell and cries, 'Fetch Père Adam.' The good Father is ready immediately, and they play at chess together. I stood by Monsieur de Voltaire and put him in tune. He spoke sometimes English and sometimes French. He gave me a sharp reproof for speaking fast. 'How fast you foreigners speak!' 'We think that the French do the same.' 'Well, at any rate, I don't. I speak slowly, that's what I do'; and this he said with a most keen tone. He got into great spirits. I would not go to supper, and so I had this great man for about an hour and a half at a most interesting téte-à-téte. I have written some particulars of it to Temple, and as our conversation was very long, I shall draw it up fully in a separate paper. When the company returned, Monsieur de Voltaire retired. They looked at me with complacency and without envy. Madame Denis insisted that I should sup; I agreed to this, and a genteel table was served for me in the drawing-room, where I eat and drank cheerfully with the gay company around me. I was very lively and said, 'I am magnificence itself. I eat alone, like the King of England.' In short this was a rich evening.

From Boswell to William Temple, 28 December 1764 [Château de Ferney]

I returned yesterday to this enchanted castle. The magician appeared a very little before dinner. But in the evening he came into the drawing-room in great spirits. I placed myself by him. I touched the keys in unison with his imagination. I wish you had heard the music. He was all brilliance. He gave me continued flashes of wit. I got him to speak English, which he does in a degree that made me now and then start up and cry, 'Upon my soul this is astonishing!' When he talked our language he was animated with the soul of a Briton. He had bold flights. He had humour. He had an extravagance; he had a forcible oddity of style that the most comical of our dramatis personae could not have exceeded. He swore bloodily, as was the fashion when he was in England. He hummed a ballad; he repeated nonsense. Then he talked of our Constitution with a noble enthusiasm. I was proud to hear this from the mouth of an illustrious Frenchman. At last we came upon religion. Then did he rage. The company went to supper. Monsieur de Voltaire and I remained in the drawing-room with a great Bible before us; and if ever two mortal men disputed with vehemence, we did. Yes, upon that occasion he was one individual and I another. For a certain portion of time there was a fair opposition between Voltaire and Boswell. The daring bursts of his ridicule confounded my under-standing. He stood like an orator of ancient Rome. Tully was never more agitated than he was. He went too far. His aged frame trembled beneath him. He cried, 'Oh, I am very sick; my head turns round,' and he let himself gently fall upon an easy chair. He recovered. I resumed our conversation, but changed the tone. I talked to him serious and earnest. I demanded of him an honest confession of his real sentiments. He gave it me with candour and with a mild eloquence which touched my heart. I did not believe him capable of thinking in the manner that he declared to me was 'from the bottom of his heart'. He expressed his veneration – his love – of the Supreme Being, and his entire resignation to the will of Him who is All-wise. He expressed his desire to resemble the Author of Goodness by being good himself. His sentiments go no farther. He does not inflame his mind with grand hopes of the immortality of the soul. He says it may be, but he knows nothing of it. And his mind is in perfect tranquillity. I was moved; I was sorry. I doubted his sincerity. I called to him with emotion, 'Are you sincere? are you really sincere?' He answered, 'Before God, I am.' Then with the fire of him whose tragedies have so often shone on the theatre of Paris, he said, 'I suffer much. But I suffer with patience and resignation; not as a Christian – but as a man.'

Temple, was not this an interesting scene? Would a journey from Scotland to Ferney have been too much to obtain such a remarkable interview? I have given you the great lines. The whole conversation of the evening is fully recorded, and I look upon it as an invaluable treasure. One day the public shall have it. It is a present highly worthy of their attention. I told Monsieur de Voltaire that I had written eight quarto pages of what he had said. He smiled and seemed pleased. Our important scene must not appear till after his death. But I have a great mind to send over to London a little sketch of my reception at Ferney, of the splendid manner in which Monsieur de Voltaire lives, and of the brilliant conversation of this celebrated author at the age of seventy-two.

Friday 28 December 1764

He was bad today and did not appear before dinner. We dined well as usual. It was pleasant for me to think I was in France. In the afternoon I was dullish. At six I applied to the secretary for a volume of Voltaire's plays, and went to my room, and read his Mahomet in his own house. It was curious, this. A good, decent, trusty servant had fire and wax candles and all in order for me. There is at Ferney the true hospitality. All are master of their rooms and do as they please ... Monsieur de Voltaire was sick and out of spirits this evening, yet I made him talk some time. His conversation shall be all collected into one piece. I may perhaps insert it in this my journal. I supped at the table tonight. It hurt me to find that by low spirits it is possible for me to lose the relish of the most illustrious genius. Hard indeed!

Notes of Voltaire's English Conversation, Saturday 29 December 1764

BOSWELL. 'When I came to see you, I thought to see a very great, but a very bad, man.'

VOLTAIRE. 'You are very sincere.'

BOSWELL. 'Yes, but the same [sincerity] makes me own that I find the contrary. Only, your *Dictionnaire philosophique* [troubles me]. For instance, *Ame*, the Soul –'

VOLTAIRE. 'That is a good article.'

BOSWELL. 'No. Excuse me. Is it – [immortality] – not a pleasing imagination? Is it not more noble?'

VOLTAIRE. 'Yes. You have a noble desire to be King of Europe. [You say,] "I wish it, and I ask your protection [in continuing to wish it]." But it is not probable.'

BOSWELL. 'No, but all cannot be the one, and may be the other. [Like Cato, we all say] "It must be so," till [we possess] immortality [itself].'

VOLTAIRE. 'But before we say that this soul will exist, let us know what it is. I know not the cause. I cannot judge. I cannot be a juryman. Cicero says, *potius optandum quam probandum* [matter of faith, rather than of demonstration]. We are ignorant beings. We are the puppets of Providence. I am a poor Punch.'

BOSWELL. 'Would you have no public worship?'

VOLTAIRE. 'Yes, with all my heart. Let us meet four times a year in a grand temple with music, and thank God for all his gifts. There is one sun. There is one God. Let us have one religion. Then all mankind will be brethren.'

BOSWELL. 'May I write in English, and you'll answer?'

VOLTAIRE. 'Yes. Farewell.'

Well, I must here pause, and as an impartial philosopher decide concerning myself. What a singular being do I find myself! Let this my journal show what variety my mind is capable of. But am I not well received everywhere? Am I not particularly taken notice of by men of the most distinguished genius? And why? I have neither profound knowledge, strong judgment, nor constant gaiety. But I have a noble soul which still shines forth, a certain degree of knowledge, a multiplicity of ideas of all kinds, an original humour and turn of expression, and, I really believe, a remarkable knowledge of human nature. This is different from a knowledge of the world as much as is

the knowledge of a florist, who understands perfectly the works of
Nature, from that of him who understands flowers formed by art. The
florist perceives in general that the artificial flowers are not natural,
but whether they are made of gummed linen, of china, or of copper,
he cannot tell. So I know in general your men of the world to be
artificial, but am not able to develop their different qualities. What is
really Man I think I know pretty well. With this I have a pliant ease
of manners which must please. I can tune myself so to the tone of any
bearable man I am with that he is as much at freedom as with another
self, and, till I am gone, cannot imagine me a stranger. Perhaps my
talents are such as procure me more happiness than those of a more
elevated kind. Were it not for my black hypochondria, I might be a
practical epicurean.

I departed from this château in a most extraordinary humour,
thinking hard, and wondering if I could possibly, when again in
Scotland, again feel my most childish prejudices.

Italy 1765

With his father's permission to visit Italy for four months in hand, and his
interviews with Rousseau and Voltaire still thrilling his imagination, Boswell
turned south to the classic ground of Italy. His plan was to spend several months
there learning about classical Italian history and art and, not least, tasting the
country's more contemporary pleasures in the shapes of Italian women. The
splendour and spectacle of the Roman Catholic church also spurred his imagination
and lifted his spirits. After Italy, he would sail to Corsica where he hoped to
meet and interview General Pasquale de Paoli, the rebel Corsican leader then
engaged in a war of liberation against the Genoese. It would be another conquest,
another feather for his cap, but the quest for Paoli also appealed to his growing
enthusiasm for liberty from oppression on any level, from personal to national.
His sojourn in the south continued to be lengthened month after month until it
stretched out for more than a year, much to the exasperation and anger of his
father, who not unjustifiably felt that his son was stealing a mile from the
inch that he had been given.

While there are surviving fully-written sections of the Italian journal, it has large gaps filled by detailed memoranda from which Boswell hoped later to (but did not) write up full journal entries. The highlights of this year include his quarrels with Lord Mountstuart (Lord Bute's son), a love affair with the married Girolama Piccolomini ('Moma'), meetings with John Wilkes in Rome and Naples, and his adventurous excursion to Corsica.

The selections below begin with an intimate specimen of autobiographical narrative, Boswell's summary of nine months in Italy which he wrote for Rousseau from Lucca, just before embarking for Corsica. It is as confessional and honest as anything he ever wrote, reminiscent of the shorter and more general 'Sketch of My Life' that he wrote for Rousseau at Môtiers just before meeting him.

1765

From Boswell to Jean-Jacques Rousseau, 3 October 1765 [Lucca]

IF IT WERE POSSIBLE, ILLUSTRIOUS PHILOSOPHER! to write to you without that respect which hinders the imagination by introducing a degree of fear, I should flatter myself that I could entertain you with an account of my tour of Italy. I shall do my best; and if I am not successful you will know what to ascribe my failure to. You were indeed right to congratulate me when my father gave me permission to travel in Italy. Nine months in this delicious country have done more for me than all the sage lessons which books, or men formed by books, could have taught me. It was my imagination that needed correction, and nothing but travel could have produced this effect.

I carried over the Alps ideas of the most rigorous morality. I thought of myself as a penitent who must expiate the sins which he had confessed to you in your sacred retreat; I felt like a hero of austerity in a dissolute age. But the ladies of Turin were very beautiful, and I thought that I might allow myself one intrigue in Italy, in order to increase my knowledge of the world and give me a contempt for shameless women. So I made myself into a gallant; but I was too modest a gallant to succeed with ladies who scorned the detours of delicacy, and who thought anyone a peasant or an imbecile who did not head straight for the main chance. Moreover, I had a heart. I was seized by passion, I could not hide it; and that was not reconcilable with the decorum which had to be maintained in public. In short, I had no success at all with the ladies of Piedmont. A French officer who was my instructor in gallantry, mortified by finding me *so young*, consoled me by procuring willing girls.

Thus, Sir, did I carry out the good resolutions I had made at Môtiers. I wrote on a piece of paper, 'O Rousseau! How am I fallen since I left you!' Yet my principles remained firm. I considered that I had done wrong. I summoned my inclinations back to virtue, and at Parma M. Deleyre[6] strengthened me in my resolutions. I was charmed by the fine mind and the finer soul of that amiable Frenchman; and the sincere evidence which he gave of his attachment to me brought me back again to the opinion that I was something above the crowd of mankind. You told me when I was about to leave you, 'Sir, all you lack is a knowledge of your own worth.' Believe me, illustrious philosopher! there is a great deal in that remark. I know my worth sometimes, and I think and act nobly. But then melancholy attacks me, I despise myself, and it seems to me a waste of time to try to improve so petty a thing. [*Continued below*]

Tuesday 22 January 1765 [Turin]

I set out at eleven [for Milan]. As I went out at one of the ports, I saw a crowd running to the execution of a thief. I jumped out of my chaise and went close to the gallows. The criminal stood on a ladder, and a priest held a crucifix before his face. He was tossed over, and hung with his face uncovered, which was hideous. I stood fixed in attention to this spectacle, thinking that the feelings of horror might destroy those of chagrin. But so thoroughly was my mind possessed by the feverish agitation that I did not feel in the smallest degree from the execution. The hangman put his feet on the criminal's head and neck and had him strangled in a minute. I then went into a church and kneeled with great devotion before an altar splendidly lighted up. Here then I felt three successive scenes: raging love – gloomy horror – grand devotion. The horror indeed I only should have felt. I jogged on slowly with my *vetturino* [coachman], and had a grievous inn at night.

Letter to Rousseau, continued

I was well enough on my trip from Turin to Rome...

I entered Rome with full classical enthusiasm, but when I arrived at my inn and found myself surrounded by the landlord, by *valets de place*, by scoundrels, my fantastic sensibility was wounded, and at first I was in a bad humour. I had an odd thought which now makes me laugh heartily. As I was walking along the streets of Rome, which are very little different from those of any other city, I said to myself, 'Was the Epistle of St Paul to the Romans written to the inhabitants of this city? And did I use to be so terrified by it?' At once the Epistle of St Paul seemed to me to be just an ancient writing by some ecclesiastical zealot. The word of God was no longer in it. Great chemist of human nature! you see how a mind can be changed. Ah, we must analyse with the most delicate nicety.

Within a few days I set out for Naples, where I was richly entertained with the variety of interesting things to be seen there, especially in the environs. I found the famous Mr Wilkes in his exile, and despite his sharp attacks on the Scots, we got along very well together. All theories of human nature are confounded by the resilient spirit of that singular factionary, who has experienced all the vicissitudes of pleasure and politics without ever having suffered a moment of uneasiness. He is a man who has thought much without being gloomy, a man who has done much evil without being a scoundrel. His lively and energetic sallies on moral questions gave to my spirit a not unpleasant agitation, and enlarged the scope of my views by convincing me that God could create a soul completely serene and gay notwithstanding the alarming reflection that we all must die. Wilkes pretended to be angry with you for having referred to him in so uncompromising a style in a note to one of your *Letters from the Mountain*. He even said boldly that he would write a public letter to you on this subject, which would be entitled, *A Letter from the Other Man of the Mountain*. [Continued below]

Wednesday 6 March 1765 Memorandum

Yesterday ... visits of English and Wilkes[7].
WILKES. 'I wish I could write in any language as well as you.'
BOSWELL. '[Such complaisance is] not in character.'
WILKES. 'Yes. [I] always tell truth – for which I'm [exiled] here.'

BOSWELL. 'Had you told such [flattering] truths to Government, [you] had not been here.' ...

WILKES. 'I make it a rule to abuse him who is against me or any of my friends point-blank. If I find two or three faults, he's good for nothing.'

BOSWELL. 'But Johnson, a respectable character in the world of literature.'

WILKES. 'Oh, I abuse Johnson as an impudent pretender to literature, which I don't think, but 'tis all one ... At school and college [I] never read; always among women at [the University of] Leyden. My father gave me as much money as I pleased. Three or four whores; drunk every night. Sore head morning, then read. I'm capable to sit thirty hours over a table to study. Plan for North Briton: grave revolutionary paper seasoned each time with a character from the Court list ...'

Boswell to John Wilkes, 22 April 1765 [Rome]

DEAR SIR, The many pleasant hours which we passed together at Naples shall never be lost. The remembrance of them shall inspirit this gloomy mind while I live. Even your compliments were excellent, and had full effect. You told me I was 'the most liberal man you had ever met with, a citizen of the world, free from the prejudices of any country, who would be liked in France as much as in Britain'. You called me 'My old Lord of Scotland', and you said I looked as if I had a thousand men at my back. Had it been your chiefest interest to make Boswell satisfied with himself, you could not have done it better. But I set a higher value on your parting words, which you pronounced with such a tone that I almost believed you: 'I shall never forget your civilities to me. You are engraven upon my heart.' Was you really in earnest? ...

Letter to Rousseau, continued

I went little into company at Naples, and remember solely that the Neapolitan ladies resembled country chamber-maids. I was there during Lent when there are no public entertainments. During my stay at Naples I was truly libertine. I ran after girls without restraint. My blood was inflamed by the burning climate, and my passions were violent. I indulged them; my mind had almost nothing to do with it. I found some very pretty girls. I escaped all danger. I have nothing to say about this period; I merely describe it for you as it occurred.

I returned to Rome for Holy Week. I grew calm. The solemn services of the Roman Catholic Church made a serious impression on me. I began to be a little melancholy and I recalled with religious regret how I had once been, like you, in the bosom of the faithful. But your Savoyard doctrines came to my aid and made me see a church even more catholic than that which I revered: the entire Universe, all souls being emanations of the Eternal Being. On Easter I was in St Peter's and in that superb temple I saw noble and mystical adorations offered to the Supreme Being. I was penetrated with devotion. I was sure that the revelation given by Jesus was true; and when I saw the Christian High Priest with venerable magnificence elevate before the Eternal Justice a Sacrifice for the sins of the whole world, I fell to my knees among the throng of my fellow men who remained fixed in respectful silence; I struck my breast, and with all the ardour of which my soul was capable I prostrated myself at the feet of my Father 'who is in Heaven', convinced that, by varied ways of which we know nothing clearly, he would one day lead all his creatures to happiness. Let cold beings sneer; I was never more nobly happy than on that day...

I must admit that in the midst of my Roman studies I indulged in sensual relaxations. I sallied forth of an evening like an imperious lion, and I had a little French painter, a young academician, always vain, always alert, always gay, who served as my jackal. I remembered the rakish deeds of Horace and other amorous Roman poets, and I thought that one might well allow one's self a little indulgence in a city where there are prostitutes licensed by the Cardinal Vicar. Thus does an ill-regulated mind assemble scattered ideas and compose from them a principle for action. I was, however, brought to a halt by an unpleasant occurrence which all libertines have to reckon with. When we walked in your room, disputing about the commerce of the sexes, you said to me with a smile, 'Watch out for Italian girls – for several reasons.' I discovered at Rome that your advice was very sound...

Until Holy Week, I had seen little of my countrymen in Italy. I was looked upon as an odd creature who studied a great deal and was very proud. I was presented to the Pope. I went to *conversazioni* in the palaces of Roman nobles, where there was a great deal of formality and also a certain air of pleasing richness and grandeur. At Rome everything is external. They have scarcely any real society ... I do not know that I did well in avoiding my compatriots so completely. I had good reason to devote myself entirely to learning the language, studying the genius, and absorbing the thought of the Italian people. But in doing this I almost isolated myself. I formed exaggerated ideas of myself, and when I fell in with Englishmen was raw and irritable, and by too great a sensitivity I was inferior in social life to mediocre young men who were accustomed to live in general society.

I could not think of placing myself so soon on the footing of a philosopher who wishes to retire from the world. I had to accustom myself to being with my equals. I had to think of establishing some political connection.

I found all these advantages happily combined. I formed a close connection with Lord Mountstuart, eldest son of the worthy Lord Bute, intimate friend of our King. My Lord Mountstuart is a young nobleman who merits his being of the blood of the ancient kings of Scotland. He deserves my drawing his portrait for you. He is handsome, has elegant manners, and a tempestuously noble soul. He has never applied himself earnestly to anything, but he is not without knowledge and has an excellent mind. He has, though to a lesser degree, the same defect that I have, weak nerves; but he does not suffer from them, for although he is no metaphysician, he is a practical philosopher. He finds himself placed in an elevated rank. He enjoys his real advantages without worrying about imaginary ills. His money is for him in civilised society what physical strength is to a savage. His servants are his arms, his horses his legs, and he can count as surely on them as the savage on the parts of his body – more, even, for he can replace them when they fail, which savages cannot do. He calmly follows his inclinations: when he wishes to study, he reads; when he is indolent, he lies on a sofa. Sometimes he speaks in company, sometimes he says nothing. Sometimes his passion for women is very strong, and he pursues them with the greatest liveliness. He has even had several affairs, although rather from vanity than from genuine feeling. Sometimes he cares nothing for any kind of love; then he enjoys talking about his adventures, and wonders most gravely how he could have been so carried away by his inclinations. He is never out of sorts with himself, because he never disputes with himself. He made me a great deal more sociable. He often said to me, 'Boswell, I will teach you how to live,' and really he did me good ...

My Lord Mountstuart insisted that I accompany him on the remainder of his tour of Italy, and I consented. He was already accompanied by a Scottish colonel, a very worthy man, and by M. Mallet, sometime professor from Geneva, who had been given a good pension in return for giving my Lord lessons in history. It would have been impossible to conceive of a more prudent or more agreeable project than ours ... But matters did not go well. I found myself in my Lord's suite, and when I heard him hold forth on the pleasures of grandeur I began to wish for employment at Court. I thought of his great interest. Insensibly I tried to please him and was afraid of offending him. He soon noticed it, and could not keep from profiting a little from it. I realised it too. I was highly shocked by it. What! Boswell, *the man of singular merit!* The friend of Rousseau! Is Boswell so far overcome by vile interest as to depend on the moods of a young Lord? I recollected myself. I made my Lord realise that I was as proud as ever. I did it too emphatically. We began to dispute about our characters, and each stated bluntly all the other's defects and all his own merits. You can imagine that between two young men, both of whom have a good deal of temperamental warmth, such a dispute, so conducted, could not but occasion many disagreeable moments. Finally our spirits subsided, and we were sometimes on a basis of puerile familiarity, and sometimes in the vilest humour possible, even to the point of not speaking to each other. I always had a great advantage, for I was four years older than my Lord, and was possessed of a little philosophy ... Mallet, from whom we had taken hardly any lessons since we left Rome, became irritated with me because I never ceased attacking his opinions and discovering his tricks; and to tell you the truth, there were never four men who travelled so ill together. It was indeed ridiculous, and my Lord and I in our hours of good humour were sometimes ready to burst with laughing.

We went to Venice ... I paid court to a noble lady, a little advanced in years ... It was an affair of pure vanity, so I gave myself little concern over it. My fancy was stirred by the brilliant stories I had heard of Venetian courtesans. I went to see them, *et militavi non sine gloria* ['And I fought, not without glory'[8]], but the wounds of my Roman wars were scarcely healed before I received fresh ones at Venice. What is worse, my Lord Mountstuart was of the party. He saw that I was agitated, and demanded to know what I was intending to do. I told him I was going out to look for girls, to taste the pleasures of Venice and learn the fashion; but I begged him not to go. You can well imagine that we went together. A pretty dancer was our common flame, and my Lord was taken in as I was. A fine piece of thoughtlessness. M. Mallet had fine sport with me then; the Colonel took me seriously to task. When a man is in any way the cause of a misfortune, even though it is entirely unintentional, he is nevertheless always regarded as guilty. Thus I felt on this occasion, and was mortified by it. Behold now your philosopher, the steady young man who was to help Lord Mountstuart to improve himself!

... M. Mallet and I quarrelled more than ever. He discovered how little I had studied either of science or of history, and he said to me, 'If I were as ignorant as you are, I should be ashamed to show my face.' The truth is that because of the hypochondria I told you of, and which I inherit from my mother, my mind has been so restless and so distracted that I have never been capable of genuine application. I have studied languages and *belles lettres*, and because of the strength and vivacity of my mind in its lucid moments I have picked up enough philosophy to make me appear much better instructed than I really am. I maintained against M. Mallet that I had as many ideas as he had, and I give you my word that during the greater part of the time that we were together I felt myself his superior. It is the soul, Sir, it is the celestial fire that gives a man his worth. One idea possessed by me has more value than a throng of ideas possessed by the majority of men. Yet M. Mallet is intelligent, and he is a fellow hypochondriac.

During that period I felt more discontented than I had been since I began my travels. In my black moments when I judged myself by the opinions of others, I was a libertine and an ignoramus. I was bashful, and distrustful of my ability to distinguish myself in my own country. I foresaw differences of opinion between me and my father. I needed relief, and, according to the state of my circulation, I was servile or proud with Lord Mountstuart. I experienced a fluctuation of conduct which was very disagreeable for a man who has an idea of uniform dignity of character. Here, Sir, are very subtle shades of character. [Mountstuart is recalled to England, so Boswell continues his travels alone.]

From Parma I went to Florence, where I remained a fortnight, to see the curiosities and a little of the society, which I did not find very agreeable. The Florentines (especially the Florentine women) are very proud and very mercenary. I shall not give you a detailed report on all the cities where I passed some time and in which I saw the nobility.

I found in Florence one of the best teachers of the flute in Europe, Dothel, a Lorrainer. He gave me several lessons, and started me on a good plan of study.

From Florence I went to Siena, where I passed a portion of my existence in perfect felicity. The nobility there form a society of the most amiable sort. They have a simplicity, an openness, a gaiety which you cannot imagine without having been there. They have no society manners, none of that affected air which to the philosopher betrays artificial beings. You, Sir, as delicate as you are, could live in the society of Siena...

I had excellent apartments at Siena. I ate well. The wine of the district was very good, and on holidays I regaled myself with delicious Montepulciano. The air is fresh, and the weather is always fine. My health was very quickly restored...

But, Sir, I must tell you of more interesting things. Your Scot was very attentive to the ladies at Siena. I found that people lived there in a completely natural fashion, making love as their inclinations suggested. It was the custom of the society in which I lived. I yielded to custom. I allowed myself to become all sensation and immediate feeling. I did not wish to extend my mind to encompass a series of prudent considerations. I did not wish to be more profound than the others. To enjoy was the thing. Intoxicated by that sweet delirium, I gave myself up, without self-reproach and in complete serenity, to the charms of irregular love...

I was wicked enough to wait at the same time on a very amiable little woman to whom I made declarations of the most sincere passion, as can be easily done when one feels only a slight inclination. I fancied that she had no heart, and as I believed everything fair in the war of gallantry, I lied to her certainly no fewer than a hundred times a day. Behold me, then, very busy indeed, with two affairs going at the same time. It required an unparalleled dexterity, and I had it. Then nothing was difficult for me. I drifted pleasantly between my two loves, and my *valet de place*, a lout who could neither read nor write, was dispatched with his face turned towards the east to carry a letter for Signora A. in his right-hand pocket and a letter for Signora B. in his left.

In a fortnight Signora B., who was the most trusting of persons, and with whom I had used the full force of my reasoning powers to prove that in me she would have the most faithful of lovers, but that my sufferings were so excruciating that, if she did not soon assure me of her affection, I feared so much the sad effects of a strong passion on a melancholy mind that I was determined to set out at once – and what a pity it would be to miss in this short life so fine an occasion for mutual happiness. This amiable person, whose heart was already touched, listened to me kindly and granted me all, saying, '*Ebbene, mi fido a voi com a un galantuomo*' ['Good enough, I trust myself with you as a man of honour']. My conscience reproached me. It happened that Signora A. revealed her character to me. I saw that she conducted intrigues strictly according to the rules, without being touched by love. I abandoned my design upon her. I attached myself completely to my dear little mistress, through a principle of true gratitude.

I studied her character. I found many good qualities in her. I even found charms in her which the dissipation of my spirit had caused me to overlook previously; and with extraordinary joy I found myself truly in love with her. I opened my heart to her, made a full confession of the deceit I had practised on her, while assuring her that she had gained my love. I enjoyed with her the exquisite pleasure of Italian gallantry, whose enchantments I had heard so much of; and I swear to you that experiencing them measured up to my ideas. She was struck with what I had told her. She reproached me tenderly for my treachery. But from that time on she had complete confidence in me. I was utterly happy and I risked nothing...

I loved her more and more. She had a natural *allegria* which never changed and which so alleviated my sombre humour that it buoyed me up until I was quite free of melancholy. I found her a woman made for a life of virtue. When I explained to her the sweet and durable bonds of the conjugal union, she was enchanted and regretted infinitely that she could not experience them, insisting strongly on the advantage which a virtuous mother of a family must enjoy in old age. But said she, 'They took me out of the convent and married me at sixteen, when I did not have the slightest idea what marriage meant.' ... 'I am married,' she continued, 'to a man considerably older than myself; a man whom I not only cannot love but whom I cannot even respect, for to tell the truth he has no liveliness of mind at all, and he is very coarse.'

Hear me, illustrious philosopher! I dare ask you to tell me honestly without prejudice whether that woman was really married, whether she had made a true contract, whether she was obliged to remain faithful to a man to whom her parents had bound her, whether it was her duty to sacrifice her finest inclinations to the hard circumstances in which she found herself. I could not answer her arguments, but in my moments of virtue and piety I warmly repeated to her the common sentiments against adultery. She was very fond of your works. I read to her with a grave and serious air the beautiful and affecting words of Juliet on that terrible vice. I was so moved by them that she could not but feel something. But an onrush of passion overcame me. I embraced her with a kind of frenzy and repeated our criminal ecstasies. She said, '*Voi siete precisamente quel Rousseau. Tale quale. Parlate moltissimo della virtu, e pero fate il male.*' [You are yourself precisely that Rousseau. Just like him. You talk a great deal about virtue, and yet you do wrong.'] I was stirred by a pride of sentiment. She confessed to me all the love affairs in which she had engaged. She told me the names of her lovers, one of whom was always at our *conversazioni*. I wished him dead many and many a time. My extreme jealousy was tormented even by what no longer existed.

My Signora was sorry that I felt so. She assured me that I was the first for whom she had felt a true passion, because it was the first time that love had made her uneasy. The same thing, indeed, has happened to women of intrigue many times. I wished to believe her. But I could not endure the thought that she had been the mistress of others. Ah, I groaned from the heart...

Thus my life slipped away in a delicious dream, while my principles of systematic morality were melted down by the fire of a heated imagination. But time was fleeing. My father was in momentary expectation of news of my arrival in France, and before going there I had secretly resolved to make a tour of Corsica. How was I to decide? My inclination, and, according to the principles of true gallantry, my duty – for vice, when it is social, has its principles also – demanded that I remain with a woman who had made me happy and to whom I owed so much. I thought also that a being who has had so sad an existence as mine would do badly not to profit as much as possible from happiness which he had finally found – if he did not drink from the stream of pleasure as long as Heaven caused it to flow. I was utterly happy. Everything seemed agreeable to me. Even God took on for me the most agreeable aspect, as he will appear to us when at the end our souls will be all purified and exalted into the divine perfection. O dear St Preux! Yes, my soul is bound to yours. I have loved like you, I am pious like you. If we have committed crimes, we have also expiated them.

I resolved to leave Siena, and I told Signora _ a week beforehand. I was firm though sad. Her good sense was such that she admitted my reasons for leaving were irrefutable. But she could not but complain of her lot, which had made her taste real happiness only to feel its loss. When we enjoyed those delicious murmurs which your divine delicacy prefers to the moment of ecstasy itself, she said, 'Ah, io piangero questi momenti' ['Ah, I shall lament these moments']. Her sighs pierced my heart...

O love, passionate fever of the soul, meteor of joy whose essence it is to be brief, how dearly we buy your transports! I tried to console us both for the sadness of parting by depicting the beautiful prospect of an eternal friendship. But the Signora insisted absolutely that she must see me again...

[After his blissful affair with 'Moma' in Siena, Boswell has to tear himself away from her to complete his tour of Italy and make his way to Corsica via Lucca.]

Boswell to Girolama Piccolomini ('Moma') (original in French), 27 September 1765 [Siena]

I AM STILL IN SIENA. I am leaving neither today nor tomorrow. Let us enjoy in peace the time remaining to us. Never in my life have I spent a more delicious day than yesterday. Yes, we are married. My heart and my soul cry out against unjust laws, and a sweet and generous emotion unites us for ever. I do not expect a reply. I simply wish to greet you.

Sunday 29 September 1765 Memorandum

Yesterday morning rose by eight. Was firm and philosophical and calm; put all in order. At ten, Momina. She was quite tendered down, for she had not slept. You told her you was resolved. She said: 'You go to greater and greater happiness, but you leave me here to go continually from bad to worse; for after a few years my youth will be gone, &c., and I am among people for whom I care nothing.' ... You took her to bed, and with mild courage did it fine. Both happy. She

begged return from Leghorn, but you was reserved. She shed tears
without affectation and promised fidelity. Her *allegria* returned by fits.
You was like Spanish cavalier and promised eternal friendship. You had
been in Cathedral first. Leave quite in confusion. At twelve, found
chaise at Porta. Half well, half ill all night. Night, bad inn.

Corsica, France, and back to London 1765–1766

Friday 11 October 1765 Memorandum [Leghorn]

   After a few hours of sleep, was called at six by Signor Giuliano and
another Corsican, who beat at my door ... This day there was little
wind. I was sick a very short while and threw up a little, but felt firm
nerves in comparison of myself on the passage to Holland. A Corsican
played a sort of guitar or lute, and I played my flute, and so did Jacob
[his Swiss servant]. The bark belonged to a Corsican of Pino. He carried
wine to Leghorn. He spoke English. To save himself, he had the Tuscan
flag (the Emperor's), and a Leghorn shipmaster, Ignazio Gentili. I lay
down in the cabin bed, but was eat up by mosquitoes and other
vermin. I eat cold tongue and bread and some of the crew's rice. There
were ten aboard: two poor Corsican merchants, six Corsican sailors,
the master, and a boy from Leghorn. I tried to read a little the disputes
of Corsica, but could give no attention. Thought hardly any, and was
content to be so. Jacob was firm and felt no sickness but wished to
have a long voyage, and at night was delighted to see nothing but the
sky and the sea. They laid a mattress on the provision chest, and hung
a sail on the side of the bark and on four chairs, and under this tent
you slept. At the Ave Maria they all kneeled, and with great fervency
said their evening orisons to the Queen of Heaven. It affected you a
good deal.

[*Boswell was not exaggerating the dangers on Corsica. Apart from its political
and military skirmishes, the island teemed with 'banditii' and he had to
watch out for the ubiquitous threat of the 'vendetta'. Once on the island, he*

walked across it bravely (if recklessly) to reach Paoli, with very little time to write in his journal. He found time only for extensive notes. It was only later, back in Scotland, that he wrote up these notes into An Account of Corsica: The Journal of a Tour to that Island; and Memoirs of Pascal, which he published to critical acclaim in 1768. Thereafter he became something of a celebrity, known across Europe as 'Corsica Boswell'.

Because there are no separate journal entries in Corsica and Boswell's Account is one of the three major books he wrote, the reader will find Part II of it later in this volume and may wish to turn to it now to maintain chronological progress through Boswell's life. The journal entries below pick him up as he begins his voyage home to Britain from Corsica.]

Tuesday 10 December 1765 [Genoa]

After a tolerable night's sleep, I was called at seven by the sailors and went with them to the port, but the courier was not yet come; so I strolled about a little in the city, and went into a church and paid my devotions to Him who rules the sea. At eight we sailed[9]. The felucca was a very good, well-built vessel. It had a railing of wood to cover it in, over which might be thrown canvas to defend the passengers from the sun or from rain, and from the night air when they choose to sleep aboard. It had twelve sailors: the master and boy and ten rowers ... We had a fine calm sea and for an hour and a half we had a brisk gale directly for us; the motion of the felucca was sound and smooth and I was not sick, but had a very good appetite and eat a bit with great pleasure. Between three and four the wind changed against us, so we were obliged to put ashore at Vado, ten leagues from Genoa. My dog[10] began to grow sick, so I threw him into the sea, thinking that when he had swum ashore he would follow the boat; but instead of that he ran off like a criminal back to Savona. The courier went off by land, and I was left to manage as I could with the master of the felucca.

I found a very tolerable inn at Vado and got some fresh fish ... I sent an express to Savona, who brought me for answer that my dog had been seen at the butchers' stalls; but it was too late to find him. However, as the gates were shut, he could not be gone out of the town, and therefore I might have him by sending next morning before the gates could be opened. Jacob slept in the same room with me. He told me he had bought malaga at two livres four sols a bottle. I was in a great passion with him and said, 'It makes me angry to have a servant who spends money in such a fashion.' Upon this he told me he had bought a capon which cost him two livres, and said, 'All the other gentlemen buy provisions. They are right-thinking people. I shall always preserve my health, since I see that I am to be given nothing to pay the doctors.' (This was a hint to me that I had not paid for the curing of his fever at Rome; however, as he has made enough by me, I took no notice of what he said.) I found myself so fortified by agitation that, although I was conscious that I had neither a genteel nor rational conduct in being thus levelled with my own servant, who really thought with more justness than I did, it gave me no concern, and I fell asleep in most easy indifference.

Wednesday 11 December 1765 [Vado]

Early this morning I dispatched my servant with a guide to Savona. I had here (at Vado) as good a clean bed as I could wish; so I lay comfortably till near nine, when my envoys returned without the dog, who had not been heard of since last night ... I composed myself, thinking that Mr Hollford would get him for me and send him by sea to England. The sea was so rough that the felucca could not go. I inclined to go by land; but, as I heard the roads were so bad that I could not get to Antibes in less than four days, I thought it better to wait a day for the chance of going by sea in four and twenty hours ... At eleven came three men from Savona bringing my dog along with them. The principal person among them said he had bought my dog for six francs from a butcher. I, overjoyed to have him again, gave the money without considering that the fellow had no right to sell a dog which was not his own. Thus was I cheated by a crafty Ligurian. I considered, however, that if I had made him be sent after me, it would have cost more. I was in rage against the brute for running away and plaguing me, and I resolved to punish him sufficiently, so I took him to the inn, tied him to a bedstead, and beat him without mercy ...

Jacob was very rude in talking of my severity to Jachone: 'If my brother did a thing like that, I would thrash him.' Thus talked with rough manner my Swiss peasant. I made him hold his tongue, but was really fretted. I continued to beat Jachone from time to time, and gave him nothing to eat, so that I humbled him very well.

Thursday 12 December 1765

Early this morning the sailors called me. The master told me it was good wind, and I, eager to go, agreed to pay him six sequins passage, and, if we could not advance, four. The rogue took me in; for the wind fell as we advanced and then was contrary, and this he must have known.

We went up three leagues and put in at Noli. I still starved Jachone, and discharged [forbade] Jacob to give him any victuals. I stepped down on shore (after being drawn to land by the sailors, which I called [the] best manner of going in [a] boat), and when I returned I found Jacob feeding my dog. I called to him, 'How dare you give anything to that dog when I forbade it?' He replied, 'Yes, I have given him something, sacré dieu!' as if he had been speaking to a brother peasant. I said, 'Upon my word, you are a fine man!' 'Well,' said he, 'I am a man. I am not a fool.' You said, 'You are the most impertinent rascal I have ever known.' He said, 'Sir, you knew that long ago. You should not have taken me with you.' Such changling passed between a master and his servant. Shameful! I could do nothing as I owed the fellow thirty louis, but I resolved if possible to borrow money at Antibes and turn him off from thence.

I determined to go by land, so left Jacob and my baggage in the felucca, and desired the master to call in at Razzi and Monaco and one or two of the other ports, if I should make him a sign from any of them. I took Jachone with me, pulling him along with a good cord, and, whenever he was rebellious, beating him sorely. I even hung him fairly up twice upon trees for half a minute, but he grasped them with his feet and saved his neck[11]. I walked five miles to Finale (the first post, which a punster would say should be the last).

Wednesday 18 December 1765

Jogged most sluggishly along. Disputed with Jacob, who said he knew me perfectly and that it was impossible for servants to live well with me, as I was not, like other gentlemen, content with external acquiescence, but would always show them clearly that they were wrong. He is very right. I am always studying human nature and making experiments on the lowest characters, so that I am too much in the secret with regard to the weakness of man in reality, and my

honest, impetuous disposition cannot take up with that eternal repetition of fictitious minutiae by which unthinking men of fashion
preserve a great distinction between master and servant. By having
Jacob so free with me, I have felt as servants do, and been convinced
that the greatest part of them laugh in their sleeve very heartily at the
parade of their lords, knowing well that eating, drinking, sleeping,
and other offices of nature are common to all. Jacob said, 'I believe,
Sir, that you have been badly brought up. You have not the manners
of a nobleman. Your heart is too open.' I confessed to him that I was
two and twenty before I had a servant. Said he, 'The son of a gentleman
ought to be accustomed early to command a servant, but reasonably,
and never to joke with them; because each must live in his state
according to his quality. You, Sir, would live just like a peasant. And
you force a servant to speak in a way he shouldn't, because you
torment him with questions. You want to get to the bottom of things.
Sir, I do not think you should marry. At least, if you marry, you should
not live in the same house with your wife; otherwise, ma foi! there
will shortly be disputes, and a quarrel which cannot be made up. Sir,
this is what you should do: marry a lady, give her a certain allowance,
and let her have her house where you can go when you find it
agreeable and not be inconvenienced; and you must never see your
children, or otherwise they will be as badly brought up as you. I hope,
Sir, you will not take this in bad part.' The fellow talked thus with so
much good sense, so much truth, and with so natural an air, that upon
my word I admired him; I, however, hoped that a few years more
would temper all that impetuosity and remove all that weakness which
now render me inconstant and capricious. At any rate, I have a singular
kind of philosophy which will make me content to be whatever I shall
turn out.

I came at night to a tolerable inn. I sat up too late writing, and I
suppose astonished the people of the house, who are used to see their
guests tumble into bed immediately after supper. By the by, the French
soft feather beds are destroying me by relaxing my nerves. The inns
of this light-headed nation are very seldom good, for the rooms are
cold and comfortless and dirty, the sheets damp, and snuffers difficult
to be found. Old England lives for ever, for thy inns are more excellent
than are palaces anywhere else.

Saturday 21 December 1765 [Marseilles]

... The stage of Marseilles is always crowded with gentlemen, a sad abuse which destroys the very essence of a dramatic entertainment ... The French squeaking and grimaces were insufferable to a man just come from the operas of Italy. O Italy! Land of felicity! True seat of all elegant delight! My mind shall ever soothe itself with the image of thy charms. Thy divine music has harmonised my soul. That nature, that sweet simplicity, that easy grace which has pleased me so often in thy theatres, shall never fade from my memory.

The gallant Duncan Drummond had told me at Genoa of a very good girl whom he had kept a long time, and had with him eight months at Minorca. Since I arrived at five and twenty, I have determined never again to risk my constitution with women. But Drummond having assured me that Mlle Susette was honest, safe, and disinterested, and counselled me to put in at that port, I went to her ... My *valet de place* was a German who spoke French and English, a tall and decent pimp. He showed me her lodgings. I found her a fine little lively girl, with hardly any of the vile cant of prostitutes. After examining me very shrewdly if I was really a friend of Drummond's, she agreed to let me pass the night with her. I went home and supped, and returned to her. She had a handsome bedroom prettily furnished. She was so little that I had an idea as if she was a child, and had not much inclination for her. I recalled my charming Signora at Siena, and was disgusted at all women but her, and angry at myself for being in the arms of another. Susette chatted neatly and diverted me. I sacrificed to the graces. I think I did no harm.

1766

Friday 3 January 1766

The surgeon of a *charité* here came and dressed my feet[12]. He was a fat and an alarming dog, for he very gravely advised me to pull out my nail altogether, 'because', said he, 'in so doing, you will have no more risk of ever being troubled with it'. As well might he have advised me to cut off my hand, had I hurt it. He gave me a softening plaster for my toe and bid me wait till I got to Paris to have it cured.

[The full journal lapses into a condensed form after he arrives in Paris. He had
hoped to see Rousseau there but he had already left for London. He met Wilkes
there, however. He also had a letter from his father confirming a report in the
paper that his mother had died and pleading with him to return home
immediately. One consequence of this was that he could not revisit Zélide, though
once he arrived in London he dithered there for ten days. Most surprising was
finding Thérèse Le Vasseur (Rousseau's housekeeper) in Paris. He looked her up
at the Hôtel Luxembourg and on her suggesting it, they agreed to travel to
London together. In the course of the eleven-day, rain-drenched trip he had sex
with her. She appears not to have been impressed with his love-making and
gave him some instructions.]

Monday 27 January 1766 [Paris]

. . . At Wilkes's saw in St James's Chronicle [a notice of] Mother's death.
Quite stunned; tried to dissipate [grief] . . .

Tuesday 28 January 1766

. . . got letter from Father, written by David. Too true; Mother gone.
Was quite stupefied. In all morning. Wept in bursts; prayed to her like
most solemn Catholic to saint. Roused philosophy; sung Italian gently
to soothe. But would not have hurt prejudices by doing so before
others.

Friday 31 January 1766

Yesterday morning after having been up all night and written sixteen
or seventeen letters, and felt spirits bound in veins, kept post-horses
waiting from six till nine, then was still in confusion. Cried, 'Is it
possible that my mother is dead?' Set out, and at Hôtel Luxembourg
took up Mademoiselle. Was serious and composed . . . was mild but
gloomy, and now and then thought Mother alive and gave starts [of
grief]. Night was manly, but hurt by Mademoiselle's mean kindness to
servants, &c. Talked of Rousseau always.

Wednesday 12 February 1766 [Dover]

Yesterday morning had gone to bed very early, and had done it once [with Thérèse]: thirteen in all. Was really affectionate to her. At two set out in fly; breakfasted Rochester on beefsteaks ... Mademoiselle was much fatigued. Came to London about six, to Swan at Westminster Bridge. Was now so firm that London made no impression.

Thursday 13 February 1766 [London]

... Back to London. Immediately to Johnson; received you with open arms. You kneeled, and asked blessing. Miss Williams glad of your return. When she went out, he hugged you to him like a sack, and grumbled, 'I hope we shall pass many years of regard.' You for some minutes saw him not so immense as before, but it came back ...

He said, 'Now you have five and twenty years, and you have employed 'em well.'

BOSWELL. 'Oh, no! Do I know history, mathematics, law, &c.? No.'

JOHNSON. 'Why, Sir, though you may know no science so well as to be able to teach it, and no profession so well as to be able to follow it, yet your general mass of knowledge of books and men renders you very capable to study any science or follow any profession.' (This was enough.) ...

Talking of Corsica and your scheme of publishing some account of it, he said, 'You cannot go to bottom [of the subject] but all you tell us is what we don't know. Give us as many anecdotes as you can.'

Sunday 16 February 1766

You went to Mitre; had engaged Mr Johnson ... You quoted Wilkes for something.

JOHNSON. 'It seems you have kept very good company abroad – Wilkes and Rousseau!'

BOSWELL. 'My dear Sir, you don't call Rousseau bad company? Do you really think him a bad man?'

JOHNSON. 'Sir, if you are to talk jestingly of this, I don't talk with you. If you would be serious, I think him one of the worst of men; a rascal who ought to be hunted out of society as he has been. Three or four nations have expelled him; and it is a shame that he is protected in this country.' [The English Government had given Rousseau a pension.] . . . You said, 'Sir, I don't deny but his novel may do harm, but I cannot think his intention was bad.'

JOHNSON. 'Sir, that will not do. We cannot prove any man's intention to be bad. You may shoot a man through the head, and say you intended to miss him, but the judge will order you to be hanged. The want of intention, when evil is committed, will not be sustained in a court of justice. If you are no better lawyer than that, we must send you back to Utrecht. Sir, Rousseau is a very bad man. I would sooner sign a sentence for his transportation than for that of any felon who has gone from the Old Bailey these many years. Yes, I should like to have him work in the plantations.'

BOSWELL. 'Sir, do you think him as bad a man as Voltaire?'

JOHNSON. 'Why, it is difficult to settle the proportion of iniquity between 'em . . . My dear Bozzy, let us have no more of this. It is extremely disagreeable to me. You are making nothing of this argument. I had rather you'd whistle me a Scotch tune.'

[*After writing to William Pitt, asking for an interview so he could convey Paoli's thoughts on the Corsican situation, he was allowed into Pitt's house in Bond Street.*]

Sunday 23 February 1766

PITT. 'Mr Boswell, I am very happy to make your acquaintance. I had heard of you before. I had seen an account in the foreign papers of your being in Corsica.[13] (He had indeed asked some questions before the company.) 'Now, Sir, I will explain to you how I cannot properly receive communications from General de Paoli, for I am a Privy Councillor, and have taken an oath to hear nothing from any foreign power that may concern Great Britain without declaring it to the King and Council. Now, Sir, it is in your breast to judge whether what you have to say is of a nature fit to be told or not. I shall be very happy to hear your accounts of the island as a traveller. Some time hence things may turn about, and I may be at liberty to receive communications from Corsica, and then I shall be very happy to hear all you have to say. I am now just a private member of Parliament. I had once, Mr Boswell, something to do in the affairs of this nation.

But when they had come to me in distress and in perplexity, "Think for us, act for us, venture for us!" and I had thought, acted, and ventured – for 'em then to come and tell me, "Now you must think as we choose!" When I had rolled the stone to the top of the hill, then! My Lord Temple and I were the only two in the Council that stood firm. We waited to see if this would last, and, finding a change of measures, and that I could be of no farther use, I resigned[14]; and ever since I have known no more of what has been doing in the Cabinet than the most remote man in the Kingdom. I know not what Genoa has been able to obtain by means of France.'

BOSWELL. 'Sir, that the General – Paoli – felt severely: to be given into the bargain that poor Corsica should be considered as nothing.'

PITT. 'Mr Boswell, I own it appears strange that an island of so great consequence to the navigation in the Mediterranean should be neglected. How are their harbours?'

BOSWELL. 'One or two excellent, with some expense.'

PITT. 'Sir, that is of great consequence to a fleet on some grand enterprise. We have no such place on Italy.'

BOSWELL. 'Sir, General de Paoli said –'

PITT. 'Sir, you'll remember my situation.'

BOSWELL. 'Pray, Sir, may I ask you if you never received a letter from General de Paoli?'

PITT. 'Never, Sir.'

BOSWELL. 'Why then, Sir, after the Proclamation he wrote to you, and, as he has the highest admiration of your character, he was most sensibly hurt to be neglected by Mr Pitt.'

PITT. 'Sir, I never received his letter. I suppose *those next the King* have taken care it should not be delivered. I could not have answered it – could not have been in correspondence with General de Paoli, but I should have taken care to let him know my regard for him. Sir, I should be sorry that in any corner of the world, however distant or however small, it should be suspected that I could ever be indifferent to the cause of liberty.'

You met at Mitre Dr Goldsmith whom you had before called upon. You both went to Mr Johnson's, who was still bad and would not come out. 'Come then,' said Goldie, 'we will not go to the Mitre tonight, since we can't have the big man with us.' But we had sent for Davies, and I insisted on going. Goldsmith said, 'I think, Mr Johnson, you don't go near the theatres. You give yourself no more concern about a new play than if you had never had anything to do with the stage.'

JOHNSON. 'Why, Sir, our tastes alter. The lad does not care for the child's rattle, and the old man does not care for the young man's whore.'

GOLDSMITH. 'Nay, but, Sir, your Muse was not a whore.'

JOHNSON. 'Sir, I don't think she was. But as we advance in the journey of life, we drop some of the things which have pleased us; whether it be that we are fatigued and don't choose to carry so many things any farther, or that we find other things which we like better.'

BOSWELL. 'But, Sir, why don't you give us something in some other way?'

GOLDSMITH. 'Ay, Sir, we have a claim upon you.'

JOHNSON. 'No, Sir, I am not obliged to do any more. No man is obliged to do as much as he can do. A man is to have part of his life to himself. If a soldier has fought a good many campaigns, he is not to be blamed if he retires to ease and tranquillity. Sir, a physician who has long practised in a great city may be excused if he retires to a small town and takes less practice. Sir, the good I can do by my conversation bears the same proportion to the good I can do by my writings that the practice of a physician, retired to a small town, does to his practice in a great city.'

BOSWELL. 'But I wonder, Sir, you have not more pleasure in writing than not.'

JOHNSON. 'Sir, you *may* wonder.' In short, Goldsmith and I could make nothing against him.

He talked of making verses. He said, 'The great matter is to know when you have made good ones. I generally have 'em in my mind, perhaps fifty at a time, walking in my room; and then write 'em, and often from laziness wrote only the half lines. Sir, I have written a hundred lines a day. I remember I wrote a hundred lines of *The Vanity of Human Wishes* in a day. Doctor, I made one line t'other day, but I made out no more.'

GOLDSMITH. 'Let us hear it, and we'll put a bad one to it.'

JOHNSON. 'No, Sir, I have forgot it.'

We left him, and as we were going along Fleet Street, Goldsmith very gravely said, 'Don't you think that head's failed – wearing, eh?' O fine!

BOSWELL. 'No, Sir, I think he is rather more impatient of contradiction than he was.'

GOLDSMITH. 'Sir, no man is proof against continual adulation.'

THREE

Settling Down
1766–1769

When Boswell arrived back home, he had three goals predominantly in his mind: find a wife, complete certain formalities for admission to the Scottish bar, and keep up his Corsican enthusiasm and eventually write his book about the island. The second went smoothly and on 29 July 1766 he was formally admitted to the bar, within weeks sensationally and indiscreetly taking on his first criminal client. Once he got to it, he wrote his book on Corsica rapidly and efficiently saw to its publication. This was in spite of Samuel Johnson's discouragement, who wrote to him on 2 September 1766: 'You have, somehow or other, warmed your imagination. I wish there were some cure, like the lover's leap, for all heads of which some single idea has obtained an unreasonable and irregular possession. Mind your own affairs, and leave the Corsicans to theirs.'

Finding a wife was more difficult. His progress in the marriage stakes, watched intensely by his father who expected him to add profitably to the Auchinleck estate through his choice, proved to be a comic saga, worthy of Restoration comedies, Shakespeare, Fielding and Sterne all put together. His search for a wife was complicated by a lengthy affair he carried on with the Circean Mrs Dodds with whom he had taken up in Moffat and who followed him to Edinburgh. On the whole, he showed himself in the process to be a conspicuously poor judge of women.

To begin with, we can follow his journey in all three areas through his letters, mainly to Temple, which he wrote with the dramatic brilliance of his best journal entries. After a hiatus, he resumed his journal in January 1767, then let it lapse again in June until the new year, when he picked it up again energetically for three months, a period that included a lively trip to London and wild extremes of behaviour. For a wife he finally settled on his childhood sweetheart, who through no fault of her own drove him even further apart from his father.

1766

Boswell to William Temple, 28 April 1766 [Auchinleck]

My ever dear Temple: Many a curious letter have you had from me in my different situations. A more extraordinary one than this you have never had. I write to you while the delirium is really existing. In short, Sir, the gardener's daughter who was named for my mother, and has for some time been in the family as chambermaid, is so very pretty that I am entirely captivated by her. Besides my principle of never debauching an innocent girl, my regard for her father, a worthy man of uncommon abilities, restrains me from forming the least licentious thought against her. And therefore in plain words I am mad enough to indulge imaginations of marrying her. Only think of the proud Boswell with all that you know of him, the fervent adorer of a country girl of three and twenty. I rave about her. I was never so much in love as I am now. My fancy is quite inflamed: it riots in extravagance.

I know as well as you can tell me that a month's or perhaps ten days' possession of this angelic Creature would probably make her appear to me insipid ... I have a clear remembrance of my being tormented with many such passions, all which went off in a little time, and yet Temple I am still dreaming of delightful nuptials. She and I were in a manner brought up together. As far back as I can remember we used to build houses and make gardens, wade in the river and play upon the sunny banks. I cannot consider her as below me. For these six or seven years past I have seen her little. Before I went abroad she had begun to be timid and reserved, for Lord Eglinton admired her extremely, and wanted to seduce her. For my part, I saw nothing more about her than in many good-looking girls in the neighbourhood. But since my return from my travels, I have been quite enchanted with her. She has a most amiable face and the prettiest foot and ankle. She is perfectly well made, and has a lively genteel air that is irresistible.

I take every opportunity of being with her when she is putting on fires or dressing a room. She appears more graceful with her besom [broom] than ever shepherdess did with a crook. I pretend great earnestness to have the library in good order and assist her to dust it. I cut my gloves that she may mend them. I kiss her hand. I tell her what a beauty I think her. She has an entire confidence in me, and has no fear of any bad design, and she has too much sense to form an idea of having me for a husband. On the contrary, she talks to me of not refusing a good offer if it is made to her. Enchanting Creature! Must she be enjoyed by some schoolmaster or farmer? Upon my honour it cuts me to the heart. If she would not marry any body else, I think I could let her alone. That we may not be too often seen together she and I write notes to each other which we lay under the cloth which covers my table. This little curious correspondence which to her is an innocent amusement makes my heart beat continually. She has a fine temper. She has read a great deal, for I always supplied her with books. In short she is better than any lady I know.

What shall I do, Temple? Shall I lay my account with all its consequences and espouse her? Will not the exquisite languish of her eyes charm away repentance? Shall I not pass a life of true natural felicity with the woman I love and have a race of healthy and handsome children? Good heavens! What am I about? It would kill my father. Have I returned safe from London, from Italy, and from France to throw myself away on a servant maid? . . .

I have got a lock of her hair which I dote upon. She allowed me to cut if off. If I should marry her, I would never suffer her to dress better than she does now. I think I could pass my whole life agreeably with her assistance. I am not fit for marriage in all the forms. A lady would not be compliant enough, and would oblige me to harass myself with an endless repetition of external ceremony and a most woeful maintaining of proper conduct. Whereas my dear girl would be grateful for my attachment, would be devoted to me in every respect, would live with me just as a mistress, without the disgrace and remorse. After all my feverish joys and pains, I should enjoy calm and permanent bliss in her arms. Was there ever such madness? . . . When dusting the rooms with my Charmer, am I not like Agamemnon amongst the Thracian girls? All this may do for a summer. But is it possible that I could imagine the dear delirium would last for life? I will rouse my philosophic spirit, and fly from this fascination. I am going to Moffat for a month[1]. Absence will break the enchantment. I charge you in honour not to mention it. Write me how you are affected by this letter.

Boswell to William Temple, 17 May 1766 [Moffat]

I have been a week here, and ... let me tell you at once that my love for the handsome chambermaid is already like a dream that is past. I kept the extravagant epistle which was to inform you of it till I should see if absence would not free me from the delirium. I can now send you with a good grace what would certainly have alarmed you, but will now be truly amusing. Romantic as I am, it was so strange a scene in the play of my life that I myself was quite astonished at it. I give you my word of honour it was literally true. There are few people who could give credit to it. But you, who have traced me since ever I fairly entered upon the stage, will not doubt of it. It is a little humbling, to be sure. It was the effect of great force and great weakness of mind. I am certainly a most various composition ... I can tell you though, Temple, such a man as I am must be very much upon his guard. I believe my safest way will be to give you a promise that I never will marry without your approbation...

I came to Moffat to wash off a few scurvy spots which the warmer climates of Europe had brought out on my skin. I drink the waters and bathe regularly and take a great deal of exercise, and have a fine flow of spirits. I am as happy as an unmarried man can be...

1767

Boswell to William Temple, 1 February 1767 [Edinburgh]

... My friend, I am happy enough to have a *dear infidel*[2], as you say. But don't think her unfaithful. I could not love her if she was. There is a baseness in all deceit which my soul is virtuous enough ever to abhor, and therefore I look with horror upon adultery. But my amiable mistress is no longer bound to him who was her husband. He has used her shockingly ill. He has deserted her. He lives with another. Is she not then free? She is. It is clear, and no arguments can disguise it. She is now mine, and were she to be unfaithful to me, she ought to be pierced with a Corsican poniard. But I believe she loves me sincerely. She has done everything to please me. She is perfectly generous, and would not hear of any present. She has hitherto been boarded here, which lays us under a restraint. I have found out a sober widow, in whose house is the rendezvous of our amours. But I have now prevailed with my love to let me take a house for her, and as it will be my family I shall provide what is necessary. In this manner I am safe and happy and in no danger either of the perils of Venus or of desperate matrimony.

Boswell to William Temple, 4 March 1767 [Edinburgh]

In a former part of this letter I have talked a great deal of my sweet little mistress. I am, however, uneasy about her. Furnishing a house and maintaining her with a maid will cost me a great deal of money, and it is too like marriage, or too much a settled plan of licentiousness. But what can I do? I have already taken the house, and the lady has agreed to go into it at Whitsunday. I cannot in honour draw back. Besides, in no other way can I have her. But I have had more intelligence of her former intrigues. I am hurt to think of them. I cry, 'Damn her, lewd minx.' I am jealous. What shall I do?

Oh, my friend! were you but here; but, alas! that cannot be. Mamhead is not within a call[3]. It ought to be so, for you should always be my pastor; and I might now and then be yours. Friend of my youth, explain to me how we suffer so severely from what no longer exists. How am I tormented because my charmer has formerly loved others! I am disgusted to think of it. My lively imagination often represents her former lovers in actual enjoyment of her. My desire fails, I am unfit for love. Besides, she is ill-bred, quite a rompish girl. She debases my dignity. She has no refinement. But she is very handsome, very lively, and admirably formed for amorous dalliance. What is it to me that she has formerly loved? So have I. I am positive that since I first courted her at Moffat she has been constant to me. She is kind. She is generous. What shall I do? I wish I could get off, and yet how awkward would it be! And, after all, can I do better than keep a dear infidel for my hours of Paphian bliss? But, alas, since yesterday I am cooled ... This is a curious epistle to a clergyman. Admonish me, but forgive me...

Boswell to William Temple, 8 March 1767 [Edinburgh]

What is to be thought of this life, my friend? Hear the story of my last three days. After tormenting myself with reflecting on my charmer's former loves and ruminating on parting with her, I went to her. I could not conceal my being distressed. I told her I was very unhappy, but I would not tell her why. She took this very seriously, and was so much affected that she went next morning and gave up our house. I went in the afternoon and secured the house, and then drank tea with her. She was much agitated. She said she was determined to go and board herself in the north of England, and that I used her very ill. I expostulated with her. I was sometimes resolved to let her go, and sometimes my heart was like to burst within me. I held her dear hand. Her eyes were full of passion. I took her in my arms. I told her what made me miserable. She was pleased to find it was nothing worse. She had imagined that I was suspicious of her fidelity, and she thought that very ungenerous in me, considering her behaviour. She said I should not mind her faults before I knew her, since her conduct was now most circumspect. We renewed our fondness. She owned she loved me more than she had ever done her husband. All was again well. She said she did not reproach me with my former follies, and we should be on an equal footing. My mind all at once felt a spring. I agreed with her. I embraced her with transport.

That very evening I gave a supper to two or three of my acquaintance, having before I left Scotland laid a guinea that I should not catch the venereal disorder for three years, which bet I had most certainly lost and now was paying. We drank a great deal, till I was so much intoxicated that instead of going home I went to a low house in one of the alleys in Edinburgh where I knew a common girl lodged, and like a brute as I was I lay all night with her. I had still so much reason left as not to 'dive into the bottom of the deep', but I gratified my coarse desires by tumbling about on the brink of destruction. Next morning I was like a man ordered for ignominious execution. But by noon I was worse, for I discovered that some infection had reached me. Was not this dreadful? I had an assignation in the evening with my charmer. How lucky was it that I knew my misfortune in time. I might have polluted her sweet body. Bless me! What a risk! But how could I tell her my shocking story? I took courage. I told how drunk I had been. I told the consequences. I lay down and kissed her feet. I said I was unworthy of any other favour ... I hoped she would consider my being drunk as a fatal accident which I should never again fall into. I called her my friend in whom I had confidence, and entreated she would comfort me.

How like you the eloquence of a young barrister? It was truly the eloquence of love. She bid me rise; she took me by the hand. She said she forgave me. She kissed me. She gently upbraided me for entertaining any unfavourable ideas of her. She bid me take great care of myself and in time coming never drink upon any account...

Tell me sincerely, do I right to insist that my dear little woman shall stay? She was married very young. But she has three children. I hate to think of it. No matter. She is like a girl of eighteen. She has the finest black hair, she is paradisial in bed. Is it not right I should have a favourite to keep me happy? But, alas, I love her so much that I am in a kind of fever. This is unworthy of Paoli's friend[4].

Boswell to William Temple, 30 March 1767 [Auchinleck]

What say you to my marrying? I intend next autumn to visit Miss Bosville in Yorkshire[5]. But I fear, my lot being cast in Scotland, that beauty would not be content. She is, however, grave. I shall see. There is a young lady[6] in the neighbourhood here who has an estate of her own between two and three hundred a year, just eighteen, a genteel person, an agreeable face, of a good family, sensible, good-tempered, cheerful, pious. You know my grand object is the ancient family of Auchinleck, a venerable and noble principle. How would it do to conclude an alliance with this neighbouring princess, and add her lands to our dominions? I should at once have a very pretty little estate, a good house, and a sweet place. My father is very fond of her. It would make him perfectly happy. He gives me hints in his way: 'I wish you had her.' No bad scheme this. I think a very good one. But I will not be in a hurry...

...My fair neighbour was a ward of my father's. She sits in our seat at church in Edinburgh. She would take possession here most naturally. This is a superb place: we have the noblest natural beauties, and my father has made most extensive improvements. We look ten miles out upon our own dominions. We have an excellent new house. I am now writing in a library forty foot long. Come to us, my dearest friend. We will live like the most privileged spirits of antiquity. I am now seriously engaged in my Account of Corsica. It elevates my soul, and makes me *spernere humum* [spurn the earth]. I shall have it finished by June.

Tuesday 28 April 1767

At night I received a packet of papers brought from Holland by Captain Kinloch. But my [Dutch] Journal was a-missing. I was much vexed. I figured its being exposed to a hundred enemies. I wrote immediately to Mr Brown at Utrecht, and to Mr Kinloch of Gilmerton, the Captain's father.

Boswell to William Temple, 12 June 1767 [Edinburgh]

The lady in my neighbourhood is the finest woman I have ever seen. I went and visited her, and she was so good as to prevail with her mother to come to Auchinleck, where they stayed four days, and in our romantic groves I adored her like a divinity. I have already given you her character. My father is very desirous I should marry her. All my relations, all my neighbours approve of it. She looked quite at home in the house of Auchinleck. Her picture would be an ornament to the gallery. Her children would be all Boswells and Temples, and as fine women as these are excellent men.

[On the eve of his brother David's departure, in October 1767, for Spain, where he would remain for more than a decade, Boswell wrote for him this juvenile 'oath' swearing his fealty to Auchinleck and its ancestry. David thought it was all ridiculous, as did James Bruce, the overseer at Auchinleck, who with his family had to witness it. But Boswell was in earnest.]

OATH OF DAVID BOSWELL

I, David Boswell, youngest son of the Right Honourable Alexander Boswell, Lord of Session and Justiciary, present representative of the family of Auchinleck, do by these presents declare that, according to the usage of the family when any branch of it is sent forth into the world, I have stood upon the old castle of Auchinleck and have there solemnly promised to stand by these old walls with heart, purse and sword, that is to say, that in whatever part of the globe my fortune should place me, I should always be faithful to the ancient family of Auchinleck, and give a reasonable obedience to the representative thereof. In consequence of which I was invested with a ring according to the usage of the family. All this was done upon the nineteenth day of October in the year of our Lord one thousand seven hundred and sixty-seven years, in presence of James Boswell, Esquire, my eldest brother and heir of the family; the Reverend Mr John Dun, minister at Auchinleck, and the Reverend Mr Joseph Fergusson, minister at Tundergarth, chaplains appointed for the occasion; I departing for Valencia in Spain, there to settle as a merchant. Also in presence of Mr James Bruce, overseer at Auchinleck, and Alexander, John, Andrew, and James Bruces, his sons, all present having with one voice wished the continuance and prosperity of the ancient family of Auchinleck, and that the family of Bruce might ever flourish there. In testimony of which I now subscribe these presents, and seal them with the seal of my investiture, they being written by the said James Boswell, Esquire, and subscribed on the twenty-seventh day of the said month and in the said year of our Lord. Amen.

Boswell to William Temple, 24 December 1767 [Edinburgh]

In my last I told you that after I had resolved to give up with the Princess [Catherine Blair] for ever, I resolved first to see her, and that when I did see her I was so lucky as to have a very agreeable interview, and was convinced by her that she was not to blame. This happened on a Thursday. That evening, her cousin and most intimate friend, the Duchess of Gordon, came to town. Next day I was at the concert with them and afterwards supped at Lord Kames's. The Princess appeared distant and reserved. I could hardly believe that it was the same woman with whom I had been quite easy the day before. I was then uneasy.

Next evening I was at the play with them. It was *Othello*. I sat close behind the Princess, and at the most affecting scenes I pressed my hand upon her waist. She was in tears, and rather leaned to me. The jealous Moor described my very soul. I often spoke to her of the torment which she saw before her. Still I thought her distant, and still I was uneasy.

On Sunday ... I met the Princess at church. She was distant as before. I passed the evening at her aunt's, where I met a cousin of my Princess, a young lady of Glasgow who had been with us at Adamton.

She told me she had something to communicate, and she then said that my behaviour to the Princess was such that Mrs Blair and her daughter did not know how to behave to me. That it was not honourable to engage a young lady's affections while I kept myself free. In short, the good cousin persuaded me that the Princess had formed an attachment for me, and she assured me the Nabob [a rival suitor] had been refused. On Monday forenoon I waited on Miss Blair; I found her alone, and she did not seem distant. I told her that I was most sincerely in love with her, and that I only dreaded those faults which I had acknowledged to her. I asked her seriously if she now believed me in earnest. She said she did. I then asked her to be candid and fair as I had been with her, and to tell me if she had any particular liking for me. What think you, Temple, was her answer? No. 'I really,' said she, 'have no particular liking for you. I like many people as well as you.'

(Temple, you must have it in the genuine dialogue.) BOSWELL. 'Do you indeed? Well, I cannot help it. I am obliged to you for telling me so in time. I am sorry for it.'

PRINCESS. 'I like Jeanie Maxwell (Duchess of Gordon) better than you.'

BOSWELL. 'Very well. But do you like no man better than me?'

PRINCESS. 'No.'

BOSWELL. 'Is it possible that you may like me better than other men?'

PRINCESS. 'I don't know what is possible.' (By this time I had risen and placed myself by her, and was in real agitation.)

BOSWELL. 'I'll tell you what, my dear Miss Blair, I love you so much that I am very unhappy. If you cannot love me, I must if possible endeavour to forget you. What would you have me do?'

PRINCESS. 'I really don't know what you should do.'

BOSWELL. 'It is certainly possible that you may love me, and if you shall ever do so I shall be the happiest man in the world. Will you make a fair bargain with me? If you should happen to love me, will you own it?'

PRINCESS. 'Yes.'

BOSWELL. 'And if you should happen to love another, will you tell me immediately, and help me to make myself easy?'

PRINCESS. 'Yes, I will.'

BOSWELL. 'Well, you are very good' (often squeezing and kissing her fine hand, while she looked at me with those beautiful black eyes).

PRINCESS. 'I may tell you as a cousin what I would not tell to another man.'

BOSWELL. 'You may indeed. You are very fond of Auchinleck; that is one good circumstance.'

PRINCESS. 'I confess I am. I wish I liked you as well as I do Auchinleck.'

BOSWELL. 'I have told you how fond I am of you. But unless you like me sincerely, I have too much spirit to ask you to live with me, as I know that you do not like me. If I could have you this moment for my wife I would not.'

PRINCESS. 'I should not like to put myself in your offer, though.'

BOSWELL. 'Remember, you are both my cousin and my mistress. You must make me suffer as little as possible. As it may happen that I may engage your affections, I should think myself a most dishonourable man if I were not now in earnest, and remember I depend upon your sincerity; and whatever happens you and I shall never again have any quarrel.'

PRINCESS. 'Never.'

BOSWELL. 'And I may come and see you as much as I please?'

PRINCESS. 'Yes.'[7]

My worthy friend, what sort of a scene was this? It was most curious. She said she would submit to her husband in most things. She said that to see one loving her would go far to make her love that person; but she could not talk anyhow positively, for she never had felt the uneasy anxiety of love ...

Amidst all this love I have been wild as ever. I have catched another memorandum of vice, but a very slight one ... My black friend has brought me the finest little girl I ever saw[8]. I have named it Sally. It is healthy and strong. I take the greatest care of the mother, but shall have her no more in keeping.

1768

[John Raybould, an Englishman, had been convicted of forgery by the Court of Session. Boswell was not emotionally involved in this case because of Raybould's gentility and obvious guilt. Here he conducts himself almost like a prison *chaplain, but he is also fascinated with the spectacle of a man's behaviour when confronted with execution.*]

Sunday 21 February 1768 [Edinburgh]

In all forenoon, I had dreamt of Raybould under sentence of death. I was gloomy. Afternoon, church. Tea home, then visited Raybould, that my gloomy imagination might be cured by seeing the reality. I was shown up to him by Archibald, the soldier who was to be tried for murder. The clanking of the iron-room door was terrible. I found him very composed. I sat by him an hour and a half by the light of a dim farthing candle. He spoke very properly on religion. I read him the 4 Chapter of the 1 Epistle of John and lectured upon it. On verse 18 I discoursed on fear very appositely, by an illustration taken from Robert Hay, the soldier who was hanged last year. 'There, John,' said I, 'did he lie quite sunk, quite desperate, and neither would eat nor drink, and all for fear, just terror for dying. But the comfortable doctrine of Christianity prevents this.' I was quite firm, and I was astonished to compare myself now with myself when a boy, remarkably timorous. Raybould seemed wonderfully easy. I therefore talked quite freely to him. 'But, John, have you no fear for the immediate pain of dying?' 'No,' said he, 'I have had none as yet. I know not how it may be at the very moment. But I do think I shall be quite composed.' I looked steadfastly at him during this and saw he was speaking truly. One certain sign of his being much at ease was the readiness with which his attention was diverted to any other subject than his own melancholy situation; for when a man is much distressed he is still fixed in brooding over his calamity. But Raybould talked of his wife's journey down in all its particulars, just as if he had been an indifferent, ordinary man.

He told me when he came first to Scotland he did not know the difference between an agent and an advocate[9]. I saw him beginning to smile at his own ignorance. I considered how amazing it would be if a man under sentence of death should really laugh, and, with the nicest care of a diligent student of human nature, I as decently as possible first smiled as he did, and gradually cherished the risible exertion, till he and I together fairly laughed. How strange! He very calmly examined whether a man dying of sickness or one in his situation was worst. He said one in his situation. I argued that one dying of sickness was worst, because he is weakened and unable to support the fear of death, whereas one in his situation was quite well but for the prospect before him. Raybould, however, maintained his proposition, because, he said, the man weakened by sickness was brought to a state of indifference. I bid him farewell. It was truly a curious scene.

Wednesday 24 February 1768

I went to see Raybould's execution. I was invited up to the window of one – a merchant ... who knew me. I tried to be quite firm and philosophical, and imagined Raybould in some future period telling what he felt at his execution. The most dreadful event seems light when past, and I made it past by imagination. I felt very little; but when he stood long on the ladder I grew impatient, and was beginning to have uneasy sensations. I came home.

[Boswell set off on a visit to London on 18 March 1768.]

Saturday 19 March 1768 [York]

Shall my mind ever be all solid and rational? Yes. A room which is hung with the slightest chintz and gaudiest paper may by and by be hung with substantial velvet or even thick arras hangings with Scripture stories wrought upon them. My walls are good, so they will bear any sort of hangings. Often have they been substantially hung. But as yet I have changed my furniture as whim suggested...

...I felt myself quite strong, and exulted when I compared my present mind with my mind some years ago. Formerly my mind was quite a lodging-house for all ideas who chose to put up there, so that it was at the mercy of accident, for I had no fixed mind of my own. Now my mind is a house where, though the street rooms and the upper floors are open to strangers yet there is always a settled family in the back parlour and sleeping-closet behind it; and this family can judge of the ideas which come to lodge. This family! this landlord, let me say, or this landlady, as the mind and the soul are both she. I shall confuse myself with metaphor. Let me have done with it. Let me then have done with it. Only this more. The ideas – my lodgers – are of all sorts ... I am forced to own that my rooms have been occupied by women of the town, and by some ladies of abandoned manners. But I am resolved that by degrees there shall be only decent people and innocent, gay lodgers.

Wednesday 23 March 1768 [London]

I had this morning been at Tyburn seeing the execution of Mr Gibson, the attorney, for forgery, and of Benjamin Payne for highway robbery. It is a curious turn, but I never can resist seeing executions. The Abbé du Bos ingeniously shows that we have all a strong desire of having our passions moved, and the interesting scene of a man with death before his eyes cannot but move us greatly. One of weak nerves is overpowered by such spectacles. But by thinking and accustoming myself to them, I can see them quite firmly, though I feel compassion. I was on a scaffold close by. Payne was a poor young man of nineteen. He was pale as death, and half a corpse before the rope was put round his neck. Mr Gibson came in a coach with some of his friends, and I declare I cannot conceive a more perfect calmness and manly resolution than his behaviour. He was dressed in a full suit of black, wore his own hair cut round and a hat, was a man about fifty, and as he drove along it was impossible to perceive the least sign of dejection or gloom about him. He was helped up on the cart. The rope was put round his neck, and he stood with the most perfect composure, eat a sweet orange, and seemed rationally devout during prayers by Mr Moore, the ordinary of Newgate, who is really a good man and most earnest in the duties of his sad office, which I think a very important one. Stephen Roe, the last ordinary, was but a rough-spun blade. Never did I see death without some horror but in the case of Mr Gibson. It seemed a very easy matter. I always use to compare the conduct of malefactors with what I suppose my conduct might be. I believe I confounded the people about me by my many reflections. I affected being shocked that punishment might have an effect on their minds, though it had none upon my own. I never saw a man hanged but I thought I could behave better than he did, except Mr Gibson, who, I confess, exceeded all that I could ever hope to show of easy and steady resolution.

Saturday 26 March 1768 [Oxford]

On my coming to London I had called on Mr Samuel Johnson, but found he was gone to Oxford and was living at New Inn Hall. I was very anxious to see again my revered friend. I had written him many letters and had received none from him of a long time. I had published my *Account of Corsica*, in which I had spoken very highly of him, yet he had taken no notice of it. I had heard he was displeased at my having put into my book a part of one of his letters to me. In short, I was quite in the dark concerning him. But, be it as it would, I was determined to find him out, and if possible be well with him as usual. I therefore set out early this morning in the Oxford fly . . .

. . . We stopped at the gate of Magdalen College . . . I immediately had some coffee and then got a guide to show me New Inn Hall . . . by and by arrived the great man. He took me all in his arms and kissed me on both sides of the head, and was as cordial as ever I saw him. I told him all my perplexity on his account, and how I had come determined to fight him, or to do anything he pleased. 'What,' said he, 'did you come here on purpose?' 'Yes, indeed,' said I. This gave him high satisfaction. I told him how I was settled as a lawyer and how I had made two hundred pounds by the law this year. He grumbled and laughed and was wonderfully pleased. 'What, Bozzy? Two hundred pounds! A great deal.' . . .

He put me in mind of our journey to Harwich, and we recalled many a circumstance. He also renewed his promise of coming to Scotland and visiting with me some of the Western Isles.

Monday 28 March 1768 [Oxford]

We talked of adultery. Mr Johnson showed how highly criminal it was, because it broke the peace of families and introduced confusion of progeny. 'These constitute the essence of the crime, and therefore a woman who breaks her marriage vows is so much more criminal than a man. A man, to be sure, is criminal in the sight of God, but he does not do his wife a very material injury if he does not insult her; if, for instance, from mere wantonness of appetite, he steals privately to her chamber-maid. Sir, a wife ought not greatly to resent this. I should not receive home a daughter who had run away from her husband on that account. A wife should study to reclaim her husband by more attention to please him. Sir, a man will not once in a hundred instances leave his wife and go to a harlot, if his wife has not been negligent of pleasing.' 'Upon my word,' said I, 'he is grown liberal upon our hand.' 'But,' said Mr Chambers, 'suppose a husband goes a-whoring, and then poxes his wife.' 'Why Sir, if he poxes her, it is a bodily injury, and she may resent it as she pleases.'

I asked him if it was not hard that one deviation from chastity should so absolutely ruin a woman. JOHNSON. 'Why, no, Sir; the great principle which every woman is taught is to keep her legs together. When she has given up that principle, she has given up every notion of female honour and virtue, which are all included in chastity.' I argued that virtue might be found even in a common street-walker. He laughed, and as I had told him of my Dutch lady, 'Why,' said he 'I shall have the Dutch lady; you can get a wife in the streets.' I told him my objections to the Dutch lady were her superior talents. 'O Sir,' said he, 'you need not be afraid, marry her; before a year goes about you'll find that reason much weaker, and that wit not near so bright.' O admirable master of human nature!

[Boswell left London on 9 June to return to Edinburgh and Auchinleck. He wrote out this endearing and charming make-believe 'agreement' for his poor cousin and dear childhood friend Margaret to sign sometime that summer. A playful extension of their childhood intimacy, it is a sign of his simple fondness for her.]

Agreement between James Boswell and Margaret Montgomerie

At Edinburgh, the eighth day of August one thousand seven hundred and sixty-eight years, I, Margaret Montgomerie, sister of the late James Montgomerie of Lainshaw, Esquire, considering that Mr James Boswell, advocate, my cousin, is at present so much in love with me that I might certainly have him for my lawful husband if I choose it, and the said James being of a temper so inconstant that there is reason to fear that he would repent of his choice in a very short time, on which account he is unwilling to trust himself in my company; therefore, I, the said Margaret Montgomerie, hereby agree that in case I am married to the said James Boswell any time this year, or insist upon his promise thereto within the said time to take place any time thereafter, I shall submit to be banished out of Great Britain during all the days of my life. In witness whereof I have subscribed this paper written by the said James Boswell.

[Later that summer, Boswell met a rich sixteen-year-old Irish girl called Mary Ann Boyd, a cousin of his cousins, the Montgomeries of Lainshaw, not far from Auchinleck. He promptly fell in love with her, his 'la belle Irlandaise', and was invited to visit her family in Ireland the following spring, which he resolved to do, fairly certain that he would end up marrying this teenager 'formed like a Grecian nymph, with the sweetest countenance, full of sensibility, accomplished, with a Dublin education ...'. Margaret Montgomerie agreed to travel with him.]

1769

Tuesday 25 April 1769

Miss Montgomerie and I set out from Auchinleck [for Lainshaw]. My father was so averse to my Irish expedition that she had not resolution to agree to accompany me ... My father walked out, and I did not take leave of him. It was a delightful day.

Thursday 27 April 1769 [Lainshaw]

I was quite drunk. I am sorry for it. I behaved ill to Margaret, my own affectionate friend. Such terrible effects may intoxication have.

Friday 28 April 1769

I rose with a headache and the disagreeable reflection that I had offended Margaret. When she came down I found her so much hurt that she would not have set out on our Irish jaunt, had she not been so kind that she would not assign the cause of her staying. I was very sorry, and resolved to make up to her for what she had suffered by my future good behaviour ... Margaret and I on bad terms were yet driving in one chaise, and going on a jaunt of pleasure all the way to Dublin. But the quarrels of friends never last ... It was a charming day, and Margaret and I became gentle and complacent.

Saturday 29 April 1769

I felt myself in love with another woman [Margaret] than Marianne. She is always my friend and comforter. She and I were now admirable company. I observed that there were few people but were mixed characters, like a candle: half wax, half tallow ... I observed that she and I had more enlarged views, as we had fancy to look beyond what really is ours — like one whose house has a prospect not only of his own lands, but of many beautiful objects at a distance ... When I talked that Corsica was a very hilly country, Margaret observed that the French would have uphill work there.

Sunday 30 April 1769

... my serious passion came into my mind with more force than ever. I imagined that Miss Montgomerie knew the lady's [Mary Ann Boyd's] mind, and from some things she said I concluded that the lady was engaged. I was amazingly affected. I cried bitterly, and would not speak to my companion. I, who was on an expedition to court a pretty young lady at Dublin, and had with me a most agreeable companion was miserable from love of another woman, and would not speak to my companion. Such a mind! I never was in greater torment, nor indulged gloomier schemes. We had a good inn at Ballantrae. For ten minutes I continued as bad as in the chaise, till Miss Montgomerie by chance discovered the cause of all my misery, and with her usual kindness assured me that I was mistaken. I then enjoyed the most delightful calm after a dismal storm. We drank tea comfortably after our journey, read part of the evening service, had some agreeable religious conversation, and then supped cheerfully. I was so much rejoiced that, after she went to bed, I got Mactaggart the landlord to drink with me till I staggered. Such wild transitions! A punster would say the landlord might be called Macstaggered.

Monday 1 May 1769 [Portpatrick]

... We engaged a boat, the James and —, Captain Cosh, commander, to carry us to the other side of the water. As we knew we would be sick, we determined to sail that night and try to sleep, as there was a good cabin ... At twelve my companion and I went aboard. I tried to brave it out for a while, but grew very sick. She was better than I. Only I got some sleep, which she did not. Nothing can be severer than to be sick at sea, for one has no hope that immediate relief may come, as in other sicknesses. One grows quite weak. I thought my Irish jaunt madness, and that I would not try another. Such are our minds at times. It was a very moderate breeze. We got over in about five hours.

Boswell to William Temple, 3 May 1769 [Donaghadee]

I am fairly landed in the kingdom of Ireland, and am tomorrow to proceed for Dublin to see my sweet Mary Ann. But, my worthy friend ... I must tell you that I am accompanied by my cousin Miss Montgomerie, whom I believe you saw at Edinburgh, and she perhaps may and perhaps ought to prevent my Hibernian nuptials. You must know that she and I have always been in the greatest intimacy. I have proved her on a thousand occasions, and found her sensible, agreeable, and generous. When I was not in love with some one or other of my numerous flames, I have been in love with her; and during the intervals of all my passions Margaret has been constantly my mistress as well as my friend. Allow me to add that her person is to me the most desirable that I ever saw. Often have I thought of marrying her, and often told her so. But we talked of my wonderful inconstancy, were merry, and perhaps in two days after the most ardent professions to her I came and told her that I was desperately in love with another woman. Then she smiled, was my confidante, and in time I returned to herself. She is with all this, Temple, the most honest, undesigning creature that ever existed.

Well, Sir, being my cousin german, she accompanies me on my Irish expedition. I found her both by sea and land the best companion I ever saw. I am exceedingly in love with her. I highly value her. If ever a man had his full choice of a wife, I would have it in her. But the objections are she is two years older than I. She has only a thousand pounds. My father would be violent against my marrying her, as she would bring neither money nor interest. I, from a desire to aggrandise my family, think somewhat in the same manner. And all my gay projects of bringing home some blooming young lady and making an éclat with her brilliant fortune would be gone.

But, on the other hand, my cousin is of a fine, firm, lively temperament, and never can be old [melancholic]. She may have as many children as I wish, and from what she has already done as an aunt I am sure she would make a very good mother. Would not my children be more obliged to me for such a mother than for many thousands? Then, she has much to say with my father, who could not reasonably be enraged, at having his niece for daughter-in-law. She would live in such a manner that at my death my family may be richer than if I married a fortune; and for the gay projects of fancy, is there any doubt that they are nothing when compared with real happiness? Many men seek to form friendships with the great, the embroidered, the titled. If they succeed, are they as happy as I am in the friendship of Temple? I fear that if I marry any other woman, my love for my cousin may often distract me. And what weighs much with me, Temple, is that amidst all this merriment and scheming, I really imagine that she truly loves me, that by my courting her so often she is so attached to me that she would silently suffer very severely if she saw me irrevocably fixed to another.

And yet my charming seraph, my Marianne, melts my heart. Her little bosom beats at the thoughts of seeing me – forgive my vanity – you know, strange as it may be, that women of all tempers and ages have been fond of me. Temple, you never failed me yet. What shall I do? This is the most delicate case of the many that I have laid before you. I must, however, tell you that my father is quite averse to Marianne, and declares he never will agree to it. But if her father gives me a round sum, I do not fear mine. But if I am certain that my cousin sincerely loves me, wishes to have me, and would be unhappy without me, what should I do? Should I be hard-hearted enough not to give happiness to the woman I love, and the friend I can trust? for such she literally is. And if I think of my own happiness, whether do you think that she or the seraph is most certain? And how shall I do not to hurt either of the two? Never did there live such a man as myself.

[Annoyingly, the journal stops at this point, resuming five weeks later, but we know that by the time Boswell reached Mary Ann he had abandoned any idea of marrying her. He had almost made up his mind to marry Margaret by the time he returned to Scotland on 7 June, but on his return to Edinburgh he was assaulted with doubts and attacks of gonorrhoea and hypochondria.]

Thursday 13 July 1769 [Edinburgh]

At night I had a serious conversation with my father. He talked of my not minding affairs at home. That gave me a good opportunity to say that I really had no encouragement as I was in so uncertain a way, and that he even talked *de se remarier*. He in a manner acknowledged his having such views. I spoke in the strongest terms, and fairly told him he should be no more troubled with me. I was really calm and determined. It is wonderful to think how he and I have differed to such a degree for so many years. I was somewhat hurt to find myself again thrown loose on the world. But my love of adventure and hope made me surprisingly easy. My great unhappiness was thinking of M[argaret]. And yet in any way she could not but suffer, for I could not think of marriage when he exposed himself at his years and forgot my valuable mother. O unfeeling world! I declare I am not, nor ever could be, so much so. And yet, honest man! he talked of his affection for me and what he had suffered on my account with a tone that moved me, though I was quite irritated against him now. I am truly a composition of many opposite qualities.

Sunday 16 July 1769

After a wretched, feverish night I awaked in a dreadful state. I have no doubt that evil spirits, enemies to mankind, are permitted to tempt and torment them. 'Damn him [his father]. Curse him,' sounded somehow involuntarily in my ears perpetually. I was absolutely mad. I sent for worthy Grange, and was so furious and black-minded and uttered such horrid ideas that he could not help shedding tears, and even went so far as to say that if I talked so he would never see me again. I looked on my father's marrying again as the most ungrateful return to me for my having submitted so much to please him. I thought it an insult on the memory of my valuable mother. I thought it would totally estrange him from his children by her. In short, my wild imagination made it appear as terrible as can be conceived. I rose and took a little broth, and, in order to try if what I liked most could have any effect on me when in such a frame, I went to the chapel in Carrubber's Close, which has always made me fancy myself in heaven. I was really relieved. I thought of M. and loved her fervently. But I was still obstinate.

Boswell to Margaret Montgomerie, 10 July 1769 [Edinburgh]

My dear cousin, I know I shall have a friendly and affectionate answer to the last letter which I wrote to you. But in the meantime, I am going to write you a calm and determined epistle, in few words but of infinite importance to us both.

You never knew till we were in Ireland that I had at different periods of my life been deeply in love with you. That has, however, been the case; and had not vanity or some other artificial motive made me, from time to time, encourage my fancy in other schemes, the genuine inclinations of my heart would ever have been constant to my dear Peggie Montgomerie. As it was, you know how fond I have been of you, and how I have at different times convinced you that my love for you was truly sincere. While wavering in my resolutions, I was always determined that if your happiness depended upon having me, I would not hesitate a moment to make my best friend happy. And I accordingly begged in a late letter that you would tell me freely if that was the case.

I was at the assembly last night, and saw a variety of beauties. I was not inconstant to you for a moment. Indeed, after standing the trial you did in Ireland, there could be little fear. Any other person than you would be apt to disregard what I say in my present situation. But I think I may trust to the generosity of a noble-minded woman, as Dempster calls you. I therefore make you this proposal. You know my unhappy temper. You know all my faults. It is painful to repeat them. Will you, then, knowing me fully, accept of me for your husband as I now am – not the heir of Auchinleck, but one who has had his time of the world, and is henceforth to expect no more than £100 a year? With that and the interest of your £1,000, we can live in an agreeable retirement in any part of Europe that you please. But we are to bid adieu for ever to this country. All our happiness is to be our society with each other, and our hopes of a better world. I confess this scheme is so romantic that nothing but such love as you showed at Donaghadee could make you listen to it. Nor ought I to be surprised if a woman of your admirable sense and high character with all who know you should refuse to comply with it, should refuse to sacrifice every prudent consideration to me. But as I love you more than I can express, you will excuse me for making this proposal. I am ready upon these terms to marry you directly. And, upon my honour, I would not propose it

now, were I not fully persuaded that I would share a kingdom with
you if I had it. I also solemnly promise to do everything in my power
to show my gratitude and make you happy. Think seriously of this.
Give me any positive answer you honestly can. But I insist on no
mediocrity, no reasoning, no hesitation. Think fully, and one way or
other tell me your resolution.

Saturday 29 July 1769

It is impossible to put upon paper an exact journal of the life of
man. External circumstances may be marked. But the variations within,
the workings of reason and passion, and, what perhaps influence
happiness most, the colourings of fancy, are too fleeting to be recorded.
In short, so it is that I defy any man to write down anything like a
perfect account of what he has been conscious during one day of his
life, if in any degree of spirits. However, what I put down has so far
an effect that I can, by reading my Journal, recall a good deal of my
life.

Boswell to Margaret Montgomerie, 21 August 1769 [Edinburgh]

I do not wonder at your panic and reluctance to go to Auchinleck.
Nobody but such as know my father's way perfectly can imagine how
hard it must be upon you. For the truth is that his manner of keeping
people in awe, joined with his peculiar talent of putting what he
pleases in a contemptible light, is galling beyond expression to a
feeling mind. The best remedy which I have found against the effects
of this has been to prepare myself calmly for it, as for a piece of
caricatura which I am certain is unjust but which may entertain me. A
great part of the happiness of lovers and friends consists in the high
opinion which they entertain of each other. In what particular way
you think of me, I cannot know; but am convinced that you have a
value for me, as I have for you, as much as ever man had for woman,
and for which I have often given you the best reasons. Now how
terrible must it be for any one of us to have the other represented as
a very inconsiderable being. However, allowance must be made. No
other person can think equally high of us as we do of each other, and
my father less so perhaps than anybody else. Let us bear it patiently,
and hope to make him by degrees think better of us.

I approve of your not being in too great a hurry to go to Auchinleck. I have written to my father telling him that, as I now look upon you as my *wife*, it will be very obliging to me if he will send his chaise for you, or at least write to you, and behave to you with kindness as his daughter-in-law. My letter will be with him this afternoon. You may wait a day or two, and see what effect it produces. As this is our sacrament week at Auchinleck, he may put off sending for you till next week. But if you do not hear from him by Friday, I would have you send your letter to him. You will observe that I have shortened it considerably and have struck out the paragraph justifying yourself as to our marriage. I think you have no need of a justification. Are not you my equal? Are not you his own niece? Keep in mind your own value, my dearest. Keep in mind that you are my spouse, the woman whom I have preferred to all others for her real merit. Will you forgive me for rejoicing in my reformation? and let me add the woman whom I have preferred to the temptations of fortune? for so you know to be true. On my account, as well as your own, I will not suffer you to write to my father as if you were a milliner or a tenant's daughter whom his son had married in a foolish fit of love. Remember you are my *lady*. I have also thought it best to keep out the paragraph as to some of your relations having contributed to prejudice him against you. Let all these things be forgotten. My life for it, we shall hear no more of them now. I have taken the same liberty with the expression, 'If you admit me into your family', because I wish if possible that he should invite us rather than that we should propose it. With the alterations I have made, I am of opinion your letter will be of service to prepare him for receiving you.

I do really believe that the reason of his asking you to come to him is to talk with you calmly, and judge how far it will be proper for him to have us to live in family with him...

I should not imagine he will ... be inquisitive as to when I made my proposals, and all the circumstances of our attachment. If it should so happen, you must tell him that in the very time of my schemes for heiresses, I used often to make strong professions of love to you, to tell you that I would marry you rather than any other woman, were it not that I was resolved to have £10,000 with a wife. That, at the same time, I bid you not mind me; and that accordingly you considered all I said to be words of course. That when you was at Auchinleck last spring, I paid you more than ordinary attention. That before you was aware, this made some impression on you. That you concealed your sentiments, as you knew I was upon another scheme, and besides imagined that he would not approve of a match for me by which I got neither money nor any new connections that could be of use to me. That you wished much to avoid going to Ireland, but that I insisted on it, and got your sister and the Captain to join their influence. That on the journey to Ireland I became unusually thoughtful and uneasy, told you that you was the woman on earth whom I really loved, that I had been in love with you in my earliest years and twenty times since, that you was my friend whom I valued, and that I was miserable to think that I was going to marry another, which was at the same time not honourable, considering my love for you. That you then began to think me serious, but still resolved to keep your mind to yourself, and, though you should be unhappy, let me do what was most for my interest. That at Donaghadee I put myself in such a passion with you at your declining to go to Dublin that you was so much affected as to let me know the impression I had made upon your mind, though you at the same time continued your resolution to keep both our secrets. That in Dublin I saw everything fair for me; but confessed to you that although I was distracted between gay views of fortune and real attachment, the latter would prevent me at that time from making any advances to the Heiress.

That my passion continued in the same way till we returned to Lainshaw. But you did not allow yourself to reckon on me as yours, though we corresponded very frequently this summer. That you received a letter from me, telling you that my father was going to marry again, which hurt me so much that I was to leave Scotland for ever, and that I then owned to you that I durst not see you, because I had been indulging hopes of getting his consent to marry you, and that to see you in view of parting for ever would almost turn me mad. That you was shocked with this letter, wrote to me in the most earnest terms and used every argument to reconcile me to my father's scheme; but in vain. That your affection for me was such that you wished to let me know that you would go with me. That while you was in that situation, you received a letter from me, telling you that if I were not conscious I would share a crown with you if I had it, I would not make the proposal I was going to make: which was that if you chose to join the interest of your £1,000 to my £100 a year, and would go with me to some agreeable retirement, I was ready to marry you directly. That you readily accepted my proposal, trusting to God's providence which extends over all the earth. That I was most grateful for this ... That this having accordingly taken place, and my father having kindly told me that he would give his consent to our marriage, I came to you at Lainshaw, and then we solemnly engaged ourselves *as we should answer to God.*

This, my dear Peggie, is, I think, a just and true abstract of our story. It does you great honour, and I appear a better man than people have imagined. Take courage, and tell this slowly to my father, and I am almost sure it will please him. Take care, at the same time, to let him know that as you have always been my confidante, and are therefore the best judge of me, you can assure him I never was before in the style in which you now know me to be. Do as I direct you, and there will be no room for dissimulation. Be rather silent and reserved, and let him take the lead. What a comfort would it be if you and I could make him happy, and prevent his doing a very improper thing which would lessen his character and estrange him from me...

I have now fixed Monday for setting out on my London journey.

[Boswell leaves for London on 28 August. His stated reason for going was to seek medical attention for his gonorrhoeal infection from a Dr Kennedy, renowned for his Lisbon Diet Drink, 'to purify my blood from every remain of vicious poison'. But it really was a last fling before his marriage. Margaret did not want him to go, but she gave in graciously. The main event on this visit was an excursion to Stratford-upon-Avon for David Garrick's bonanza, the Stratford Jubilee, celebrating Shakespeare. Boswell in exhibitionist fashion decided to attend in the costume of a Corsican chief, which he prepared before leaving London. The Jubilee turned into something of a nightmare for Garrick when torrential rains descended on the events. But Boswell was undeterred. Back in London, the highlight (apart from speaking to Johnson) was his reunion with Paoli, who after his defeat by the French had escaped from Corsica and taken up his exile in London.]

Boswell to Margaret Montgomerie, 5 September 1769 [Oxford]

I believe you and I differ as to shows and grand occasions. This Jubilee, which makes all my veins glow, will make little impression on you ... I assure you my Corsican dress will make a fine, striking appearance. My gun slung across my shoulder, my pistol at one side and stiletto at another, with my bonnet or kind of short grenadier cap, black, with *Viva la Libertà* (that is, 'Long live liberty', or as the English say, 'Liberty for ever') embroidered upon its front in letters of gold, will attract much noise. I have that kind of weakness that, when I looked at myself in the glass last night in my Corsican dress, I could not help thinking your opinion of yourself might be still more raised: 'She has secured the constant affection and admiration of so fine a fellow'.

Wednesday 6 September 1769 [Stratford]

... I went immediately to the great church[10]. It was surrounded by a crowd of people; and, as objects anyhow similar call up similar circumstances, I could not help thinking of the Monday's meeting after giving the sacrament in a country church in Scotland. I was exceedingly dirty; my hair hung wet about my ears; my black suit and the postilion's grey duffle above it, several inches too short every way, made a very strange appearance. I could observe people getting together and whispering about me, for the church was full of well-dressed people. At last Mr Garrick observed me. We first made an attitude to each other and then cordially shook hands. I gave him a line I had written to let him know I was incognito, as I wished to appear in the Corsican dress for the first time they should know me. Many of those who had stared, seeing that I was intimate with the steward of the Jubilee, came up to him and asked who I was. He answered, 'A clergyman in disguise.' To see a noble band of the first musicians from London with Dr Arne at their head, Mr Garrick, a number of nobility and gentry and of the learned and ingenious assembled to do honour and Shakespeare in his native place, gave me much satisfaction.

Thursday 7 September 1769 [Stratford]

... This was the night of the ball in mask, when I was to appear as a Corsican chief. I had begun some verses for the Jubilee in that character but could not finish them. I was quite impatient. I went home and forced myself to exertion, and at last finished what I intended. I then ran to Garrick, read them to him, and found him much pleased ... There was a fellow called Fulke Weale here, who advertised 'printing at an hour's notice', I suppose taking it for granted that Stratford would produce a general poetical inspiration which would exert itself every hour. To him I went. But Mr Angelo's fireworks turned his head, and made him idle. He preferred them to all poetical fire. I then went to the bookseller and printer of the place, Mr Keating. He had a lad from Baskerville's at Birmingham, of Scots extraction, his name Shank. I found him a clever, active fellow, and set him to work directly. He brought me a proof to the masquerade ball about two in the morning. But could not get my verses thrown off in time for me to give them about in my Corsican dress.

... My Corsican dress attracted everybody. I was as much a favourite as I could desire ... I pleased myself with a variety of ideas with regard to the Jubilee, peculiar to my own mind. I was like a Frenchman at an ordinary, who takes out of his pocket a box of pepper and other spices, and seasons a dish in his own way.

Friday 8 September 1769 [Stratford]

We did not get home, many of us, till past six in the morning. I got about three hours' sleep ... The true nature of human life began now to appear. After the joy of the Jubilee came the uneasy reflection that I was in a little village in wet weather and knew not how to get away, for all the post-chaises were bespoke, I don't know how many times over, by different companies. We were like a crowd in a theatre ...

I then took the parish clerk and went into the great church, and viewed calmly and solemnly the tomb of Shakespeare. His wife lies buried beside him. I observed with pleasure that she was seven years older than he, for it has been objected that my valuable spouse is a little older than I am.

Friday 22 September 1769 [London]

I then went to Old Bond Street and called on Paoli. A footman who opened the door said he was not well and could not see company, and made a great many difficulties. 'Stay,' said I. 'Get me a bit of paper and pen and ink, and I'll write a note to him.' His *valet de chambre* came down. Seeing something about him like what I had been used to see in Corsica, I asked him in Italian if he was a Corsican. He answered,

'Yes, Sir.' 'Oh, then,' said I, 'there is no occasion to write. My name is Boswell.' No sooner had I said this than Giuseppe (for that was his name) gave a jump, catched hold of my hand and kissed it, and clapped his hand several times upon my shoulders with such a natural joy and fondness as flattered me exceedingly. Then he ran upstairs before me like an Italian harlequin, being a very little fellow, and, opening the door of the General's bedchamber, called out, 'Mr Boswell'. I heard the General give a shout before I saw him. When I entered he was in his night-gown and nightcap. He ran to me, took me all in his arms, and held me there for some time. I cannot describe my feelings on meeting him again. We sat down, and instantly were just as when we parted. I found myself much rusted in my Italian ... He looked very well, having recruited wonderfully upon his journey. He told me he would have written to me, had he not expected to see me soon ... He insisted on my dining with him, ill dressed as I was...

   ...I felt myself just as when at Sollacarò. As I hardly hoped to meet Paoli in this world again, I had a curious imagination as if I had passed through death and was really in Elysium. This idea made me not afraid of actual death, of which I think so often, just as my grandfather Mr James Boswell did. I was filled with admiration whenever the General spoke. I said that after every sentence spoken by him I felt an inclination to sing Te Deum. Indeed, when he speaks it is a triumph to human nature and to my friendship...

   ...I then went to Dempster's, and finding no letter from my dearest Peggie, I was really uneasy. I sat down and wrote to her, which did me good. The General's arrival obliged me to alter my retired, frugal system. It was my duty to attend upon him, and be genteelly dressed accordingly. So I ordered a genteel, plain, slate-blue frock suit, and a full suit of a kind of purple cloth with rich gold buttons, and Mr Dilly supplied me with a silver-hilted sword. Paoli said he was sorry he had not room for me in the house with himself. I could have wished it. But I did my best, and immediately took very handsome lodgings within a few doors of his, at a M. Renaud's, an old Swiss, whose wife kept a milliner's shop. She was a well-behaved, obliging woman. The Bishop of Peterborough had been her lodger many years. Indeed the apartments were excellent. I had a large dining-room with three windows to Old Bond Street, a bedchamber, and a dressing-room, both looking into Burlington Gardens. So that I saw a pretty large extent of green ground and stately trees in the very centre of the court end of the town ... I paid for my apartments in Old Bond Street a guinea and a half a week, only the half of what they bring in winter.

MARRIAGE CONTRACT BETWEEN JAMES BOSWELL, ESQ. AND MISS PEGGIE MONTGOMERIE, 1769.

This is the marriage contract between James Boswell, Esquire, eldest son to the Right Honourable Alexander Boswell, Esquire, of Auchinleck, one of the Lords of Session and Justiciary in Scotland, and Miss Peggie Montgomerie, daughter to the late David Montgomerie of Lainshaw, Esquire.

The said parties do hereby agree that, in consideration of the sincerest mutual love and regard, they will, on or before the holy festival of Christmas next to come, be united to each other by marriage.

They solemnly engage to be faithful spouses, to bear with one another's faults, and to contribute as much as possible to each other's happiness in this world; hoping through the merits of their blessed Saviour, Jesus Christ, for eternal happiness in the world which is to come.

In faith of which, this paper, written by the said James Boswell, Esquire, is subscribed by him at London on the thirty-first day of October in the year of our Lord one thousand seven hundred and sixty-nine, before these witnesses: Pascal Paoli, General of the Corsicans, and Samuel Johnson, Doctor of Laws, and author of The Rambler and other works. JAMES BOSWELL

FOUR

Early Marriage Years

1770–1774

One of the unfortunate results of Boswell's marriage was that for two and a half years his happiness and new stability caused him to neglect his London friends, his writing interests (though he wrote a little for the London Chronicle and the London Magazine, and, above all, his journal. Married life and intense and successful work as an advocate simply put out of his mind that pre-marriage world of confusion and identity crisis. In the almost complete absence of a journal from his marriage until 1772, therefore, the chief sources regarding his state of mind during these years are his letters, mainly to Grange and Temple.

If this pattern had continued, it would have been sad indeed for British literature. But the real Boswell must inevitably re-emerge, and re-emerge he did in the spring of 1772 when he made his first trip to London and Johnson since just before his marriage. And with this visit his journal was re-ignited. He fully recorded these weeks in London, composing dialogue that achieves a new level of immediacy and power, though once he returned home in May he continued the journal fitfully. During that summer, autumn and winter in Edinburgh there were signs of boredom: too much drinking and gaming, and even one or two visits to a prostitute for the first time since his marriage. His legal practice, however, was highly successful.

In the spring of 1773, just a few day after the birth of his first daughter Veronica, he again headed south, released like a coiled spring from his confining Edinburgh box of legal duties and married life. Margaret allowed it but grumbled, and his father (who remarried on the very day of his son's wedding) saw it as confirmation that his son would never reform. But because of it, the journal again springs to life, a vivid account of his frenetic life and of the panorama of London seething with energy, great conversation, beauty and the incongruously unsavoury. Profoundly devoted to his wife, he nonetheless threw to the winds the last remnants of his resolution to be faithful to her. He no longer pretended to himself that he could abstain from sex with other women, mostly prostitutes. The journal may read like a disillusioning failure to live out the marriage contract he drew up for himself and Margaret, but the richness of these London journals, if they do not redeem this particular behaviour, remind us where his genius lay as a writer.

Back in Edinburgh, he again lost interest in the journal, a sad loss that is gloriously recovered when Johnson joins him in August 1773 for their historic tour of the Hebrides. His Hebridean journal is a triumph of journalising, which Johnson vigorously encouraged as they made their way through the Highlands. He published a revision of the journal in 1785, but as the manuscript version contains a richness of a personal nature that he excluded from the published version, I have decided to include selections from it here as part of the chronological progress of the larger journal instead of in a separate section. Also included here are several passages taken from his published account.

Boswell took with him from Edinburgh on his Hebridean journey two blank notebooks which he may have thought would see him through to the end. But although in the first days out of Edinburgh his notes were rough and abbreviated, he soon began to write full entries in complete sentences. In six weeks he had filled both notebooks and Johnson had to supply him with a third, smaller one in which, against his normal manner of writing in a large, sprawling hand, he had to write in a very small script. In a couple of weeks he had filled that notebook and was lucky on the isle of Coll to be able to buy loose paper at a lonely shop. He recorded the rest of the trip on these loose leaves – the last two weeks again only with notes. The irony is that none of these loose leaves appears to be missing, while seventy-four pages out of a total of 675 in the notebooks are. Unlike most of Boswell's other writings, the journals were exposed to damp – perhaps in the cardboard croquet box in which they were discovered at Malahide in 1930 – so that about one third of the leaves are damaged, with some small portions of the text. Boswell wrote continuous text, incidentally, without paragraphs, so the version below follows the journal's first editors who took their lead for paragraphing from the published Tour in 1785.

Few periods in Boswell's life were so troubled mentally, bleak with strident hypochondria, as the year in Edinburgh following the tour. There were periods when scarcely a day went by without his getting drunk, as he was swallowed up by Edinburgh society. It was his first significant attack of hypochondria since his marriage, severely aggravated by his decision not to visit London in the spring of 1774. His wife was pregnant again (his second daughter Euphemia was born in May) and he painfully concluded that he could not justify leaving her then. His journal begins in detail again in June; this period is the first in his native city which he recorded copiously. It is therefore a mine of information about his domestic, personal and professional life. He was heavily and successfully involved in the Court of Session, notably with criminal causes (that of the sheep-stealing John Reid was the most notorious), but on the whole this is not a period that makes for happy reading: the bright intervals are like rays shining through a thick cloud cover — few, short-lived, and not very bright.

1770

Boswell to William Temple, 6 October 1770 [Edinburgh]

... You cannot say too much to me of my wife ... I am fully sensible of my happiness in being married to so excellent a woman, so sensible a mistress of a family, so agreeable a companion, and above all so affectionate and peculiarly proper helpmate for me. I own I am not so much on my guard against fits of passion or gloom as I ought to be; but that is really owing to her great goodness. There is something childish in it I confess. I ought not to indulge such fits. It is like a child that lets itself fall purposely, to have the pleasure of being tenderly raised up again, by those who are fond of it. I shall endeavour to be better. Upon the whole, I do believe I make her very happy.

1771

Boswell to Grange, 20 October 1771 [Auchinleck]

Since we parted at the foot of the Bow, I believe I may say at the foot of the gallows[1], I have been as well as you could wish me. The complaint[2] which I had is quite removed by sober regular living, country air and exercise. I have been serving an apprenticeship with my father in the art of pruning, and I hope in time to be a skillful and diligent Guardian of the trees here. My father has been as good as his word, in giving me a college [tutorial] upon the Election-Law of Scotland, mixed with its antiquities, which illustrate it in an entertaining manner, and without which one cannot have a full and clear knowledge of it. My father just dictated to me a system, which I took down in writing, and which will be a valuable collection. I can say with truth that I have been employing my time to good purpose.

At the same time, I must tell you that I have suffered much more than any body would imagine, on account of so long a separation from my wife[3]. You know my worthy friend with what uncommon affection and true happiness she and I live together. To be deprived of that inestimable blessing for day after day and week after week (for so I have counted the time though it is not four weeks yet since I left her) has seriously distressed me. I have been seized with fits of impatience and my heart has fluttered like a bird confined in a cage, and I have had the most anxious apprehensions about her, while my strong imagination has in the silence and solitude of night presented to me such dreary thoughts as are the more afflicting that we can have no certainty but they may be realised. Thank God she is in much better health than when I left her; and although I find that she has been suffering in the same manner with myself, I please myself with the cheerful prospect that when we meet all our uneasiness will at once fly away and its remembrance only serve to increase our happiness. This, my good friend, is not a very polite letter, as it is all taken up in my writing about my wife; but I know how much you rejoice in my happiness.

1772

Saturday 14 March 1772 [Edinburgh]

I was in a flutter to a certain degree at the thoughts of setting out for London, for which I have always had an enthusiastic fondness. I was at the same time seriously concerned at parting with my wife. Everything depends upon our ideas; and I could with truth describe what passed in my mind this day in such a manner as to furnish out a narrative like that of the Londoner in the Idler who gives a dreadful detail of the disasters which befell him on a jaunt into the country, such as rain falling upon him from the heavens and many other circumstances[4]. My parting with my wife this day would make just such a figure should I describe it as I really felt it; for to part with a valuable friend and constant companion and go four hundred miles from her, though but for two months, is something considerable to a domestic man who has any turn to anxiety of mind.

Sunday 21 March 1772 [London]

I went to Johnson's Court, Fleet Street, and was happy enough to find Mr Johnson at home. Frank, his black, who had left him for some years, was returned to him, and showed me up to his study. Frank and I were pleased to renew our old acquaintance. I waited a little and then heard the great man coming upstairs. The sound of his feet upon the timber steps was weighty and well announced his approach. He had on an old purple cloth suit and a large whitish wig. He embraced me with a robust sincerity of friendship, saying, 'I am glad to see thee, I am glad to see thee. Come sit you down. You have not had my letter?' 'No, Sir.' (I shall give what passed, as much as I can, in the way of dialogue.) 'Well, I am glad you are come, and glad you are come upon such an errand' (meaning, to support the schoolmaster of Campbeltown in the House of Lords⁵). 'I hope, Sir, there will be no fear of him. It is a very delicate matter to interfere between a master and his scholars; nor do I see how you can fix the degree of severity that a master may use.'

JOHNSON. 'No, Sir. Till you fix the degree of negligence and obstinacy of the scholars, you cannot fix the degree of severity of the master. Severity must be continued until obstinacy be subdued and negligence cured.'

BOSWELL. 'To speak candidly, Sir, this man was rather too severe.'

JOHNSON. 'Has he broke any bones?'

BOSWELL. 'No.'

JOHNSON. 'Has he fractured any skulls?'

BOSWELL. 'No.'

JOHNSON. 'Then, Sir, he is safe enough. My master at Lichfield, Hunter, used to beat us unmercifully. He erred in not making a distinction between mistake and negligence; for he would beat a boy equally for not knowing a thing as for neglecting to know it. He would have asked a boy a question, and if he did not answer it, he beat him, without considering whether he had an opportunity of knowing how to answer it. Now, Sir, if a boy could answer every question, there would be no need of a master to teach him'. . .

I said, 'Hunter is a Scotch name. So this master who beat you so severely has been a Scotsman. I can now account for your prejudice against Scotsmen.'

JOHNSON. 'No, Sir, he was not Scotch; and, in abstracting from his brutality, he was a very good master'...

He then spoke of St Kilda [in the Hebrides]. I told him I thought of buying it. 'Pray do,' said he. 'We shall go and pass a winter amid the blasts there. We shall have fine fish, and we shall take some dried tongue with us and some books. We shall have a strong-built vessel and some Orkney men to navigate her. We must build a tolerable house. But we may carry with us a wooden house ready made and nothing to do but to put it up. I remember there was a gentleman going to North America who had a curiosity to see me, and I gave him that advice, as he was going to a country where they cut down wood only to get rid of it. Consider, Sir, by buying St Kilda you may keep the people from falling into worse hands. We must give them a clergyman, and he shall be one of Beattie's choosing. I'll be your Lord Chancellor or what you please.'

BOSWELL. 'Are you serious, Sir, in advising me to buy St Kilda's? For if you should advise me to go to Japan, I believe I should do it.'

JOHNSON. 'Why, yes, I am serious.'

BOSWELL. 'Why, then I'll try it'...

Thus have I collected this day's conversation ... He seemed happier to see me than ever. He said, 'I do love thee. I do love thee'; and when I left him he said, 'Good-night, dear Sir. I am glad to see you again, very glad to see you again.'

Thursday 26 March 1772

I must now remark that since I came last to London I have indulged myself with several interviews with women of the town, from a kind of inclination to entertain my curiosity, without deviating from my fidelity to my valuable spouse. This night completing a week in London, I solemnly resolved to indulge myself so no more; because I could learn nothing but what I had formerly heard over and over again, their stories being mostly the same; and because there was a degree of depravity in associating with them, and, as the idea of the distance between me and them now was lessened by my seeing them familiarly, I might fall into an infidelity which would make me very miserable. The heat of the theatre, eating and drinking a variety of things some of which had not suited my constitution, and the cold of the streets had made me ill, and when I got home I was very uneasy.

Tuesday 31 March 1772

I have a constant plan to write the life of Mr Johnson. I have not told him of it yet, nor do I know if I should tell him. I said that if it was not troublesome and presuming too much, I would beg of him to tell me all the little circumstances of his life, what schools he attended, when he came to Oxford, when he came to London, etc., etc. He did not disapprove of my curiosity as to these particulars, but said, 'They'll come out by degrees'...

Tuesday 7 April 1772

...In the evening I met at the Queen's Arms in St Paul's Churchyard with the rest of the partners of The London Magazine. It was truly satisfactory to me to find myself the only Scotsman among a company of English, and at the same time the distinction quite forgotten from our union of interest and from my perfect art of melting myself into the general mass. Most individuals when they find themselves with people of a different country cannot get free of their own particular national distinction. The individual, instead of being melted down, as I have remarked of myself, remains as hard as a piece of iron in a crucible filled with lead or silver. I should not wish to be melted so as not to be again separated from the mass. But when the heat is over, I gather myself up as firm as ever, with perhaps only a small plate or thin leaf of the other metal upon me sufficient to make me glitter, and even that I can rub off if I choose it. Our consultations this evening for the good of our magazine, with every monthly publication lying on the table before us, was quite in the style of London editors. I delighted in looking through our record, seeing the succession of proprietors and conductors, the rises and falls of our magazine in peace and in war, in short the whole circumstances of an undertaking which for so many years has entertained the public. I had more enjoyment in thinking of my share of the profits of this than if I had been to draw ten times the sum out of an estate. We had an admirable supper. Our first toast was 'The London Magazine' in a bumper, and every partner present had a crown given him for his attendance by our Treasurer and Secretary ... I was a man of considerable consequence. The place of our meeting, St Paul's Churchyard, the sound of St Paul's clock striking the hours, the busy and bustling countenances of the

partners around me, all contributed to give me a complete sensation
of the kind. I hugged myself in it. I thought how different this was
from the usual objects of a Scots laird. I had a joy in indulging my
own humour. I drank more than I had done since I had come last to
London, though not to excess. I was, however, heated a little; and
Tom Becket the bookseller would fain have had me along with him, I
suppose to stop by the way at another tavern, for Tom is too much
given to his cups. However, my good friend Mr Dilly insisted on my
going home with him, which I did.

Friday 10 April 1772

I dined at General Oglethorpe's[6], at his house in Lower Grosvenor
Street. His lady, whose fortune is his support while our court shamefully
neglects him, was a good civil old lady, with some affectation of wit,
with which, however, she troubled us but little. Mr Johnson and Dr
Goldsmith and nobody else were the company. I felt a completion of
happiness. I just sat and hugged myself in my own mind. Here I am
in London, at the house of General Oglethorpe, who introduced
himself to me just because I had distinguished myself; and here is Mr
Johnson, whose character is so vast; here is Dr Goldsmith, so distinguished in literature. Words cannot describe our feelings. The finer
parts are lost, as the down upon a plum; the radiance of light cannot
be painted . . .

I started the question if duelling was lawful. The brave old General
at once fired at this and said that undoubtedly a man had a right to
defend his honour. Goldsmith said, 'I ask you first, what you would
do if you was affronted?' I answered, 'No doubt I would fight.' 'Why,
then', said Goldsmith 'that solves the question'. 'Nay, Sir,' said Mr
Johnson, 'it does not follow that what a man would do is therefore
right.' I said I wanted to know if duelling was consistent with
Christianity. Mr Johnson took up the question and indeed treated it in
a masterly manner; and so far as I have been able to recollect[7], his
thoughts were these: 'Sir, as men become in a high degree refined,
various causes of offence arise which are considered to be of such
importance that life must be staked to atone for them, though in reality
they are not so. A body that has received a very fine polish may be
easily hurt. Before men arrive at this artificial refinement, if one tells
his neighbour he lies, his neighbour tells him he lies; if one gives his

neighbour a blow, his neighbour gives him a blow; but in a state of highly polished society, an affront is held to be a serious injury. It must, therefore, be resented, or rather a duel must be fought upon it; as men have agreed to banish from their society one who puts up with an affront without fighting a duel. Now, Sir, it is never unlawful to fight in self-defence. He, then, who fights a duel does not fight from passion against his antagonist but out of self-defence; to avert the stigma of the world and to prevent himself from being driven out of society. I could wish there was not that superfluity of refinement; but while such notions prevail, no doubt a man may lawfully fight a duel.'

Wednesday 15 April 1772

I breakfasted by appointment with Mr Garrick ... Mr Garrick complained of a passage in Mr Johnson's preface to his Shakespeare, in which he insinuates that Mr Garrick (for he chiefly has the old editions of Shakespeare) was not very ready to communicate them. 'Now,' said he, 'not only did his black get any old plays that he sent for, but the key of them was left with the maid, with orders to have a fire and every convenience for Mr Johnson.' I was sorry to find any coldness between Mr Johnson and Mr Garrick. They had misunderstood one another. Mr Garrick had imagined that showing his old plays was a favour. I have since learnt from Mr Johnson that his idea was that Garrick wanted to be courted for them, and that on the contrary he ought rather to have courted him and sent him the plays of his own accord. He denied that his black ever got any of them. Mr Johnson may perhaps be insensibly fretted a little that Davy Garrick, who was his pupil and who came up to London at the same time with him to try the chance of life, should be so very general a favourite and should have fourscore thousand pounds, an immense sum, when he has so little. He accordingly will allow no great merit in acting. Garrick cannot but be hurt at this, and so unhappily there is not the harmony that one would wish...

I pressed Mr Garrick to come to Scotland, and said we had a right to a visit from him; that he had favoured Ireland with his presence, and why not Scotland?' 'Sir,' said he, 'when I went to Ireland, I went to get money. It was harvest time then with me. But when the barn's full' (stretching himself in his chair) 'one grows lazy.' 'Well, Sir,' said

I, 'but you have not yet had the harvest of oats. you must come and get that.' ... Mr Garrick said I had done very well in the House of Lords, only might have been a little more animated. 'But', said he, 'you considered that they would be expecting to see the bold Boswell, and so you restrained yourself.' That was really the case.

Monday 20 April 1772

... my most attentive and indefatigable friend Mr Dilly had procured me a ticket to my Lord Mayor's dinner and ball at the Mansion House ... Before dinner, Mr Dilly and I went in to the Egyptian Hall and viewed the tables, which were indeed grand. We then waited at the door and saw dinner carried in. The review of dishes was prodigious. Everybody was kept out of the hall till dinner was set, the door being guarded by men with great staves, I suppose City officers. Then the Lord Mayor and Alderman and ladies and their attendants or partners went in, and then the door was left free. As there were a good many more tickets given out than there were places in the hall, there was a terrible struggle who should get in first among us who had to shift for ourselves. I was sadly squeezed and not a little concerned lest I should lose Dilly, he being a very little man. However he and I got in soon enough to get good places. It was truly a superb entertainment, and made the metropolis of Great Britain appear in a respectable light. There was a great number of foreigners of distinction there. We had everything in the way of meat and drink that could be found, fruits, confections, ices in perfection. Burgundy and champagne were called for as we pleased. I had before me a bottle of each. During our entertainment a band of music played, and from time to time the crier announced a toast. There were three tables with about a hundred people at each. The Lord Mayor sat at the table in the middle. The company retired just as they chose, without any order.

The Lord Mayor and Aldermen and a select party adjourned to another room, where were a couple of long tables, with a range of bottles. I had not met with John Wilkes[8] since I left him at Paris in spring 1766. I thought this a good opportunity to do it accidentally. So when Dilly and I came into this room, I said with an audible voice, 'This is excellent; this is like ourselves, quite Scotland.' Wilkes turned about, and seeing me, we instantly shook hands ... 'Well,' said Wilkes, 'Boswell, you was a pleasant fellow when I knew you. But now you're grown the gravest of grave mortals. You should have come and seen a friend in gaol.' Said I: 'I do assure you I am glad to meet with you, but I cannot come to see you. I am a Scotch laird and a Scotch lawyer and a Scotch married man. It would not be decent.' 'Do you remember,' said he, 'how melancholy you was at Paris, when the news came of the Old Pretender's death? I kept your secret.' 'Upon my word,' said I, 'you had a grand entertainment here today.' Said he, 'You did not see the sheep's-head. You did not see the haggis.'

1773

Boswell to Oliver Goldsmith, 29 March 1773 [Edinburgh]

Dear Sir, I sincerely wish you joy on the great success of your new comedy, She Stoops to Conquer or The Mistakes of A Night. The English nation was just falling into a lethargy. Their blood was thickened and their minds creamed and mantled like a standing pool; and no, the wonder – when their comedies which should enliven them, like sparkling champagne, were become mere syrup of poppies, gentle soporific draughts. Had there been no interruption to this, our audiences must have gone to the theatres with their nightcaps. In the opera houses abroad, the boxes are fitted up for tea-drinking. Those at Drury Lane and Covent Garden must have been furnished with settees and commodiously adjusted for repose. I am happy to hear that you have waked the spirit of mirth which has so long lain dormant, and revived natural humour and hearty laughter. It gives me pleasure that our friend Garrick has written the prologue for you. It is at least lending you a postilion, since you have not his coach; and I think it is a very good one, admirably adapted both to the subject and to the author of the comedy.

You must know my wife was safely delivered of a daughter the very evening that She Stoops to Conquer first appeared. I am fond of the coincidence. My little daughter is a fine, healthy, lively child and, I flatter myself, shall be blessed with the cheerfulness of your comic muse. She has nothing of that wretched whining and crying which we see children so often have; nothing of the comédie larmoyante. I hope she shall live to be an agreeable companion and to diffuse gaiety over the days of her father, which are sometimes a little cloudy.

I intend being in London this spring and promise myself great satisfaction in sharing your social hours. In the meantime, I beg the favour of hearing from you. I am sure you have not a warmer friend or steadier admirer. While you are in the full glow of theatrical splendour, while all the great and the gay in the British metropolis are literally hanging upon your smiles, let me see that you can stoop to write to me.

Tuesday 3 March 1773 [Boswell is about to leave for London.]

I had felt a kind of dreary reluctance the night before when I looked forward to the fatigues of my journey, especially the little sleep which one is allowed when travelling by the fly. But the agreeable prospect of being in London, which includes so many interesting and favourite objects, prevailed over the mists of apprehension; though I had still the awful thought that I might never return to Scotland and meet my dearest wife. Either of us might die during our separation. This thought, when it presses strongly upon the mind, is terrible. It is enough to make one never separate from a valuable spouse. Yet how weak would it be to be so influenced. I cannot explain how the mind takes different degrees of firmness and vigour at different times. I walked down the High Street of Edinburgh, which has a grand appearance in the silence and dusky light of three in the morning, and felt myself like an officer in a campaign. When the fly had rumbled me a mile or two, rational and manly sensations took the place of tender and timid feebleness. I considered that I had left my wife and little daughter well. That I was going to London, whither so many Members of Parliament, lawyers, merchants, and others go and return in safety to their families. I saw nothing dangerous, nothing melancholy. I had taken leave of my wife last night, which had affected my spirits a good deal. She is of an anxious temper at all times; but being not yet fully recovered from child-birth, she was more anxious than usual. Luckily she did not wake when I set out this morning, so that we had not a second farewell interview.

Thursday 1 April 1773

I travelled alone all this day, except for about half a stage when I had for my companion the chambermaid of the inn at Tuxford, who was returning home from a visit to her relations, and about the third of a stage when I had a good gentlewoman who was going to Newark. I remember the time when my mind was in such a state of fermentation that whenever the lid put upon it by the restraint of company was removed, it was like to boil over, or rather, to use a better metaphor, when not stirred by company but left to stagnate in solitude, it soon turned up the fret. But now it has wrought itself into such a sound state that it will keep for a long time. The satisfaction which I feel from the comparison of my present with my former self is immense; though I must own that during my fermentation there were grand ebullitions and bright sparkles which I can no longer perceive.

Monday 5 April 1773 [London]

I know not how it is, but I am less anxious in being absent from my valuable spouse this year than I was last. Perhaps her having a little daughter to amuse her makes the scene more lively to my imagination; but then ought I not to feel a double anxiety this year, when I am absent both from a wife and a child? In whatever way it is to be explained, I have mentioned the fact. Yet I am certain that I am as fond of my wife as I was last year; nor do I know that my mind is become more rational so as to throw off any vain fears that may arise, as sparks of water are thrown from a grindstone. I wish I may continue as I am while absent from my family...

[At the House of Commons] I was ... fortunate enough to hear Mr Edmund Burke speak twice. It was a great feast to me who had never heard him before. It was astonishing how all kinds of figures of speech crowded upon him. He was like a man in an orchard where boughs loaded with fruit hung around him, and he pulled apples as fast as he pleased and pelted the Ministry. It seemed to me, however, that his oratory rather tended to distinguish himself than to assist his cause. There was amusement instead of persuasion. It was like the exhibition of a favourite actor. But I would have been exceedingly happy to be him ... Speaking in Parliament appeared to me to be not very difficult. If a man knows pretty well the subject of debate and has good animal spirits, he may make a very good appearance.

Wednesday 7 April 1773

I had called on Dr Goldsmith at his chambers in Brick Court in the Temple as I passed along in the morning. He was not up, and I was shown into his dining-room and library. When he heard that it was I, he roared from his bed, 'Boswell'. I ran to him. We had a cordial embrace. I sat upon the side of his bed and we talked of the success of his new comedy, which he saw that I sincerely enjoyed, and of his beating Evans the publisher. He said there was no other method left; and he was determined to follow it. He showed me in some newspaper two paragraphs of scandal about Mr Johnson and Mrs Thrale[9]: how an eminent brewer was very jealous of a certain author in folio, and perceived a strong resemblance to him in his eldest son. 'Now,' said he, 'is not this horrid?' 'Why,' said I, 'no doubt though to us who know the characters it is the most ludicrous nonsense, yet it may gain credit with those who do not' ... He rose and came to breakfast, and I sat by him. He is the most generous-hearted man that exists; and now that he has had a large supply of gold by his comedy, all the needy draw upon him.

Friday 9 April 1773

To my astonishment Mr Johnson asked me to dine with him on Sunday. I never supposed he had a dinner at home. 'Sir', said he, 'I generally have a pie on Sunday.' I most readily accepted the invitation.

[Easter] Sunday 11 April 1773

When I came to Mr Johnson's, he was not yet come home. By and by he arrived. I had gratified my curiosity much in dining with Rousseau, and I thought it as curious to dine with Mr Johnson. I supposed we should hardly see knives and forks, and only have the pie which he mentioned. But to my surprise I found everything in very good order. He and I and Mrs Williams and a Miss — were the company. We had a very good soup, a boiled leg of lamb and spinach, a veal pie, an excellent rice pudding, pickled walnuts and onions, porter and port wine. I dined as well as ever I wished to do ...

He told me he had twelve of fourteen times attempted to keep a Journal, but never could persevere. 'The great thing', said he, 'is the state of your own mind; and you ought to write down everything that you can, for you cannot judge at first what is good or bad; and write immediately while the impression is fresh, for it will not be the same a week after.' I told him how uneasy I was at having lost eight hundred pages of my Journal, which were sent from Utrecht, where I had left them, and that I was chiefly uneasy for fear that somebody had them, as they really contained a full state of my mind when in a deep melancholy. He comforted me by saying that probably they had fallen into the hands of somebody who could not understand them, and would be destroyed as waste-paper. I am, however, much vexed at this loss, and at the apprehension that they may be lying concealed.

I asked him if he could tell when he was born, when he came to London and such things. Said he, 'You shall have them' (or 'I'll give you them') 'all for twopence. I hope you shall know a great deal more of me before you write my Life.' ... I talked of going to see the Reverend Mr Adams at Shrewsbury, who was Mr Johnson's tutor at Oxford. 'Sir', said he, ''tis not worth while. You know more of me than he does.'

[On Friday 23 April Goldsmith (at Johnson's request) nominated Boswell for membership of the exclusive Literary Club, founded by Johnson and Reynolds in 1763. The original members included Topham Beauclerk, Bennet Langton, Burke, Goldsmith, and Sir John Hawkins (eventual biographer of Johnson).]

Friday 30 April 1773 [from the Life of Johnson]

On Friday 30 April I dined with him [Johnson] at Mr Beauclerk's[10] ... As I was this evening to be balloted for as candidate for admission into that distinguished society. Johnson had done me the honour to propose me, and Beauclerk was very zealous for me ... The gentlemen went away to their club, and I was left at Beauclerk's till the fate of my election should be announced to me. I sat in a state of anxiety which even the charming conversation of Lady Di Beauclerk could not entirely dissipate. In a short time I received the agreeable intelligence that I was chosen. I hastened to the place of meeting [Turk's Head in Gerard Street, Soho], and was introduced to such a society as can seldom be found ... Upon my entrance, Johnson ... placed himself behind a chair, on which he leant as on a desk or pulpit, and with humorous formality gave me a *Charge*, pointing out the conduct expected from me as a good member of the Club.

[*In August Johnson travelled north to Edinburgh for the long-awaited tour of the Hebrides.*]

Boswell to Bennet Langton[11], 14 August 1773 [Edinburgh]

I am in very high spirits at present. Mr Johnson is actually come as far north as Newcastle; and I expect to have him under my roof this night. We shall set out on Wednesday next on our wild expedition to the highlands and some of the Hebrides. What an intellectual feast is before me! I shall never murmur though he should at times treat me with more roughness than ever. His roughness is an indication of the vigour of his genius. You know you and I differ a little upon this head. But I am keen for my own opinion. That however is too ample a subject for a letter. I must only say that I cannot help having a kind of joy in recollecting that you with all your timid caution got a drubbing at Dilly's. The truth is, it was observed when you was here that you assumed a kind of superiority over me, as if you was never touched by that awful rod, which has so often been applied to my back. It is natural then for me to feel some satisfaction in thinking that you had your share. I shall keep a full and exact Journal of this Johnsonian Tour, which will be very valuable.

[*The selections that follow are from either the manuscript journal that Boswell kept during the Hebridean journey, or from the published* Tour.]

Saturday 21 August 1773 [Included in the Tour]

We had tedious driving this afternoon, and were a good deal drowsy. Last night I was afraid Mr Johnson was beginning to faint in his resolution, for he said, 'If we must *ride* much, we shall not go; and there's an end on't.' Today when he talked of Skye with spirit, I said, 'Why, sir, you was beginning to despond yesterday. You're a delicate Londoner – you're a macaroni! You can't ride!' JOHNSON. 'Sir, I shall ride better than you. I was only afraid I should not find a horse able to carry me.' I hoped then there would be no fear of fulfilling our wild Tour.

We got to Aberdeen half an hour past 11. The New Inn, we were told, was full. This was comfortless. The waiter, however, asked if one of our names was Boswell, and brought me a letter left at the inn. It was from Mr Thrale, enclosing one to Mr Johnson. Finding who I was, we were told they would contrive to lodge us by putting us for a night into a room with two beds. The waiter said to me in strong Aberdeenshire, 'I thought I knew you, by your likeness to your Father.' My father puts up at the New Inn when on his circuit. We had a broiled chicken, some tarts, and crabs' claws. Little was said tonight. I was to sleep in a little box-bed in Mr Johnson's room. I had it wheeled out into the dining-room, and there I lay very well.

Thursday 26 August 1773

We got to Forres[12] at night. Found an admirable house kept by Lawson, wine-cooper from London. By the road I had, from that strange curiosity which I always have about anything dismal, stepped out of the chaise and run up close to the gallows where Kenneth Leal hangs in chains for robbing the mail. As he had not hung but about two months, the body was quite entire. It was still a man hanging. The sight impressed me with a degree of gloom. Mr Johnson did not know of this, or, he told me afterwards, he would not have talked as he did, for he diverted himself with trying to frighten me, as if the witches would come and dance at the foot of my bed. I said he would be the most frightened of the two. But that I would rather see three witches than one of anything else. I was really a little uneasy. However, the door of my room opened into his. This gave me a security, and I soon fell asleep.

Sunday 29 August 1773 [Inverness]

Mr Johnson told me that all the aid he had in compiling the Dictionary was having about twenty etymologies sent him by an unknown hand at the time, which he afterwards learned was Dr Pearce, Bishop of Rochester. Some of them he adopted. He never lived a great deal with Lord Chesterfield[13], nor was there any particular incident that produced a quarrel between them, as has been erroneously propagated. My lord had made him great professions. Yet for years, while Mr Johnson was engaged in his immense undertaking, the

Dictionary, my lord never took the least notice of him. When the work came out, my lord fell a-scribbling in the *World* about it. Mr Johnson, with a just indignation and contempt, wrote to him a letter which was civil but showed him that he did not mind what he said or wrote, and that he had done with him. Mr Johnson kept no copy of the letter. He could repeat it, and was once persuaded to write it down from memory, but he believes he has lost the copy. I have heard Langton repeat some of it; in particular a sentence to this purpose: that Lord Chesterfield, after leaving him to struggle with the waves unassisted, stretched out his hand to welcome him on shore.

Tuesday 31 August 1773 [Glenmoriston] [Included in the Tour]

We had tea in the afternoon, and our landlord's daughter, a modest civil girl very neatly dressed, made it to us. She told us she had been a year at Inverness and learnt reading and writing, sewing, knotting, working lace, and pastry. Mr Johnson made her a present of a book of arithmetic which he had bought at Inverness.

The room had some deals laid as a kind of ceiling. There were two beds in the room. A woman's gown was hung on a rope to make a curtain of separation between them. Joseph[14] had the sheets which we brought with us laid on them. We had much hesitation whether to undress or lie down with our clothes on. I said at last, 'I'll plunge in! I shall have less room for vermin to settle about me when I strip!' Mr Johnson said he was like one hesitating whether to go into the cold bath. At last he resolved too. I observed he might serve a campaign. Said he, 'I could do all that can be done by patience. Whether I should have strength enough, I know not.' He was in excellent humour. To see the Rambler as I saw him tonight was really a curiosity. I yesterday told him I was thinking to write an Epistle to him on his return from Scotland, in the style of Mrs Gulliver to Captain Lemuel Gulliver—

Sullen you turn from both and call for oats. He laughed and asked in whose name I'd write it. I said Mrs Thrale's. He was angry and said, 'Sir, if you have any sense of decency or delicacy, you won't do that.' 'Then,' said I, 'let it be Cole, the landlord of the Mitre Tavern.' 'Ay, that may do,' said he.

Tonight each offered up his private devotions. After we had chatted a little from our beds, Mr Johnson said, 'GOD bless us both for Jesus Christ's sake. Good night.' I pronounced 'Amen'. Mr Johnson fell asleep immediately. I could not have that good fortune for a long time. I fancied myself bit by innumerable vermin under the clothes, and that a spider was travelling from the *wainscot* towards my mouth. At last I fell into insensibility.

Wednesday 1 September 1773 [Rattachan and Glenelg] [Included in the Tour]

...We rode on well till we came to the high mountain called the Rattachan, by which time both Mr Johnson and the horses were a good deal fatigued. It is a terrible steep to climb, not withstanding the road is made slanting along. However, we made it out. On the top of it we met Captain MacLeod of Balmeanach (a Dutch officer come from Skye) riding with his sword slung about him. He asked, 'Is this Mr Boswell?' which was a proof that we were expected[15]. Going down the hill on the other side was no easy task. As Mr Johnson was a great weight, the two guides agreed that he should ride the horses alternately. Hay's were the two best, and Mr Johnson would not ride but upon one or other of them, a black or a brown. But as Hay complained much after ascending the Rattachan, Mr Johnson was prevailed with to mount one of Vass's greys. As he rode upon it downhill, it did not go well, and he grumbled. I walked on a little before, but was excessively entertained with the method taken to keep him in good humour. Hay led the horse's head, talking to Mr Johnson as much as he could; and just when Mr Johnson was uttering his displeasure, the fellow says, 'See such pretty goats.' Then *whu!* he whistled, and made them jump. Little did he conceive what Mr Johnson was. Here was now a common ignorant horse-hirer imagining that he could divert, as one does a child, Mr *Samuel Johnson!* The ludicrousness, absurdity, and extraordinary contrast between what the fellow fancied and the reality, was as highly comic as anything that I ever witnessed. I laughed immoderately, and must laugh as often as I recollect it.

It grew dusky; and we had a very tedious ride for what was called five miles, but I am sure would measure ten. We spoke none. I was riding forward to the inn at Glenelg, that I might make some kind of preparation, or take some proper measures, before Mr Johnson got up, who was now advancing in silence, with Hay leading his horse. Mr Johnson called me back with a tremendous shout, and was really in a passion with me for leaving him. I told him my intentions. But he was not satisfied, and said, 'Do you know, I should as soon have thought of picking a pocket as doing so.' 'I'm diverted with you,' said I. Said he, 'I could never be diverted with incivility.' He said doing such a thing made one lose confidence in him who did it, as one could not tell what he would do next. I justified myself but lamely to him. But my intentions were not improper. I wished to be forward to see if Sir A. Macdonald had sent his boat; and if not, how we were to sail, and how we were to lodge, all which I thought I could best settle myself, without his having any trouble. To apply his great mind to minute particulars is wrong. It is like taking an immense balance, such as you see on a quay for weighing cargoes of ships, to weigh a guinea. I knew I had neat little scales which would do better. That his attention to everything in his way, and his uncommon desire to be always in the right, would make him weigh if he knew of the particulars; and therefore it was right for me to weigh them and let him have them only in effect. I kept by him, since he thought I should.

As we passed the barracks at Bernera, I would fain have put up there; at least I looked at them wishfully, as soldiers have always everything in the best order. But there was only a sergeant and a few men there. We came on to the inn at Glenelg. There was nothing to give the horses, so they were sent to grass with a man to watch them. We found that Sir Alexander had sent his boat to a point which we had passed, at Kintail, or more properly at the King's house – that it had waited several days till their provisions run short, and had returned only this day. So we had nothing to say against that Knight. A lass showed us upstairs into a room raw and dirty; bare walls, a variety of bad smells, a coarse black fir greasy table, forms of the same kind, and from a wretched bed started a fellow from his sleep like Edgar in *King Lear*: 'Poor Tom's a-cold.' The landlord was one Munro from Fort Augustus. He pays £8 to MacLeod for the shell of the house, and has not a bit of land in lease. They had no bread, no eggs, no wine, no spirits but whisky, no sugar but brown grown black. They prepared some mutton-chops, but we would not have them. They killed two hens. I made Joseph broil me a bit of one till it was black, and I tasted it. Mr Johnson would take nothing but a bit of bread, which we had luckily remaining, and some lemonade which he made with a lemon which Joseph had for him, and he got some good sugar; for Mr Murchison, factor to MacLeod in Glenelg, sent us some, with a bottle of excellent rum, letting us know he was very sorry that his servant had not come and informed him before we passed his house; that we might have been there all night, and that if he were not obliged to set out early next day for Inverness, he would come down and wait upon us. I took some rum and water and sugar, and grew better; for after my last bad night I hoped much to be well this, and being disappointed, I was uneasy and almost fretful. Mr Johnson was calm. I said he was so from vanity. 'No,' said he, ''tis from philosophy.' It was a considerable satisfaction to me to see that the Rambler could practise what he nobly teaches.

I resumed [talking of] my riding forward, and wanted to defend it. Mr Johnson was still violent upon that subject, and said, 'Sir, had you gone on, I was thinking that I should have returned with you to Edinburgh and then parted, and never spoke to you more.'

I sent for fresh hay, with which we made beds to ourselves, each in a room equally miserable ... Mr Johnson made things better by comparison. At Macqueen's last night he observed that few were so well lodged in a ship. Tonight he said we were better than if we had been upon the hill. He lay down buttoned up in his greatcoat. I had my sheets spread on the hay, and having stripped, I had my clothes and greatcoat and Joseph's greatcoat laid upon me, by way of blankets. Joseph lay in the room by me, upon a bed laid on the floor.

Thursday 2 September 1773 [Armadale] [Included in the Tour with omissions]

I had slept ill. Mr Johnson's anger had affected me much. I considered that, without any bad intention, I might suddenly forfeit his friendship. I was impatient to see him this morning. I told him how uneasy he had made me by what he had said. He owned it was said in passion; that he would not have done it; that if he had done it, he would have been ten times worse than me. That it would indeed, as I said, be 'limning in water', should such sudden breaks happen (or something to that effect); and said he, 'Let's think no more on't.'

BOSWELL. 'Well then, sir, I shall be easy. Remember, I am to have fair warning in case of any quarrel. You are never to spring a mine upon me. It was absurd in me to believe you.'

JOHNSON. 'You deserved about as much as to believe it from night to morning.' Mr MacLeod of Drynoch, to whom we had a letter from Kenneth Macaulay, breakfasted with us.

A quarter before nine we got into a boat for Skye. It rained much when we set off, but cleared up as we advanced. One of the boatmen who spoke English said that a mile at land was two miles at sea. I then said to him that from Glenelg to Armadale in Skye, which was our sail this morning and is called twelve, was only six miles. But this he could not understand. 'Well,' said Mr Johnson, 'never talk to me of the native good sense of the Highlanders. Here is a fellow who calls one mile two, and yet cannot comprehend that twelve such miles make but six.' It was curious to think that now at last Mr Johnson and I had left the mainland of Scotland and were sailing to the Hebrides, one of which was close in our view; and I had besides a number of youthful ideas, that is to say, ideas which I have had from my youth about the Isle of Skye. We were shown the land of Moidart where Prince Charles first landed. That stirred my mind.

We reached the shore of Armadale before one. Sir Alexander came down and received us. He was in tartan clothes. My lady stood at the top of the bank and made a kind of jumping for joy. They were then in a house built by a tenant at this place, which is in the district of Sleat. There was a house here for the family, which was burnt in Sir Donald's time. But there is really a good garden and a number of trees of age and size, mostly ash, and that too of a particular kind, the wood of which is very compact. There is a kind of recess here of land, as well as a kind of bay of the sea, more indeed the former. It is a pretty warm exposure. There is a little brook runs down from the hill through a tolerable bank of wood. I am a very imperfect topographer. The house is a very good tenant's house, having two storeys and garrets, but seemed very poor for a chief. Mr Johnson and I were to have had but one room. But I made the plan be altered; so one of the beds was taken out of his room and put into the next, in which I and the overseer of the farm were to lie; but happily Joseph was put in the overseer's place...

We had an ill-dressed dinner, Sir Alexander not having a cook of any kind from Edinburgh[16]. I alone drank port wine. No claret appeared. We had indeed mountain and Frontignac and Scotch porter. But except what I did myself, there was no hospitable convivial intercourse, no ringing of glasses. Nay, I observed that when Captain Macdonald and Mr Macqueen came in after we were sat down to dinner, Sir Alexander let them stand round the room and stuck his fork into a liver pudding, instead of getting room made for them. I took care to act as he ought to have done. There was no wheat-loaf, but only a kind of bannock or cake, raw in the heart, as it was so thick. Sir Alexander himself drank punch without souring and with little spirits in it, which he distributed to those men who were accustomed even in their own houses to much better. He gave it with a pewter dividing-spoon which had served the broth. At tea there were few cups and no tea-tongs nor a supernumerary tea-spoon, so we used our fingers.

I was quite hurt with the meanness and unsuitable appearance of everything. I meditated setting out the very next day ... When Mr Johnson and I retired for rest, he said it grieved him to see the chief of a great clan in such a state; that he was just as one in a lodging-house in London. However, he resolved that we should weather it out till Monday.

Friday 3 September 1773

After dinner the Knight and I met in Mr Johnson's room, where I was looking for pen and ink. I fell upon him with perhaps too great violence upon his behaviour to his people; on the meanness of his appearance here; upon my lady's neither having a maid, nor being dressed better than one. In short, I gave him a volley. He was thrown into a violent passion; said he could not bear it; called in my lady and complained to her, at the same time defending himself with considerable plausibility. Had he been a man of more mind, he and I must have had a quarrel for life. But I knew he would soon come to himself. We had moor-fowl for supper tonight, which comforted me.

Tuesday 7 September 1773 [Coirechatachan]

It was a very wet, stormy day. So we were obliged to remain here, as it was impossible to cross the sea to Raasay. Mr Johnson called me to his bed-side this morning, and to my astonishment he took off Lady Macdonald leaning forward with a hand on each cheek and her mouth open – quite insipidity on a monument grinning at sense and spirit. To see a beauty represented by Mr Johnson was excessively high. I told him it was a masterpiece and that he must have studied it much. 'Ay,' said he.

Thursday 16 September 1773 [Dunvegan, Isle of Skye]

...Mr Johnson said he would go to Sweden with me. I said we should like to be with the King. Said Mr Johnson, 'I doubt if he would speak to us'. Said the Colonel, 'I'm sure Mr Boswell would speak to him.' This was a good remark as to my forwardness. He added with a genteel civility, 'and with great propriety.' Let me value my forwardness. It has procured me much happiness. I do not think it is impudence. It is an eagerness to share the best society, and a diligence to attain what I desire. If a man is praised for seeking knowledge though mountains and seas are in his way, is it not laudable in me to seek it at the risk of mortification from repulses? I have never yet exerted ambition in rising in the state. But sure I am, no man has made his way better to the best of company. Were my places to be ranged after my name, as 'Member of the Club at the Turk's Head', etc., I should make as great a figure as most peers. There is a meaning in this if it were well expressed.

After the ladies were gone, we talked of the Highlanders' not having sheets; and so on we went to the advantage of wearing linen ... then he came out with this saying: 'I have often thought that if I kept a seraglio, the ladies should all wear linen gowns, or cotton; I mean stuffs made of vegetable substances. I would have no silk; you cannot tell when it is clean. It will be very nasty before it is perceived to be so. Linen detects its own dirtiness.'

To hear Mr Johnson, while sitting solemn in arm-chair, talk of his keeping a seraglio and saying too, 'I have often thought,' was truly curious[17]. Mr Macqueen asked him if he would admit me. 'Yes,' said he, 'if he were properly prepared; and he'd make a very good eunuch. He'd be a fine gay animal. He'd do his part well.' 'I take it,' said I, 'better than you would do your part.' Though he treats his friends with uncommon freedom, he does not like a return. He seemed to me to be a little angry. He got off from my joke by saying, 'I have not told you what was to be my part' – and then at once he returned to my office as eunuch and expatiated upon it with such fluency that it really hurt me. He made me quite contemptible for the moment. Luckily the company did not take it so clearly as I did. Perhaps, too, I imagined him to be more serious in this extraordinary raillery than he really was. But I am of a firmer metal than Langton and can stand a rub better.

Sunday 19 September 1773 [Dunvegan]

...He came to my room this morning before breakfast to read my Journal, which he has done all along. He often before said, 'I take great delight in reading it.' Today he said, 'You improve. It grows better and better.' I said there was a danger of my getting a habit of writing in a slovenly manner. 'Sir,' said he, 'it is not written in a slovenly manner. It might be printed, were the subject fit for printing.' ... He asked me today how we were so little together. I told him my Journal took up so much time. But at the same time, it is curious that although I will run from one end of London to another to have an hour with him, I should omit to seize any spare time to be in his company when I am in the house with him. But my Journal is really a task of much time and labour, and Mr Johnson forbids me to contract it...

I was under the greatest apprehensions for fear of the itch, which is really very common in these parts (especially among the young people), and very little minded. I this day perceived several pimples or rather blisters on the palm of my right hand, which were hot, painful, and itchy; but I was assured it never began so. I was, however, uneasy. The horror of having so vile a distemper and carrying it home made me shudder. I may appear to talk in too strong terms of a minor disease. But I feel what I write. As yet in the Highlands I was only bit with fleas at Anoch and Glenelg, and when changing my shirt at Armadale I found what I thought a bug sticking fast on my left arm. Perhaps it was some other sucking animal.

Monday 27 September 1773 [Coirechatachan] [Included in the Tour]

He read tonight, as he sat in the company, a great deal of this volume of my Journal, and said to me, 'The more I read of this, I think the more highly of you.' 'Are you in earnest?' said I. Said he, 'It is true, whether I am in earnest or no.' I went to bed at two in the morning, but the rest of the company sat still. They drank on and sung Erse songs till near five. I lay in great uneasiness. I was quite sombre in the dark, and could get no rest. I tried to think how long I had been free [from hypochondria] now, but all the gloomy chances that imagination can figure disturbed me. I had the utmost impatience to get home. I was tormented for some time, till at last those who lay in the same room with me came up. Unluckily Coll[18] found a bottle of punch standing; upon which in tumbled all the company, and they drank it, and another which Coirechatachan brought. They made many apologies for disturbing me. I said I once thought of rising and going down to them. Honest Corry said that to have had me do that, he would have given a cow. I thought I suffered so much tonight that the scene would make a figure in my Journal, but it makes but a wretched one.

Tuesday 28 September 1773 [Coirechatachan]

...As we were going, the Scottish phrase of 'honest man', which signifies kindness and regard, was often and often repeated by many of Mr Johnson. I myself was shown as much kindness and regard as I could desire; and I must take some merit from my assiduous attention to him, and the happy art which I have of contriving that he shall be easy wherever he goes, that he shall not be asked twice to eat or drink anything (which always disgusts him), that he shall be provided with water at his meals, and many such little things, which, if not attended to, would fret him. I have also an admirable talent of leading the conversation; I do not mean leading as in an orchestra, by playing the first fiddle, but leading as one does in examining a witness: starting topics, and making the company pursue them. Mr Johnson appeared to me like a great mill, into which a subject is thrown to be ground. That is the test of a subject. But indeed it requires fertile minds to furnish materials for this mill. It vexes me when I see it unemployed, but sometimes I feel myself quite barren, and have nothing to throw in. I know not if this mill be a good figure; Pope makes his mind a mill for turning verses. It is fine to see how the nonsense is thrown off from Mr Johnson's mill, or specious error crushed.

Monday 4 October 1773 [Coll]

...At night I was a little disconcerted. There were but three rooms or divisions in the house. The Captain and Mrs Maclean had one. Mr Johnson had another, with Joseph on a straw-bed beside him. And in the room where we sat all day were two beds. Simson and Macdonald had the one. The other was for young Coll and me. I have a mortal aversion at sleeping in the same bed with a man; and a young

Highlander was always somewhat suspicious as to scorbutic symptoms. I once thought of sleeping on chairs; but this would have been uncivil and disobliging to a young gentleman who was very civil and obliging to us. Upon inspection, as much as could be without his observing it, he seemed to be quite clean, and the bed was very broad. So I lay down peaceably, kept myself separated from him, and reposed tolerably.

Monday 11 October 1773 [Coll]

The morning was fine and the wind fair and moderate. My mind was sound as ever, and the enamel of philosophy entire. It had not been broke, I take it, for it is not easily repaired. Coll was in a hurry to get us down to the harbour where the ship lay. But he was too late of beginning. We did not get away till about eleven . . . to the harbour; but before we reached it, so violent a storm came on that we were obliged again to take shelter in the house of Captain Maclean, where we dined and passed the night.

Friday 15 October 1773 [Erray]

After I had tossed long in weariness, Joseph came and called me and let in light. I would have risen, but was afraid to put my hand anywhere in the dark, for fear of spiders, or some uncleanly circumstance of sloth. I was not well at all, but I got up, sat down to my Journal, and soon was better. Another damp to my gay prospect of advancing with celerity occurred. There was a violent storm of wind and rain. We should have been wet to the skin immediately had we set out; but it was absolutely impossible for us to get forward, because the rivers were swelled. There was no help for it. We were doomed to stay here all this day. I could hardly keep from repining indecently. Mr Johnson said, 'Now that I have had an opportunity to write to the mainland, I'm in no such haste.' I wrote to my dear wife. It was a relief to me to think that she would hear of me, though I could not hear of her till I got to Inverary. I also wrote to my father. I told him that, having been now for some time in countries where great attention is paid to dreams, I had been gloomy from having dreamt that I had lost him. I hoped in GOD he was well, and longed much to see him. It gives me pain to consider that there is much doubt if he has now that warm affection for me which he once had, and which I really have for him. I have now made up to him for all the uneasiness which my follies gave him. The satisfaction which I feel on his living till that was the case, is very great. I shall do my part now as well as I can; and shall never check my sincere affection for him (an affection which has much of the tenderness of a child) though he should appear cold.

Monday 18 October 1773 [Inchkenneth]

We had agreed to pass this day with Sir Allan[19]; and he engaged to have everything in order for our journey tomorrow [to Icolmkill or Iona[20]]. Before breakfast, I repaired to the chapel, knelt at the ruined altar, and prayed in a pleasing holy frame, 'with a sense of gratitude and joy,' as Parnell[21] says. I thought I had so steady, so certain a prospect of celestial felicity that I should never again be vicious and could die with perfect peace. LORD, grant that when the period of my dissolution arrives, I may be in the same state! 'Thou wilt keep him in perfect peace, whose mind is stayed on thee,' etc...

I this morning got a spade and dug a little grave in the floor of the chapel, in which I carefully buried what loose bones were there. I said, 'Rest in peace, so far as I can contribute to it.' I said I hoped somebody would do as much for me. JOHNSON. 'Well said.' He praised me for what I had done, though he said he would not do it. He showed, in the chapel at Raasay, his horror at dead men's bones...

I was very much taken with Inchkenneth. I said I was resolved to have it for an elegant retreat for our family during a month or two in summer. Sir Allan said, if he recovered it from the Duke of Argyll, I should have it on my own terms. I really indulged serious thoughts of buying it. My brother David always talked of purchasing an island. 'Sir,' said Mr Johnson, 'so does almost every man, till he knows what it is.' Sir Allan and he and I walked awhile on the shore under the houses. We looked at a cave or cleft or recess of a rock, in which Sir Allan keeps his peats dry. We looked at a bed of oysters, which I had never seen anywhere before. I took up one, broke it between two stones, and eat it, by way of having a proof how I could live if I were thrown upon a coast where I could get only raw shell-fish; and I thought I could do. Mr Johnson and I were also occupied in gathering little yellow shells like a more elegant species of whelks. Mr Johnson gathered for little Miss Thrale, I for my father...

Mr Johnson takes a kind of pleasure in laughing at his friends in trifles. There was a mere black barren rock in our view today as we sailed. He called to me, 'This shall be your island, and it shall be called Inch Boswell'; and then he laughed, with a strange appearance of triumph.

Tuesday 19 October 1773 [At sea, from Mull to Iona]

Mr Johnson said, as we were going up the narrow sound between Mull and Nun's Island, with solemn-like rocks on each side of us, and the waves rising and falling, and our boat proceeding with a dancing motion, 'This is roving among the Hebrides, or nothing is.' A man has a pleasure in applying things to words, and comparing the reality with the picture of fancy. We had long talked of 'roving among the Hebrides'. It was curious to repeat the words previously used, and which had impressed our imaginations by frequent use; and then to feel how the immediate impression from actually roving differed from the one in fancy, or agreed with it. It will be curious too, to perceive how the impression made by reading this my Journal some years after our roving will affect the mind, when compared with the recollection of what was felt at the time. Mr Johnson said I should read my Journal about every three years. Joseph made a very good observation. 'Your journey,' said he, 'will always be more agreeable to you.' ...

[On Iona] ... The seeing of Mr Samuel Johnson at Icolmkill was what I had often imaged as a very venerable scene. A landscape or view of any kind is defective, in my opinion, without some human figures to give it animation. What an addition was it to Icolmkill to have the Rambler upon the spot! After we landed, I shook hands with him cordially.

Wednesday 20 October 1773 [Iona]

We walked down again to our barn, where breakfast was prepared – milk, cheese, eggs, bread and butter. I slipped away and returned to the cathedral and its environs to perform some pleasing serious exercises of piety. I knelt before St Martin's Cross and said a short prayer. I went to the black stone on which the islanders of old used to swear. I had been shown a greyish piece of freestone, which they said was it; and I adopted their inaccurate information. I put my knees to this greyish freestone and said, 'I here swear with all the solemnity that any honest, honourable, and brave man ever swore upon this stone, that I will stand by Sir Allan Maclean and his family.' I had told Sir Allan that I would swear a covenant with him upon the black stone. I could not easily get him with me privately; so I went alone, and told him what I had done, which pleased him mightily; and I hope I shall have it in my power to convince him of my sincerity and steadiness...

I then went into the cathedral, which is really grand enough when one thinks of its antiquity and of the remoteness of the place; and at the end, I offered up my adorations to GOD. I again addressed a few words to Saint Columbus; and I warmed my soul with religious resolutions. I felt a kind of exultation in thinking that the solemn scenes of piety ever remain the same, though the cares and follies of life may prevent us from visiting them, or may even make us fancy that their effects were only 'as yesterday when it is past', and never again to be perceived. I hoped that ever after having been in this holy place, I should maintain an exemplary conduct. One has a strange propensity to fix upon some point from whence a better course of life may be said to begin. I read with an audible voice the fifth chapter of St James, and Dr Ogden's[22] tenth sermon. I suppose there has not been a sermon preached in this church since the Reformation. I had a serious joy in hearing my voice, while it was filled with Ogden's admirable eloquence, resounding in the ancient cathedral of Icolmkill...

[Two days after this last entry Boswell's manuscript Hebridean journal on the journey ends; he did not resume it from his notes until 1779 and later. What follows is taken from the Tour.]

Tuesday 2 November 1773 [Auchinleck]

We were now in a country not only 'of saddles and bridles,' but of post-chaises; and having ordered one from Kilmarnock, we got to Auchinleck before dinner.

My father was not quite a year and a half older than Dr Johnson ... His age, his office, and his character had long given him an acknowledged claim to great attention, in whatever company he was; and he could ill brook any diminution of it. He was as sanguine a Whig and Presbyterian as Dr Johnson was a Tory and Church of England man; and as he had not much leisure to be informed of Dr Johnson's great merits by reading his works, he had a partial and unfavourable notion of him, founded on his supposed political tenets, which were so discordant to his own that, instead of speaking of him with that respect to which he was entitled, he used to call him 'a Jacobite fellow'. Knowing all this, I should not have ventured to bring them together, had not my father, out of kindness to me, desired me to invite Dr Johnson to his house.

I was very anxious that all should be well; and begged of my friend to avoid three topics, as to which they differed very widely: Whiggism, Presbyterianism, and Sir John Pringle[23]. He said courteously, 'I shall certainly not talk on subjects which I am told are disagreeable to a gentleman under whose roof I am; especially, I shall not do so to your father.'

Our first day went off very smoothly. It rained, and we could not get out; but my father showed Dr Johnson his library, which, in curious editions of the Greek and Roman classics, is, I suppose, not excelled by any private collection in Great Britain. My father ... was a sound scholar, and, in particular, had collated manuscripts and different editions of Anacreon, and others of the Greek lyric poets, with great care; so that my friend and he had much matter for conversation, without touching on the fatal topics of difference...

Thursday 4 November 1773

Dr Johnson was pleased when I showed him some venerable old trees under the shade of which my ancestors had walked. He exhorted me to plant assiduously, as my father had done to a great extent.

As I wandered with my revered friend in the groves of Auchinleck, I told him that if I survived him, it was my intention to erect a monument to him here, among scenes which, in my mind, were all classical; for in my youth I had appropriated to them many of the descriptions of the Roman poets. He could not bear to have death presented to him in any shape, for his constitutional melancholy made the king of terrors more frightful. He turned off the subject, saying, 'Sir, I hope to see your grandchildren!'

Saturday 6 November 1773

I cannot be certain whether it was on this day or a former that Dr Johnson and my father came in collision. If I recollect right, the contest began while my father was showing him his collection of medals; and Oliver Cromwell's coin unfortunately introduced Charles the First, and Toryism. They became exceedingly warm and violent, and I was very much distressed by being present at such an altercation between two men, both of whom I reverenced; yet I durst not interfere. It would certainly be very unbecoming in me to exhibit my honoured father and my respected friend as intellectual gladiators, for the entertainment of the public; and therefore I suppress what would, I dare say, make an interesting scene in this dramatic sketch – this account of the transit of Johnson over the Caledonian Hemisphere...

In the course of their altercation, Whiggism and Presbyterianism, Toryism and Episcopacy, were terribly buffeted. My worthy hereditary friend, Sir John Pringle, never having been mentioned, happily escaped without a bruise.

My father's opinion of Dr Johnson may be conjectured from the name he afterwards gave him, which was 'Ursa Major.' But it is not true, as has been reported, that it was in consequence of my saying that he was a constellation of genius and literature. It was a sly abrupt expression to one of his brethren on the bench of the Court of Session, in which Dr Johnson was then standing, but it was not said in his hearing.

Monday 22 November 1773

I have now completed my account of our tour to the Hebrides. I have brought Dr Johnson down to Scotland, and seen him into the coach which in a few hours carried him back into England. He said to me often that the time he spent in this tour was the pleasantest part of his life, and asked me if I would lose the recollection of it for five hundred pounds. I answered I would not; and he applauded my setting such a value on an accession of new images in my mind.

Had it not been for me, I am persuaded Dr Johnson never would have undertaken such a journey; and I must be allowed to assume some merit from having been the cause that our language has been enriched with such a book as that which he published on his return[24]; a book which I never read but with the utmost admiration, as I had such opportunities of knowing from what very meagre materials it was composed.

1774

Saturday 25 June 1774 [Edinburgh]

I found a letter from Mr Samuel Johnson, informing me that the first sheets of his *Journey to the Hebrides* were sent to the press. This gave me a lively joy; and I was much elated by his writing, 'I have endeavoured to do you some justice in the first paragraph.'[25] One must pause and think, to have a full feeling of the value of any praise from Mr Johnson. His works and his majesty of mind must be kept in view. I had the same sensation tonight as on hearing from General Oglethorpe: that it was hard that I should not be in London. It is true Hume, Robertson, and other greater geniuses than I am prefer Scotland. But they have neither that peculiar and permanent love of London and all its circumstances which I have; nor are they so much in unison with the English as I am, which I have clearly perceived, and of which Mr Johnson has assured me.

Saturday 30 July 1774

John Reid's trial was to come on next Monday[26]. Michael Nasmith, who at my desire was agent for him, seemed anxious. I promised to him what I had resolved in my own mind: that I should taste no wine till the trial was over. In the afternoon I went with my wife and Veronica to Heriot's Gardens, which soothed and refreshed me. Veronica walked briskly, with a little help, pulled flowers, and I held her up till she pulled a cherry for the first time. I played a party at bowls with Adam Bell and so many more, drank tea at home calmly, as I had dined, and made up for yesterday's excess. In the evening when it was dusky I visited John Reid. I felt a sort of dreary tremor as he and I walked together in the dark in the iron room. He would own nothing to me ... I sent for a pot of lenitive electuary at night, that I might open and cool my body, and took a part of it. I had not taken physic before for two years...

Monday 1 August 1774

Michael Nasmith came home with me between five and six, when we dined, drank some porter and port and a bottle of claret. I was in a kind of agitation, which is not without something agreeable, in an odd way of feeling. Having heard that a verdict was found against John Reid, I went at eight to Walker's Tavern, where the jury were met (I having first visited my client and intimated his fate to him), and being elated with the admirable appearance which I had made in the court, I was in such a frame as to think myself an Edmund Burke – and a man who united pleasantry in conversation with abilities in business and powers as an orator. I enjoyed the applause which several individuals of the jury now gave me and the general attention with which I was treated. The Crown entertains the jury on an occasion of this kind, and the bill is authenticated by the initials of the chancellor. We drank a great deal, and by imposing a fine of a pint of claret on any man who mentioned the trial, bets, etc., we had six pints of claret secured for a future meeting ... I was much in liquor, and strolled in the streets a good while – a very bad habit which I have when intoxicated. I got home before one. My dear wife had been very anxious.

Wednesday 10 August 1774

In the forenoon I had visited John Reid, whom I found very composed. He persisted in averring that he got the sheep from Gardner. I really believed him after I had adjured him, as he should answer to GOD, to tell me the truth. I told him that I was of opinion that a petition to the King [to save Reid from the death penalty] would have no effect, but that his wife had applied to me, and I should draw one which he should sign; but that he must not expect anything but death. He very calmly assured me he would expect nothing else. I wondered at my own firmness of mind while I talked with a man under sentence of death, without much emotion, but with solemnity and humanity. I desired John to write his life very fully, which he promised to do ... It will be a curious thing if he gives a narrative of his life.

Saturday 20 August 1774

This morning I drew a petition to His Majesty for John Reid. I could think of nothing else; so Mr Charles Hay and I read no law, but went with it to Michael Nasmith's, who was very much pleased with it, and undertook to have two fair copies on large paper ready to go by the post at night. Charles went with me to see John. His wife was with him. I adjured him not to say that he was innocent of the theft found proved against him if he was not so; that I had put into the petition what he says, but he would have as good, if not a better, chance by fairly confessing to His Majesty. Charles very properly said to him, 'Take care and do not fill up the measure of your iniquity by telling a lie to your Sovereign.' I in the strongest manner assured him that I thought the petition would have no effect – that I wrote it only because I had promised to do it; but that I really thought it would be better not to send it, as it might make him entertain vain hopes and prevent him from thinking seriously of death. John professed his conviction that the chance was hardly anything, but was for using the means. I could not therefore refuse him. Charles again addressed him as to his telling a lie, and said, 'I may say, you are putting your salvation against one to ten thousand; nay, against nothing.' John expressed his willingness to submit to what was *foreordained* for him. 'John,' said I, 'this would not have been *foreordained* for you if you had not stolen sheep, and that was not *foreordained*. GOD does not foreordain wickedness. Your Bible tells you that.' I then took it up and read from the Epistle of James, Chap. I, v. 13 and 14: 'Let no man say when he is tempted, I am tempted of GOD; for GOD cannot be tempted with evil, neither tempteth he any man. But every man is tempted, when he is drawn away of his own lust, and enticed.' This seemed to satisfy him. But people in his situation are very apt to become predestinarians...

Thursday 25 August 1774

I communicated to Crosbie a scheme which I had of making an experiment on John Reid, in case he was hanged, to try to recover him. I had mentioned it in secrecy to Charles Hay and Mr Wood the surgeon, who promised me assistance. Crosbie told me that he had lately had a long conversation on the subject with Dr Cullen, who thought it practicable. It was lucky that I spoke of it to Crosbie, for he was clear for trying it, and threw out many good hints as to what should be done. I resolved to wait on Dr Cullen and get his instructions. I was this forenoon at the burial of a daughter of the late Mr Sands, bookseller here. There is something usefully solemn in such a scene, and I make it a rule to attend every burial to which I am invited unless I have a sufficient excuse; as I expect that those who are invited to mine will pay their piece of decent attention.

Monday 29 August 1774

A very curious whim had come into my head: that I would have a portrait of John Reid as my first client in criminal business and as a very remarkable person in the annals of the Court of Justiciary. Keith Ralph, a young painter ... had drawn Mr Lawrie's picture very like. I had him with me this forenoon, and he agreed to paint John. He desired to see him today, to have an idea of his face, to see what kind of light was in the room where he lay, and to judge what should be the size of the picture. Accordingly I went with him. I had before this given a hint of my design to Richard Lock, the inner turnkey, a very sensible, good kind of man; and he had no objection. Accordingly we went up. Mr Ritchie, a kind of lay teacher who humanely attends all the people under sentence of death, was with John. I was acquainted with Mr Ritchie, as he had called on me about my client Agnes Adam. After standing a little and speaking a few words in a serious train, I addressed myself to Ritchie in a kind of soft voice and mentioned my desire to have a remembrance of John Reid, by having a picture of him; that Mr Ritchie and I could sit by and talk to him, and that I imagined John would have no objection, as it would not disturb him. Ritchie said he supposed John would have none; that he was so much obliged to me, he would do much more at my request; and he would come and be present. Next morning between nine and ten was fixed.

Tuesday 30 August 1774

At ten o'clock I was with John Reid. Before I got there, Ralph was begun with his chalk and honest Ritchie was exhorting him quietly. I was happy to see that this whim of mine gave no trouble to John. One of his legs was fixed to a large iron goad, but he could rise very easily; and he at any rate used to sit upon a form, so that he just kept his ordinary posture, and Ritchie and I conversed with him. He seemed to be quite composed, and said he had no hopes of life on account of the dreams which he had. That he dreamt he was riding on one white horse and leading another. 'That,' said he, 'was too good a dream, and dreams are contrary.' He said he also dreamt a great deal of being on the seashore and of passing deep waters. 'However,' said he, 'I allwaye (always) get through them.' 'Well,' said I, 'John, I hope that shall not be contrary; but that you shall get through the great deep of death.' I called for a dram of whisky. I had not thought how I should drink to John till I had the glass in my hand, and I felt some embarrassment. I could not say, 'Your good health'; and 'Here's to you' was too much in the style of hearty fellowship. I said, 'John, I wish you well,' or words pretty much the same, as 'Wishing you well' – or some such phrase. The painter and Mr Ritchie tasted the spirits. Richard the gaoler makes it a rule never to taste them within the walls of the prison...

Ritchie and I sat awhile with him after the painter was gone, the first sitting being over. John said, 'Death is no terror to me at present. I know not what it may be.' Said Ritchie, 'You must either be infatuated, or you have, by grace, a reliance on the merits of Jesus Christ.' John said he trusted to the mercy of GOD in Christ; that he had been an unfortunate man, and insinuated that his fate was foreordained. Ritchie quoted the passage in James which I had quoted; but he seemed to be much hampered with Calvinistical notions about decrees, while he struggled to controvert John's wickedness being foreordained. Indeed the system of predestination includes all actions, bad as well as good. Ritchie pressed John much to make an authentic last speech. I told him that if he was guilty of the crime for which he was condemned, it was his duty to his country and the only reparation he could make, to acknowledge it, that his example might have a proper effect. He persisted in his denial, and did not seem willing to have any speech published...

It was a very wet day. I grew dreary and wanted either Charles Hay or Grange to dine with me, but neither of them could come. I took a little bowl of warm punch by myself, except a glass which Veronica drank. Her sweet little society was a gentle relief, but I was too dismal to enjoy it much ... I had by sympathy sucked the dismal ideas of John Reid's situation, and as spirits or strong substance of any kind, when transferred to another body of a more delicate nature, will have much more influence than on the body from which it is transferred, so I suffered much more than John did.

Wednesday 31 August 1774

I spoke to him [Reid] of his execution, thinking it humane to familiarise his mind to it. I asked him if he was here when Murdison died[27]. He said no, and on my saying, 'So you did not see him die,' told me that he had never seen an execution. 'No?' said I. 'I wonder you never had the curiosity.' He said he never had. That once, as he and some other drivers of cattle were coming from Yorkshire, they stopped at Penrith in Cumberland, where there was a man to be executed for murder next day; that some of his companions stayed to see it, but he and the rest did not. I then spoke of the way in England of having a cart and ours of having a ladder, and that it was said ours was the easiest way. 'I take it, John,' said I, 'I shall die a severer death than you.' 'I dinna (do not) think,' said he, 'they can feel much; or that it can last ony (any) time; but there's nane (none) of them to tell how it is.' ...

... I was desirous to have his picture done while under sentence of death and was therefore rather desirous that, in case a respite was to come, it should not arrive till he had sat his full time. It was finished today and was a striking likeness, a gloomy head. He asked if it would not be better to have had on his bonnet, and said he should have had on a better waistcoat. He asked too if his name would be upon it. I said it would be on the back of it. Said he: 'I thought it would have been on the fore (front) side of it.' There was vanity again. As the painter advanced in doing it, I felt as if he had been raising a spectre. It was a strange thought. Here is a man sitting for his picture who is to be hanged this day eight days. John himself seemed to wonder somewhat at the operation, and said, 'I'm sure you maun hae an unco (must have a strange) concern about this,' or words to that purpose. When it was finished and hung upon a nail to dry, it swung, which looked ominous, and made an impression on my fancy. I gave John a dram of whisky today again. When I got home I found several vermin upon me which I had attracted while in the gaol. It was shocking. I changed all my clothes.

Thursday 1 September 1774

...After taking a tolerable dose of law, Mr Hay and I went for a walk to Heriot's Garden, and then I dined with him. He had Dr Monro and several more company with him, and it was concerted that we should get information from the Anatomical Professor as to recovering a hanged person, which would be useful to Reid ... He said in his opinion a man who is hanged suffers a great deal; that he is not at once stupefied by the shock, suffocation being a thing which must be gradual and cannot be forced on instantaneously; so that a man is suffocated by hanging in a rope just as by having his respiration stopped by having a pillow pressed on the face, in Othello's way, or by stopping the mouth and nostrils, which one may try; and he said that for some time after a man is thrown over he is sensible and is conscious that he is hanging; but that in three minutes or so he is stupefied. He said that it was more difficult to recover a hanged person than a drowned, because hanging forces the blood up to the brain with more violence, there being a local compression at the neck; but that he thought the thing might be done by heat and rubbing to put the blood in motion, and by blowing air into the lungs. And he said the best way was to cut a hole in the throat, in the trachea, and introduce a pipe. I laid up all this for service in case it should be necessary...

Friday 2 September 1774

...John Reid had got a respite for fourteen days ... I was put into great agitation. All my nerves started. I instantly dressed ... We went up to John, whom we found in a dreadful state. He was quite unhinged. His knees knocked against each other, he trembled so; and he cried bitterly. I spoke to him in most earnest manner and told him, since the respite was only for fourteen days, the judges would be consulted and they would report against him. He must therefore consider that he had just fourteen days more allowed him to prepare for his awful change. He moaned and spoke of his being 'cut off after all, with a hale (whole) heart'. I said he must compose himself. He said he hoped he should, if it pleased GOD to continue him in his senses, as he had hitherto done. I said, 'You would make this application, though I told you I thought it would have no effect. If you suffer from it, it is owing to yourself.' It was striking to see a man who had been quite composed when he thought his execution certain become so weak and so much agitated by a respite. My wife put a construction on his conduct which seemed probable. She said it was plain he had all along been expecting a pardon and therefore was composed, but that now when he found that only a respite for fourteen days had come and that inquiry was to be made at the judges, he for the first time had the view of death. But if I can judge of human nature by close observation, I think he was before this time reconciled to his fate, and that the respite affected him by throwing him into a wretched state of uncertainty. I gave him a shilling to get some spirits as a cordial.

    ... my wife, who never favoured John Reid and who was sorry to see me so much interested about him, told me that she had heard some decent-looking men talking tonight on the street against him. One of them said, 'I think no laws will get leave to stand now. I wish the law of Moses may get leave to stand.'

Wednesday 7 September 1774 [Boswell had just come by some information strongly suggesting Reid's guilt.]

I went up to John a little before two, with the messenger's letter in my hand. Seeing me have a paper, he gave an earnest look, I suppose in expectation that it was his pardon. But I at once accosted him as a dying man, upbraided him with having imposed on me, and said to him what I and Mr Nasmith had concluded from perusal of the letter. He calmly explained his conduct. 'Sir,' said he, 'Gardner had before this time come to my house and owned to me that he had stolen the sheep, and promised me great rewards if I would not discover him. Therefore, when I was taken up, I would not speak out against him, but wanted him to be apprehended, that he and I might concert what was to be done to keep ourselves safe. But he was but a very little time with me, and then was carried to Stirling.' I was not much convinced by this account of the matter. I had wrought myself into a passion against John for deceiving me, and spoke violently to him, not feeling for him at the time. I had chosen my time so as to be with him when two o'clock struck. 'John,' said I, 'you hear that clock strike. You hear that bell. If this does not move you, nothing will. That you are to consider as your last bell. You remember your sentence. On Wednesday the 7 of September. This is the day. Between the hours of two and four in the afternoon; this is that very time. After this day you are to look upon yourself as a dead man; as a man in a middle state between the two worlds. You are not in eternity, because you are still in the body; but you are not properly alive, because this is the day appointed for your death. You are to look on this fortnight as so much time allowed to you to repent of all your wickedness, and particularly of your lying to me in such a way as you have done. Think that this day fortnight by four o'clock you will be rendering an account to your Maker. I am afraid that you are encouraged by your wife to persist in obstinacy, not to disgrace her and your children. But that is a small consideration to a man going into eternity. I think it your duty to own your being guilty on this occasion if you be really so, which I cannot but think is the case. By doing so you will make all the atonement in your power to society. But at any rate I beseech you not to deny your guilt contrary to the truth.' This was as vehement and solemn a harangue as could be made upon any occasion. The circumstance of the clock striking and the two o'clock bell ringing were finely adapted to touch the imagination. But John seemed to be very unfeeling today. He persisted in his tale. There was something approaching to the ludicrous when, in the middle of my speech to him about his not being properly alive, he said very gravely, 'Ay; I'm dead in law.' I was too violent with him. I said, 'With what face can you go into the other world?' And: 'If your ghost should come and tell me this, I would not believe it.' This last sentence made me frightened, as I have faith in apparitions, and had a kind of idea that perhaps his ghost might come to me and tell me that I had been unjust to him. I concluded with saying, 'You have paper, pen, and ink there. Let me have a real account of everything.' He said he would . . .

Mr Nasmith met me when I came out of prison and was very impatient to hear about John . . . after drinking a bottle of port between us, a curious thought struck me that I would write the case of John Reid as if dictated by himself on this the day fixed for his execution. I accordingly did it, and hit off very well the thoughts and style of what such a case would have been.

Sunday 18 September 1774

It gave me much concern to be informed by my dear wife that I had been quite outrageous in my drunkenness the night before; that I had cursed her in a shocking manner and even thrown a candlestick with a lighted candle at her. It made me shudder to hear such an account of my behaviour to one whom I have so much reason to love and regard; and I considered that, since drinking has so violent an effect on me, there is no knowing what dreadful crime I may commit. I therefore most firmly resolved to be sober. I was very ill today...

Tuesday 20 September 1774

Before breakfast I received a very good letter from Mr Nasmith dissuading me from the scheme of recovering John Reid [after his execution], but he did not persuade me. Mr Hay came and he and I called on Mr Nasmith and took him with us to look for a place where the corpse might be deposited. We walked about the Grassmarket and Portsburgh, and saw some small houses to let. Mr Nasmith proposed that we might take one till Martinmas; but then it occurred that the landlord would make a noise if a hanged man was put into it. In short, we were in a dilemma. I thought of the Canongate Kilwinning Lodge, of which I was Master and could excuse myself to the brethren for taking liberty with it; but it was too far off. I did not think it right to trust a caddie, or any low man, with the secret. I asked John Robertson the chairman if he could find a house that would take in the corpse till the mob dispersed. He thought none would do it. Mr Nasmith went out of town. Mr Hay, after a short party at bowls, went with me and called for Mr Innes, Dr Monro's dissector. Mr Wood had not yet spoken to him; but he very readily agreed to give his help. He however could not help us to get a house. I called on Wood. Neither could he help us as to that article; and he began to doubt of the propriety of the scheme. I however remained firm to it, and Mr Hay stood by me. Mr Innes suggested one George Macfarlane, a stabler, where a puppet-show had been kept. Mr Hay and I went to the Grassmarket, where he lived. But first it occurred to me that there was one Andrew Bennet, a stabler, whom I had lately got out of prison. We went to him. He had no family but his wife, and they were both fools. They were prodigiously grateful to me, called me his Grace, Andrew having reproved his wife for calling me only his Honour. I told them that the friends of the poor man who was to be executed next day were anxious to lodge his body in some place till the mob should disperse, and, as he was a client of mine, I was desirous to assist them; so I hoped Andrew would let them have his stable for that purpose. He agreed to it, though his wife made some objection, and though he said he would rather let his *craig* (throat) be cut than allow it, unless to oblige me. I sounded them as to letting the body into their house; but Mrs Bennet screamed, and Andrew said very justly that nobody would come to it any more if that was done. It is amazing what difficulty I found in such a place as Edinburgh to get a place for my purpose. The stable here entered by a close next entry to the door of the house, and had no communication with the house; so that the operators must be obliged to take their stations in the stable some time before the execution was over. It was a small stable, and there was a smith's shop just at the door of it; so that we could not be private enough. However, I was glad to have secured any place...

When I came to the prison I found that John Reid's wife and children were with him. The door of the iron room was now left open and they were allowed to go and come as they pleased. He was very composed. His daughter Janet was a girl about fifteen, his eldest son Benjamin about ten, his youngest son Daniel between two and three. It was a striking scene to see John on the last night of his life surrounded by his family. His wife and two eldest children behaved very quietly. It was really curious to see the young child Daniel, who knew nothing of the melancholy situation of his father, jumping upon him with great fondness, laughing and calling to him with vivacity. The contrast was remarkable between the father in chains and in gloom and the child quite free and frolicsome. John took him on his knee with affection. He said to me that his daughter Jenny was the only one of his children whom he had named after any relation; and he went over all the names of the rest. They had almost all Old Testament names. They were seven in all. I again exhorted him to truth...

Mr Hay went with me again to Mr Innes, who was satisfied with Bennet's stable and desired that there should be a blanket and a good quantity of warm salt prepared. We went again to Bennet's, and took a dram of whisky of his own distilling; and he and his wife promised to have the blanket and the salt in readiness, I having said that some surgeon had advised his friends to rub the body with warm salt to preserve it, as it was to be carried to the country. Bennet, though a fool, had smoked what was intended; for he said, 'Could they not cut him down living?' I said that would be wrong. I should have observed, when I was with John this evening, it gave me some uneasiness to think that he was solemnly preparing for an awful eternity while at the same time I was to try to keep him back. He spoke himself very calmly of the corpse, by which he meant his own dead body; for I spoke to his wife before him about it: that I had secured a place for it, but I wished she could get a better place for it to be laid in till the mob dispersed. She said she would try Mrs Walker at the sign of the Bishop in the Grassmarket, who was very friendly to her. It was comfort to me that neither John nor his wife had the least idea of any attempt to recover him.

Mr Hay and I met my worthy friend Grange in the Grassmarket tonight. He was much against the attempt. After supper Mr Wood called and told me that he had the proper apparatus ready; that he had also engaged Mr Aitkin, another surgeon, to attend, and that, if I insisted on it, he was willing to make the experiment, but that as a friend he could not but advise me against it; that it would be impossible to conceal it; the mob would press upon us, and continue looking in at the door. A great clamour would be made against me as defying the laws and as doing a ridiculous thing, and that a man in business must pay attention in prudence to the voice of mankind; that the chance of success was hardly anything, and this was to be put in the scale against a certainty of so many disagreeable consequences. But he suggested another thought which had great weight with me. 'This man,' said he, 'has got over the bitterness of death; he is resigned to his fate. He will have got over the pain of death. He may curse you for bringing him back. He may tell you that you kept him from heaven.' I determined to give up the scheme...

Wednesday 21 September 1774

...I was not much affected when I saw him [Reid] this morning in his usual dress. But now he was all in white, with a high nightcap on, and he appeared much taller, and upon the whole struck me with a kind of tremor. He was praying; but stopped when we came in...

I once more conjured him to tell the truth ... I thus pressed him; and while he stood in his dead clothes, on the very brink of the grave, with his knees knocking together, partly from the cold occasioned by his linen clothes, partly from an awful apprehension of death, he most solemnly averred that what he had told concerning the present alleged crime was the truth...

Two o'clock struck. I said, with a solemn tone, 'There's two o'clock.' In a little Richard came up. The sound of his feet on the stair struck me. He said calmly, 'Will you come awa now?' This was a striking period. John said yes, and readily prepared to go down. Mr Nasmith and I went down a little before him. A pretty, well-dressed young woman and her maid were in a small closet off the hall; and a number of prisoners formed a kind of audience, being placed as spectators in a sort of loft looking down to the hall. There was a dead silence, all waiting to see the dying man appear. The sound of his steps coming down the stair affected me like what one fancies to be the impression of a supernatural grave noise before any solemn event. When he stepped into the hall, it was quite the appearance of a ghost. The hangman, who was in a small room off the hall, then came forth. He took off his hat and made a low bow to the prisoner. John bowed his head towards him. They stood looking at each other with an awkward uneasy attention. I interfered, and said, 'John, you are to have no resentment against this poor man. He only does his duty.' 'I only do my duty,' repeated the hangman. 'I have no resentment against him,' said John. 'I desire to forgive all mankind.' 'Well, John,' said I, 'you are leaving the world with a very proper disposition: forgiving as you hope to be forgiven.' ... The hangman advanced and pinioned him, as the phrase is; that is, tied his arms with a small cord. John stood quiet and undisturbed. I said, 'Richard, give him another glass of wine.' Captain Fraser, the gaoler, had sent him the night before a bottle of claret, part of which Richard had given him, warmed with sugar, early in the morning, two glasses of it in the forenoon, and now he gave him another. John drank to us. He then paused a little, then kissed his wife with a sad adieu, then Mr Ritchie kissed him ...

The mob were gone from the prison door in a moment. Mr Nasmith and I walked through the Parliament Close, down the Back Stairs and up the Cowgate, both of us satisfied of John Reid's innocence, and Mr Nasmith observing the littleness of human justice, that could not reach a man for the crimes which he committed but punished him for what he did not commit.

We got to the place of execution about the time that the procession did. We would not go upon the scaffold nor be seen by John, lest it should be thought that we prevented him from confessing. It was a fine day. The sun shone bright. We stood close to the scaffold on the south side between two of the Town Guard. There were fewer people present than upon any such occasion that I ever saw. He behaved with great calmness and piety. Just as he was going to mount the ladder, he desired to see his wife and children; but was told they were taken care of. There was his sister and his daughter near to the gibbet, but they were removed. Dr Dick asked him if what he had said was the truth. He said it was. Just as he was going off, he made an attempt to speak. Somebody on the scaffold called, 'Pull up his cap.' The executioner did so. He then said, 'Take warning. Mine is an unjust sentence.' Then his cap was pulled down and he went off. He catched the ladder; but soon quitted his hold. To me it sounded as if he said, 'just sentence'; and the people were divided, some crying, 'He says his sentence is just.' Some: 'No. He says unjust.' Mr Laing, clerk to Mr Tait, one of the town clerks, put me out of doubt, by telling me he had asked the executioner, who said it was unjust. I was not at all shocked with this execution at the time. John died seemingly without much pain. He was effectually hanged, the rope having fixed upon his neck very firmly, and he was allowed to hang near three quarters of an hour; so that any attempt to recover him would have been in vain. I comforted myself in thinking that by giving up the scheme I had avoided much anxiety and uneasiness...

It was now about eight in the evening, and gloom came upon me. I went home and found my wife no comforter, as she thought I had carried my zeal for John too far, might hurt my own character and interest by it, and as she thought him guilty. I was so affrighted that I started every now and then and durst hardly rise from my chair at the fireside.

FIVE

Boswellian Extremes
1775–1778

The two to three years following the Hebridean journey proved to be more unhappy and emotionally violent than any Boswell had ever known. Missing London in 1774 was deeply depressing for him. His legal work (in spite of the Reid cause) became even more like drudgery, his relationship with Margaret was often argumentative and sometimes almost violent – though he kept reminding himself how much he loved and depended on her – and he fell into a pattern of gaming that with his drinking loomed as a great trial for his marriage and an ominous threat to his fortunes. The deterioration of his relationship with his father kept pace with the decline in his father's health. He managed London in the spring of 1775 and 1776, but he felt increasingly cut off from Dr Johnson and London. And even London seemed more commonplace to him, more like a place to live than where, as in the past, to travel deliriously in the realms of cosmopolitan literary gold. Still, London was his salvation and his journal during his visits sparkles with lively conversation on an extraordinary diversity of subjects. The two highlights of his 1776 visit were his excursion to Lichfield and Ashbourne with Johnson and his interview with the notorious Mrs Rudd that is reminiscent of his courtship of the actress 'Louisa' in 1762.

In the thick of severe depression and unhappiness in Edinburgh, he keeps at his journal heroically, often falling behind by days and weeks but nonetheless vividly chronicling his 'angst'. With a growing family on her hands, Margaret seems helpless to do anything about his condition. At times she explodes angrily, at times he retaliates with his own outbursts. But she continues to encourage, console, and care for him. She emerges from his journal as a stable, wise, forgiving, yet enigmatic, figure.

The behaviour that his journal for the rest of the 1770s records may be characterised as morbid insipidity, a type of wasting debility or weakness of will, that gradually begins to wear him down. He is not able to sustain his many happy and exuberant moments and periods, especially in London and on excursions with Johnson; they vie unsuccessfully with the more dominant pattern of despondency, listlessness and dissipation. The oscillations are sudden and dramatic. When an entry begins you can never be sure what his state of mind will be at the end of it. Because these unexpected twists of temper and conduct fascinated him, the journal is thrilling, like an existential novel with little preparation of character to explain action. We see and feel the destructiveness of it all, intrigued by the process, as was he. Nonetheless, much in his happier stretches, like the hectic 1778 London visit, is exhilarating. And it was all written furiously fast, as if he were travelling wildly on a post-chaise out of control.

Paradoxically, the furious pace of Boswell's life during these years, leading up to his father's death in 1782, proceeds as he struggles (for the most part successfully) against the rage for alcohol and sex. The struggle against addiction heightens his nervous energy, raises his social temperature, so that his behaviour is often absurd and amusingly extreme. His sobriety, dating back to promises to Temple and Paoli, is also a major factor in his writing memorable prose, abundantly detailed and marvellously thorough in his rendering of conversations. A classic example is his interview of the dying David Hume, which shows his melancholic fascination with death and his profound need to be assured of immortality. Hume's persistent scepticism plunged him into a dreadful period of gloom lasting several months. Another significant theme in his journal and letters is his strong pro-Americanism. So although Boswell's friends said from time to time that his writing would suffer if he abstained entirely from wine, it is nonetheless true that a degree of sobriety during these years accounts for much of his control over his prose: his steady and patient hand in recalling scene, imagery, incident and dialogue.

1775

Tuesday 10 January 1775 [Edinburgh]

Not having slept quite well, I got up somewhat gloomy. Knowing that I would be immediately relieved when I got to town, I indulged hypochondria, which I had not felt of a long time. I called up into my fancy ideas of being confined all winter to an old house in the north of Scotland, and being burdened with tedium and gnawed with fretfulness. It is humiliating for me to consider that my mind is such that I can at any time be made thus wretched, merely by being placed in such a situation. But let me comfort myself that I can keep out of it. My body would be tormented were it put into a fire, as my mind would be tormented in such a situation. But as the one thought gives me no uneasiness, neither should the other. As I would not wish to have my body of stone, so I would not wish to have my mind insensible.

Wednesday 18 January 1775

...Mr Johnson's *Journey to the Western Islands* of Scotland came to me in thirteen franks. I have still a kind of childish satisfaction in seeing many packets come to me, and thinking that I appear important at the post-office. I opened the franks with impatience, read a short letter from Mr Johnson and a part of the book; and, as I had received it the very day on which it was published at London, I was pleased at my being so privileged ... [Later] I came home as early as I could, sat down by the drawing-room fire, and read on till I had reached the end of the *Journey*. It was then about three in the morning, and the fire was very low and the night very cold...

Wednesday 15 February 1775

...Life is like a road, the first part of which is a hill. A man must for a while be constantly pulling that he may get forward, and not run back. When he has got beyond the steep, and on smooth ground – that is, when his character is fixed – he goes on smoothly upon level ground. I could not help indulging Asiatic ideas as I viewed such a number of pretty women, some of them young gay creatures with their hair dressed with flowers. But thoughts of mortality and change came upon me, and then I was glad to feel indifference...

Sunday 5 March 1775

Stayed at home in the forenoon. My wife with great justice complained that my conversation with her was never rational, but merely childish nonsense. It is not easy to give a distinct specimen of that puerile jocularity in which alone I exert myself at home. The reason of it may be partly indolence, to avoid thought; partly because my wife, though she has excellent sense and a cheerful temper, has not sentiments congenial with mine. She has no superstition, no enthusiasm, no vanity; so that to be free of a disagreeable contrariety, I may be glad to keep good humour in my mind by foolish sport.

Wednesday 8 March 1775

...I was quite in love with her [Margaret] tonight. She was sensible, amiable, and all that I could wish, except being averse to hymeneal rites. I told her I must have a concubine. She said I might go to whom I pleased. She has often said so. I have not insisted on my conjugal privilege since this month began, and were I sure that she was in earnest to allow me to go to other women without risk either of hurting my health or diminishing my affection for her, I would go. Thus I thought; but I was not clear, for though our Saviour did not prohibit concubinage, yet the strain of the New Testament seems to be against it, and the Church has understood it so. My passion, or appetite rather, was so strong that I was inclined to a laxity of interpretation, and as the Christian religion was not express upon the subject, thought that I might be like a patriarch; or rather, I thought that I might enjoy some of my former female acquaintances in London. I was not satisfied while in this loose state of speculation. I thought this was not like Izaak Walton or Dr Donne. But then the patriarchs, and even the Old Testament men who went to harlots, were devout. I considered indulgence with women to be like any other indulgence of nature. I was unsettled.

[On Wednesday, 15 March, Boswell left for another jaunt to London.]

Friday 24 March 1775 [London]

I had found Percy¹ in his study at Northumberland House in the forenoon. He told me Mr Johnson spoke of me with more affection than he had heard him do of almost anybody. Before Mr Johnson came to The Club this night, I said he was only willing to believe the second sight. I really believed it. The evidence was enough for me. What could not fill a quart bottle might fill a pint bottle. I was filled with belief.

This night, as well as some former ones, I had wandered about with women of the town pretty late, but had not proceeded to completion.

I was alarmed at finding myself approaching to viciousness, and
resolved to shun such temptations; for my arguments in favour of
concubinage had, either from their own weakness or by being met by
prejudice from long habit, ceased to appear even plausible to me now.
Besides, concubinage was something settled. This was approaching to
vaga Venus. I this night went to my lodgings.

Friday 31 March 1775

At eleven I insisted to go to The Club ... [and] having either been
told or fancied that Mr Johnson was not to be there, I was forsooth
so full of wisdom and abilities that I would, as I thought, supply his
place. But I found him sitting there, and intoxication could not keep
off awe. I made a foolish attempt to combat with him. Went and stood
leaning over his chair. 'Why, Sir, did you go to Mrs Abington's benefit?
Did you see?'
JOHNSON. 'No.'
BOSWELL. 'Did you hear?'
JOHNSON. 'No.'
BOSWELL. 'Why, then, did you go?' (roaring boisterously).
JOHNSON. 'Because she is a favourite of the public; and when the
public cares the thousandth' (I think) 'part about you that it does
about her, I'll go to your benefit too.' This was a good lick. I cried,
'Well, I'm satisfied, and shall now go and eat my pigeon in peace,' a
dressed pigeon having been brought for me to a side table. I eat it
heartily and drank small beer. Then returned to the table. I remember
there were, besides Mr Johnson, Charles Fox, Percy, Langton. I was
sadly in liquor, and harangued Fox, who sat next me, about his
certainly being Prime Minister; but that then he would not have the
same pleasure from his speaking as now, as he would imagine the
applause was given to the Minister. Whereas now he was sure it was
to Mr Fox. He did not like my vinous compliments, and went to
another part of the table from that where I sat. Worthy Langton very
attentively and kindly put the bottle past me, that I might drink no
more, though indeed it would have been better that I had taken as
much as would have knocked me up quite, so that I might have been
carried to bed; for I got into the streets, and wandered among the
women of the town, first with one, then with another; but had reason
enough left to prevent me from proceeding to the last risk.

Thursday 6 April 1775

...Burke and his brother came and sat awhile in the Court of Chancery ... I maintained a strange proposition to Burke: that it was better for a Scotsman and an Irishman to preserve so much of their native accent and not to be quite perfect in English, because it was unnatural. I would have all the birds of the air to retain somewhat of their own notes: a blackbird to sing like a blackbird, and a thrush like a thrush, and not a blackbird and other birds to sing all like some other bird. Burke agreed with me. Englishmen would laugh heartily, and say, 'Here an Irishman and a Scotsman, each with his own country tone strong, attempt to prove that it is better to have it.' I said it was unnatural to hear a Scotsman speaking perfect English. He appeared a machine. I instanced Wedderburn. 'A man of wood,' said I, 'or a man of brass.' 'Ay, a man of *brass*,' cried Burke. Lord Lisburne and I had afterwards a dispute on this subject! My metaphor of the birds he opposed by saying, 'A Scotsman may do very well with his own tone in Coll; but if he comes into the House of Commons, it will be better if he speaks English. A bagpipe may do very well in the Highlands, but I would not introduce it into Bach's concert.' 'This,' said I, 'shows what it is to argue in metaphors. One is just as good as another.' But I maintained to my Lord that it put me in a passion to hear a Scotsman speaking in a perfect English tone. It was a false voice. He speaks as if he had some pipe or speaking instrument in his mouth. And I thought always, 'Can't he take this confounded pipe out, and let us hear him speak with his own organs?' I do still think I am right...

Saturday 8 April 1775

Wrote my journal at Dilly's quietly in the forenoon. Tom Davies called. I said, 'I am quite full of Mr Johnson's sayings. I am tapping myself.' 'Well,' said he, 'it will be good wine to draw off for the public.' I dined at Mr Thrale's by invitation...

Mr Thrale told me, I am not sure what day, that there is a book of Johnsoniana kept in their family, in which all Mr Johnson's sayings and all that they can collect about him is put down ... I must try to get this *Thralian* miscellany, to assist me in writing Mr Johnson's life, if Mrs Thrale does not intend to do it herself. I suppose there will be many written...

Tuesday 11 April 1775

...At this time in London I was wearing out as my dressed suit an old crimson suit embroidered with silver, made at Dublin in 1769. It was now old-fashioned, though a good handsome dress. I said, 'I feel myself quite different in this suit from what I am in my frock' (meaning that I felt myself better). Said Beauclerk: 'So should I feel myself quite different, but I should not feel agreeably' (meaning that I was ridiculous). He has a fine malignity about him...

Thursday 13 April 1775

Walked in the park up by Buckingham House, and went to Mrs Stuart's². Found Mrs Chancellor, the great lace-woman in Duke Street, with her ... Drank a great deal of tea, and was entertained by looking at a variety of beautiful laces ... My valuable spouse never yet would allow me to buy her a suit of laces. I determined to do it now, while her friend should approve of my choice. I mounted up gradually from sixteen guineas to thirty. I wished to have a suit not merely genteel but rich. I was flattered by the speeches which the old beldame made to me, who even called me a *handsome* gentleman. I was quite a fine fellow this morning. I was all levity and did not care how much money I spent. It was amazing with what copiousness and variety of expression Mrs Chancellor set off her laces. 'This,' said she, 'is *innocent*. This is *grand*.' 'Oh,' said I, 'we're past innocence. I'll have the grand.' I wanted to have a suit for the lady of a *baron*. I said to Mrs Stuart, 'This is just contracting thirty guineas of more debt. You must become bound to pay it in case I die in ten years, and then I can make myself easy by thinking that, by taking this lace, I do not make my creditors worse.' Accordingly she wrote a note declaring that she was bound for thirty guineas if I died within ten years without paying my debts; and Miss Hale, who came in, signed witness. Mrs Stuart and she and I drove to the Green Park and walked a good while. I was now quite well and in delightful spirits. (When I told Mr Johnson of the lace, he said, 'Well, you've done a wise thing and a good thing.' 'I've done a good thing,' said I, 'but I don't know if I've done a wise thing.' 'Yes, Sir,' said he. 'No money is better spent than what is laid out for domestic satisfaction. A man is pleased that his wife is dressed as well as other people, and a wife is pleased that she is dressed.')

Tuesday 18 April 1775

As a curious instance how little a man knows, or wishes to know, his own character in the world, or perhaps as a convincing proof that Johnson's roughness was only external, and had no participation with his heart, the following dialogue actually passed between us: JOHNSON. 'It is wonderful, Sir, how rare a quality good humour is in life. We meet with very few good-humoured men.' I mentioned four of our friends, none of whom he would allow to be good humoured. One was *acrimonious*, another was muddy, and to the others he had objections which have escaped me. Then, shaking his head and stretching himself at his ease in the coach, and smiling with much complacency, he turned to me and said, 'I look upon *myself* as a good-humoured fellow.' The epithet *fellow* applied to the great lexicographer, the stately moralist, the masterly critic, as if he had been *Sam* Johnson, a mere pleasant companion, was highly diverting; and this light notion of himself struck me with wonder. I answered, also smiling, 'No, no, Sir; that will *not* do. You are good-natured, but not good-humoured. You are irascible. You have not patience with folly and absurdity. I believe you would pardon them if there were time to deprecate your vengeance; but punishment follows so quick after sentence that they cannot escape.'

[*Boswell's journal lapsed when he returned to Edinburgh in May, but he summarised the period with the following.*]

'REVIEW OF MY LIFE DURING THE SUMMER SESSION 1775'

I do not remember any portion of my existence flatter than these two months. I was indolent in body and in mind; and the scenes of most lively enjoyment that I had were two dinners in the Castle with the mess of the 66 Regiment. Dr Samuel Johnson being on a jaunt in different parts of England, I had not a single letter from him during this Session; so that my mind wanted its great SUN. Some letters from Temple and one from my brother David were comforts. My father's coldness to me, the unsettled state of our family affairs, and the poor opinion which I had of the profession of a lawyer in Scotland, which consumed my life in the mean time, sunk my spirits woefully; and for some of the last weeks of the session I was depressed with black melancholy. Gloomy doubts of a future existence harassed me. I thought myself disordered in mind. Yet I was able to discharge my duty as a lawyer, wrote sixty papers, though none of them were very long indeed, and got one hundred and eighteen guineas and one pound in fees...

Boswell to William Temple, 19 June 1775 [Edinburgh]

...My father is most unhappily dissatisfied with me. My wife and I dined with him on Saturday. He did not salute her; though he had not seen her for three months; nor did he so much as ask her how she did; though she is pretty big with child. I understand he fancies that if I had married another woman, I might not only have had a better portion with her, but might have been kept from what he thinks idle and extravagant conduct. He harps on my going over Scotland with 'a Brute' [Johnson] (think how shockingly erroneous) and wandering (or some such phrase) to London. In vain do I defend myself. Even the circumstance that my last jaunt to England did not cost me £20, as I got 42 guineas in London, does not affect him. How hard is it, that I am totally excluded from parental comfort. I have a mind to go to Auchinleck next Autumn and try what living in a kind of mixed stupidity of attention to country objects, and restraint from expressing any of my own feelings, can do with him. I always dread his making some bad settlement...

Boswell to William Temple, 12 August 1775 [Edinburgh]

My dearest friend: I have had a pretty severe return this summer of that melancholy or Hypochondria, which is inherent in my constitution, and from which I have suffered miserably in former years, though since my marriage I have been wonderfully free from it. Your languor and discontent are occasioned by a gentler species of the distemper. You have a slow fever, I a raging one. While gloomy and fretful, and grossly indolent, I was shocked with the recollection of my good spirits, gayety and activity, as a man with a headache is shocked by bright sunbeams ... Nobody here but my wife and worthy Johnston had the least notion of my being at all uneasy; for I have been remarkably busy this summer ... The Court rose yesterday and this day the clouds have begun to recede from my mind, I cannot tell from what cause. My promise under the solemn Yew[3], I have observed wonderfully, having never infringed it, till the other day, that a very jovial company of us dined superbly at a tavern; and I unwarily exceeded my bottle of old hock, & having once broke over the pale, I run wild. But I did not get drunk. I was however intoxicated, and very ill next day. I ask your forgiveness; and I shall be more strictly cautious for the future. The drunken manners of this country are very bad. *Huzza! Huzza! Huzza!*

Tell me My Dear Temple, if a man who receives so many marks of more than ordinary consideration, can be satisfied to drudge on in an obscure corner, where the manners of the people are disagreeable to him? You see how soon I revive again. Could I but persuade my father to give me £400 a year and let me go to the English bar, I think I should be much better. That, however, seems to be impossible. As he is bound for £1,000 which I owe, he has resolved to lessen his allowance to me of £300 to £200. I must not dispute with him ...

I am growing more and more an American. I see the unreasonableness of taxing them without the consent of their Assemblies. I think our ministry are mad in undertaking this desperate war ...

Boswell to William Temple, 2 September 1775 [Auchinleck]

Here I am, according to my purpose. I came to Auchinleck on Monday last, and I have patiently lived at it till Saturday evening ... It is hardly credible how difficult it is for a man of my sensibility to support existence in the family where I now am. My father whom I really both respect and *affectionate* (if that is a word: for it is a different feeling from that which is expressed by *love*, which I can say of you from my soul) is so different from me, – we *divaricate* so much, as Dr Johnson said, that I am often hurt, when I dare say he means no harm, and he has a method of treating me, which makes me *feel* myself like a *timid boy*, which to *Boswell* (comprehending all that my character does, in my own imagination and in that of a wonderful number of mankind) is intolerable. His wife too, whom in my conscience I cannot condemn for any capital bad quality, is so narrow-minded, and I don't know how, so set upon keeping him totally under her own management, and so suspicious, and so sowrishly tempered, that it requires the utmost exertion of practical philosophy to keep myself quiet. I however have done so, all this week to admiration, nay I have appeared good-humoured; but, it has cost me drinking a considerable quantity of strong beer, to dull my faculties. The place [Auchinleck] is greatly improved. It is really princely. I perceive some dawnings of taste for the country. I have sauntered about with my father; and he has seen that I am pleased with his works. But what a discouraging reflection is it, that he has in his possession a renunciation of my birthright, which I madly granted to him, and which he has not the generosity to restore, now that I am doing beyond his utmost hopes; and that he may incommode and disgrace me by some strange settlements, while all this time, not a shilling is secured to my wife and children, in case of my death...

Thursday 19 October 1775

The great lines of characters may be put down. But I doubt much if it be possible to preserve in words the peculiar features of mind which distinguish individuals as certainly as the features of different countenances. The art of portrait painting fixes the last, and musical sounds with all their nice gradations can also be fixed. Perhaps language may be improved to such a degree as to picture the varieties of mind as minutely. In the mean time we must be content to enjoy the recollection of characters in our own breasts, or by conversation and gestures with people acquainted with the particular persons as much as we are.

Friday 10 November 1775

After breakfast my father and Lady Auchinleck paid us a visit. He was very guarded last night against expressing joy on the birth of my son[4], and today when he saw him he said very little. I however flattered myself that I detected symptoms of satisfaction in his behaviour...

...I got into a Highland humour and drank first plentifully of port and then of claret, which cost only £16 a hogshead; and, as intoxication rose, I disregarded my solemn engagement of sobriety to my friend Temple, and pushed the bottle about with an improper keenness, as I was not the entertainer. About nine Graham and I drank tea with Mr and Mrs Mackenzie. I was able to be decent then. But when I got into the street I grew very drunk and miserably sick, so that I had to stop in many closes in my way home; and when I got home I was shockingly affected, being so furious that I took up the chairs in the dining-room and threw them about and broke some of them, and beat about my walking-stick till I had it in pieces, and then put it into the fire and burnt it. I have scarcely any recollection of this horrid scene, but my wife informed me of it. She was in great danger, for it seems I had aimed at her both with chairs and stick. What a monstrous account of a man! She got me to bed, where I was excessively sick.

Monday 4 December 1775

... When I came home, I found that my wife had been reading this journal, and, though I had used Greek letters[5], had understood my visits to —. She spoke to me of it with so much reason and spirit that, as I candidly owned my folly, so I was impressed with proper feelings; and, without more argument than that it was disagreeable to so excellent a spouse, resolved firmly to keep clear. And when I reflected calmly, I thought it lucky that my journal had been read, as it gave an opportunity to check in the beginning what might have produced much mischief. I wondered at my temporary dissipation of thought when I saw the effects of my conduct. I valued and loved my wife with renewed fervour.

Friday 22 December 1775

It is a certain fact that I have a mind incapable, or at least ill disposed, for science of any kind. I always remember Sir John Pringle's saying to me some years ago in London, 'You know nothing.' And now the remark is as just as then. There is an imperfection, a superficialness, in all my notions. I understand nothing clearly, nothing to the bottom. I pick up fragments, but never have in my memory a mass of any size. I wonder really if it be possible for me to acquire any one part of knowledge fully. I am a lawyer. I have no system of law. I write verses. I know nothing of the art of poetry. In short I could go through everything in the same way.

Sunday 31 December 1775

My wife went to church in the afternoon. I got up to tea, and afterwards I took from my drawers the account of our family drawn up by my grandfather, and read it with more attention than I had ever done; and I discovered that in fact my great-grandfather had got little better than a bankrupt estate from his uncle, and that it was so burdened with debt that it appeared to me a question if, at that period, when money was scarce in Scotland and interest high, it was prudent to take it. This at once, like a blaze of light, showed me that I had been in an error as to an obligation in justice to give the succession all along to heirs male, seeing that we had not received it as a sacred trust with that view; and if principle was removed, I could yield my inclination and agree with my father. I was apprehensive that this sudden light would not be steady, and was only struck out by my father's threatenings; at least that my mind was much biased by them. I therefore resolved to wait for some time and to consult Dr Johnson. My wife, who was pleased not a little, cherished the discovery and suggested that if I had any scruple remaining, I might settle my estate of Dalblair[6] on heirs male for ever. I was wonderfully relieved tonight. My feudal enthusiasm for the heirs male of our founder, Thomas Boswell, remained. But this I could yield or modify.

1776

Sunday 14 January 1776

I this day read over this volume of journal and was pleased upon the whole with my life. But it occurred to me that if I keep in constant remembrance the thoughts of my heart and imaginations of my fancy, there will be a sameness produced, and my mind will not have free scope for alteration; so that I had better lay by my journal and read masses of it at distant intervals. However, I am persuaded that a man who mixes at all in society or has business to manage cannot have a sameness of mind. One new idea or former one revived will introduce a group. Nay, a monk of La Trappe, who never hears anything but prayers and memento mori, will, by the very change of seasons, of his health, and from memory, have his mind affected with alterations.

Tuesday 27 February 1776

From some time past my mind has been in a troubled, fretful state. I had a fit of gloomy passion this morning at breakfast, and threw a guinea note in the fire because my wife objected to my subscribing three shillings for a miscellany by a Miss Edwards. However I rescued the note with the tongs before it was consumed, and, though a good part of it was burnt, I got its value from the Royal Bank. This incident shocked me, because it made me dread that I might in some sudden rage do much worse ... I wondered when I recollected how much of my life since my marriage had been free from hypochondria; and it galled me that at present I was so afflicted with it that I had no just ideas or sensations of any kind. I was anxious to be with Dr Johnson; but the confused state of my affairs, and my tender concern at being absent from my wife and children, distressed me. I was exceedingly unhappy ...

Sunday 10 March 1776

My wife was a little indisposed. I was at the New Church in the forenoon. Between sermons I went up to my father's. I had not resolution to tell him that I was to set out for London next day. I took Lady Auchinleck into another room, acquainted her of it, and asked her 'friendly advice' how to proceed; told her that it distressed me to give any uneasiness to my father, but that I was convinced my going to London was for my interest. She said that my father looked on it as idle and expensive, and that I had formerly given him reason to think in that manner; but upon my giving her my reasons she seemed to be convinced that I was right, and she engaged to communicate the matter to him first, and then I might call on him in the evening. I was for the first time on a confidential footing with her, and I was sincere; but I saw she doubted my sincerity. I told her so. She owned it; but said that it never made any odds on her conduct. I assured her that she was wrong. That indeed I had once hated her; but that I now thought very differently, and she must have no longer any suspicion of me; that I had great faults, but was upon the whole one of the best men that ever lived; that it gave me uneasiness to be at enmity with anybody. She said, 'You cannot be a better man than I wish you, on many accounts.' She said that she had for some time been pressing my father to give up his Justiciary gown if something could be got for me; and that he was willing, but doubted of my prudence to negotiate the affair. It was a new and comfortable kind of feeling which I had now.

[On 19 March Boswell and Johnson embark on a ten-day excursion to Lichfield (Johnson's birthplace) and Ashbourne via Oxford, Stratford, Henley and Birmingham.]

Friday 22 March 1776 [Birmingham.]

After a sound sleep [at Henley] we got up well refreshed. Before we set out, Dr Johnson resumed the subject of my melancholy, and was displeased with my notion of thinking down that malady. He said, 'I have not been more shocked with anything that I have heard of a long time.' 'Sir,' said I, 'it was spirit and resolution.' 'Ay,' said he, 'but it was the spirit and resolution of a madman.' I said I had been in a mistake, for I imagined that he approved of that method. While we were in the chaise driving to Birmingham to breakfast, he said, 'When you have a place in the country, lay out twenty pounds a year upon a laboratory. It will be an amusement to you.' I said I had last summer taken a course of chemistry. 'Sir,' said he, 'take a course of chemistry, or a course of rope-dancing, or a course of anything to which you are inclined at the time. Contrive to have as many retreats for your mind as you can, as many things to which it can fly from itself.' There was a liberal philosophy in this advice which pleased me much. I thought of a course of concubinage, but was afraid to mention it...

...Amidst all this I had high happiness, and was warmly pious. Nothing disturbed me but a degree of unsettledness as to the consistency of concubinage, or rather occasional transient connexions with loose women, and Christian morals. I was sensible that there was a great weight of interpretation against such licence. But as I did not see precisely a general doctrine for practice in that respect in the New Testament, and some Christians, even Luther, did not think it an indispensable duty to cohabit only with one woman, and my appetite that way was naturally strong and perhaps rendered stronger by encouragement, I could not decide against it. I must venture to consult

Dr Johnson upon it. For he can, by his noble counsel, make my judgement clear and my resolution vigorous . . .

. . . 'I suppose', said I, 'there are fifty women with whom a man may be as happy as with any one in particular'. 'Ay, fifty thousand,' said he. I doubted if he was right. I have a strong imagination that I could not have been so happy in marriage with any other woman as with my dear wife. I cannot tell why, so as to give any rational explanation to others. I only know or fancy that there are qualities and compositions of qualities (to talk in musical metaphor) which in the course of our lives appear to me in her that please me more than what I have perceived in any other woman, and which I cannot separate from her identity.

Sunday 24 March 1776 [Lichfield]

Miss Seward[7] was rather a pretty woman. She had bright eyes but I thought a bad mouth. I thought one might make an epigram in the old style of conceit, and compare her eyes and mouth to lights placed at the mouth of a coal-pit. Dr Johnson had jocularly proposed to me to write a prologue to be spoken before the play on Monday, which we were to attend: 'A Prologue by James Boswell, Esq., from the Hebrides'. I really did think of writing one after he gave the hint. I was for 'Prologue spoken before Dr Johnson at Lichfield', like 'Prologue before the Duke of York' in Charles II's time. Much might be said of what Lichfield had done for Shakespeare by Johnson and Garrick.

[Towards the end of his London visit, the record of which (because of his hectic social whirl) he fell behind by more than forty days and brought up to date with extensive conversation from rough notes, Boswell's curiosity regarding the notorious Mrs Margaret Caroline Rudd led to the interview with her which follows. Men could not resist her and he wanted to know what the nature of her attraction was, and whether he would be attracted. In March 1775 she had been caught forging bonds and promissory notes with the two Perreau brothers, Daniel and Robert. They were convicted and hanged, but she languished in prison for six months until her trial in which she defended herself and apparently charmed the judges into acquitting her. On the afternoon of 22 April, only three months after her acquittal, Boswell called on her on the strength of a feeble recommendation. He thought the interview was remarkable enough to write up, *strangely enough, for his wife. He thought better of sending it to her, however; he sent it to Temple instead.*]

Monday 22 April 1776 [London]

...Then I heard her coming up stairs. I was all impatience and trepidation, when there entered rather a little woman, delicately made, not at all a beauty, but with a very pleasing appearance and much younger than I imagined. In short, the first view of her surprised me somewhat, as it was not by any means such as to strike me with the awe either of dignity or of high elegance. She was dressed in black clothes, with a white cloak and hat. I begged pardon for intruding upon her, but I was a friend of Mr Macqueen's, and though I had no indirect instructions from that family, she might believe that they would be glad to have accounts of her. She said she was much obliged to me for my civility. We sat down opposite to one another at a little distance, and I asked her how she was now. She said, 'As well as could be expected,' and immediately entered upon her unhappy story, which she told (I went to bed when I had written to the foot of the last page; I now continue my narrative, 24 April, between nine and ten in the morning) with wonderful ease and delicacy and an air of innocence quite amazing when one thought of what had been proved. She said the *Perreau* family (as she called it) was a little commonwealth, it was so numerous and so spread over England and Ireland, and that all the connexions endeavoured to throw the guilt upon her. I said it was shocking that the Perreaus had died denying as they did. 'Yes,' said she, 'it must shock everybody who has any tenderness of conscience. They should have died in silence.' She said she was to carry on a suit against Sir Thomas Frankland [her accuser] by which, if she got the full value of what he carried off belonging to her, she would recover £5,000 besides high damages.

She spoke with much earnestness of her anxiety to know whether her Husband Mr Rudd was alive or not, and said she would go to Ireland to see if a man whom some would have to be he, and others an impostor, was he or not, though she thought that his long neglect of her set her free from him. But she would not think of marrying again after having been twice so unlucky; and indeed, unless it was a man of rank and fortune that could bear her up notwithstanding what had happened to her, she should not think of marriage. She said she loved reading, and that if she had not had resources in her own mind, she must have been very unhappy. She said her confinement was very severe upon her. She had formerly been consumptive two years. She was almost blind when she came out again to the light, and her eyes, I saw, were still weak. When I looked at her narrowly she seemed to have some flushy heat on her cheeks, her nose contracted as she breathed, and she spoke through her teeth. Yet there was upon the whole ... something so pleasing and insinuating that I could believe her power to be what we have read. I said she was reckoned quite a sorceress, possessed of enchantment. She smiled and did not contradict me as to the past, but said she could enchant nobody. I begged her pardon and, with exquisite flattery, said, 'My dear Mrs Rudd, don't talk so. Everything you have said to me till now has been truth and candour'; and I told her I was convinced she could enchant, but I begged she would not enchant me too much, not change me into any other creature, but allow me to continue to be a man with some degree of reason. I was as cautious as if I had been opposite to that snake which fascinates with its eyes. Her language was choice and fluent and her voice melodious. The peculiar characteristic of her enchantment seemed to be its delicate imperceptible power. She perfectly concealed her design to charm. There was no meretricious air, no direct attempt upon the heart. It was like hearing the music of the spheres which poets feign, and which produces its effect without the intervention of any instrument, so that the very soul of harmony immediately affects our souls. She said she had formerly deluded herself with hopes of enjoying happiness. She now was satisfied with insensibility, not however in the extreme, but comparatively speaking. 'You must not be insensible,' said I, and rose and seized her silken hand, and afterwards, upon the argument being renewed a little, kissed it. This was all experiment, and she showed neither prudery nor effrontery, but the complaisance, or compliance if you please, of a woman of fashion.

She ... said she liked Scotland and would perhaps visit it again ... She spoke of our New Town with commendation ... We talked then on forming a character by habit, and she said we might be anything we pleased. This is Dr Johnson's opinion ...

I sometimes kept silence on purpose to observe how she would renew the conversation. She never let the pause be long, but with admirable politeness, when she found that I did not begin again to speak and might perhaps be embarrassed, said something quite easily, so as not to have the appearance of abruptness, to make me feel that I had stopped short, but rather of a continuation of our discourse, as if what she then said had grown out of what we had talked of before. Another thing which I remarked was that she did not aim at being witty. She did not dazzle with brilliance, but cheered one with a mild light. And what I thought also an uncommon excellence, she did not whine about her distress or affect to be plaintive, for she was sensible that the representation of unhappiness gives a certain degree of pain, and though pity is said to be akin to love, gaiety is a much more engaging relation. Seeing her eyes weak, I set the candles upon a table at some distance from her, but as she was then in such obscurity that I could hardly discern the pretty turns of her countenance as she talked, I soon brought back one of them to a table near her, saying that I must not deny myself altogether the pleasure of seeing her ... 'It is amazing,' said I, 'with what confidence people will tell lies, but there is a vanity in being thought to know particularly about a lady so celebrated as you.' Said she: 'People are apt to form an idea of one whom they have never seen. A gentleman told me he had imagined that I was old and ugly.' 'Why,' said I, 'that was very extraordinary, though indeed it may have been owing to the reputation of your enchantment, as witches were said to be old and ugly. You are, however, much *younger* than I supposed.' 'But,' said she, 'I am not a young woman. I am nine-and-twenty, and I do not think that young.'

... I spoke of her pedigree. She said, 'They would not allow me to be a gentlewoman and said my pedigree was forged – as if one would forge a pedigree when certainly one cannot raise money upon it.' The easy, unconcerned pleasantry with which she talked of forgery was wonderful.

While she ... said something about her confinement and trial, she showed a pretty little foot, and I got up in a kind of lively sudden surprise and said, 'I cannot believe that you have gone through all this. Are you really Mrs Rudd?' She smiled and said, 'I *am* Mrs Rudd.' I said she must forget all the ill that had passed and be happy for the future, and I thought love would be the best remedy for her. She said very gently she did not think so. I run out in the commonplace style upon the happiness of love, but said she must now be very cautious in her choice. I said I hoped she would forgive the liberty I had taken in waiting upon her ... She made me very welcome and said she was always at home. I returned her a thousand thanks.

During all this interview I was quite calm and possessed myself fully, snuffed the candles and stirred the fire as one does who is at home, sat easy upon my chair, and felt no confusion when her eyes and mine met. Indeed her eyes did not flash defiance but attracted with sweetness, and there was the reason of the difference of effect between her eyes and those of more insolent or less experienced charmers. She was not a robber but a thief. I wished her good night with a kiss which she received without affectation of any kind. I was then a little confused ... I thought of Mrs Rudd's fame for enchantment and all her history. I concluded from every circumstance that she was now upon the town, though her conversation was so superior to that of common women. But I might be mistaken, for I never hinted at an intrigue. I wondered what she thought of me. I imagined I was very agreeable, and it pleased me much that she never asked my name or anything at all about me, which showed perfect good breeding. I would not for a good deal have missed this scene. We crowd to see those who excel in any art, and surely the highest excellence of art is the art of pleasing, the art of attracting admiration and fondness.

'An Account of my Last Interview with David Hume, Esq.' (Partly recorded in my Journal, partly enlarged from my memory, 3 March 1777 [Edinburgh].)

ON SUNDAY FORENOON the 7 of July 1776, being too late for church, I went to see Mr David Hume, who was returned from London and Bath, just a-dying. I found him alone, in a reclining posture in his drawing-room. He was lean, ghastly, and quite of an earthy appearance. He was dressed in a suit of grey cloth with white metal buttons, and a kind of scratch wig. He was quite different from the plump figure which he used to present. He had before him Dr Campbell's Philosophy of Rhetoric. He seemed to be placid and even cheerful. He said he was just approaching to his end. I think these were his words. I know not how I contrived to get the subject of immortality introduced. He said he never had entertained any belief in religion since he began to read Locke and Clarke. I asked him if he was not religious when he was young. He said he was, and he used to read The Whole Duty of Man; that he made an abstract from the catalogue of vices at the end of it, and examined himself by this, leaving out murder and theft and such vices as he had no chance of committing, having no inclination to commit them. This, he said, was strange work; for instance, to try if, notwithstanding his excelling his schoolfellows, he had no pride or vanity. He smiled in ridicule of this as absurd and contrary to fixed principles and necessary consequences, not adverting that religious discipline does not mean to extinguish, but to moderate, the passions; and certainly an excess of pride or vanity is dangerous and generally hurtful. He then said flatly that the morality of every religion was bad, and, I really thought, was not jocular when he said that when he heard a man was religious, he concluded he was a rascal, though he had known some instances of very good men being religious. This was just an extravagant reverse of the common remark as to infidels.

I had a strong curiosity to be satisfied if he persisted in disbelieving a future state even when he had death before his eyes. I was persuaded from what he now said, and from his manner of saying it, that he did persist. I asked him if it was not possible that there might be a future state. He answered it was possible that a piece of coal put upon the fire would not burn; and he added that it was a most unreasonable fancy that we should exist for ever. That immortality, if it were at all, must be general; that a great proportion of the human race has hardly any intellectual qualities; that a great proportion dies in infancy before being possessed of reason; yet all these must be immortal; that a porter who gets drunk by ten o'clock with gin must be immortal; that the trash of every age must be preserved, and that new universes must be created to contain such infinite numbers. This appeared to me an unphilosophical objection, and I said, 'Mr Hume, you know spirit does not take up space.' . . .

I asked him if the thought of annihilation never gave him any uneasiness. He said not the least; no more than the thought that he had not been, as Lucretius observes. 'Well,' said I, 'Mr Hume, I hope to triumph over you when I meet you in a future state; and remember you are not to pretend that you was joking with all this infidelity.' 'No, no,' said he. 'But I shall have been so long there before you come it will be nothing new.' In this style of good humour and levity did I conduct the conversation. Perhaps it was wrong on so awful a subject. But as nobody was present, I thought it could have no bad effect. I however felt a degree of horror, mixed with a sort of wild, strange, hurrying recollection of my excellent mother's pious instructions, of

Dr Johnson's noble lessons, and of my religious sentiments and affections during the course of my life. I was like a man in sudden danger eagerly seeking his defensive arms; and I could not but be assailed by momentary doubts while I had actually before me a man of such strong abilities and extensive inquiry dying in the persuasion of being annihilated. But I maintained my faith. I told him that I believed the Christian religion as I believed history. Said he: 'You do not believe it as you believe the Revolution.' 'Yes,' said I 'but the difference is that I am not so much interested in the truth of the Revolution; otherwise I should have anxious doubts concerning it. A man who is in love has doubts of the affection of his mistress, without cause.'

He had once said to me, on a forenoon while the sun was shining bright, that he did not wish to be immortal. This was a most wonderful thought. The reason he gave was that he was very well in this state of being, and that the chances were very much against his being so well in another state; and he would rather not be more than be worse. I answered that it was reasonable to hope he would be better; that there would be a progressive improvement. I tried him at this interview with that topic, saying that a future state was surely a pleasing idea. He said no, for that it was always seen through a gloomy medium; there was always a Phlegethon or a hell. 'But,' said I, 'would it not be agreeable to have hopes of seeing our friends again?' and I mentioned three men lately deceased, for whom I knew he had a high value: Ambassador Keith, Lord Alemoor, and Baron Mure. He owned it would be agreeable, but added that none of them entertained such a notion. I believe he said, such a foolish, or such an absurd, notion; for he was indecently and impolitely positive in incredulity. 'Yes,' said I, 'Lord Alemoor was a believer.' David acknowledged that he had some belief...

It was amazing to find him so keen in such a state. I must add one other circumstance which is material, as it shows that he perhaps was not without some hope of a future state, and that his spirits were supported by a consciousness (or at least a notion) that his conduct had been virtuous. He said, 'If there were a future state, Mr Boswell, I think I could give as good an account of my life as most people.'

Friday 23 August 1776

And thus on Saturday the 24 of August I have once more brought up my journal, which had fallen sadly behind. My low spirits this

summer have been very severe upon me. I complained to Dr Samuel
Johnson. He first wrote to me rather harshly, but soon wrote in a
gentler strain. I have been too long without writing to him. Day after
day I have been vexed because I failed to write to him and to Mr and
Mrs Thrale and to Mr Langton, to all of the three last of whom I owe
letters; but an inexplicable dilatory disease prevents me. My Con-
sultation Book too, in which I engross all my fees from loose leaves
in which they are marked at first, is many, many sessions behind. I
wonder if I shall ever be able to bring up the several things which
ought to be done, so as to have only to upbraid myself with the neglect
of what *it were better to do*, such as writing every year some book, or at
least publishing some selection, arranging my letters to and from
different persons, and several other things. But my fear is that I shall
continue to be in a confused state, with nothing clear and finished and
distinct, but all my affairs in a sort of hurried irregularity, all my
exertions being occasional and forced...

Monday 26 August 1776

...My wife had been ill during the night with a cough, pain in her
breast, and sweatings; and as she was apprehensive of a consumption,
she was much distressed[8]. The jaunt was therefore put off, and I took
her out an airing in a post-chaise with Veronica, and went to a garden
at Restalrig, and pulled gooseberries. This did her good...

Friday 6 September 1776

Laboured some. In the evening was seized with a restless rage for
tavern company. Complained very absurdly to my wife that no care
was taken to study my humour and make me happy, when in reality
I do not believe that any woman on earth could have indulged me so
much and made me so happy as she does ... I proposed to call at
different taverns, and, if I could find a good company, to join it. But
I thought this would expose me. My wife, with a ready cheerfulness,
offered to go and sup with me at a tavern, where I might take a hearty
glass. I grew quiet at last, played at brag, supped well, drank strong
negus, and recovered my spirits. What strange weaknesses will come
upon one at times!

Friday 4 October 1776 [near Auchinleck]

...My spirits were high. I was made landlord, and I promoted drinking till we were too much intoxicated ... A wild thought seized me. I would try if I was sober; and the experiment was if I could walk across a narrow wooden bridge without rails, over the water of Doon, running rapid and pretty deep. If I did this and returned, it was to be a proof I was sober. I did not consider what would be my fate if I failed. Joseph followed me as I staggered down. I ordered him back. He could not apprehend what I was going to try. I accomplished my perilous exploit. I shudder to think of it. What an unhappy wife and helpless children might I in this drunken delirium have made! I surely should of all men guard against intoxication. Let this be the last instance. I sat a little with the company at cards. Felt myself very uneasy. Went to my room, got rid of the wine, and went into bed between seven and eight. I say into because it was truly a refuge.

Monday 25 November 1776 [Edinburgh]

...I went out a little fretted with some trifling dispute with my wife, saying I would not dine at home. I took myself just as I got into the street, but could not yield. I thought I would punish myself by walking in the fields and fasting; but I had not resolution, so dined at my father's. Claud was there. I drank little, and cannot say I was intoxicated; but my fretfulness worked me, and as I was coming home at five, I met a young slender slut with a red cloak in the street and went with her to Barefoots Parks and madly ventured coition. It was a short and almost insensible gratification of lewdness. I was vexed to think of it.

Sunday 1 December 1776

...About eight I got into the street and made Cameron, the chairman, inquire for Peggy Grant at a house in Stevenlaw's Close where she had told me she lived. He brought her out, and I took her to the New Town, and in a mason's shade in St Andrew's Square lay with her twice. I grew pretty sober by the time I got home, but was in a confused, feverish frame. My dear wife asked me if I had not been about mischief. I at once confessed it. She was very uneasy, and I was ashamed and vexed at my licentiousness. Yet my conscience was not alarmed; so much had I accustomed my mind to think such indulgence permitted.

Sunday 8 December 1776

My wife had been much fatigued by want of sleep, as I myself indeed was. I was too late for church ... I dined at my father's between sermons. Effie was there, and Sandy for a little[9]. In the evening my wife insisted to read this journal, and finding in it such explicit instances of licentiousness, she was much affected and told me that she had come to a resolution never again to consider herself as my wife; though for the sake of her children and mine, as a *friend*, she would preserve appearances. When I saw her in great uneasiness, and dreaded somewhat – though not with much apprehension – her resolution. I was awaked from my dream of licentiousness, and saw my bad conduct in a shocking light. I was really agitated, and in a degree of despair. She comforted me with hopes of my amendment ...

Saturday 28 December 1776

My wife, with too much keenness but with a good deal of justice, gave me this morning literally a curtain lecture upon the coarse, ill-bred, and abusive style of conversation which I now habitually practised. She said that it was so disagreeable and provoking that my company could not be liked, and that I had not the tenth part of the invitations now that I had before I was married. I was very sensible of my fault, but my invitations being less frequent was owing to my having refused many, and by degrees dropped many of my dining visitors. The roughness of manners amongst the Scotch lawyers made me assume that style in self-defence, and I have carried it to excess, as I do everything. I resolved to amend.

1777

Thursday 6 February 1777

...I had lately a thought that appeared new to me: that by burning all my journal and all my written traces of former life, I should be like a new being; and how soon may this be done; nay, how soon might all the libraries in Britain be destroyed! Were I just now to go and take up house in any country town in England, it would be just a different existence. Might it not be proper to change one's residence very frequently, so as to be literally a pilgrim upon earth? for death would not be such a violent circumstance, as one would not be strongly fixed...

Thursday 20 March 1777 [Auchinleck]

...I rode briskly to Auchinleck; felt my heart warm as I approached it. Found my father and the ladies arrived a little before me; was well received and was in a better frame than ordinary. I was not come to make a long stay, so I had no great weight of time upon my imagination as I have almost always had on arriving there. I therefore was easy. I thought that if I travelled frequently between Auchinleck and Edinburgh, I might dispel that imaginary cloud which the notion of a change of life for a considerable time gives me, and I projected doing this. Local impressions are nobly supported by Dr Johnson in his *Journey* at Icolmkill [Iona]. But they may be too strong, as odours may overpower.

Friday 21 March 1777 [Auchinleck]

(Writing from memory on Friday 4 April.) It was a fine day. I took James Bruce with me and walked fully round the plantations from the Hern to the Corbiecraighead. Was pleased to find the fences in decent order and the plantations properly thinned. My mind was quite sweet and pure, without fretfulness, and without trouble of any kind. I loved the country after the labour of a Winter Session, and I had solid notions as a country gentleman. The experience of such a state of mind should quiet me on other occasions, since I find that a man may, after the severest perturbations, be quite easy. When the sea is calm and smooth in fine weather, the agitations of past storms have no connexion with it. Let me look up to that blessed state of being in a future life. Those who remark their religious experiences are generally looked on with ridicule; but very unreasonably, for they are experimental philosophers upon the most important subject.

Monday 24 March 1777

(Writing on Sunday 13 April at Edinburgh.) My imagination preserves beauty and every amiable quality, so that if it has once existed in an object, and touched my senses, it is embalmed for ever...

Saturday 29 March 1777 [Edinburgh]

Grange dined with us. Poor little David[10] had been very ill for some days of a teething fever which was very severe on his delicate frame. Grange and I went and brought Mr Wood after dinner. He said he could do nothing for the child. I drank tea with Grange, but was called home before it was finished, the child having grown worse. I found him in sad distress, and his anxious mother in much affliction. I had not before been seriously alarmed for him, as he had struggled on wonderfully. But I was now affected to the heart, and to make my wife easy, I sent for Dr Young. He bathed his limbs in warm water, which relieved him a little. But he was pale and feeble, though in as much pain as he apparently could suffer. The Doctor then put a blister on his back. But it had no effect, and he expired a little before nine. I was calm as I could wish, and resigned to the dispensations of GOD. My wife was in real grief, but composed her mind better than I could have expected. His nurse was sincerely sorry. Grief appeared strongly in her countenance, though her behaviour was quiet. I carried the little corpse on my arms up to the drawing-room and laid it on a table covered with a table-cloth, parts of which again I spread over my child. There was something of dreariness in the blank in our nursery. Yet the gentle death of the sweet innocent, and his appearance like waxwork and at peace after his sufferings, affected us pleasingly...

Sunday 30 March 1777

... This morning Veronica and Effie would see their little brother. Veronica calmly kissed him. But Effie was violently affected, kissed him over and over again, cried bitterly, 'O my poor billy [brother] Davie,' and run to his nurse, who had also been hers, and clung about her, blubbering and calling to her, 'O come and take him off the table. Waken him, waken him, and put him in his cradle.' With much difficulty we got her pacified. I shall regard her all my life for the strength of her affection. She will take the greatest care of me in my old age, though Veronica may be the most pleasing companion when I am well. Veronica is of my temper. Euphemia of her mother's. Yet I was tenderer today than I imagined, for I cried over my little son and shed many tears. At the same time I had really a pious delight in praying with the room locked, and leaning my hands on his alabaster frame as I knelt. I prayed for his spirit, but chiefly to it as in the region of felicity, looking to a beautiful sky. There was not the least horror of death in this scene. My wife was shocked by seeing him ... ·

Sunday 20 April 1777

(Writing from notes on Sunday 4 May.) ... On the forenoon of this day, or a former forenoon, I had a most pleasing conversation with my dear Veronica, sitting with her on the floor of my dining room while the sun shone bright. I talked to her of the beauties and charms of Heaven, of gilded houses, trees with richest fruits, finest flowers, and most delightful music. I filled her imagination with gay ideas of futurity instead of gloomy ones, and she seemed to lift her eyes upwards with complacency. Yet when I put it to her if she would not like to die and go to Heaven, the natural instinctive aversion to death, or perhaps the acquired, by hearing it mentioned dismally, made her say, 'I hope I'll be spared to you.' I for the first time mentioned Christ to her; told her that he came down to this world for our good; that ill men put him to death; that then he flew up with silver wings and opened the great iron gates of Heaven, which had long been shut, and now we could get in. He would take us in. She was delighted with the idea, and cried, 'O I'll kiss him.' One cannot give rational or doctrinal notions of Christianity to a child. But it is a great blessing to a child to have its affections early engaged by divine thoughts.

'Suppose,' said I, 'Veronica, when you come to Heaven, you do not find me there. What would you do?' Said she: 'I would cry, "Angels! where's my papa?"' She said this with such an enchanting earnest vivacity, as if she had really been addressing herself to the *celestial ministers*, that I was quite happy. 'But,' said I, 'suppose they should let you see me walking upon wild mountains and shut out because I had not been good enough?' Said she: 'I would speak to GOD to let you come in.' I kissed her with the finest fondness. The brilliant light shone into my very soul. I was all hope and joy. I trusted that I should yet have supreme felicity with Veronica in a better world. I looked at her sweet little mild countenance with steadfast speculation. And may not her prayers to GOD avail much for me yet? Much good is gained to us in this state of being by others; and why not in the next?...

[*Because Boswell did not manage a visit to London in the spring* 1777, *he arranged to rendezvous with Dr Johnson for two to three weeks at John Taylor's home in Ashbourne. It was some compensation for a long arid period without London stimulation. As usual, his spirits suddenly soared as he left Edinburgh and, except in a couple of instances, they stayed high in Johnson's company.*]

Saturday 13 September 1777

(Writing at Ashbourne on Thursday 18 September.) I carry my own sheets and pillow-slips with me when I travel, that I may be sure my bed-linen are clean and dry. When the maid was taking them off the bed early this morning, she looked so inviting, and my desire was so strong, that after being allowed liberties enough I attempted to lie with her; but to this she would not consent. In a moment after I was shocked to think of the risk I had run. Perhaps I should not put such things as this into my journal...

Wednesday 17 December 1777 [Ashbourne]

... I said, in writing a life, a man's peculiarities should be mentioned, because they mark his character. He [Johnson] said there was no doubt as to peculiarities; the question was if a man's vices should be mentioned; for instance, if it should be mentioned that Addison and [Thomas] Parnell were drunkards, for that people would more easily indulge in drinking from knowing this; so that more ill might be done by the example than good by telling the whole truth ... Dr Johnson maintained that if a man is to write a panegyric, he may keep vices out of sight; but if he professes to write a life, he must give it as it really was; and when I objected the danger of telling that Parnell was a drunkard, he said that it would produce an instructive caution to avoid drinking when it was seen that even the learning and genius of Parnell could be debased by it; and in the Hebrides he maintained (as appears from my journal) that a man's intimate friend should mention his faults if he writes his life...

Friday 19 September 1777 [Derby]

I talked one morning of the difficulty of rising in the morning. Dr Johnson said that the learned Miss [Elizabeth] Carter [the poetess], when she was eager in study, did not awake as early as she wished, and she therefore had a contrivance that at a certain hour her chamber light should burn a string to which a heavy weight was suspended, and which then fell with a strong sudden noise, which roused her from sleep, and then she had no difficulty in getting up. But I said that was my difficulty, and I wished there could be some medicine invented which would make one rise without pain, which I never did, unless after lying in bed a very long time. Perhaps there may be something in the stores of Nature which can do this. I have thought of a pulley to raise me gradually; but that would give me pain, as it would counteract my internal inclination. I would have something that can dissipate the vis inertiae, and give elasticity to the body. As I imagine that the body may be put, by the operation of other substances, into any state in which it has ever been, and as I have experienced a state in which rising from bed was not disagreeable, but easy – nay, sometimes agreeable – I suppose that this state may be produced if we knew by what. We can heat the body, we can cool it, we can give it tension or relaxation; and surely we may bring it into a state in which rising from bed will not be a pain.

Monday 22 September 1777

... At breakfast I unguardedly said to Dr Johnson, 'I wish I saw you and Mrs Macaulay together.'[11] He grew very angry, and after a pause, while a cloud gathered on his brow, he burst out, 'No, Sir. You would not see us quarrel to make you sport. Don't you see that it is very uncivil to pit two people against one another?' Then, taking himself, and wishing to be more gentle, he added, 'I do not say you should be hanged or drowned for this, but it is very uncivil.' Dr Taylor thought him in the wrong and spoke to him privately of it. But I afterwards acknowledged to him that I was to blame. For that I candidly owned I meant to express a desire to see a contest between Mrs Macaulay and him; but then I knew how the contest would end, so that I was to see him triumph. He said, 'You cannot be sure how a contest will end; and no man has a right to engage two people in a dispute by which their passions may be inflamed, and they may part with bitter resentment against each other. I would sooner keep company with a man from whom I must guard my pockets than with a man who contrives to bring me into a dispute with somebody, that he may hear it.' This he said was Langton's great fault: endeavouring to introduce a subject on which two people in the company differ. 'But,' said I, 'he told me he did it for instruction.' 'Sir,' said Dr Johnson, 'whatever the motive be, the man who does so is very pernicious. He has no more right to instruct himself at such a risk than he has to make two people fight a duel, that he may learn how to defend himself.' . . .

[During the next few months in Edinburgh Boswell is hypochondriac, attending to business in a desultory and lacklustre manner, and ill much of the time (as is Margaret). His father is as cold and hostile as ever. Until March 1778, his journal entries are mostly short, not much more than notes.]

1778

Monday 5 January 1778

Wife better, so that Wood between eight and nine said if weather was good and we had her in motion, would be as well as ever. And I tried *volupt.* [sex], which brought on spitting of blood about midnight. O direful! thought herself gone. Prospects gloomy and dark. I miserable. Went to Wood. Brought him. He was calm and mild, but alarmed. I followed to door and cried bitterly, and loved him for his friendship.

He said, 'You'll have a great charge.' But he hoped there might be only blood from throat. We had a sad night. I regretted that I had not been so good to her as she deserved, and that she had not been mistress of Auchinleck. She slept none and I very little. Prayed earnestly. Was in state of wildness.

Friday 13 March 1778 [Edinburgh]

Veronica cried enchantingly when I spoke of my going to London. She walked out with me to my father's, and being soon cheerful again, when I resumed the story of my leaving her, she bid me not speak of it again, for it made her cry. I was delighted with her. It was agreeable to have her with me when I took leave of my father, for he never cordially approves of my going to London; and by the influence of habit since ever I remember him, I am depressed in his presence and cannot get free of the imagination that I am still a boy, or at least a youth, and that, too, pretty much 'void of understanding'. Having a child of my own before me elevates me to the rank of a father and counteracts the depressing imagination to a certain degree. It is like having a little footstool to raise one...

[On 13 March 1778 Boswell is off to London for two and a half months.]

Thursday 9 April 1778 [Sir Joshua Reynolds's house, London]

...Drawing-room, how rich! Besides dinner company, Garrick, Harris, Miss Hannah More, Dr and Mrs Percy, Dr Burney, rich widow —, Mrs Cholmondeley. Langton and [I] sat a little quiet and enjoyed the scene, the lustre in light and in genius. I said, 'Not true, man never is [blest]: we are.' He agreed, pretty much at least...

I went up to Garrick. He hardly took notice. Ridiculous importance. Vexed me a little, I'm ashamed to say so. Talked a few words with Mrs Cholmondeley, then joined Johnson, Garrick, and Harris. Garrick said to Johnson, 'Here, Sir, is the great Boswell from Scotland, as sublime as ever' (ridiculously). I was a little angry. However, down on settee beside them, Johnson and he agreeing most men worse of drinking. I mentioned to Garrick his being my tempter two years ago.

JOHNSON. 'Had I made a resolution and been driven from it so, should have hid my head for a year.'

GARRICK. 'It gave all the company a better opinion of you that you yielded.' (To Johnson.) 'Sir, there was he drinking water, with his book to take down our conversation.'

JOHNSON. 'I do not approve of ... [water-drinkers] ...'

GARRICK. 'Let it be a law of The Club, either drink or we'll search him, that he mayn't have book. If he won't let wine search him, we will.' Nonsense: as if I had book and wrote in company and could not carry in my head...

Friday 10 April 1778

... On this or some other topic I troubled him [Johnson] with too many questions, asking, 'What did you do?' and so on. The Doctor grew enraged and said, 'Don't you consider, Sir, these are not the manners of a gentleman? What man of elegant manners teases one with questions so? I will not be baited with what: what is this? what is that? why is a cow's tail long? why is a fox's tail bushy?'

BOSWELL. 'Why, Sir, you are so good.'

JOHNSON. 'My being so good is no reason why you should be so ill.'

BOSWELL. 'Sir, I stop whenever you give me a hint, whenever you put a lock upon the well.'

JOHNSON. 'But that is forcing one to do a disagreeable thing.' (Then he said, I believe, about the cow's tail and the fox's tail.)

BOSWELL. 'Nay, Sir, if you put a lock on the well so that I cannot drink, do not make the water play upon me and wet me.' ...

Sunday 12 April 1778

... Found Burke [at his house in the Broad Sanctuary, Westminster]. For a little (for the first time I ever found it) he did not burst forth; his genius was not impatient of restraint like a strong spring from a rock. And he was somewhat flat. But he was shaving, and might have cut himself had he not been quiet. I found myself sadly empty and unsettled as to public affairs ... He said Great Britain had a right to bind her colonies. But that is to be exercised according to circumstances. 'I at my farm have a right over my cows and my sheep and my hogs. But I exercise it for my advantage, with proper allowance. I have a right to shear my hogs. But it would be absurd to do it.'

BOSWELL. 'How, then, are you to govern?'

BURKE. 'As you find the people inclined.'

BOSWELL. 'This is not governing, 'tis salmon-fishing. You let out your line by the wheel and draw it in, and play with the salmon. You would fish with a single hair. Johnson would take a strong line, a cable rope, and pull them out.'

BURKE. 'I do not wish for a better illustration than your simile of salmon-fishing. You cannot govern men as you do boys. This force may do at Eton, at Edinburgh, or at Glasgow. But you will get few salmon with the cable rope. I would not like to trust my dinner to these professors at Glasgow. There are proper seasons for salmon-fishing, and you must carefully adapt your fly. You must not fish with a mayfly in autumn. An ignorant, violent man would say, "Damn your bloods, salmon, come out!" and he'd laugh at you for taking such pains, sorting feathers of birds and bits of silk and such things. But he'd make nothing of it.' He mentioned nets. 'No, no,' said I, ''tis fishing with the rod. You must be an *angler*.' 'Ay, or a *dangler*,' said Burke. A tolerable conceit, as one who tries to win a lady is called a dangler.

Good Friday 17 April 1778

...Walked deliberately for Dr Johnson's ... Found Dr Johnson and Mrs Desmoulins at breakfast. A larger cup, such as I had asked the last time, was ready for me. Eat cross-buns and drank plentifully of tea. I observed the Doctor chose to abstain from milk on this fast morning ... He eat some cross-bun. I talked a good deal myself this morning...

I said to him, 'What would I have given some years ago to be assured of this intimacy with Dr Johnson. Sir, there is none of your friends on whom you could depend more than on me.'

JOHNSON. 'No, Sir, none who would do more for me of what I'd wish to have done. Were you to die, it would be a limb lopped off. And remember, I tell you this that you may not always be wishing for kind words.'

BOSWELL. 'Sir, you are very good. If you were to die, there would be such a blank to me as I cannot express. But one of us must survive the other.'

JOHNSON. 'Yes, Sir...'

Tuesday 15 September 1778 [Edinburgh]

The birth of another son is a new era in my life; and I flatter myself that I may continue my journal from this day on which my son *James* was born, with more constancy than I have done for some time past. I had rested ill all night, having been disturbed by being raised from bed with my wife, and having more than ordinary anxiety about her, as she had been very ill and apprehensive of being in a consumption at the time she fell with child. I rose between nine and ten. She was in great distress all the forenoon. I prayed earnestly for her to GOD and to Jesus Christ, and I addressed myself (if I could be heard by them) to the Virgin Mary, to my dear mother, to my grandfather and hers, and to her father and mother for their intercession. About ten minutes after two she was safely delivered of a fine, big, stout boy, and she herself was better than ever she had been on such an occasion. She however had suffered so severely that she told me she had now for the first time expressed a wish that she might have no more. I was satisfied to think she should not.

Sunday 27 September 1778

... a wanton-looking wench catched my eye in the street. I accosted her, but without intention to transgress. She endeavoured to hold me, and named me, 'Mr Boswell'. This was a proof to me that I must not suppose I am not known by such creatures in Edinburgh, so that if other motives fail, a regard to my reputation as a man of some decency may restrain me. Grange supped in my wife's room. I now slept with her.

SIX

In the Middle of Life's Journey
1779–1782

The journals from this point to his father's death in 1782 are weak on plot, high on incident and process. Ideas, fears, hopes, joys and depression crowd in on each other in so unpredictable and unstable a pattern that there is no escaping the conclusion that the 'enamel' of his mind is cracking. He does not know where he is heading. He is full of indecision and uncertainty. Incongruities have always been a keynote of Boswell's life and thought, but now in the journal they shove each other off the stage with a kind of organic rapidity, an honest immediacy that makes for tragic but fascinating reading. The formlessness of it all is a great paraphrase of his life and mind at this time.

Nonetheless, there are recurring themes that trace some pattern in his existence. The main one is the developing rancour of his family life, even as his family grows. His love for his wife, in spite of continuing arguments, is seldom in doubt and his love for his children is touchingly precious, but the serpents in that Eden are his father and stepmother, the 'noverca' as he fashions her. In the journal he unsparingly cites chapter and verse of offence and insult that he experiences at his father's hands. But that is always warring with a love for his father that he attempts to salvage. The 'noverca' is another matter. She is the ugly witch, the icy wind that he is convinced freezes relations between him and his father.

As his father's health declines, Boswell's legal practice declines. He sees no hope in it for advancement and he languishes. He is forced by finances to stay in Edinburgh and push on with his career, but he constantly fantasises about London. There appears to be no way out and hypochondria plays havoc with him.

He also doubts himself socially. Is he a success socially, or not? His erratic and heavy drinking illustrates his lack of belief in himself. At times, though, he is convinced that he has a genius for conviviality and grace. Back and forth he rocks from one extreme to another.

On the positive side — ironically since he seldom derives sustaining satisfaction

from his talents as a writer — he feels literary pride. He writes monthly articles
for the London Magazine; boasts to himself of a galaxy of eminent literary
friends and acquaintances; is sure that one day he will write the great biography
of Johnson; and has projected a number of other biographies of the famous. Most
of all, he knows he is good at writing his journal and has faith in it, although
he constantly questions its validity and purpose. He never takes it for granted,
measuring it from any number of points of view. He reads his old journals, a
severe test if there ever was one, to see if they are any good. And so the days
unfold, not bringing him any closer to his preconceived ideas of social and
financial success but inexorably taking him to the pivotal moment when his
father dies and, at long last, he inherits Auchinleck.

1779

[An anti-papist riot broke out in Edinburgh in the evening of 2 February 1779,
in response to recent relaxation of the penal laws against Roman Catholics
adopted by the General Assembly of the Church of Scotland. Characteristically,
Boswell was drawn to the scene of mob violence.]

Tuesday 2 February 1779 [Edinburgh]

I went close to the scene of action and found so many both of the
Town Guard and the Fencibles standing with their arms, which made
me suppose that the people whom I heard knocking in the house in
flames were extinguishing the fire. But to my astonishment I soon
perceived that they were throwing in fuel, and the Lord Provost did
not think it prudent to attack them. I was really shocked, and having
called silence, I harangued to them a little very keenly; said I loved a
mob, but was ashamed of them now, for what could the papists do
worse than this? ... A fellow who did not know me said, 'You had
better not speak so among the mob.' I said, 'I'm not afraid of the
mob.' One who knew me called out with a significant look and
manner, 'Mr Boswell, you know we're in the right,' and then was
great huzzaing and no more could be said. It hurt me to see a large
book, perhaps some venerable manuscript, come flaming out at one
of the windows. One of the mob cried, 'They' (i.e., the papists) 'burnt
us: We'll burn them.' Another cried, 'Think what they did to our

worthy forefathers.' It was striking to see what one has read of religious fury realised.

Sunday 14 February 1779

Paid a visit to my father, whom I had not visited since Sunday last. My two daughters and Sandy followed me, and though it came on a pretty heavy rain, they were sent away without the coach. Such cold and unfeeling treatment shocked me. I went home with them. I was feeble and sunk. My father was failed, and his appearance affected me gloomily. Yet I envied the steady, regular, prudent conduct he had maintained through life, and did not think with any pleasure of the superior warmth of enjoyment in various ways which had been my lot. I drank coffee and grew a little better at night. Was affectionate to my wife and children.

[In April 1779 the Rev. James Hackman shot and killed Martha Ray, the Earl of Sandwich's mistress, and attempted to kill himself. She had obdurately declined his offer of marriage. Boswell wrote magazine articles on the incident after Hackman was convicted of murder, representing the condemned man's humanity and misery.]

Friday 16 April 1779 [London]

As the – I know not what word to use, whether dispute, contest, or altercation – between Johnson and Mr Beauclerk at the Literary Club, 16 April 1779, has been much talked of and may be misrepresented, I think it right to write down exactly what passed.

We were talking of Hackman. Dr Johnson argued, as Judge Blackstone had done, that his having two pistols with him was a proof that he meant to shoot two people. Mr Beauclerk said no. For that whoever intended to kill himself took two pistols that he might be sure of doing it at once. Lord [Charles] Spencer's cook shot himself with one pistol, and lived ten days in great agony. Mr Delmis, who loved buttered muffins but durst not eat them because they disagreed with his stomach, resolved to shoot himself; and then he eat three buttered muffins for breakfast before shooting himself, knowing he should not be troubled with indigestion. He had two charged pistols. One was found lying charged upon the table by him after he had shot himself with the other. 'Well,' said Dr Johnson with an air of triumph. 'You see here one pistol was sufficient.' (With great deference to him, his conclusion was not just, because it only so happened that one *was* sufficient. Two might have been necessary.) Mr Beauclerk replied smartly, 'Because he was dead.' And either then or a very little after, being in anger at Dr Johnson's triumphant remark, said, 'This is what you don't know, and I know.' There was then a cessation of the dispute; and some minutes intervened, during which dinner and the glass went on cheerfully. When all at once, Dr Johnson abruptly said, 'Mr Beauclerk, how come you to talk so petulantly to me as, "This is what you don't know and I know"? One thing I know which you don't know: that you are very uncivil.' Mr Beauclerk said, 'Because you began by being uncivil (which you always are).' The words in parenthesis were, I believe, not heard by Dr Johnson. Here again there was a cessation of arms. Dr Johnson told me that the reason why he waited some time at first without taking any notice of what Mr Beauclerk said was because he was thinking whether he should be angry. But when he considered that there were present a young lord (Lord Althorp) and Sir Charles Bunbury, men of the world to whom he was little known, they might think they had a right to take such liberties as Beauclerk did, and therefore he would not let it pass. A little while after this, the conversation turned on the violence of Hackman's temper. Dr Johnson then said, 'It was his business to command his temper, as my friend Mr Beauclerk should have done a little ago.' 'I should learn of you,' said Mr Beauclerk. Dr Johnson answered, 'You have given me opportunities enough of learning, when I have been in your company. No man loves to be treated with contempt.' Beauclerk (with a polite inclination towards the Doctor) said, 'You have known me twenty years and however I may have treated others, you may be sure I could never mean to treat you with contempt.' 'Sir,' said the Doctor, 'you have said more than was necessary.' Thus it ended; and Beauclerk's coach not having come for him till very late, Dr Johnson, with Mr Steevens, sat with him a long time after the rest of the company were gone; and he and I dined at Beauclerk's on the Saturday se'nnight thereafter.

Boswell to William Temple, 3 May 1779 [London]

Had you been in London a week ago, you would have seen your friend sadly changed for a little. So trifling a matter as letting the nails of my great toes grow into the flesh, particularly in one foot, produced so much pain and inflammation and lameness and apprehension that I was confined to bed, and my spirits sank to dreary dejection ... I am now much better, but still unable to walk. And having received a very wise letter from my dear, sensible, valuable wife, that although my father is in no immediate danger, his indisposition is such that I ought to be with him, I have resolved to set out tomorrow, being the very first day, after completing another term at the Temple.' ...

Friday 25 June 1779 [Edinburgh]

... This week, and particularly this day, [legal] fees came in so well that I got up again in spirits as to my practice at the bar ...

I was now in very good spirits. But what was I doing? I was engaged in no sort of study. I was not improving my mind. I had a fine letter this week from my friend Temple which humbled me. For it showed me that he continued constant to literature, so that in himself he was much my superior. But then as a social being I had the advantage of him. I was doing pretty well as an advocate. I was bringing up my children ... I was to succeed to an estate of £1500 a year. It however hurt me to be sensible that I was deficient in vigour of mind, was not enough a man.

Sunday 19 December 1779

(Writing on Monday the 20th.) It was a very wet day. So I stayed at home and made the children say divine lessons. In the afternoon I read one of Mr Carr's sermons aloud, and my wife another. At night after we were in bed, Veronica spoke out from her little bed and said, 'I do not believe there is a GOD.' 'Preserve me,' said I, 'my dear, what do you mean?' She answered, 'I have thinket it many a time, but did not like to speak of it.' I was confounded and uneasy, and tried her with the simple argument that without GOD there would not be all the things we see. 'It is He who makes the sun shine.' Said she: 'It shines only on good days.' Said I: 'God made you.' Said she: 'My mother bore me.' It was a strange and alarming thing to her mother and me to hear our little angel talk thus. But I thought it better just to let the subject drop insensibly tonight. I asked her if she had said her prayers tonight. She said yes, and asked me to put her in mind to say them in the morning. I prayed to GOD to prevent such thoughts from entering into her mind...

Monday 20 December 1779

(Writing Tuesday the 21.) By talking calmly with Veronica, I discovered what had made her think there was not a GOD. She told me, she 'did not like to die'. I suppose as she has been told that GOD takes us to himself when we die, she had fancied that if there were no GOD, there would be no death; so 'her wish was father to the thought' – 'I wot through ignorance.' I impressed upon her that we must die at any rate; and how terrible would it be if we had not a Father in Heaven to take care of us.

Tuesday 28 December 1779

(Writing on Wednesday the 29th.) I must remark a curious incident. I dreamt that I saw the cause of my toe being so painful: viz., a piece of the nail sticking in the flesh.[2] When I took off the poultice this morning, I observed a piece of nail appearing through the ball of my toe. Dr Gillespie called. He desired to see it. He said it should be pulled out with a forceps. I took hold of it with my finger and thumb, and out it came. I was then at once easy, except that the wounded flesh smarted a little. Wood called, and I showed him how I was relieved. I had now only to let the wound heal.

1780

Thursday 6 January 1780

My passion [anger] on Wednesday night was occasioned by a very trifling cause, which is not worth mentioning. Yet it was shockingly violent, and was directed against my dear wife, who, though now in good health, was with child, and required tender treatment. I was much vexed with myself both last night and this morning. Yet I was this morning in an obstinate fit, and would take no breakfast till my wife came and solicited me after hers was over, though I had a headache. I insisted with her that she ought in duty as a wife to be ever attentive, ever ready to soothe my temper and be complaisant. She said very sensibly that she had been educated without that timorous restraint in which I had been kept, and that it was much easier for me not to insist on subjection than on her to submit to it. But she was certainly wrong in contradicting my favourite notions and partialities. In particular, she was much to blame in endeavouring to counteract the principle of family which has prevailed in the family of Auchinleck from generation to generation. She said, and perhaps with some truth, that our pride and high estimation of ourselves as if German princes (my phrase) was ridiculous in the eyes of other people, who looked upon us not only as no better than any other gentleman's family, but as a stiff and inhospitable family. But as I have great enjoyment in our fancied dignity, and cannot be persuaded but that we do appear of more consequence in the country than others, from a certain reserve which has always been maintained, and am also of opinion that this pride makes us act in a nobler manner, I wish to encourage it; and my wife therefore should at least not oppose it. My son Sandy seems to imbibe it as I could desire. I catechise him thus: 'What is your first duty?' 'My duty to GOD.' 'What is your second duty?' 'My duty to the family of Auchinleck.' 'Who was the first laird of Auchinleck?' 'Thomas Boswell.' 'From whom did he get the estate?' 'From his king.' 'Who was his king?' 'King James the IV of Scotland.' 'What became of Thomas Boswell?' 'He was killed at Flodden Field fighting with his king against the English, for Scotland and England were then two kingdoms.' 'Who was Thomas Boswell's son?' 'David.' 'What became of him?' 'He fought for his sovereign, Queen Mary, at the Battle of Langside, lived a worthy gentleman, and died at Auchinleck.' He seems much pleased with this genealogical instruction. I shall go on with it and habituate him to think with sacred reverence and attachment of his ancestors and to hope to aggrandise the family.

Sunday 9 January 1780

(Writing on Monday the 10th.) ... I kept the house all day, and heard the children say divine lessons. I told them in the evening so much about *black angels* or *devils* seizing bad people when they die and dragging them down to hell, a *dark* place (for I had not yet said anything of *fire* to them, and perhaps never will), that they were all three suddenly seized with such terror that they cried and roared out and ran to me for protection (they and I being in the drawing-room), and alarmed their mother, who came upstairs in a fright, and she ... took them downstairs. This vexed me. Yet without mixing early some *fear* in the mind, I apprehend religion will not be lasting.

Thursday 3 February 1780

I thought I would look into my journal in London in 1762, that I might console myself in Edinburgh by being reminded that I had been as weary and melancholy in London as here ... This was wrong. I was sickened in mind by reviewing my own sickly weakness. Yet I thought that it was not fair to judge of London now to me by what it was when I had a narrow acquaintance in it. For now how delightful is it to me! And I can scarcely imagine that it would not continue to be so were I constantly there.

Saturday 11 March 1780

(Writing on Monday the 13th.) Was somewhat uneasy that my fees this Session amounted to less than they had formerly done. Apprehended a failure of my practice now that my father did not attend the Court, and thought I should be unhappy for want of business.[3] Yet I was sensible that a great deal of the coarse labour of law in Scotland would hurt my mind; and I should have considered that one of my fortune should be satisfied with little practice. I however dreaded insignificance, while at the same time I had all this year as yet been so averse to the business of the Court of Session that I had no keenness for it, as I once had, and wished always to have anything I had to do decently over. I saw no opportunity for ambition in this narrow sphere. What practice I had, I had with the dignity of a gentleman; not having used the artifices which many advocates have done, and not debasing myself by familiarity with vulgar agents. Fain would I have indulged gay, animating hopes of exerting myself in London. But I felt indolence and gloom too heavy upon me, and I was conscious that I could not persist in uniform application. Then I considered that the expense of living in London would impoverish me, and that I might perhaps in my hypochondriac discontent wish for the home of Edinburgh. I was sick-minded today. The Session rose, which was rather dispiriting to me, as I was not to go to London[4] and would mould in inactivity.

I dined at my father's. Lady Auchinleck had a headache and did not dine with us. But she with venom talked to me of people being quick to see others failed, which was not a sign of a good disposition.[5] She plainly meant my being sensible of my father's failure, which it is possible she does not perceive clearly, and wishes not to see, as her consequence depends on his life. I kept my temper. My father was very ungracious. I came home today quite sunk, as I often do from my father's, which is really sad.

Saturday 15 April 1780

(Writing on Monday the 17th.) My dear wife has for some months been troubled with a cough, sometimes better, sometimes worse. This morning she had a severe fit, so that she spit some blood. This frightened her and made me uneasy. But I hoped that the blood came only from her throat.

Wednesday 19 April 1780

I drank tea with Mrs Mitchelson and talked a great deal of nonsense which vexed me afterwards. I then wandered an hour in the streets and followed girls, but happily did not go with any of them or run any kind of risk. It was however very disagreeable to think that I had from intoxication (writing on Saturday the 22nd) been so foolish as to debase myself by intruding at Mitchelson's, and so gross as to follow after low Edinburgh whores. I had been cutting my great toe-nails this week and had hurt the flesh, and by walking a good deal today they were both inflamed. The toe which troubled me before was much swelled and very painful. I put a poultice to it and went to bed. My dear wife had soup ready for me, which I took comfortably amidst my contrition.

Wednesday 9 August 1780

... I called on my father, and he was confidential with me about John.[6] I respected his calm solid sense, though I could not but regret his feeling so little. We were well together for a little by ourselves, he having called me into his room with him. I said I hoped he was now pleased with me. He said, 'Yes,' but not with warmth. I said if he would tell me anything, it should be done. He said the great point was to be frugal and sober. I spoke of how much he had done. He said he had been lucky in having a good wife – two good wives, he might say. I said he was better now than he had been five years ago ... I wished to hear him talk on religion, but saw no fair opening. When we returned to the drawing-room, I proposed to Lady Auchinleck to take Sandy with them. She said she had care enough without him, and said (I think) she had no wish to live but to take care of my father, and in a whimpering tone talked of his being the worse of being at Auchinleck. She said that perhaps, being overjoyed at my brother's return[7], I might think it was to be a merry meeting at Auchinleck. But it was quite different. My father went there to be quiet and retired. That company disturbed him, especially at night; and why have people who wanted to drink and be merry and would go away and say he was useless? It was hard, when people were willing to give up the world, that they could not be allowed to live in their own way. She said she was glad she had spoken to me. I said, 'Well then, I give you my word of honour I shall not invite anybody. If you will be so kind as mention anything, it shall be done.' I wanted to know if my father's bonds to my children did not leave them independent of me. She said she had never read them. But she should look them out. But I would not, she said, have my father to write them over again now. She was for people making settlements when in good health, but not to be troubled when indisposed. I said it was proper to alter what was wrong in settlements. She said she never had been so anxious. In short she talked absurdly. I kept my temper finely, and I was really disposed for peace.

[From 17 August to 16 September, Boswell was at Auchinleck with his brother David, his father and his stepmother, trying to recover his sense of the preciousness and sacredness of his youth there. His wife and children were not invited. David was on the whole a disappointment to him, lacking that Romantic enthusiasm that Boswell treasured and hoped his brother, on his return from Spain, would share with him. And despite moments of warmth from his father, his relations with him and his stepmother remained cool or unfriendly.]

Monday 11 September 1780 [Auchinleck]

... I had a conversation of some length with my brother David in my room. He talked *rationally* of my flights, but was in the extreme opposite to imagination and gay frankness. I however now think him a good deal more agreeable than I did at Edinburgh, though his cool, attentive conduct to the *noverca*, and insensibility to her sour, resentful behaviour to a brother who had been all along warmly kind and generous to him, could not but give me uneasiness. I have had satisfaction in contemplating him at this time at Auchinleck as *constantly* neat and accurate; of which I have no idea from my own experience, but the reverse. Little circumstances present him to my mind in the most lively manner, as I believe is the case with everything. I mark then my sitting in his room with him, he intense upon some calculation, I reading his Spanish almanac or calendar and having foreign ideas. It is impossible to record fully one's life if all sensations are to be minutely described.

Friday 17 November 1780 [Edinburgh]

When I do not mention the day on which I write, it is to be understood that I write of the date. I was very unwilling to rise this morning, but was obliged to be in the Court of Session. Last night the street was covered with snow. This morning there was a thaw and all was black and wet. My spirits were low as upon many former occasions. I had a poor opinion of myself. I however was not deeply miserable ... How insignificant is my life at present! How little do I read! I am making no considerable figure in any way, and I am now forty years of age. But let me not despond. I am a man better known in the world than most of my countrymen. I am very well at the bar for my standing. I lead a regular, sober life. I have a variety of knowledge and excellent talents for conversation. I have a good wife and promising children. Sandy, upon being told some days ago that the Devil was once an angel in Heaven and thrown down for disobedience, asked me, 'Who was Devil before him?' I said there was none. But I thought the existence of an evil principle a curious investigation.

1781

Boswell to Sir Joshua Reynolds, 27 February 1781 [Edinburgh]

During the long intervals of my absence from London, I have often wished to have the pleasure of hearing from you; and when we last shook hands at parting you said, 'Write to me, and I'll answer you' – yet by some strange imbecility or distraction of mind though I have many a time sat down to begin a letter to you this (if I shall make it out) will be the first that I have ended. The truth is that in this dull northern town, I am not the same man that you see in the metropolis. I have not that jocund complacency that eager gayety which you have frequently cherished. Allow me Dear Sir to begin our correspondence with returning you my most sincere thanks for your goodness to me, which has increased every year since I was fortunate enough to be introduced to your acquaintance. To make this grateful acknow-ledgement is a real satisfaction.

I long much for more of our wonderful (mirabilis) friend Dr Johnson's Prefaces to the Poets. The criticism and biography of these I have read delight me more and more. What a pity it is that he loathes so much to write and since that is the case what a pity it is that there [is] not constantly with him such a recorder of his conversation as I am. I hope next month to be again in London and resume that office.

I hope when we meet I shall receive from you some valuable additions to my Boswelliana.

Wednesday 28 March 1781 [London]

At our club on Tuesday Sir Joseph Banks, whom we call our Chancellor of the Exchequer, opened the budget; that is to say, he is our treasurer and gave us a state of our affairs. We buy our own wine and pay the master (or rather mistress, the man being dead) 1/6 for each bottle of claret we drink, and 1/- for each bottle of port. Taxes are levied annually for this wine. We had all the matter done today in parliamentary form. We had two guineas apiece to pay for the current year. But there was a question as to arrears. The first defaulter was Charles Fox: unanimously ordered that he should pay. Then I was read out. Upon which Mr Burke, who sat next me, said, 'By all means let him pay. If we can get anything out of Scotland, let us have it. We get a little land tax' (he had said before). 'But by the Customs and Excise we some years literally don't get a shilling. Besides,' said he, 'the Scotch were so violent for taxing their brethren in America that they should certainly be taxed themselves. The Club will consider of this. For I know no other reason why Mr Boswell should pay for last year when he was not in London.' It carried that I should not pay, because I held no place under Government, which Dunning, upon my telling him what had passed, said was the case with very few of my countrymen ... Dr Johnson was excused because of his not drinking wine; and my account of his swallowing it greedily was considered by Burke as representing him rather under a kind of disease, a rage, as the French say; and that till he could drink as an honest fellow he was not to be reckoned among the taxed. Sir Robert Chambers was going to be excused. 'What!' said Burke, 'a man who is in the very centre of wealth, and absent to get money? No.' It was agreed he should be taxed. Somebody suggested that he might commute his arrears by sending a hogshead of wine. I moved that it should be a hogshead of Madeira that had been in the East Indies; and it being ordered that this should be intimated to him, it was afterwards suggested that a hogshead was not a Madeira measure, but a pipe. I moved that the word 'hogshead' be erased and instead thereof be inserted the word 'pipe'. Dr Adam Smith came last; and Burke and I were clear that a Commissioner of the Customs, who holds a lucrative place and was absent only because he is a tax-gatherer, should be taxed; which was ordered. Dr Johnson did not relish a repetition from me of this pleasantry. He said, 'I am glad I was not there.' Yet it was very well, I thought. Gibbon alone stickled for Smith, because he is a brother infidel. He is a disagreeable dog, this Gibbon. Mrs Thrale said, 'He squeaks like Punch. I imagine he'll squeak [confess] indeed before he dies, as he had a religious education.' 'Yes,' said I ludicrously, 'he is an infidel puppet: *le marionet infidel.*'

Monday 9 April 1781 [Boswell is returning to London from an overnight excursion to Woodford.]

Preston was in my room. 'James, get up. I have got a place in the coach for you.' I was alert, jumped up, and my heels beat on the floor responsive to his call. I was in an agreeable feverishness from yesterday's generous living. Tom, Mr Foulis's black boy, attended me well and put on my wig. I got a basin of tea. The coach came to the door, which hurried me. I took the basin of tea in my hand as I walked to the coach door, that it might cool in the air. Drank it off, and then throwing three shillings into the basin, called, 'Here, Tom, take you the grounds.' A smart, lively young gentleman of Woodford, who had something of Wilkes's manner, was in the coach. We talked away. We took in a plump servant-maid, whom I kissed and was gay with, and by degrees the coach was quite full. I joked on everything we saw. There was 'Eve's Manufactory'. That, I supposed, must be aprons. All jokes do in a hackney-coach. There came on a pretty smart rain. A well-looked, stately woman who sat on the coach-box begged as a favour we would make room for her in the coach. I told her all the seats were filled. But if she chose to sit on my knee, and the company had no objection, she was heartily welcome. This being agreed, in she came, and I had a very desirable armful. She was a widow with three children. She had suckled the son of Mr ———, brewer in Winchester Street, and continued in his service. But having had ill health, went to a friend's at Woodford for country air, was going up to her master's for a single day and night, and then to return to Woodford. I grew very fond of her, cherished her in the coach, and when she went from us, kissed her repeatedly and warmly, and wished to be better acquainted with her. Such incidents are marrow to my bones.

Wednesday 30 May 1781 [London]

... I then drove in the General's [Paoli's] chariot to Court. It was a very full levee. The inner room was crowded to the door. Colonel Stopford and I walked in the outer room. At length the King came to the door, and bowed a signal to us in our turns to approach. I stood in some uneasiness lest he should not speak to me, as he first spoke to a gentleman on my left hand and then to Stopford on my right. But he relieved me. When I approached him, the following conversation took place. (I mark it before dinner on my return home.) KING. 'When must you be in Scotland for your law?' BOSWELL. 'The 12 of June, Sir. Our term begins that day.' KING. 'Have you practised the law long? Ever since you returned from abroad?' BOSWELL. 'Yes, Sir.' KING. 'Ever since you came from Corsica?' BOSWELL. 'Your Majesty is pleased to recollect my having been there.' KING. 'When did you see General Paoli?' BOSWELL. 'I saw him today, Sir. I live in his house.' KING. 'Do you? That's but fair. I think him a man of an excellent heart.' BOSWELL. 'He is indeed, Sir; and is always very sensible of Your Majesty's goodness to him. But though Your Majesty is pleased to make him very comfortable as a private gentleman, I, who have seen him in Corsica, am sensible that it is a sad change.' KING. 'Was it not like to kill him at first? But I believe he is a philosopher.' BOSWELL. 'He is, Sir. But I remember when he was amongst our mountains (for he came down to us to Scotland), I heard him have this soliloquy: "*Ah, que cela me fait souvenir que je ne suis plus rien.*"[8] KING. 'When he saw your hills?' BOSWELL. 'Yes, Sir.' KING. 'He has very good sense.' BOSWELL. 'He has, Sir. Old Ambassador Keith said of him at my house, "This is the most sensible man I ever saw."' KING. 'I believe he was a greater politician than a soldier.' BOSWELL. 'The French have been at great pains to depreciate him as a soldier. But from what I have been informed, I trust he had courage enough' (or 'acted very well'). KING. 'I don't mean he was deficient. But that his forte was being a legislator – in short, putting law into a people who were lawless.' 'Yes, Sir,' said I, 'and he did it with great ability.' After saying that General Paoli had an excellent heart, His Majesty added, 'He is a great deal better than the people among whom he was. They were wild' (or some such word). 'They were a brave people, Sir,' said I. I was exceedingly happy at being allowed thus to talk with the Sovereign. I even felt some allowable vanity. Colonel Stopford said, 'You've had a long conversation with the King.' 'Yes,' said I. 'He is a very sensible (or 'a very agreeable') man. I wish to be acquainted with him.'

Thursday 26 July 1781 [Edinburgh]

... Was sadly dispirited; thought myself insignificant and subjected to a wretched destiny. Had no clear thoughts of anything, no consoling pious feelings ... Was saddened by speculative clouds composed of the uncertainty of life, the forgetfulness of things years after their happening, and such dreary truths. Wondered how I had ever been active and keen in anything.

Thursday 23 August 1781

(Writing on Friday the 24th.) It rained all day ... I know not how it happened, but I had a complete relief from melancholy for an hour or two, and enjoyed some of Dr Johnson's *Lives of the Poets* fully. We played a rubber at whist. My wife, who had been a little hoarse for some time, spit some blood, which alarmed both her and me. I persuaded her to go to bed early. She said my father and I were quite different. My spirits required agitation, no matter by what. His did not. I was brandy kindled, the flames of which, if not stirred, went out. He was a good coal fire, which burnt steady.

Monday 3 December 1781

... I am too fat at present. My belly is more swelled than I ever remember it; and perhaps my humours are gross. I have a torpidity of mind that I have not often experienced. I have not 'a lively hope of immortality'. It occurred to me today that perhaps a man is immortal or not as he happens to die in a dull or a lively frame. I have often been an immortal soul. At present it seems to me that I am not of celestial fire. I am quite sensual, and that, too, not exquisitely but rather swinishly.

1782

Monday 7 January 1782

(Writing on the 10th.) I had resolved to have no company as long as her [Margaret's] illness continued. She had no spitting of blood. But had a severe hollow cough in the night-time, unless when quieted by laudanum, and sweatings every night. Also at times during the day heats all over her body and a quick pulse. Also swellings in her legs; and she was very, very thin, and had pains shooting through her neck and breast. All these symptoms might be nervous. But both she and I dreaded the consumption, the fatal disease of her family. The apprehension of losing her and being left with five young children was frightfully dreary. All my affection for her and gratitude to her, and the consciousness of not having acted as her husband ought to do, overwhelmed me; and several times I cried bitterly, and one night lay long awake in misery, having wild schemes of desperate conduct floating in my imagination upon supposition of her death. The consideration of her cold, unworthy treatment by my father added much to my distress. It hurt me deeply to think that she should have been my wife only during my narrow and dependent state, and not have lived to be lady of Auchinleck. My views of futurity too were dim. In short I was very wretched ... I prayed to GOD in his mercy to restore my wife to health.

Wednesday 27 February 1782

... (Writing 4 March.) I do not recollect anything more except that either yesterday or today I left this my journal lying open in the dining-room while I went downstairs to look for some book or paper, and my dear wife having taken it up, read the account of my life on Monday the 18⁹, with which she was shocked, and declared that all connexion between her and me was now at an end, and that she would continue to live with me only for decency and the sake of her children. I was miserably vexed and in a sort of stupor. But could say nothing for myself. I indulged some glimmering of hope, and just acquiesced in my fate for the present. I was still heated with wine.

Boswell to Edmund Burke, 18 March 1782 [Edinburgh]

Will you now My Dear Sir give me leave to apply to you on my own account. I allow that I have no other right to do so, but that Imperfect right as we lawyers speak arising from your having shown me much kindness upon every occasion, which naturally founds an expectation of more. When a Lady disappoints such an expectation she is called a Jilt. I believe there is no particular epithet for a Friend who does so. I am also aware that fancy grafted on a good stock of self opinion produces fallacious blossoms in many cases both of Love and

Friendship. But I will venture to trust to those which your beams have cherished in my mind.

When I was last in London, you asked me on one of our pleasant evenings over your homebrewed, 'how I *could* live in Edinburgh?' I answered, 'Like a cat in an airpump.' In short in so narrow a sphere, and amongst people to whom I am so unlike, my life is dragged on in languor and discontent. What more years may do I cannot tell. But as yet I do not feel myself a bit easier ... May I not now assure myself that you are near your Apotheosis, as poor Goldsmith said of you poetically several years ago; for experience proved that his eye was only 'in a fine frenzy rolling'. If it is now to be real, may I not desire to be remembered by you? I ardently wish for occupation of more consequence than drudging at the bar in Scotland; and I think I should be very happy in exerting what talents I have, under your auspices.

The late Sir John Pringle said to me last autumn when he was here, 'I know not if you will be in rest in London. But you will never be at rest out of it.' And I recollect Dr Johnson observing one day at Sir Joshua Reynolds's upon the subject of a London life 'that every body is at rest in its proper place. They who are content to live out of London have minds fitted for it.' Pray be good enough to afford me a little consideration, and tell me as a Philosopher and Friend if my restlessness out of the great scene of exertion be not 'the divinity that stirs within me' and points out the line I should take? Would there not be something generous in your giving me your aid to attain greater happiness? You told me £600 a year would defray the difference between keeping house in London and in Edinburgh. How shall I contrive to get £600 from government? Would the King, with whom I related to you an excellent conversation, but of himself transplant me into a better climate, how pleasant would it be! But I wish not to indulge romantic visions. I am advancing to be called to the English bar, as another string to my bow. In short I am eagerly looking out.

Tuesday 7 May 1782

Up in good calm spirits. Called. Found *noverca* alone. SHE. 'What, not gone? [to Auchinleck]' I. 'No. I think I could not well go after what you told me yesterday.' (Repeated what she had said.) 'I thought my father's son might have been at least as well taken care of as Mr Stobie.¹⁰' She was fluttered, and I think for the first time I saw her blush. SHE. 'What was I to do? What was I to order?' I. 'You know that best.' SHE. 'You might have ordered what you pleased.' I. 'I should not have presumed. I should have expected common civility.' SHE. 'You seem not to think it necessary to acknowledge my Lord or me. If you had asked if there would be proper accommodation for you —' I. 'I mentioned my going. I resolved to say nothing about my accommodation, but leave that to you.' SHE. 'I only meant to put you on your guard in case you had taken people there.' I. 'I certainly should not have done that. So far from inviting, I have begged people not to come, even when the family was there; and far less would I invite when the family is not there.' SHE. 'There is a way of asking company not to come which may make people ridiculous.' I. 'One does not know what to do.' SHE. 'It is plain enough what to do when there's kindness.' Father came to door. She went and told him. He came in. She said with a sneer, 'I've been telling him you're angry I did not make preparations.' I. 'I am not angry now. I was angry. I thought my father's son might have been as well taken care of as Mr Stobie.' Father stood by fire and said nothing. Before he came in, she said, 'What's all this now? You said nothing yesterday.' I. 'I was angry yesterday. I don't like being angry, and I went away till I should cool.' She was so plausible and my feelings are so tender that I declare I was sorry for her, and thought she might not intend any ill. But on recollection I saw her devilish insolence.

Thursday 4 July 1782

... I made a good many excerpts from Tom Jones. My wife disliked Fielding's turn for low life; as I have observed yesterday. But it is human nature. She has nothing of that English juiciness of mind of which I have a great deal, which makes me delight in humour. But what hurts me more, she has nothing of that warmth of imagination which produces the pleasures of vanity and many others, and which is even a considerable cause of religious fervour. Family, which is a high principle in my mind, and genealogy, which is to me an interesting amusement, have no effect upon her. It is impossible not to be both uneasy and a little angry at such defects (or call them differences); and at times they make me think that I have been unlucky in uniting myself with one, who, instead of cherishing my genius, is perpetually checking it. But on the other hand, I consider her excellent sense, her penetration, her knowledge of real life, her activity, her genuine affection, her generous conduct to me during my distracted love for her and when she married me, and her total disinterestedness and freedom from every species of selfishness during all the time she has been my wife. And then I value her and am fond of her, and am pained to the heart for having ever behaved in a manner unworthy of her merit. I also consider that a woman of the same imagination with myself might have encouraged me in whim and adventure, and hurried me to ridicule and perhaps ruin, whereas my excellent spouse's prudence has kept me out of many follies, and made my life much more decent and creditable than it would have been without her. She was very apprehensive today and sadly dejected ... She has always a dreary terror for death. Indeed he is the King of Terrors. She said yesterday it was desirable to live long for one reason: because old people come to be as little afraid of death as children are...

I find the life which I now lead, upon the whole, the most agreeable to me. I am calm, I am heavenly-minded. Shall I end my days in a convent? This often seems probable to me. My dear wife's illness was more distressing to me that I reflected she had never had the advantages to which the match she had made entitled her, my father having kept me upon a small allowance, and he and his women having treated her with shameful coldness. When I thought she might perhaps die before my coming to the estate of Auchinleck, which would place her in a situation which she so well deserves, I was grievously vexed; and as a wife is to be preferred to a father, especially when he lives only to continue the harsh and unjust power of a stepmother, I could not help viewing his death as a desirable event. I know not what to think of this. Certainly the death of a father may be a desirable event. It is nice to determine in what cases. A son should be able to give strong reasons. I have given mine; and I do not see as yet that I am in the wrong. It is not on my own account that the wish rises. It is a wish formed upon the principle of choosing the least of two evils.

Boswell to Hester Thrale, 9 July 1782 [Edinburgh]

Last night's post brought me your kind letter informing me of Dr Johnson's being so much better since his jaunt to Oxford [in June]. I kissed the subscription, 'H. L. Thrale', with fervency. The good news elated me; and I was at the same time pleasingly interested by the tender wish which you express to relieve my anxiety as much as you can. My dear Madam, from the day that I first had the pleasure to meet you, when I jumped into your coach, not I hope from impudence, but from that agreeable kind of attraction which makes one forget ceremony, I have invariably thought of you with admiration and gratitude. Were I to make out a chronological account of all the happy hours which I owe to you, I should appear under great debt, and debt of a peculiar nature, for a generous mind cannot be discharged of it by the creditor.

May I presume still more upon your kindness, and beg that you may write to me at more length? I do not mean to put you to a great deal of trouble; but you write so easily that you might by a small expense of time give me much pleasure. Anecdotes of our literary or gay friends, but particularly of our illustrious Imlac, would delight me.

I hope you have not adopted a notion which I once heard Dr Johnson mention, that for fear of tempting to publication it was his study to write letters as ill, I think, or as dryly (or jejunely) I am not sure of the very phrase, but it meant as insipidly as he could. He said this last year at Mr Dilly's in company with Mr Wilkes, if I am not mistaken. I suggested to him that his writing so would most certainly make his letter be preserved and published for it would be a choice curiosity to see Dr Johnson write ill.

Monday 19 August 1782

... A very disagreeable scene of ill humour in my father happened after dinner. For all the money that is spent by his women, there is a meanness at his table ill grudging claret, which very seldom appears. When Dr Webster is there a bottle is set down to him; and as it is a great chance no more will be allowed, I generally never take any of it. Today I chose a glass of it, and said easily, 'Doctor, will you give me a glass of your wine?' He made me welcome, to be sure. As I was taking the bottle to me, my father said with a snarl, 'That's Dr Webster's bottle, man.' 'I know,' said I. 'But the Doctor makes me welcome, and I like to take a glass of claret when I'm with a man who can afford it. But if it is disagreeable to you, I shall not take any of it.' He was ashamed when I thus spoke out. But he looked displeased. I repeated, 'If it is disagreeable to you that I should drink claret, I shall let it alone.' He wished to have the meanness concealed, and said, 'Never fash [bother] your head.' So I drank claret. Lady Auchinleck called for another bottle of claret. This roused him, and with a vengeance he filled my glass with sherry. I was stunned, and hesitated for a little what to do. I once thought of instantly leaving the company. But I luckily restrained myself; said, 'It's all one'; and then putting some claret into my glass, said, 'I'll make burgundy of it.' After this the other bottle of claret was decanted; I partook of it as if nothing had happened, and he was quiet. It was really wretched treatment ... My dear wife was hurt by my father's treatment of me and thought I should have instantly resented it, because submitting to it seemed mean. She said, 'If a father slaps his son in the face, when he is a man, the son ought not to bear it peaceably.'

[Boswell is suddenly called to his father's deathbed. For this week he kept only notes in his journal.]

Thursday 29 August 1782

... Went upstairs ... Went in. He took no notice as I passed, curtains open. Went round; she [stepmother] sitting by curtains. Shook hands. I asked if in pain. 'Has the pains' (or 'struggles' or some such word) 'of dissolution on him.' Her hardness was amazing. I wished to go near. She said, 'It will confuse his head. Don't torture him in his last moments.' I was benumbed and stood off. Wept; for, alas! there was not affection between us ... Lady Auchinleck, [when I asked to] see if he could speak, [said,] 'There's all that remains of him.' Wished to stay all night ... Went home to bed.

Raised. Went back. Women servants gathered ... [He was] very low. Stayed in room ... Strange thought: 'Still alive, still here! Cannot he be stopped?' Breathing [grew] high, gradually ceased. Doctor closed eyes.

Boswell to Samuel Johnson, 1 October 1782 [Auchinleck]

I came to this place, with my wife and children, on Wednesday the 18 September and took possession of the seat of my ancestors on Dr Johnson's birthday. This was no conceit of my superstitious mind: it accidentally happened by our being kept a day longer at Edinburgh by bad weather. But I own it pleases me that it has so happened. I hovered here in fluttering anxiety to be with you till Tuesday the 24; and on that day, though my dear wife had the night before a disagreeable return of her spitting of blood and was very uneasy to think of my going away, I set out. I felt myself drawn irresistibly. I imagined I could neither act nor think in my new situation till I had talked with you. I lay that night at an inn two stages off, with intention to get next morning into a fly which crosses the country there from Glasgow to London by Carlisle. But before it came up, I was stopped by an express that my wife had been seized with her alarming complaint of spitting of blood more violently than ever and that she entreated I might return. I hastened home again; and the agitation of her spirits being calmed, she has ever since been pretty easy. But that calm she owes to you. For while I was still intent on flying away to you, your most excellent letter forcibly dissuading me from deserting my station arrived, and at once settled me. My words on reading it were, 'Well, he is a most wonderful man! He can drive me to the end of the world or confine me in a dungeon.' My wife was so affected by your letter that she shed tears of grateful joy, and declared she would write to you herself. Accordingly you have enclosed the spontaneous effusion of her heart, which I cannot doubt will interest you. There is much tenderness in the passage where she bids you 'remember that delays are dangerous in her complaining state of health'. I love and value her as much as ever husband did wife; and I should upbraid myself for having resolved to leave her, had it been with any other purpose than to be with you. I flatter myself with hopes that her complaint is not of a consumptive nature. She is quite averse to travelling. The most attentive care therefore must be taken of her at home. Ease, cheerfulness, light diet, fresh air, and gentle exercise may by GOD'S blessing re-establish her health.

Now that I allow myself to look into the affairs of the estate, I find that my presence here is essentially necessary, there being several farms to let. But as I am very ignorant myself of country concerns and have very different opinions given me, I am perplexed how to act. I must do as well as I can at first and get more knowledge gradually. I am as sober as you could wish me to be. It was my determination that I should maintain the decorum of the representative of Auchinleck; and I am doing so.

Could you not without risking any injury to your health come to us here this month? Or if that is too much, may we not meet only for two days at one of the stages on the west road? In two days a fly takes me to Doncaster; in three to Stilton. Could you not come to a middle place between these? Six days' absence may be allowed me without uneasiness. My earnestness to see you this year is very strong; and we could discuss more in an hour's conversation than in a great deal of writing. Decide, I pray, as to this, and fix any day you please if you can gratify me. If you cannot, I depend on full answers to all the questions I have to put.

In the mean time, I am undecided as to the way in which it is proper for me to behave to my *noverca*. That she is *injusta* is but too clear. From my father when his faculties were sadly decayed she has instead of £150, the jointure in her contract of marriage, contrived to obtain lands now worth £325 yearly, a house worth £100 yearly, and the property of the furniture in it reckoned worth £1,000, which at double interest for her life is £100 a year more – nay, the bygone or past rents of her jointure lands, which from the indulgence of this family to the tenants will be about £500. Is not this an exorbitant plunder? Should I attempt, by a proof of my father's incapacity and of his avowed sentiments as to moderate jointures when his mind was unimpaired, attempt to set aside the deeds, which would be an indelicate, though a justifiable, suit, or shall I just acquiesce? But her greediness is not what hurts me most. I think with regret and indignation of her totally estranging my father from me and my family; and I find a large collection of family letters, particularly a most affectionate and pious correspondence between my grandfather and grandmother for many years, has been destroyed, though carefully bound up by my father for preservation. I suppose she has either destroyed it herself or persuaded my father that his son was unworthy to have it. She was cutting a valuable wood before it was ripe. She was letting leases at low rents, for what we call *grassums* or entry-money. In short, she was doing all she possibly could to hurt my interest so that if my father had lived a few years longer, I should have had but the skeleton of an estate. I have as yet behaved to her with wonderful decorum. I have been mindful of the divine precept to forgive even until seventy times seven. But it strikes me also that there is a weakness, a silliness, in not at least breaking off all intercourse with so bad a woman. The distinction between the good and the bad will be confounded if they are treated alike well. I beg to have your counsel at large upon this. The Lord Advocate, who is at the head of my father's executors, is of opinion that she might have had more. But that is only saying that my father was entirely under her influence.

When you have answered this, be so good as burn it. Indeed I have for many years so opened to you all my heart in our correspondence that I depend on your friendship to burn all my letters or to take care that in case of your death they be delivered to the representative of this family at the time.

SEVEN

Lairdship and Literature
1782–1785

With his father's death, Boswell has a new lease on life. He throws himself into Auchinleck estate affairs and eagerly assumes the mantle of a laird, for the time being casting off hypochondria and unhealthy metaphysical introspection. He almost loses sight of his former Edinburgh self of shadows and gloom. His wife's health improves and now he is able to thrive in his paternal acres with his entire family, undisturbed by the cloudy spectacle of his father and stepmother's sourness.

But that does not last, and after seven weeks he returns to Edinburgh to pick up his legal practice. Soon enough, his melancholia revisits him, along with the old pattern of trying to conquer it and essentially failing. His stamina is remarkable. But metaphysical doubts of all kinds resurface, as do his drinking, gambling and illicit sexual adventures. And there is the gnawing anxiety about Margaret's health.

On top of this he realises that his dreams of political and public advancement, through some appointment in London or election as Member of Parliament, are likely to come to nothing. It occurs to him that the great and powerful, including Edmund Burke who has worked for him in the past and will again in the future, are ignoring him and his cries for help. Because of his impulsiveness and taste for appearing in print, he is perceived as a loose cannon, a risky man to trust with responsibility.

Ultimately, as always, his literary efforts lift him up. With Dr Johnson's death, he is deprived of the chief solace outside his family, but at the same time Johnson's death ushers in for him the most important period of literary activity of his entire life. The time has finally come to do something with all the journals he has kept of Johnson's conversation. He starts with his Tour to the Hebrides, aided by the almost miraculously well-timed appearance of a literary saviour in the person of Edmond Malone, the great Shakespearean scholar. Whether the ensuing years of work on Johnson's life will bring him the lasting happiness that has eluded him remains to be seen, but at least that work *minimises his fears of his own evanescence and recurring sense of worthlessness.*

1782

Monday 18 November 1782 [Edinburgh]

[Lord Kames][1] had been so ill, was said to be dead; had come to town night before. Went to him at night. His clerk was reading *Cecilia* to him.[2] 'My Lord, I am happy to see you. How do ye do? Are you here?' 'Yes, I am here. I know I am here, as Descartes that he existed.' BOSWELL. '*Cogito, ergo sum.* I am sure you are here, for I've shaken hands with you. Well, what news from the other world?' KAMES. 'They told me it was not time for me yet.' BOSWELL. 'We're much obliged to them. We shall take as good care of you as we can.' I talked of my father's easy death. He said, 'Some men die very easily.'

I told him that I had experienced a wonderful change upon myself this autumn. I had felt a high relish of the country, of actual farming; had looked with eagerness on ploughed land, and upon a dunghill with as much pleasure as upon Lady Wallace[3]. 'I am glad of it,' said he. 'But take care lest, like a fit of enthusiasm in religion, it go off and leave you as you were.' I said I hoped not. But I was only mentioning it as an extraordinary metamorphosis. I had acquired a new sense...

He asked me to stay and sup. I said I was afraid it would be inconvenient for him. He said, 'If it were so, I would not ask you.' ... Before supper he called for a glass of port and asked me to pledge him, which I did. I declare his judgement, memory, and vivacity were the same as ever, except that there was some failure of animal spirits, as he had for some time been weakened by a looseness. It was truly a pleasant scene, and as I was in sound cheerfulness, I relished it egregiously. It was agreeable to see a man who had been tortured by Liberty and Necessity and other metaphysical difficulties sitting at his ease by the fireside.

Tuesday 10 December 1782

... I went to Lord Kames and had, I think, the most agreeable interview of any ... He was so ill on Saturday night he could not see me ... He seemed to be very low at first. I sat down on the settee by him. I said I was afraid of disturbing him. I would stay only six minutes. Said he: 'If you'll let me draw my breath sometimes, you may stay the evening.' ...

I know not how Lord Kames and I got upon the subject of a future state, or rather how I introduced it. I said it was hard that we were not allowed to have any notion of what kind of existence we shall have. He said there was an impenetrable veil between us and our future state, and being sensible of this, he never attempted to think on the subject, knowing it to be in vain. And he applied his mind to things which he could know. 'But,' said I, 'we may conjecture about it.' Said he with that spring of thought, that kind of sally for which he was ever remarkable, 'You'll not go to hell for conjecturing.' ... 'Well,' said my Lord, 'it is true this body is put into the grave. But may we not have another film, another body, more refined? The ancients,' said he, 'all describe a future state as having enjoyments similar to what we have here. Let us lay aside the prejudices which we have been taught. Suppose we have other bodies. Why may we not have all the pleasures of which we are capable here? For instance, the pleasure of eating. Why not that, in a more delicate manner?' I mentioned before he spoke of eating, our being told we are to have music. 'And,' said he (raising himself with an earnestness while I was all attention, and coming closer to me), 'and there is another pleasure'; (I thought, though I divined what he meant clearly enough, that he should speak it out plainly, so waited in silence till he proceeded) 'why not have the pleasure of women?' 'Why not,' cried I, with animation. 'There is nothing in reason or revelation against our having all enjoyments sensual and intellectual.' I mentioned advances in knowledge, and seeing our friends again and eminent men. He was calm and kindly tonight...

I told him my father's death had relieved me of the horror I used to have at the act of dying, yet there was something discouraging that one could see no appearance of transition in death. 'None to our senses,' said he. He seemed to be firm in his belief of future existence. I said to him, 'It is curious what a propensity there is in the mind of man to listen to anything like information as to the particulars of a future state. I was all attention to your Lordship just now, as if you had been there and had returned again. And yet you can tell no more about it than I can.' I laughed a little at this.

There was in his appearance tonight something that put me in mind of my father when in a calm, serious frame. He quieted me somehow. I told him I frequently could not help thinking my father was alive and that I might go and consult him; and when I was taking care of his improvements at Auchinleck I thought I was doing what he approved; and I wished always to preserve the notion of his seeing what I was about...

I was so intent on his conversation tonight I let the candles be long without snuffing. So there was a dim, solemn light, which increased my feelings as sitting with a dying man. Yet he was as much Mr Henry Home, as much Lord Kames as ever. Sometimes death is like a fire going out gradually. Sometimes like a gun going off, when the moment before the explosion all is as entire as ever.

Friday 20 December 1782

... Supped at Lord Kames's. Was shown into his room. He was sitting in his armchair ... He seemed very spiritless from bodily weakness. I wished much to hear him say something as a dying man. It was unsatisfactory to be with a very old man, and a judge, and perceive nothing venerable, nothing edifying, nothing solemnly pious at the close of his life ... I could make nothing out of him tonight. I rose to go away. He asked me to stay for supper. I said I was afraid of intruding (or being troublesome, or some such expression). He cried with keenness, 'O GOD!'

Sunday 22 December 1782

I called [on Lord Kames] between three and four. Mrs Drummond [Lady Kames] said he was as weak as yesterday, and in bed, and she desired I would go in and inquire for him. He liked it. I went to his bedside and said, 'As I was passing by, I just called to inquire for you, my Lord. I am going to dine with your old friend Lady Dundonald. 'Not at that time of day!' said he. 'Yes' said I, 'it is after three o'clock. How are you, my Lord?' 'Oh, dinna ask foolish questions. I hope to be better in the evening ... Have you been debauching with Lady Dundonald?' ... He did not speak to me any more ... And while I looked at him, I could not help wondering why he did not answer me as usual. To perceive Lord Kames, who used to be all alive, now

quiescent, was a change to which my mind could not easily agree ...
I sat a little longer by him. He twice put out his hand and took mine
cordially. I regretted that he did not say one word as a dying man.
Nothing edifying, nothing pious. His lady told me he had not said a
word to her of what he thought of himself at present. I sat a long time
with her ... And soon after, my Lord to my surprise was supported
into the room and sat down on a settee. But he did not speak and
seemed to be very uneasy, so in a few moments he made a sign to his
servant and was led away. I came home. The children said divine
lessons in the evening.

[Kames died on 27 December 1782.]

1783

Monday 17 February 1783

(Writing the 19th.) ... Was in poor spirits, but wrote an Hypochondriack
[essay][4] with curious ingenuity of thinking. I wrote chiefly to please
myself, and with a view to make out a couple of proper volumes of
that periodical paper; for my partners of the London Magazine did not
relish it much. I was not in the least affected by this, because I had no
opinion of their taste in writing, for they wished rather for a merry
essay. I wrote to Dilly that I wished to continue it to No. 70, the years
of man's life. But if the partners really thought they could find a variety
of materials all better, I should close it next month. It is wonderful
how the spur of engagement makes me write.

Sunday 23 March 1783 [London]

... I told him [Johnson] how this day in Hyde Park by reading my
overseer's letter I had found I had an anchor. He said, 'I am sorry you
should want an anchor. I doubt if your fondness for London is so
great as you talk.' 'Sir, a man must know himself if it be so.' 'I am
not sure of that.' He was in that kind of humour tonight that he had
no allowance to make for anything but the rational part of our nature,
nothing for fancy, nothing for inclination ... I spoke of building on

the old situation at Auchinleck.[5] He raged against this, and said, 'It is too late to indulge fancy. It may do in a young man, but not at your age; not in a man with a wife and five children.' He even checked every ambitious wish which started from me, and wanted to beat me down to dull content with my present state. He said, 'Talk no more in this way. People will only laugh at you, or be vexed, as I am.' In short he was in a very disagreeable frame tonight; and amidst all my admiration of his great talents, I recollected how Sir John Pringle objected that he had not wisdom for giving counsel. He meant that sagacity or common sense which is practically of more consequence than all the genius of the first writers. And I recollected also how roughly he discouraged me from my exertions in favour of the Corsicans, by which, as I myself foresaw, I raised myself twenty degrees higher in fame and in general advantage as a social man than I should have been had he been successful in repressing my generous Ardour.

Thursday 3 April 1783

After drinking coffee and tea, Langton and I went and sat awhile with Dr Johnson at Mrs Thrale's. I was easier with him in Langton's company, and talked again of my coming to settle in London. He was in a more agreeable frame than the Sunday evening when I have complained of him in this journal. He said, 'I am unwilling to repress your ambition. But it appears to me that as you would be obliged to maintain your family in some dignity here, you would find yourself embarrassed. When you come to London now and leave it because you cannot afford the expense of living in it constantly, people applaud your wisdom. Were you to settle here, they'd despise you as a man ruining himself.' This was strong sense, and it did repress my ambition. We went upstairs a little to Mrs Thrale and her daughters. I then called at Mr Burke's, who was not at home; so I walked quietly to General Paoli's, took my warm port and water with sugar and a bit of dry toast, had some good conversation with the General, who agreed with Dr Johnson, and then went to bed.

20 April Easter Sunday 1783

... I [am] an electrical eel to Dr Johnson. Also the boy in the bowling-green who gives him the bowls. Langton said it was a great deal to do this, to be always ready. And he plays with no common bowls. His the long bullets. Great rubs. Often *rides*. Seldom *draws* a cast. But gets to the jack better than anyone. Sometimes not quite safe to give him the bowls. If not in humour will toss them away or throw them at your head . . .

[From *the* Life of Johnson] I dined with him, with Mrs Williams, Mrs Desmoulins, and Mr Lowe. He seemed not to be well, talked little, grew drowsy soon after dinner, and retired. Upon which I went away.

[But Boswell did not leave, as he told his readers in the Life. Instead he then recorded, but did not include in the Life of Johnson, the following 'Extraordinary Johnsoniana — Tacenda — to be kept secret.']

After dinner, when the Doctor had retired to take a nap, I believe, and Mrs Williams also was gone, Mrs Desmoulins, Lowe, and I remained. Said Lowe: 'Now, Ma'am, let us be free. We are all married people. Pray tell us, do you really think Dr Johnson ever offended in point of chastity? For my own part I do not believe he ever did. I believe he was chaste even with his wife, and that it was quite a Platonic connexion' (grinning a smile with his one eye to me). MRS DESMOU-LINS. 'Ah, Sir, you are much mistaken. There never was a man who had stronger amorous inclinations than Dr Johnson. But he conquered them. Poor Logie[6], who was very intimate with him, knew this, and has talked to me of it. It has been said there was a criminal connexion between him and Mrs Williams; and I remember a lady observed that no woman could behave so impudently if she did not know she had this awe over his head.' BOSWELL. 'But why an awe? What need he care?' MRS DESMOULINS. 'Sir, he would not like it. But I do not believe it.' BOSWELL. 'Not indeed. I have heard people joke about it, and talk of Dr Johnson's seraglio, which included you as well as her, Madam. But nobody had a serious belief of anything for a moment.' LOWE. 'I do still think the Doctor never has had any inclination for women.' MRS DESMOULINS. 'But he has.' LOWE. 'I do not believe his marriage was consummated.' BOSWELL. 'Do you know, Ma'am, that there really was a connexion between him and his wife? You understand me.' MRS DESMOULINS. 'Yes, yes, Sir. Nay, Garrick knew it was consummated, for he peeped through the keyhole, and behaved like a rascal, for he made the Doctor ridiculous all over the country by describing him running round the bed after she had lain down, and crying, "I'm coming, my Tetsie, I'm coming, my Tetsie! ph! ph!" (blowing in his manner). She was near fifty when the Doctor married her, and he was only two-and-twenty, and I believe she never had any love for him but only to get money from him. They did not sleep together for many years. But that was her fault. She drank shockingly and said she was not well and could not bear a bedfellow. And I remember once when at Hampstead a young woman came on a visit. I lay in the room with Mrs Johnson in a small bed. She said, "It will not hold you both. So if you will promise not to tell Mr Johnson, you shall sleep with me. But if he should know this, he'd say, "If you can bear a bedfellow, why not me as well as another?" ' LOWE (waggishly). 'He has been so bad a bedfellow she could not bear him, and this has made her take to drinking. He has had no passion.' MRS DESMOU-LINS. 'Nay, Sir, I tell you no man had stronger, and nobody had an opportunity to know more about that than I had.' LOWE. 'I am sure, Madam, were I to indulge that passion, I should think you a very agreeable object.' BOSWELL. 'You'll forgive me, Madam. But from what you have said, I beg leave to ask you if the Doctor ever made any attempt upon you?' MRS DESMOULINS (Lowe and I closing in upon her to listen). 'No, Sir, I have told you he commanded his passion. But when I was a young woman and lived with Mrs Johnson at Hampstead, he used to come out two or three days in a week, and when Dr Bathurst lived there, he'd go and stay with him till two or three in the morning. The maid went to bed, as she could not be kept up, and I used to sit up for him; and I have warmed his bed with a pan of coals and sat with him in his room many an hour in the night and had my head upon his pillow.' BOSWELL. 'What, when he was in bed, Madam?' MRS DESMOULINS. 'Yes, Sir. He'd desire me to go out of the room, and he'd go to bed; but to come back in a little while and talk to him – and I have come and sat on his bedside and laid my head on his pillow.' BOSWELL. 'And he showed strong signs of that passion?' MRS DESMOULINS. 'Yes, Sir. But I always respected him as a father.' BOSWELL. 'What would he do? Come now' (Lowe like to jump out of his skin), 'would he fondle you? Would he kiss you?' MRS DESMOULINS. 'Yes, Sir.' BOSWELL. 'And it was some-thing different from a father's kiss?' MRS DESMOULINS. 'Yes, indeed.' LOWE (approaching his hand to her bosom). 'But would he? eh?' MRS DESMOULINS. 'Sir, he never did anything that was beyond the limits of decency.' LOWE. 'And could you say, Madam, upon your

oath, that you were certain he was capable?' MRS DESMOULINS. 'Y-
yes, Sir.' BOSWELL. 'But he conquered his violent inclination?' MRS
DESMOULINS. 'Yes, Sir. He'd push me from him and cry, "Get you
gone." Oh, one can see.' BOSWELL. 'So you saw the struggle and the
conquest.' MRS DESMOULINS. 'I did.'

What a curious account. That he should bring himself to the very
verge of what he thought a crime. Mr Burke, to whom I afterwards
told it, thought there was nothing very curious – just common human
nature. But it was certainly curious in so eminent a man. She said, 'I
have many times considered how I should behave, supposing he should
proceed to extremities – and as I told a lady who once put the question
to me, I do own that such was my high respect for him, such the awe
I felt of him, that I could not have had resolution to have resisted
him.' BOSWELL. 'But you never felt any inclination for him as a
woman does for a man?' MRS DESMOULINS. 'O no, Sir.' BOSWELL.
'I cannot imagine it of any woman. There is something in his figure
so terribly disgusting.' MRS DESMOULINS. 'Yet Sir, one cannot tell.
His mind is such. Now Mrs Thrale has been exceedingly fond of him,
and I am convinced now that he is in some way vexed about her.
Either she has made a proposal to him which he has thought improper
and has declined, or he, presuming on her great fondness, has made
a proposal to her, which she has rejected. But I am convinced one or
other is the case.' I mentioned the dispute between Sir Joshua Reynolds
and me whether the Doctor would yield to the amorous solicitations
of the Duchess of Devonshire. Mrs Desmoulins said he would not. He
would instantly feel such a contempt and indignation that he would
treat her with disdain. 'I believe, Madam,' said I, 'if the contempt and
indignation rose at once, as I think it would do, he would spurn her
from him. But if he at all hesitated – as the woman who deliberates is
lost – it would be the same with him.' 'Yes, Sir,' said she, 'were he to
deliberate, I allow he might yield.'

Thursday 29 May 1783

I soon announced to him that I was to set out for Scotland next day.
JOHNSON. 'Langton, Sir, is as good a man as lives.' BOSWELL. 'But
ridiculous.' JOHNSON. 'It will do him no harm in the next world.
But it makes him be laughed at in this.' BOSWELL. 'He is a man of
great knowledge.' JOHNSON. 'Yes, Sir. But it never lies straight. There

is never one idea by the side of another. 'Tis all entangled. And then he drives it in so awkwardly upon conversation.' (I had said, 'Sometimes I think of being a grave, solid man, who keeps his mind to himself; sometimes a fine, gay, flashy fellow as in the County [Ayr],' upon which it was that he introduced Langton as a foolish instance of studied behaviour: that he was first grave and silent and then gay and talkative. I said he was the reverse of the insect which is first snail then butterfly, for he was first butterfly then snail. JOHNSON. 'Who said this of him?' BOSWELL. 'I say it now.' JOHNSON. 'It is very well said.' BOSWELL. 'I say very good things sometimes.' And then I said, 'But he is a worthy man,' after which followed what is above.)

'Sir,' said I, 'It is incredible how absurd and weak I am, with talents – I mean in conduct and in speculative opinions; for I do very well when I come to an argument in law. I have not force of mind.' 'Sir,' said he, 'endeavour to get as much force of mind as you can. Live within your income. Always have something saved at the end of the year. Let your imports be more than your exports, and you'll never go far wrong.' I said I would. 'But,' said I, 'what hurts me sometimes is the question how it is to be with us. Is not the last part of our conduct of most weight? What I mean is, if there be such a thing as balancing accounts, suppose a man has been seven years good and then acts wrong, will his former good have any effect in his favour?' 'Sir,' said he, 'if a man has been seven years good and afterwards is by passion hurried to commit what is wrong, he'll have the reward of his seven years. GOD won't take a catch of him.' . . .

I asked him to come to Auchinleck. He said, 'I cannot come this year. But when I grow better, as I hope I shall, I should gladly come. I should like to totter about your Place, and live mostly on milk, and be taken care of by Mrs Boswell. We're good friends now, are we not?' I told him yes. I said to him that in the range of various people whom he had known, none had a more sincere respect and affection for him than I had. He said he was persuaded of it, and added, 'If I were in distress, there is no man I would come to so soon as you. I should come to you and have a cottage in your park.'

He advised me to set my mind on practice as a lawyer in Scotland. Every new cause would teach me more law, and the more causes I had, the less surprising it would be that I was made a judge. I should court employment by all honest and liberal means, be still more civil to agents than before, as they naturally suspect a rich man to be proud.

'Have them to dine and show them you are desirous of practice.' I was animated by his manly conversation . . .

When I told him that Mrs Strange assured me their family was kept in London for £500 a year, 'Sir,' said he, 'it may be so. But your family would not be kept in London for £500 a year, nor £1,000 neither. You would wish to make a figure suitable to your rank. Your lady would wish to do it.' 'Oh, Sir, she has nothing of that turn. I believe she has cost me less for clothes than any woman, not only of her rank, but really in any decent style.' JOHNSON. 'Ah, Sir, were she here, it would be different. And you would not be satisfied if, when she went about to the conversaziones, she were not as well dressed as other ladies.'

He was mild and cordial this morning. I felt a tender concern at parting with him, as it was very uncertain if I should see him again. I complained of not having him near me to consult upon all occasions of any difficulty. He said, 'Write.' 'Then,' said I, 'you will not be unwilling' (or slow, or some such phrase) 'in answering my letters?' He said, 'No.' I got up to part from him. He took me in his arms, and said with solemn fervour, 'GOD bless you for Jesus Christ's sake.' I then hastened away. He called after me, 'You'll see' (or 'you'll call on') 'Mrs Williams.' 'Yes, Sir,' said I. 'I intended to see her.' I did so, and sat down a little by her. She said Dr Johnson would not allow he had been very ill whenever he got pretty well again. But when his complaints returned, he was very dreary, or some such phrase. I told her he had said he would leave me my letters in case he should die before me. But I doubted he would neglect it. For he had told me since I came last to London that he had not made his will. I regretted this, and said he should be spoke to about it. She thought I ought to speak. I said it was a delicate subject. But I would write to him about it. I bid her adieu. I then gave Frank a crown and bid him drink his master's health, or take good care of him. I walked away from Dr Johnson's door with agitation and a kind of fearful apprehension of what might happen before I returned.

The day was now fair. I walked along till I came to a barber's shop near the New Church in the Strand. And there I was shaved and had my hair dressed and my clothes brushed.

Thursday 30 October 1783 [Auchinleck]

I was not at ease. I know not what had affected me. But I was irritable in a sad degree; and upon some careless expression of my dear wife's which hurt my pride, I burst into a paroxysm of horrible passion, of which I feel ... a most painful recollection. I put some shirts in my greatcoat pocket, got upon my horse, and rode out in a hurried dubiety which way I should go to be from home. Luckily I met Mr Dun in the road to the church, and returned with him and entertained him with tolerable decency. It is shocking to be subject to such fits of violence. I was harsh to the most valuable of wives, and at the same time shuddered at the apprehension of the dismal uneasiness it would give me to reflect on this, should I be unhappy enough to have her taken from me by death. I regret that she had not more acquaintance with the various workings of my mind.

Boswell to Thomas Barnard, 14 May 1784 [London]

[Barnard was Bishop of Killaloe and a member of The Club.]
... I cannot but still be dissatisfied that my talents are exerted in a narrow sphere; and I think I am now almost resolved to remove to London, for my town residence where I may possibly feed my ambition, and am sure of gratifying my taste. The Sage Johnson discourages me by two objections. One that I cannot afford the expence of keeping a family here. The other that I shall be estranged from my ancient territory of Auchinleck. To the first I answer, that a man may live here upon any scale he chooses; and neither I nor my wife are eager for 'vain shew', though I acknowledge it would please me, had I a superfluity of wealth. To the second I answer that London is now the capital of the whole Island of Britain; that the difference of going and coming between London and Auchinleck and between Edinburgh and Auchinleck is just six days in a year, and that I shall be of more consequence at home, and be of more service to my friends and neighbours by establishing myself on a good footing here. I have reasonable hopes to distinguish myself in Westminster Hall; and I have not a faint prospect of getting into Parliament. Let me sum up all with the striking thought that I have but one life in this world, and that after years of suspense, I feel that I cannot be content until I have tried my fortune upon this great scene of action.

1784

[*Edmund Burke travelled to the University of Glasgow to be installed as Rector without informing Boswell that he was going there. Hearing of Burke's visit, Boswell mounted his horse at Auchinleck and rushed to Glasgow to see him, almost killing himself in the process when he fell from his horse and a cart wheel just missed his head.*]

Saturday 10 April 1784 [Glasgow]

When I got to the Saracen's Head Inn at Glasgow, where Mr Burke was, I wrote a fair copy of the letter on the other side of this paper and sealed it, intending to have made a waiter convey it to him, without letting him know that I was in the house. But as I walked upstairs, I met his servant, who knew me and asked if I would not go in to his master. I bid him first give Mr Burke that letter.

From Boswell to Edmund Burke, Glasgow, Saturday morning, 10 April 1784

Your long silence, and particularly your not complying with my request to be informed of the time of your coming to Scotland, have made me apprehend it is possible you may have taken offence at my Tory zeal against a political system which you have supported[7]. Yet I cannot easily believe that Edmund Burke is deficient in liberality of sentiment. You will please impute partly to my anxiety, partly to your neglect, that I have for a moment entertained a fear of what I should very much regret, for your sake as well as my own. I am grateful for your kindness. I love your virtues. I admire your talents. And on hearing of your arrival, I have hastened from my seat in the country to wait on you, to show you all the respect I can, and to entreat I may have the honour to see you at Auchinleck.

But if in this cursed strife, you 'have ought against me', and will not be fully 'reconciled' with me even in this week[8], pray tell me frankly, that our difference may not be exposed to the profane, and that we may either not meet at all, or in your ever memorable words to the worthy Langton, 'live pleasant'. I am, my dear Sir, your faithful, obliged, humble servant.

No sooner had he read it than he came quickly into the parlour where I was, and approached me with all the good humour he ever showed at our meeting. We embraced complaisantly, and I said something of my apprehension, and of my joy that it was without foundation. He said, 'What has made you go so mad of late? As to quarrelling with you, that cannot happen; for as you observe as to Langton –' In short he conveyed a compliment that my pleasantry was such that one would be a loser by quarrelling with me. He said too, 'As to telling you when I should come to Scotland, I did not know myself till we were dismissed.' ... He invited me to breakfast with him directly, as he was to go to the College at ten. In a little Lord Maitland, who accompanied him, came to me, and was very polite and affable. I went and joined them at breakfast. Lord Daer, Professor Dalzel, Professor Dugald Stewart, Professor Millar and Dr Adam Smith were all of the party. I was a little flurried from the consciousness of my being in the midst of opposition. But I conducted myself very well. I had a curious feeling while I recollected that the first time I had contemplated the character of Mr Burke was at Glasgow, four-and-twenty years ago, when I was a student of law there, and viewed him like a planet in the heavens. And now here he was actually Lord Rector of that university, and sitting in the town, a reality almost as wonderful to my mind as if some eminent man of a distant age had been before my eyes. The feeling was heightened by reviving the thoughts which I had then in company with Adam Smith, and those I had now. I believe it is exceedingly rare to have the power of thus bringing together the impressions of periods of time widely separated; for in general those of an early period are obliterated when those of a period present but long posterior to it are lively. I exulted in the soundness and comparatively [sic] strength of mind of which I now was conscious.

About ten we walked to the College. I should wish to describe all that passed minutely, but life is too short. Suffice it to say that Edmund Burke looked exceedingly well in the Lord Rector's gown, and showed that so great a literary honour sat very becomingly on one who had no solemn appearance, but a pleasant air of genius....

Wednesday 23 June 1784 [London]

The anxiety of his [Johnson's] friends for preserving so valuable a life as long as human means might be supposed to have influence made them plan for him a retreat from the severity of a British winter to the mild climate of Italy. This scheme was at last brought to a very serious resolution at General Paoli's, where some of us had often talked of it. It was considered that he would be exceedingly helpless and dull were he to go alone, and therefore it was concerted that he should be accompanied by Mr Sastres the Italian master, who we were persuaded would wait on him with a very affectionate attention, and who very readily agreed to go. One essential matter however we understood was necessary to be previously settled, which was obtaining from the King such an addition to Johnson's pension as would be sufficient to put him in a situation to defray the expense in a manner becoming the first literary character of a great nation and, independent of all his other merits, the author of the DICTIONARY OF THE ENGLISH LANGUAGE. The person to whom I above all others thought I should apply to negotiate this business was Lord Thurlow, Lord High Chancellor of Great Britain, but I first consulted with Sir Joshua Reynolds, who perfectly agreed with me. I therefore, though personally very little known to his Lordship, wrote to him . . .

Sunday 27 June 1784

He this day said he should wish much to go to Italy, and that he dreaded next winter in England. I said nothing, but enjoyed a secret satisfaction in thinking that I had taken the most likely way to get him to Italy in a proper way.

[On Monday 28 June Boswell received a reply from the Lord Chancellor saying he would do what he could to obtain an addition to Johnson's pension.]

Monday 28 June 1784

This letter gave me an elevated satisfaction which has been seldom equalled in the course of the events of my life. I next day went and showed it to Sir Joshua Reynolds, who was exceedingly pleased with it, and in the warmth of his friendly joy said that he himself would undertake that Mr Sastres should have a pension of eighty pounds for his life. He thought that I should now communicate the negotiation to Dr Johnson, who might afterwards complain if the success with which it had now been honoured should be too long concealed from him. I intended to set out for Scotland next morning, but he cordially insisted that I should stay another day, that Johnson and I might dine with him, that we three might talk of his going to Italy and 'have it all out'. I hastened to Johnson and was told by him that he was rather better today. BOSWELL. 'I am really anxious about you, Sir, and particularly that you should go to Italy for the winter, which I believe is your own wish.' JOHNSON. 'It is, Sir.' BOSWELL. 'You have no objection but the money.' JOHNSON. 'Why no, Sir.' BOSWELL. 'Why then, Sir, suppose the King should give you the money? I have reason to think he will.' JOHNSON. 'Why should you think so?' BOSWELL. 'You are not to be angry with me.' JOHNSON. 'No.' BOSWELL. 'Why then I will tell you fairly what I have done. I have applied to the Lord Chancellor.' He listened with much attention while I communicated to him what had passed, then warmly called out, 'This is taking prodigious pains about a man.' 'O Sir,' said I, with most sincere affection, 'your friends would do everything.' He paused, grew more and more agitated, till tears started into his eyes, and he exclaimed with much emotion, 'GOD bless you all.' I was so affected that I also shed tears. After a little while he renewed his grateful benediction, 'GOD bless you all for JESUS CHRIST'S sake.' We remained for some time unable to speak. He got up suddenly and quitted the room [quite melted in tenderness]. He stayed out a short time till he had recovered his firmness, and I should suppose till he had offered up his solemn thanks at the throne of grace ... I secured him for Sir Joshua Reynolds's next day ...

On Wednesday 30 June he and I had the friendly confidential dinner with Sir Joshua Reynolds, nobody being present but ourselves ... Both Sir Joshua and I were so sanguine in our expectations, knowing the very high esteem which the Sovereign had expressed for him, that we expatiated with confidence on the large provision which we were sure would be made for him, conjecturing whether it would be a donation at once or an augmentation of his pension, or both. He himself yielded so much to our enthusiasm as to suppose it not impossible that our hopes might in one way or other be realised. He declared that he would rather have his pension doubled than a grant of a thousand pounds, 'for,' said he, 'though probably I may not live to receive as much as a thousand pounds, a man would have the consciousness that he should be for the rest of his life in splendour.' Considering what a moderate proportion six hundred pounds a year bears to innumerable fortunes in this country, it is shocking to think that a man so truly great should think it splendour ... We endeavoured to flatter his imagination with agreeable prospects of happiness in Italy. 'Nay,' said he, 'I must not expect that. Were I going to Italy to see fine pictures, like Sir Joshua, or to run after women, like Boswell, I might to be sure have pleasure in Italy. But when a man goes to Italy merely to feel how he breathes the air, he can enjoy very little.' ...

[In September Reynolds wrote to Boswell that the effort to obtain more money for Johnson had been unsuccessful. This infuriated Boswell but Johnson, for whom the news must have been a cruel disappointment, took it with dignity and grace.]

Boswell to William Temple, 8 July 1784 [Carlisle]

Thus far on my way to Scotland, I am waiting at an inn till the coach from London to Carlisle comes up, to carry me on. I arrived at Lichfield on Friday, and was elegantly and hospitably entertained at the Rev Mr Seward's who lives in the Bishop's Palace. He is a Canon of that Cathedral, far advanced in years, much of a gentleman ... and been besides in a great deal of high company; and he is one of the writers in Dodsley's Collection of the Female Right to Literature etc. His charming daughter has established that right in brilliant characters. Though not now a girl, she is still beautiful. Her eyes are exquisite – her en bon point delightful, her sensibility Melting. Think of your friend (you know him well) reclined upon a sofa with her, while she read to him some of the finest passages of her Louisa. How enchanting! Many moments of felicity have I enjoyed. Let me be thankful. Maupertuis thinks that human life should not be taken as a whole, but as moments of good and of evil – the latter of which he is of opinion predominates. I fear it is true as to men of delicate and keen sensations. But Dr Johnson at a choice dinner at Sir Joshua's the day before I left London just we three, asserted that though a Man should have more pain than pleasure from having his faculties finer and more improved, he should not wish they were duller. 'Be as perfect as you can' said he, 'be the consequences what they may.' A noble thought! ...

... Now that I am resolved to try my fortune at the English bar you and all my friends must encourage me, as Dr Johnson *mirabile dictu!* does in his powerful manner. He tells me, 'If you only take care not to exceed your income, you cannot be wrong. You have every chance in your favour. You will *certainly* improve your mind, and you *may* improve your fortune.' You cannot imagine with what firmness I am prepared to live in London upon a small scale for some time, and after having entertained (I may splendidly) the first company at my table, to entertain none at all. Burke says this is very manly. What a triumph shall I have if I acquire wealth and grandeur to the ancient family of Auchinleck. The difficulties are to keep the family seat in good repair, to be once a year there for some months with my family, the travelling expenses amounting to £120 annually, to get my debts kept quiet and gradually cleared off. To restrain my eagerness for variety of scenes, to conduct myself with prudence. But strict economy will, I trust, do a great deal, and a determined attendance on Westminster Hall, and a course of study and practice of the English law will give me a desirable steadiness. Your visits to town will be cordials to me. But remember you must make full allowance for the difference between your feeble and my robust constitution. I must, however, have a philosophical resolution not to be cast down though I should have no [legal] practice. Of this I am aware as a thing possible. My retreat to the bench in Scotland will, I trust, be secured. Did I mention to you that I talked over my scheme fairly to the King, and that His Majesty was graciously pleased to listen to me, and talked of it afterwards to the Lord in Waiting?

... My great consolation [for having to return to work in Edinburgh] is my permanent consequence as Baron of Auchinleck, which is believed to be of much more value than I know it to be. What pleasure shall I feel when I am free from debt! May I not indulge the ambitious hope of being a *Baron* indeed, of being created by my Sovereign *Baron Boswell of Auchinleck in the County of Ayr* . . .

I read some of my *Hypochondriacks* to Dr Johnson, and he said, 'Sir, these are very fine things; the language is excellent, the reasoning good, and there is great application of learning. I may say to you what my wife said to me after I had published four or five of my *Ramblers*. "I thought very well of you before. But I did not expect anything equal to this." I would have you publish them in a volume and put your name to them.' Now my *priest!* What say you? He is to revise them, and then I shall bring them forth in two or perhaps three elegant volumes.

[This was short-lived euphoria, for on his return to Edinburgh and Auchinleck, the realities of his finances and his wife's illness struck him forcibly and hypochondria overwhelmed him. He remained despondent for four months.]

Boswell to William Temple, 20 July 1784 [Edinburgh]

All is sadly changed. I was three nights comfortably well with my family at Auchinleck. Then my wife accompanied me to Edinburgh, where I was no sooner arrived, than at once, as if plunged into a dreary vapour, my fine spirits were extinguished, and I became low and as miserable as ever. There certainly never was a mind so local as mine. How strange, how weak, how unfortunate is it that this my native city and my countrymen should affect me with such wretchedness. I have been harassed by the arguments of relations and friends against my animated scheme of going to the English bar. I have lost all heart for it. My happiness when last in London seems a delirium. I cannot account for it. ... When I go thither at present as a gentleman of fortune, I am on a footing with the first people, easy, independent, gay. But were I settled as man of business, labouring up hill, and anxious for practice, my situation would be quite different. Add to all this, the weakness of her [Margaret's] lungs renders her very unfit to live in the smoke of London. Last night she had a return of spitting of blood. In short, my friend, I tell you in confidence I am satisfied that my airy scheme will not do.

Friday 17 December 1784 [Edinburgh]

(Writing 19th.) This must be ever remembered as a melancholy day, for it brought me the dismal news of my great and good friend, Dr Samuel Johnson. His physician, Dr Brocklesby, favoured me with a very full letter dated on Monday the 13, the night of his death. I was stunned, and in a kind of a maze. I had company engaged to sup with us; and as it might have appeared vain affectation to forbid their coming, I received them and behaved with much ease, and said nothing of the dismal news but to worthy Sir William Forbes, just as he was going away. I did not shed tears. I was not tenderly affected. My feeling was just one large expanse of stupor. I knew that I should afterwards have sorer sensations.

Saturday 18 December 1784

... In the evening I read two accounts of Dr Johnson's death in the *Public Advertiser* and *London Chronicle*. And I had a letter from Mr Dilly mentioning it, and in the true spirit of the *trade* wanting to know if I could have an octavo volume of 400 pages of his conversations ready by February. I had had a letter from him lately suggesting that I might be the editor of all his works and write his life. I answered him that I had a large collection of materials for his life, but would write it deliberately. I was now uneasy to think that there would be considerable expectations from me of memoirs of my illustrious friend, but that habits of indolence and dejection of spirit would probably hinder me from laudable exertion. I wished I could write now as when I wrote my *Account of Corsica*. But I hoped I should do better than I at first apprehended.

Boswell to Sir Joshua Reynolds, 23 December 1784 [Edinburgh]

You may believe I am exceedingly desirous to know every thing that can be told concerning our departed friend [Dr Johnson], and I therefore earnestly beg you may be so kind as indulge me with a communication of interesting particulars. It is said in the newspapers and I have no doubt is true that you are one of his executors. I trust to your honour that if my letters to him exist they will be given back to me as they were written in full confidence as to a Confessor. Probably he has burnt them as I understand he destroyed in that manner a little before his death a number of papers.[9] Pray let me know what manuscripts are saved. I shall be vexed if he has either intentionally or as the newspapers say inadvertently deprived the world of two quarto volumes of memoirs of his life a considerable part of which I have read. They indeed contained a variety of things which it would have been improper to expose to the *profanum Vulgus* but his confidential friends might have made a most valuable selection for I never saw so minute a diary as was kept of the thoughts and actions of that wonderful philosopher during certain periods for it was not continued long without interruptions. I owned to him my having read in those volumes and asked him if he thought I could have resisted the temptation when I found them lying open? He said with one of his complacent smiles, 'I believe you could not.' I told him that for once I was tempted to be a thief – to have carried them off and never seen him more and I asked how this would have affected him. He said 'It would have made me mad.' I almost regret I did not commit a *splendidum peccatum* which all of us would now have forgiven on account of the rich stores of mind which it would have preserved. I have amongst my Johnsonian collection a transcript of a few passages of his diary. My large stock of materials for writing his life I mean to arrange and publish. But I shall be in no hurry. I wish first to see many other lives of him that I may both receive additional information and correct mistakes and misrepresentations. I shall be much obliged to you, My Dear Sir, for your assistance. I have a peculiar treasure which my assiduity has secured – a great number of his conversations taken down exactly – scenes which were highly delightful at the time and will forever afford instruction and entertainment. How dismal a blank does his departure make! I stretch after him with enthusiastic eagerness. I cannot doubt that he is exalted to immortal felicity. I should think that the coldness in a certain quarter [the King] of which you informed me would now be felt with regret. What a dignified satisfaction must Lord Thurlow enjoy! Pray was the letter in the newspapers to him from Dr Johnson genuine? If it was, how came it to be made public? I left with him a half bound volume of printed essays which he undertook to revise.[10] Mrs Desmoulins knew of it. I beg you may take care of it for me. I am soon to publish my Journal of a Tour to The Hebrides in company with him. I hope you will like it.

1785

Boswell's dream, recorded Sunday 6 February 1785

Last night I dreamt that I was with my much respected friend, Dr Johnson. I saw him distinctly, sitting in a chair opposite to me in his usual dress. He talked something which I do not perfectly recollect about his library not being in such order as he could have wished, and gave as a reason his being hurried as death approached. He then

said in a solemn tone, 'It is an awful thing to die.' I was fully sensible
that he had died some time before, yet had not the sensation of horror
as if in the presence of a ghost. I said to him, 'There, Sir, is the
difference between us. You have got that happily over ...' I then felt
myself tenderly affected, and tears came into my eyes, and clasping
my hands together, I addressed him earnestly. 'My dear Sir! pray for
me.' This dream made a deep and pleasing impression on my mind. I
this morning invoked him to pray for me if he heard me and could
be of influence. He did not absolutely disapprove of invoking departed
saints. God grant us a happy meeting!

Friday 20 May 1785 [London]

Resolved to be seen at Court recently before my *warm appearance*.
Dressed in my scarlet suit. Looked like a baron, and was quite easy...
[The king] ... graciously asked me, 'How do you go on with your
account of your' (I think *great* or *old*) 'friend?' 'Sir,' said I, 'I am going
first to give my *log-book*, my journal kept *de die in diem*, of the curious
journey which Dr Johnson and I made through a remote part of *Your
Majesty's dominions*, our Highlands and Islands' (thus connecting them
with the King – throwing them into his bosom). 'It will be more a
journal of Dr Johnson than of what I saw.' I said, 'Whenever it is
finished, I shall take the liberty to present it to Your Majesty.' The King
gave a gracious nod. Said the King: 'But when are we to have' (or
'when are you to give') 'your other work?' (meaning the *Life*). 'Sir,'
said I, 'Your Majesty a little ago remarked that people were sometimes
in too great a hurry before they had collected facts. I mean to avoid
that fault, and shall take time, as I intend to give a very full account
of Dr Johnson.' KING. 'There will be many before you.' BOSWELL.
'I wish first to see them all, Sir.' KING. 'There will be many foolish
lives first. Do you make the best.' BOSWELL. 'I cannot presume to
say I can do that, Sir. But I shall do as well as I can.' KING. 'I believe
you knew him more intimately than any man.' BOSWELL. 'He was
very good to me, Sir. And I was very forward with him.' In the course
of the conversation he politely named *Dr Johnson* to the Duke of Gordon
and Lord Effingham, that they might know who was meant. KING. 'I
believe he was a very worthy man; a sincere Christian upon principle.'
BOSWELL. 'He certainly was, Sir. And a great friend to subordination'
(bowing respectfully to the Monarch), 'in which he had great merit.

As he used to say himself, "I have great merit in this. For I hardly know who was my grandfather."' KING. 'There is one question concerning him to which I have never yet been able to get an answer, which is how he was so much master of the literature of his age, and yet for the last thirty or five-and-thirty years of his life was never known to study.' BOSWELL. 'Sir, he had the quickest apprehension and the most retentive memory of any man I suppose that ever lived. And he had a faculty of scooping out the substance of any book without reading it all through. He read very few books all through.' (I think I said not above five, which was contracting too much.)

[Boswell has now fallen into a steady rhythm of working sessions with Edmond Malone, revising his Tour to the Hebrides for publication. He also makes a point of introducing himself again to the notorious Margaret Caroline Rudd, who had enchanted him in July 1776.]

Tuesday 9 August 1785

I went this very day, and as I suspected, found – Mrs Rudd. She looked as well as ever and was exceedingly agreeable ... She begged to see me sometimes, and that [I] would not forget her. It was a romantic scene.

Wednesday 10 August 1785

Malone was busy with his Shakespeare. So we did not sit upon my Tour . . .

Thursday 11 August 1785

Malone devoted the whole of this day to me, that we might get forward with my Tour. I breakfasted, dined, drank tea, and supped with him, and sat till near two in the morning. Yet we did not get a great deal winnowed, there was so very much chaff in that portion of it.

Sunday 28 August 1785

. . . Sir Joshua also talked of Mrs Rudd, and said that if a man were known to have a connexion with her, it would sink him. 'You,' said he, 'are known not to be formally accurate' (or some such phrase) 'in your conduct. But it would ruin you should you be known to have such a connexion.' I did not see why this should appear so peculiarly bad.

Wednesday 21 September 1785

Breakfasted home pretty well. Went to the levee. The King asked me when I went north. I said, 'On Saturday, Sir. My book has detained me longer than I expected. But tomorrow is *coronation* day with me too. "Finis coronat opus." It will then be finished. Your Majesty will have it tomorrow evening.'[11] I then went to Malone's and settled my title-page. Then to Baldwin's; gave all my directions as to have four books tonight for Sir Joshua, Dr Brocklesby, Dempster, Langton, all of whom Malone had kindly asked to meet me at his house at dinner next day to be impanelled on the *Tour* . . .

Thursday 22 September 1785

Dined at Malone's with the jury [reviews] on my *Tour*, who applauded it much. Had my baggage with me, and drove to Dilly's at night, having bid a cordial adieu to my kind and elegant friend Malone.[12]

Boswell to Edmond Malone, 30–31 October 1785 [Auchinleck]

. . . My wife says she wishes I would set out so as to be with you as soon as possible that we may confer as the [second] edition proceeds. It is humiliating to experience how much I depend upon *situation* for happiness. My wife says my spirits are like brandy set on fire. If not constantly stirred the flame will go out. The weather here at present is exceedingly cold – snow, frost, sleet. I suffer from it.

EIGHT

Johnsonianissimus
1786–1789

With the Tour to the Hebrides out of the way, Boswell is now free to concentrate on his magnum opus, the Life of Johnson. In 1785 he begins collecting materials from hundreds of sources that would supplement his own collection, at the centre of which, of course, is his journal. It would seem that a straight and open road lies before him to literary immortality. But there never had been, is not now, and never would be any such thing as a clear road ahead for him.

To begin with, although he wants profoundly to honour Johnson and preserve him for posterity, literary fame is not an all-consuming goal for him – less now, in fact, than ever before. He feels time is running out and yet he has not realised so many of the prizes to which he had always told himself one with his abilities and imagination was entitled: social distinction, wealth and political influence. He panics at the thought of wasting the rest of his life grinding it out as an advocate in Edinburgh, even with a huge literary project to engage his imagination and talents. He has to get to London, live there and be admitted to the London Bar as a barrister – even though he is almost totally ignorant of English law, shrinks from learning it, and is therefore highly unlikely to succeed – and take his chances with the famous and great. The city's sparkling energy and excitement will save him. His London friends – especially Edmond Malone, who saw early on that the Life of Johnson (like the Tour to the Hebrides) could be written only in London – advise caution but mostly encourage him to make the move. So in 1786 he uproots his family from Edinburgh and Auchinleck and takes them to London to take up a new life. London turns out to be less his promised land, however, than the despairing scene of shattered dreams.

1786

[Boswell has rented a house on Great Queen Street, big enough to accommodate his family; he will move into it in May and they will join him later. He is admitted to the Bar and readily continues with his hectic social life of dinner parties and other convivial social gatherings. This includes resuming a relationship with Mrs Rudd, even as he waits for Margaret's arrival.]

Sunday 26 February 1786 [London]

... I drank rather too liberally and sat too late, as I was to go to the Lord Chancellor's[1] levee. I did not get to his house till half an hour past nine. I was shown up to the drawing-room. Everybody was gone, and my Lord had left the room. But the servant said he would let his Lordship know. In a little he came, took me by the hand courteously ... CHANCELLOR. ... 'You are going to publish something more about Dr Johnson?' BOSWELL. 'Yes, my Lord. I am going to give *tota vita senis.* Your Lordship did me the honour to read my *Tour?*' CHANCELLOR. 'Yes, every word of it; and yet one cannot tell how. Why should one wish to go on and read how Dr Johnson went from one place to another? Can you give a rule for writing in that manner? Longinus could not. But indeed I always thought rules absurd.' BOSWELL. 'Your Lordship's getting through the book is as extraordinary as Dr Johnson's getting through the tour. He was a most extraordinary man; and, my Lord, as life is uncertain, and it is possible I may die or your Lordship may die before my *Life of Dr Johnson* is published, let me now have the pleasure of telling you a very high compliment which he paid your Lordship. He said, "I would prepare myself for no man in England except Lord Thurlow. But when I am to meet Lord Thurlow, I should wish to know a day before."' The Chancellor smiled complacent at this. I proceeded: 'It would be curious to conjecture how he would prepare himself.'

I then, I know not how, introduced the King's having refused an addition to Dr Johnson's pension, and I said, 'My Lord, I am a very forward man. Your Lordship will check me, or you may knock me down if I say what is improper. But I put it fairly to your Lordship: was not the King made to understand that Dr Johnson wished to have an addition to his pension to enable him to go abroad, and yet His

Majesty did not grant it?' The Chancellor admitted it was so. 'But,'
said he, 'will you make no allowance for an east wind, or any other
circumstance? A philosophical mind will do the same justice to a king
as to a beggar. In the multiplicity of applications which press upon
the King, that may not have been attended to.' In short, the Sovereign
was much obliged to his Chancellor, who shielded him very ably. I
was, however, very sorry, and mentioned Sir Joshua's saying that he
did not expect generosity from the King. But that merely as a good
economist he wondered that the application was not successful, for
how could he lay out his money so well in purchasing fame? 'Then,'
said Lord Chancellor, 'Sir Joshua is angry that the King is not so vain
as he would have him' (smiling). 'That is a good answer to Sir Joshua's
Argument.' ...

I hastened in fine spirits to communicate this good reception to
M. C. [Mrs Rudd]. I was first told not at home. 'Not at home!' said I.
'Gone to bed.' 'Gone to bed!' said I. 'At this time of night?' 'Has on
night clothes, but I dare say will see you,' says John. In I went. But
was reproved and hastened away. Supped on cold meat at Malone's
with Courtenay most agreeably.

Tuesday 7 March 1786

I ... found M. C. dressing, and was told she had sent me a note.
She would meet me at one. Never shall I forget the scene. So good,
so generous, was she. Elegantly dressed: satin *couleur de rose*; her hair in
perfect taste – not to be discomposed. A kind wish to give me felicity
before a separation.

[*The following memorandum Boswell wrote for himself, probably dating from
this period, indicates how far he had progressed with Mrs Rudd.*]

If the Roman Emperor who had exhausted delight offered a reward
for the inventor of a new pleasure, how much do I owe to thee, who
hast made the greatest pleasure of human life new to me. I used to
look on love with feverish joy or childish fondness. All madness or
folly, though delight. Thou hast shown me it rational, pure from evil.
How keen the fire that thus clears the dross from the most precious
ore!

Boswell to Edmond Malone, 31 March 1786 [Lancaster]

... And now for La Signora Piozzi. I received her[2] by the coach only last night Thursday, and her journey down cost me within 6d. of her original price. I however did not grudge the cost, and *devoured* her as you say. I had before the book arrived, two *whets* [extracts] in the [*Morning*] *Herald*. She is a little artful impudent malignant devil. She relates that Johnson in reference to her *littleness* said insects have gay colours. I will add insects are often *venomous*, have often *stings*. It is clear that she means to bite me as much as she can, that she may curry favour with Mrs Montague.[3] P. 44 is *undoubtedly* levelled at me; for it *describes* what the jade has often seen me do – but with Dr Johnson's *approbation*; for he at all times was flattered by my preserving what fell from his mind when shaken by conversation, so there was nothing like treachery. I must have the patience of *Job* to bear the Book of *Esther*. But I shall trim her *recitativo* and all her *airs*.

The *retort* upon *in vino veritas* which she affects to *remember* as if she had been *present* was told to her by myself, and she has either forgotten or misrepresented the true state of it. The argument in favour of drinking was maintained by me one evening at the Crown and Anchor where Dr Johnson supt with Lord Binning and his tutor, Langton, myself, and [one or two] more. But I have it all in writing. It was I think in [1772; my] journal will ascertain it all exactly. I am pretty certain his answer to *in vino veritas* was 'Sir a fellow is not much to be regarded who cannot speak truth till you fill him drunk.' I am *sure* he did not *point* his fire personally to *me*, till after I had teased him long, to bring out all I could. When I at last said, 'But Sir would not you drink to forget care, to forget every thing disagreeable?' JOHNS. 'Yes, – if I sat next to you.' *Madam* as *Sam* said 'has no care about truth'. We shall concert a genteel reply to her, to this effect. She should have stated *fairly* – not said by *me* as might be supposed from her manner of expressing it, but *reported* by me to have been said by Dr Johnson ...

Boswell to Margaret Boswell, 18 May 1786 [London]

My Dearest Life, you are too good to me. I had your letter of the 11th yesterday, and today I have that of the 13th. I am afraid you hurt yourself by writing to me oftener than you should do, that I may not be too much alarmed. I have been two nights in the Queen Street house[4], the solitude of which is very dreary and gives room for very uneasy thought. Your illness distresses me deeply; and the situation of my affairs is really wretched. I begin to apprehend that it was very ill-judged in me to venture to come to the English bar at my time of life. I see numbers of barristers who I really believe are much better qualified for the profession than I am languishing from want of employment. How then can I reasonably hope to be more successful than they? The encouraging speeches made me by many people I suspect were made merely to please me, or without any serious consideration. I indeed see the necessary application to be much more difficult than I imagined. Yet, on the other hand, my long-indulged notion that I might rise to wealth and honour at the English bar is not yet quite subdued; and it may be advisable to make a farther trial to get myself thoroughly satisfied, so as never again to be disturbed by it should I not succeed. In this wavering state I go on attending Westminster Hall, where, however, I own I am entertained, as business is done with so much accuracy and in so agreeable a manner. If I do not hear soon that you are better I will hasten down to you, for all considerations on earth are nothing compared with your comfort. If you should by GOD'S blessing have a speedy recovery, I should wish that you would come up by slow journeys; because if I do continue making the trial of the bar here it would be proper to attend till this and the next term are over, and to go the Home Circuit, by which means I could not get home till the middle of August, and that is a long, long time from this date. The distance at which we are is terrible. May GOD in His infinite mercy grant us a more pleasing prospect. I am quite cast down.

The difficulty of determining what to do with my sons here is another uneasy consideration. Worthy Langton is so afraid of public schools that he teaches his himself. Both of mine have such constitutions that I should think it too great a risk to board them with strangers amongst many boys, and yet I could not well have them at home. At this moment it seems to me a curse that I ever saw London, since it has occasioned so much vexation to my family and may estrange us from our own fine Place. I am not now much disturbed by apprehensions of being ashamed to return to Scotland, for during my last visit I was convinced that I can put a good face on it. But perhaps it would be better to let our children have a year or two of this place and then quietly retreat. I am pretty sure that London will not be the same to me as a settled man that it was to me as an occasional man. O! my dearest, most valuable friend, counsel me! The great consolation is that we can stop when we please...

... I have no expectation now of any continued happiness in this life, as it appears to me I shall only suffer disappointments. Let me be thankful for such a blessing as my dear, dear M. M. And such fine children.

Monday 26 June 1786

... Malone and I walked in the Temple garden [of Inner Temple Hall]. He then went home with me and had some bread and wine and water, and heard me read some Johnsoniana. He argued clearly with me not to be uneasy, for that I might be at the English bar, or the Scotch bar, or no bar at all, and nobody would trouble their heads about what I did. And I might make a trial at Westminster Hall at little expense, and have my children improved by being in London.

Boswell to Margaret Boswell, 3 July 1786 [London]

My Dearest Life, That I am very selfish you have told me, and I have acknowledged it. But I am not so excessively selfish as to resist your very strong and persuasive letter of the 23 June, in which you describe the uneasiness it would give you should our family be removed to London and the desolation of Auchinleck so feelingly, that I yield to you...

For some time past, my constitutional melancholy has been grievous. The solitude of this house has frightened me into constant dissipation. I do not mean vice but a perpetual succession of company; and my mind has been quite unhinged. My anxiety about you and the children has been dreary, and I have upbraided myself for neglecting you.

I am now convinced that there is no probability of my getting great practice at the English bar; and therefore there is not an adequate reason for putting you and my children into a state of inferiority and running the risk of their being estranged from Auchinleck.

The difficult question then is, what should be done? Lady Forbes says that if you are assured that I will return with you to Scotland in the spring you will have no objection to come to London and bring Veronica and Phemie and pass the winter; and your mind being relieved from the imagination of being banished forever from your country and friends, that much of London would do you no harm, and then I shall have made a fair trial of my chance in Westminster Hall. But, in truth, I already see clearly that I have so poor a chance that it is not advisable to persist. Mr Malone thinks otherwise, and I am loath to contradict his opinion. Yet it is shocking to me, who have been used to have a competent share of practice, to be altogether without it, and I am impatient and fretful. Lady Forbes and Sir William are full of your kind attention to them last winter, and have proposed that as it may be better for Sandy to be at the High School while we are in London, he shall be at their house as one of their own sons. How agreeable is it to be so well with them! My next consideration is Dr Johnson's *Life*, which it is necessary I should get ready for the press soon, that the public attention may not be diverted to some other object; and as I have collected a great variety of materials, it will probably be a work of considerable value. Mr Malone thinks I can write it nowhere but in London. But I feel that it is almost impossible for me to settle to it here on account of the agitation to which I have been used; and, especially in the present state of my mind, how can I settle to it, when I am in a kind of fever to think of my absence from her I love, and who is my own, and with whose illness I was lately so deeply alarmed? . . .

Tuesday 4 July 1786

. . . I sauntered into various coffee-houses 'seeking rest and finding none'. The Virginia, Maryland, and *Greenland* Coffee-house attracted my curiosity, but I found nothing particular in it. I walked on beyond Cornhill to see if there were any coffee-houses so far east. I grew somewhat weary. I perceived *Aldgate Coffee-house*. Went into it and had tea and dry toast and butter. This was poor relief. When I got into the streets again I was so depressed that the tears run down my cheeks. I thought of my dear wife and children with tender affection. I upbraided myself for being so long absent from them. I upbraided myself for neglecting Auchinleck . . . I came to my solitary house drearily, as to a prison. What a poor, wretched day!

Sunday 9, Monday 10 and Tuesday 11 July 1786

These three days I confined myself to the house and took only tea and dry toast to breakfast and boiled milk and dry toast at night, and this discipline made me quiet, and I did the first part of Dr Johnson's Life, and made arrangements for more of it. My resolution now was to put it in such a way that I could carry it on at Auchinleck, and as soon as I had it so, I was to set out, and wrote so to my wife. My brother T. D.[5] called and was earnest for my doing this; and as I was to return in November to polish and complete the Life, he was for my instantly letting my house, so as to have no kind of settlement in London, and not to bring up my wife to be in an inferior state. I was sadly dejected and very impatient to be gone. Fortunately Malone called on me on Tuesday, and with his judicious and elegant spirit roused me from despair. He urged that I must act rationally; that I must not appear so ridiculous as to fly off from Westminster Hall before there was time for its being well known that I was in it; that I must fulfil what I had proposed, and must certainly be at least one winter at the bar; that going no circuit was a kind of declaration that I did not mean to continue in the profession, therefore I must go the Home Circuit. He did not insist upon my going to every one of the towns, but I must go to one or two of them, so as that it might be said I went the Home Circuit. That I might then go to Scotland and bring up my wife and two eldest daughters for the winter and live upon a very moderate scale; and that all my notions about inferiority were pride, which ought to be repressed. He thus saved me from acting in a way of which I must have repented grievously. When the fit of melancholy was off I should have seen the despicable fickleness of my conduct and been vexed by the ridicule with which I should have perceived myself looked upon.

Wednesday 12 July 1786

My intention was to persevere in confinement and fasting for a week. But about four o'clock, in came Malone and Courtenay in good spirits and told me I must go with them and have a ramble into the country and dine at Dulwich. I was feeble in body and dim in mind. But I was complaisant to my two excellent friends, dressed quickly, and away we walked beyond Westminster Bridge, while London and all its animated objects only oppressed my sensorium. We took a hackney-coach at length, and the motion did me good. Courtenay, who while in the Ordnance made many friends, called at a Captain Dickinson's at Camberwell and got a couple of bottles of madeira for us. I had never been this way before, and I imperceptibly got some relish of the beautiful scenes around. The old College at Dulwich pleased me much. We found at this place the Greyhound, the best inn, just as ill-provided as one in the remote parts of Scotland or Ireland. However, we got bacon and eggs and mutton chops. It was curious to me after my three milk diet days to have for the first time in my mouth bacon and eggs. I eat hearty. We had a bottle of port, but it was such stuff we did not drink it. Small beer, good ale, and our admirable madeira warmed me and raised me again into temporary felicity while in such company. We walked pleasantly to London and had some cold beef and wine and water at my house.

Sunday 16 July 1786

Malone and Courtenay and young Courtenay came about one in a hackney-coach and I joined them to go, as we had fixed on Wednesday, to see Norwood[6] and dine in the open air. We clubbed our dinner. Courtenay furnished two bottles of madeira, Malone, a couple of roasted chickens. I furnished cold roast beef, some slices of ham, a loaf, two bottles of port, a bottle of cider, salt, table-cloth, plates, glasses, knives, and forks. My servant went on the back of the coach. It was a delightful day. We did not find the gipsies; indeed we did not look much for them, but dined under a tree. I wished for a room and table and chairs. We were troubled by ants. However, it was very well. We walked to the top of the hill above Dulwich, from whence we saw all London before us on one side and on the other an extensive rich country. I wished to have a house here. It was as wild as Arthur's Seat. We walked home, drank tea at Camberwell like sober citizens, and had some pickled salmon, etc., at my house.

[Boswell returns to Auchinleck on 21 August 1786 for one month, then returns to London with his entire family. His journal for the ensuing period is significantly titled, 'Full Trial of My Fortune at the English Bar'. The trial is a disaster. In late November he travels with Lord Lonsdale to Carlisle, retained by Lonsdale as counsel to the election there in mid-December. He hoped to be appointed by Lonsdale as Recorder of Carlisle, and then on the strength of that a Member of Parliament. Three weeks in Lonsdale's bullying, autocratic, and grubby company were enough to remove any of his illusions about this would-be benefactor's generosity, but he persevered in his hopes and thus created excruciating tensions for himself between his ambition and love for wife and family. Margaret grew steadily sicker as the months wore on, and in the middle of all these uncertainties and recurring hypochondria he kept at the Life. Malone even persuaded him to attend Westminster Hall 'laxly' for legal business so that he could really push on with the Life. Boswell despairs of ever obtaining any significant amount of legal business.]

1787

Friday 6 April 1787 [London]

... My wife's illness was sadly alarming. She had feverish heat and cold and sweatings in the night.

Monday 9 April 1787

... My wife was very ill. I cried bitterly. Sandy comforted me like a man older than myself, saying, 'O Papa, this is not like yourself.'

Wednesday 11 April 1787

Was shockingly ill. Walked in the streets and grew better. Went with my wife and daughters in a coach to the Green Park and walked and sat there. Captain Bruce Boswell and Colonel Craufurd dined with me. My wife was not able to appear. I was much sunk. I upbraided myself for not having made her set out for Auchinleck before, as she now thought she would not be able to go. I was overwhelmed with dismal thoughts of death. She had lamented her poor children when I talked how melancholy I was.

Monday 7 May 1787

... My wife did not spit blood ... I was sunk and dreary at night not knowing what to resolve as to my family, whether to keep them here or send part down. In short, I was very unhappy. My straitened circumstances vexed me. I felt a warm longing after old Auchinleck, but could not bear the thoughts of receiving all company that might come, and many other circumstances.

Friday 11 May 1787

In a full suit of black clothes went to His Majesty's levee, where I had not been since I brought my family to London. I wished to observe how he behaved to me, as I thought of presenting a memorial to him to have some mark of his royal favour to me. It was a delightful day. I was in fine spirits and full of courtly ideas. There were not many present. The King accosted me with a pleasing look: 'How does writing go on?' BOSWELL. 'Pretty well, Sir.' KING. 'When will you be done?' BOSWELL. 'It will be some time yet. I have a good deal to do to correct Sir John Hawkins.' KING. 'I believe he has made many mistakes.' BOSWELL. 'A great many, Sir, and very injurious to my good friend.' KING. 'I do not believe Dr Johnson was so fond of low company in the latter part of his life as Sir John Hawkins represents' ('describes', or some such word). I visited Malone.

[In December 1787 Lonsdale offers Boswell the Recordership of Carlisle and tears him from his family and Life in London to travel up to Carlisle to be 'elected'. He was gone for almost four weeks and recorded his various humiliations and frustrations under Lonsdale's thumb with painful vividness.]

Thursday 20 December 1787

I was agitated at finding now that LOWTHER [James Lowther, 1st Earl of Lonsdale] really had resolved publicly to befriend me, but I was somewhat embarrassed. I told his Lordship that I was very much obliged to him; that I should be very happy to have the honour of attending his Lordship. But that I had several engagements, and Johnson's Life to finish. However, I would try, and I begged that his Lordship would allow me till the evening to consider of it. He did so.

I ran home and talked with my wife, who was for my going. So was
T. D., who thought it *could do no harm* ... At night I returned to Lord
Lonsdale's and told his Lordship that I would wait on him. He kept
Mr Garforth and me late and then Mr Garforth and I walked through
Berkeley Square cordially. He said this was a feather in my cap.

Friday 21 December 1787

In a great hurry to be with Lord L. at nine *to a second*. Disturbed my
family and was quite uneasy as I did not reach his door till twenty-
five minutes after nine. Garforth smiled and said I would be time
enough two hours after. Was shaved in the [servants'] hall. Satterthwaite
came. Mr John Lowther[7] came about eleven knowing how it might be.
I went to Partlet's Coffee-house in Shepherd's Market and had a pot of
coffee and a muffin comfortably. Between twelve and one Colonel
Lowther came and told me the coach was at the door. We talked of
the Great Man. He said the way to get anything from him was not to
ask it but rather to have somebody to oppose it, such as saying, 'What!
would you bring Boswell into Parliament?' He seemed to think I might
have a chance for Cockermouth in room of Senhouse, who hated being
in. I objected that I should not choose to be a Member of Parliament
without any will of my own but merely to utter Lord L.'s inclination.
He said, 'He was very honourable to his Members and did not require
this.' But Satterthwaite afterwards told me sagaciously that it was
understood in all cases where a Member was brought in by any person
that he should not go against him.

When I returned there was no appearance of his coming out of his
room. The uncertain waiting was very unpleasant. Governor Penn[8]
came, and asked if that was the first set of horses, for he had known
a set changed at the door, the first having waited very long. It was
frost this morning. Penn said he knew him well, and when he was
with him, he just eat, drank, and slept as it might happen, without
any thought about the matter. 'It is a school,' said he, 'to which people
must be broke in.' ... All the things were put into the coach. He
ordered them all to be taken out again and, I suppose, packed in some
other way. At length he came to us and first took Penn into another
room, and then Garforth, who had been waiting since half past seven.
At last Satterthwaite was desired to go into the coach and to wait in it
at the corner of Davies Street, to which it drove down Charles Street.

Soon after, the Earl, accompanied by Mr John Lowther and Penn and me, walked up Davies Street and turned into Hill Street, and so got to the coach. What this round-about mode could mean was a mystery. But they told me he never went into the carriage at his own door, but had it waiting at some place out of sight. He and I sitting frontwards, and Satterthwaite and Mr John Lowther backwards, drove off. He felt himself hungry but did not stop till we came to Stevenage. There, in the kitchen, we had beefsteaks, a fowl with mushrooms, porter, and four bottles of port. He and I this day sang several of the songs in The Beggar's Opera. We stopped at night at Buckden and had tea and white-wine whey.

Saturday 22 December 1787

Satterthwaite and I had colds, his the worst. We breakfasted at Stilton. Victor, his Norman servant, rode always on and had horses at the door each stage. He made the boys drive excessively hard. We dined at Grantham but poorly, there being what is called the squires' monthly dinner in the house, which took all their best things. Ale and two bottles of port. At night we stopped at Doncaster. We had sung less today. He felt himself ill in his stomach. Would take only tea and eggs, and Satterthwaite only an egg and white-wine whey, and Mr John Lowther only tea and a jelly. There was a comfortable supper put down and I eat some veal cutlet, a grey plover and a bit of another, and a tart, and had ale and gin and water. We had sung some more Beggar's Opera today, and he had talked a good deal of bawdy.

Sunday 23 December 1787 [Doncaster]

Excessively cold. A good deal of snow had fallen for two days. He had been very ill in the night and taken forty-four drops of laudanum. He was in my room before I was up, as I had disbelieved the maid's report, and indeed Satterthwaite had put me on my guard that, after the horses were put to and his company all up and ready, he sometimes would not come down for two hours. We had breakfast before setting out. Satterthwaite was worse. He did not seem to mind him but made him go and see his things put into the coach. Victor was exceedingly sick and seemingly unable to go on and hinted piteously to get into a carriage, but in vain. He was ordered to stop at Boroughbridge and have some dinner ready for us. When we got there (Mr John Lowther having gone out at Ferrybridge), Victor said he could go on. But he of his own accord desired he might be put into a warm bed and come in the stage-coach next day, and ordered a man from the inn to ride on and order horses and send one on from next stage. The landlord, Rushton, was a stupid, miserable-looking old man.

He damned and scolded about bad beef, etc., and was irritated that a bolt of the coach was broke and had to be mended, which took some time. Two shillings were charged. He would give only one; and because the Wetherby boys had not come in less than an hour and twenty minutes he gave them only sixpence apiece and nothing to the ostler, nor would he take back a guinea in the hire, which they said was light. His way was to call, 'Boys, I'm in a great hurry. Make haste or I'll give you nothing. I am not to waste my lungs calling to you. I have looked my watch. If I have to call to you again you shall have nothing. If I must waste my lungs I must save my cash.'

Only one bottle of port today, porter, and ale. Then Gretabridge. Hard driving. Sad work for the last part of the road near to Lowther.[9] Had asked me on road, 'What will you have?' I said, 'Only a little warm milk.' Satterthwaite said the same, but when L. was out of the room complained seriously to me of giving such a precedent, and said, 'When we had had a damned bad dinner, we should have had something good at night.' George Saul[10], whom we found here, had come from Lancaster and hardly eaten all day. He durst not say he would have anything till L. was out of room, and then said if he could have had but a piece of bread and cheese. I mentioned his wish and he had it. L. took warm milk. Dreadfully cold in the waste [empty] dining-room, and there was a railing of iron painted green to keep us off the hearth that it might be clean. In this whim he was obstinate. Bedroom cold, cold.

Monday 24 December 1787 [Lowther Hall]

Satterthwaite took care that each of us should have some tea and roll and butter in our rooms, but beware telling. Breakfast not till about one: I sat a long time with Satterthwaite in his room, where he had a good fire and bid me take care to have the same, as it was the most comfortable thing I would have here. He said there was a total want of all comforts. A man for instance might be days without having his shoes cleaned. Garforth sometimes wiped his with the carpet. He spoke strongly of the Earl's want of attention to make people happy about him, and told how a gentleman observed how great a man he might be if he were but commonly civil. 'Nay,' said another, 'if he were but commonly uncivil.' He said no man of parts had ever submitted to go along with him. He said he did not wish to put those attached to him into good situations because that would make them independent. Yet, from his great fortune and influence he ought to have [have in his influence] a Lord of the Treasury, a Lord of the Admiralty, and a Commissioner both of Customs and Excise. Yet he said for himself he could not complain, for He had done very well for him. He said he talked freely to me as looking upon me now as attached to Him, and he would be glad to communicate with me.

All this struck a damp upon me, and I saw how fallaciously I had imagined that I might be raised by his interest, for I never would submit to be dependent. Satterthwaite said he thought all along that He would make me Recorder of Carlisle, for He had praised my conduct at the election and said I had gone as far for his interest as my character in my profession would allow. I now foresaw many difficulties in being Recorder, as he could not bear even decent attention to be paid to his opponents in the Corporation.

We were kept long hanging on for dinner even after it was on the table, and I believe sat down about seven. Tolerably well. Port, hermitage, frontignac, rather too much...

Wednesday 26 December 1787 [Lowther Hall]

I paused and asked myself what I had to do with such a man. All the way down I had been uneasy and anxious at being away from my dear wife and children, and to look forward to a much longer absence overwhelmed me. I also felt how unworthy it was of the Laird of Auchinleck to hang on thus upon a savage. I thought I heard my worthy father say, 'James, I left you independent.' I wished to elope from him and was quite impatient to be gone, and I studiously meditated how I should decline the Recordership. It was dismal always when I went to bed. He slept a good deal after dinner, never minding his company, and we never had wine but from his own hand.

Thursday 27 December 1787 [Lowther Hall]

... George Saul is a merchant in Lancaster. He was nine years in America. He is a large, stout man with a ruddy, good-humoured countenance and a black scratch-wig. Being in America has taught him the management of wood fires. He has for seven years been zealously attached to the interest of Lowther and has lived much with Lord Lonsdale, whom he respects and fears, yet sees his faults. There is a remarkable naivete in his manner. He holds down his head and shakes it and winks when he talks of the Earl's opponents, calling them dogs who want to pull down the king if they could. When he looked at the cold, green wood which his Lordship had insisted should burn, he said, 'If this be your fifty thousand a year, my service to it.' The Earl inquired, and good dry logs were found in the servants' hall. We had them and the fire blazed, and we were warm at last.

Dinner was between six and seven, ox-cheek broth, tripe, plum pudding, which he said no man cook could make well, but the camp butcher did. We had Nicholson today at dinner. Only two bottles of wine, I forget which. But the grievous thing was that no man could ask for a glass when he wished for it but had it given to him just when the fancy struck L. The glasses were large, eight in a bottle.

While LONSDALE was drowsy after dinner, we sat in stupid silence, and I groaned inwardly. I could not help showing impatience at this treatment. I turned myself some time restlessly upon my chair and then went up to my room, where I meditated sullenly what I should do, sometimes thinking of setting out on foot for Clifton, a village two miles off through which the mail-coach comes, and from thence getting off for London this very night, sometimes of going to bed. The immediate pressure of uneasiness was terrible, and the dreary waste of the cold house, with nobody but Saul, a sycophantish fool, to talk to made me almost desperate. I fancy my mind was in a state very similar to that of those wretched mortals who kill themselves. I did not stay long but resumed resolution and went back to the dining-room, thinking to go off next morning in daylight. No notice appeared to have been taken of my absence, and I weathered out the night till about twelve, when I got to bed.

Friday 28 December 1787 [Lowther Hall]

I had a headache in the morning, and as I had no hope of being warm but in bed and wished to escape the dreary waiting for breakfast, I resolved to be ill and lie in bed all the forenoon...

Between ten and eleven I grew weary and rose ... I walked in a troubled frame between the dining-room and my bedroom and upon the gravel before the house till it was one o'clock, and still there was no appearance of L. or of breakfast. I felt the insolence so as to meditate writing to him in the keenest terms that he did not seem to know who I was. My impatience to be gone increased. The servants, a parcel of negligent wretches unless when the Lion roared and frightened them, were always solacing themselves in their hall and other places, so that none of them were to be seen, and consequently they did not observe when anyone went out or came in. I got my travelling-bag all packed, and taking it in my hand, I walked off.

... The snow, which was lying deep, discouraged me somewhat ... I returned again for a little while to the house. But observing two men with carts going out at the gate, I went to them and was informed they were going to Clifton. So I put my bag into one of the carts and walked on before till I was out of sight of the house, and then got into another of them and sat upon a sack and drove along. Having had no breakfast, being very cold, and being sadly fretted, I was quite gloomy and could look upon nothing without disgust. A gleam of felicity came across my mind when I thought of being again with my wife, and I thought that nothing upon earth could make up to me for being absent from her, even for a week or two at a time. All my fondness for Miss Peggie Montgomerie, all her admirable conduct as a wife and mother were before me in a warm glow. But I feared that she would despise my impatience and flight, and that I should be made ridiculous on account of thus forfeiting my expectations from the Great Lowther, whom I had celebrated in lofty language. I was also not without apprehension that he might resent my abrupt departure as impertinent to him. But I thought I could write to him declining the Recordership in very smooth, respectful terms. And keep my own secret, never mentioning his intolerable behaviour.

The carts went towards Temple Sowerby, and I quitted them where they turned off from the Penrith road, and then walked on to Penrith carrying my bag, which was pretty heavy. I had seen no inn at Clifton

which looked comfortable, so luckily did not stop there. At the end of
Penrith I bought some paper at a shop and there left my bag, and then
walked into the town uncertain what I should do. I got notice at the
George Inn where Mr Saul was and, having found him, told him that
I feared Lord L. might put off from day to day going to Whitehaven
... so I was come here to take the coach. I sounded him if he thought
Lord L. would take it amiss if I went off. He was clear he would. So I
being by this time somewhat better by exercise resolved I would return
and speak to him, and I could get off by the coach any day ...

I went to the George and had a pot of coffee and muffin and toast,
the first comfortable meal I had enjoyed for some days, and I insensibly
felt myself restored. It struck me to compare my poor state at this
house now with what it was when here last with my wife, etc. The
cold and dark weather was gloomy, and for two days I had been
troubled with one of my foreteeth being half broken off yet the root
of the broken part not separated from the gum. It was a mouldering
memento of my mortality.

I walked to Lowther with Saul and carried my bag all the way. I
was fully tired and all in a sweat, so went to my room and changed
myself from head to foot and felt stout. I was glad that I had avoided
writing a letter to Lord L., for a strange one it must have been. I went
down to the dining-room and sent a message to his Lordship that I
begged leave to speak with him for a few minutes. He came instantly.
I said to him in a flurry, but composing myself as well as I could, that
I took the liberty to speak to him what I was going to have written,
that I had lain awake all night thinking of the Recordership which his
Lordship had been so good as to promise me, and that after much
wavering it did appear to me that I ought not to accept of it. That his
Lordship's having given me the preference had done me great honour;
that I was conscious of this and had the honour as much as if I had
been elected. (He very politely said it should be as I pleased and there
was no appearance of his being displeased.) I said it was happy that
the matter had not been communicated. 'No,' said He, 'it is entirely
between you and me.'

I said I would presume to speak freely. The truth was I had been of
a very good standing at the bar in Scotland. I had been flattered and
persuaded that I might succeed in England, in a wider sphere. My
ambition had led me to make the experiment. I found I had been
deceived. Jack Lee and others who had encouraged me had told me

that the difference of practice in the two countries was not great, that I had only to acquire a few elements and forms. But that I had found the difficulty very great at my time of life. That I had tried the Northern Circuit in vain, and had then gone the Home Circuit with as little success. That this of the Recordership was a *dernier ressort*, a forlorn hope, but that upon thinking it over and over again, I thought that my returning to the Northern Circuit and still having no business would make me appear in a much worse light; and that as one great motive of my wishing for the Recordership was to do what I could to promote his Lordship's interest, I thought my unfitness for the office was against that, for I should discredit his Lordship's recommendation. That there were many gentlemen who could be of much more use to him in that way, and that my being appointed, one newly come from the Scotch bar, might raise a clamour. I sincerely thanked him, was ashamed of my weakness, but thought I was now resolving for the best.

'Sir,' said he, 'you applied to me for this several times, and at last mentioned your returning to the Northern Circuit as a reason for your having it. I thought of it deliberately for some time. I never consult, neither the officers nor Garforth nor one of them. They may be partial or they may think themselves right. You applied to me several times. I gave no answer. I considered. I thought not only of myself and the Corporation but of you. It is said it is easier to get into a situation than to get well out. If a man does not get out well it is a reflection on the person who put him in. I considered your being Recorder of Carlisle. You could say to a Minister, "Here I am," and make it a step. I don't know your views. But you might go into Scotland or into some other situation. I may say without disparagement to you that there are many gentlemen on the Northern Circuit who know English law better than you. But what I should say to the Corporation: "Here is a man of great sense, of talents, who when a thing is properly prepared can judge of it with ability." And the business is all prepared by the Town Clerk. Besides, when the Recorder is consulted, other counsel are consulted at the same time.'

'Your Lordship is very kind. You put it in the most favourable light. I am now ambitious to have it. And as to the Circuit, there is no necessity for my beating the whole round. I may take more or less of it as I please. To be sure, you have many who go only to particular places. Why, Scott does not go all round. My Lord, I am very much obliged to you. Your Lordship has not only the power to give me the place but you have given me fortitude to take it. I am of an anxious temper.' 'You can think of it for four or five days or a week, and it shall be as you please. If you had had as much to do in life as I have had, you would not have that anxious temper.'

This conversation gave quite a new turn to my spirits. The Rev Dr Lowther came, and our dinner was his supper, and he was very placid and, being a new being in our sphere of existence, gave relief. We had cow-heel soup, very good, as I now thought, cow-heel dressed with white sauce, and something else; a double bottle of a rich Spanish red wine and a bottle of port; and a pint of wine and a pineapple, which pleased my senses, and I felt myself wonderfully well. I told how I had got a good dish of coffee at Penrith. 'Why,' said Lord L., 'could not you have had it here?' 'I should be very glad to have it, my Lord,' said I. Upon which the bell was rung, and Payne the butler was directed to have it well made and, just as it bubbled, to have a little hartshorn put in. So minute! It was indeed very good. Saul, who said he liked coffee, told me he never had seen it here, and that the housekeeper told him she knew of none in the house except some of her own. The relief as to the Recordership, the novelty of Dr Lowther, the little comforts of the stomach, and the prospect of moving next day to Whitehaven Castle, which I was assured was warm, made me go to bed in tranquillity. Such is the human mind. Tell it not.

1788

[In spite of Boswell's raised spirits and hopes, Lowther kept to his boorish form and Boswell was soon questioning the Recordership all over again. Lowther also kept delaying their progress to Carlisle, even though he knew Boswell was eager to return to his sick wife. Boswell persevered, however, and on 11 January 1788 was elected Recorder of Carlisle. He was back with his family in London on 14 January. But life in London continued to be a financial disaster and Margaret pressed him, for the sake of money and her health, to return to Auchinleck and take up at the Court of Session again. Boswell agreed in his heart, but his head told him he had to stay in London until he finished the Life of Johnson, on which he was now working with renewed intensity. He took to sleeping in the drawing-room because of her fevers at night.]

Boswell to Thomas Percy[11], 9 February 1788 [London]

Procrastination, we all know, increases in a proportionate ratio the
difficulty of doing that which might have once been done very easily.
I am really uneasy to think how long it is since I was favoured
with your Lordship's communications concerning Dr Johnson, which,
though few, are valuable, and will contribute to increase my store. I
am ashamed that I have yet seven years to write of his Life. I do it
chronologically, giving year by year his publications, if there were
any, his letters, his conversations, and every thing else that I can collect.
It appears to me that mine is the best plan of biography that can be
conceived; for my readers will as near as may be accompany Johnson
in his progress, and, as it were, see each scene as it happened. I am
of opinion that my delay will be for the advantage of the work, though
perhaps not for the advantage of the author, both because his fame
may suffer from too great expectation, and the sale may be worse
from the subject being comparatively old. But I mean to do my duty
as well as I can. Mrs (Thrale) Piozzi's [Mrs Thrale had married her
children's music-master, Gabriel Piozzi] collection of his letters will be
out soon, and will be a rich addition to the Johnsonian memorabilia.
I saw a sheet at the printing-house yesterday, and observed Letter
CCCXXX, so that we may expect much entertainment. It is wonderful
what avidity there still is for every thing relative to Johnson.

Friday 7 March 1788 [London]

My good friend Dilly sent me this morning Mrs Piozzi's *Letters to Dr
Johnson* a day before they were published. I read with assiduity till I
had finished both volumes. I was disappointed a good deal, both in
finding less able and brilliant writing than I expected and in having a
proof of his fawning on a woman whom he did not esteem because
he had luxurious living in her husband's house; and in order that this
fawning might not be counteracted, treating me and other friends
much more lightly than we had reason to expect. This publication
cooled my warmth of enthusiasm for 'my illustrious friend' a good deal.
I felt myself degraded from the consequence of an ancient Baron to
the state of an humble attendant on an author; and, what vexed me,
thought that my collecting so much of his conversation had made the

world shun me as a dangerous companion. I carried the volumes to Malone and drank tea with him . . .

['Oh, Mr Boswell, I fear I'm dying,' Margaret burst out one afternoon in March. Finally, she decided she could abide London no longer, and in May the entire family except for Veronica (who entered a new school) left for Auchinleck. Boswell attended the Northern Circuit in July–August and wrote apologetic letters to Malone confessing that he was making no progress whatever on the Life. On 26 October he was back in London, lonely without Margaret but with Sandy and James. Taking smaller lodgings, he laboured on with his great work.]

1789

Boswell to William Temple, 10 January 1789 [London]

Another sad interruption of our correspondence without any sufficient reason. Soon after receiving your last long, kind letter, I recovered my spirits pretty well. I know not how. A letter from my wife recommending to me to take a house in a well aired situation determined me not to sell my furniture, as my doing so after what she wrote might appear like discouraging her from coming to me, which though I could hardly hope, would have made me very happy. It is incredible what difficulty I found in several weeks wandering to find a house that would answer; and at last I fixed on one at £50 in Queen Ann Street West Cavendish Square, very small but neat. It however would not accommodate the whole of my family with even tolerable conveniency; but would serve as a sort of camp lodging till better could be had. In winter the upholsterers and brokers take numbers of houses and furnish them with old trash, and by letting them furnished get great profits. This makes it very difficult to get choice of unfurnished houses at that season. I am in a most illegal situation[12]; and for appearance should have cheap chambers in the Temple, as to which I am still inquiring; but in truth, I am sadly discouraged by having no practice nor probable prospect of it. And to confess fairly to you my friend, I am afraid that were I to be tried, I should be found so deficient in the forms the quirks and the quiddities which early habit acquires, that I should expose myself. Yet the delusion of

Westminster Hall, of brilliant reputation and splendid fortune as a barrister still weighs upon my imagination. I must be *seen* in the courts, and must hope for some happy openings in causes of importance. The Chancellor as you observe has not done as I expected. But why did I expect it? I am going to put him to the test. Could I be satisfied with being Baron of Auchinleck, with a good income for a gentleman in Scotland, I might no doubt be independent. But what can be done to deaden that ambition which has ever raged in my veins like a fever. In the country I should sink into wretched gloom, or at best into listless dullness, and sordid abstraction. Perhaps a time may come when I may by lapse of time be grown fit for it. As yet I *really from a philosophical* spirit, allow myself to be driven along the tide of life, with a good deal of caution not to be much hurt, and still flattering myself that an unexpected lucky chance may at last place me so, that the prediction by a *fortunate* cap appearing on my head at my birth will be fulfilled.

My two boys are still in the house with me. The oldest is advancing both in Latin and Greek exceedingly well, by the assistance of one of the ushers of the Soho Academy; and the other goes on in Latin with him during this hard weather; but next week I am to send him again to that Academy. I am sensible that it is a great disadvantage to them to be under my roof, as I am so much abroad, and then they must be with my Scotch housekeeper and footman whom I yet retain on account of their fidelity and moderate wages. But I am afraid to send my eldest to a public school with his rupture; the younger I shall send to one when he is a year older.

I am now very near the conclusion of my rough draught of Johnson's Life. On Saturday I finished the Introduction and Dedication to Sir Joshua both of which had appeared very difficult to be accomplished. I am confident they are well done. Whenever I have completed the rough draught, by which I mean the work without nice correction, Malone and I are to prepare one half perfectly, and then it goes to press where I hope to have it early in February so as to be out by the end of May. I do not believe that Malone's Shakespeare will be much before me. His brother Lord Sunderlin with his Lady and two sisters, came home from a long tour on the Continent in summer last, and took a country house about twenty miles from town, for six months. Malone lived with them, & so his labour was much intermitted.

Boswell to *William Temple*, 31 March 1789 [London]

... I have received very alarming accounts of the distress which my wife suffers, both in a letter from the physician, and in one from herself; her expression is 'my fever still continues, and I waste away daily'. I have been in wretched agitation since the day before yesterday when such melancholy information reached me. It is possible that a return of mild weather may relieve her, as has happened several times; but we cannot be ignorant that each repeated attack makes her less able to recover; and supposing that now the disease should increase, and as sometimes happens, should take a rapid course, she may be carried off, while I am four hundred miles from her. The alternative is dreadful, and though she with admirable generosity bids me not to be in a haste to leave London (knowing my extreme fondness for it) I should have a heart as hard as a stone were I to remain here; and should the fatal event happen in my absence, I should have a just upbraiding gloom upon my mind for the rest of my life. I have therefore resolved to set out early the day after tomorrow, and take Veronica with me...

[He found her even in a worse state than he imagined. At this critical moment Lonsdale commanded him to return to London with him on business. Shedding tears, he tore himself away from Margaret and then was subjected to numerous delays at Lowther while the unfeeling Lonsdale dithered.]

Boswell to *William Temple*, 22 May 1789 [Lowther]

... I found my dear wife as ill or rather worse than I apprehended ... No man ever had a higher esteem or a warmer love of a wife, than I of her. You will recollect, my Temple, how our marriage was the result of an attachment truly romantic. Yet how painful is it to me to recollect a thousand instances of inconsistent conduct. I can justify my removing to the great sphere of England, upon a principle of laudable ambition. But the frequent scenes of what I must call dissolute conduct are inexcusable. Often and often when she was very ill in London have I been indulging in festivity with Sir Joshua Reynolds, Courtenay, Malone &c. &c. &c and have come home late, and disturbed her repose. Nay when I was last at Auchinleck on purpose to soothe and console her, I repeatedly went from home and both on those occasions, and when neighbours visited me, drank a great deal too much wine. On Saturday last dining at a gentleman's house where I was visiting for the first time and was eager to obtain political influence, I drank so freely, that riding home in the dark, without a servant, I fell from my horse, and bruised my shoulder severely. Next morning I had it examined by a surgeon who found no fracture or dislocation, but blooded me largely to prevent inflammation. While I was thus confined to bed, came a letter from Colonel Lowther one of Lord Lonsdale's Members [of Parliament], informing me that his Lordship would set out for London as soon as I arrived at Lowther and would be glad to have my company in the carriage with him. I expected such a letter because I was engaged to appear as Recorder of Carlisle for the Corporation in a cause brought against us in the King's Bench, which I knew was to come on this month or early in June. But I was in a great dilemma what to do. I was afraid I should not be able to travel; and to leave my wife in such a state was severe. She with a spirit which I cannot enough admire, animated me to set out, which I accordingly did, resolved to return as soon as the business was over, and bring our two sons with me to be some comfort to her, while she can at all be sensible of it...

[After a week in London he received word that Margaret was dying. He and his youngest son James rushed home only to find that he was too late.]

Boswell to William Temple, 3 July 1789 [Auchinleck]

Your letter upon my late most severe loss proves that you are now the same steady and warm-hearted friend that I have ever known you. O my friend! this is affliction indeed! My two boys and I posted from London to Auchinleck night and day, in sixty-four hours and one quarter, but alas! our haste was all in vain. The fatal stroke had taken place before we set out. It was very strange that we had no intelligence whatever upon the road, not even in our own parish, nor till my second daughter came running out from our house and announced to us the dismal event in a burst of tears. O! my Temple! what distress, what tender painful regrets, what unavailing earliest wishes to have but one week, one day, in which I might again hear her admirable conversation and assure her of my fervent attachment notwithstanding all my irregularities. It was some relief to me to be told that she had after I was set out mentioned what I think I wrote to you, that she had pressed me to go up and show my zeal for Lord Lonsdale. But when on my return before the cause came on, I found that by my going away at that unlucky time I had not been with her to soothe her last moments, I cried bitterly and upbraided myself for leaving her, for she would not have left me. This reflection, my dear friend, will I fear pursue me to my grave. She had suffered a great deal from her disease for some weeks before her death. But the actual scene of dying itself was not dreadful. She continued quite sensible till a few minutes before, when she began to doze calmly and expired without any struggle. When I saw her four days after, her countenance was not at all disfigured. But alas! to see my excellent wife, and the mother of my children, and that most sensible, lively woman, lying cold and pale and insensible was very shocking to me. I could not help doubting that it was a deception. I could hardly bring myself to agree that the body should be removed, for it was still a consolation to me to go and kneel by it and talk to my dear, dear Peggie. She was much respected by all who knew her, so that her funeral was remarkably well attended. There were nineteen carriages followed the hearse, and a large body of horsemen, and the tenants of all my lands. It is not customary in Scotland for a husband to attend his wife's funeral. But I resolved if I possibly could to do her the last honours myself, and I was able to go through with it very decently. I privately read the funeral service over her coffin in the presence of my sons and was relieved by that ceremony a good deal. On the Sunday after, Mr Dun delivered almost verbatim a few sentences which I sent him as a character of her. I imagined that I should not be able to stay here after the sad misfortune. But I find that I cling to it with a melancholy pleasure.

Honest David is perpetually pressing my confining my family to Scotland. But alas, my dear friend, should I or could I now be satisfied with narrow provinciality, which was formerly so irksome and must now be much more so? I have agreed that my second daughter shall pass the winter at Edinburgh, as she has desired it, in order to finish her education. But were my daughters to be Edinburgh-mannered girls, I could have no satisfaction in their company. Veronica wishes to be boarded this winter with a lady in London. Little Betsy, who is just nine years old, goes tomorrow to a quiet boarding-school at Ayr, our county town, till I settle where to place her for a year or two. I am

thinking of a convent in France, or rather in Flanders, where she can
be well-educated a certain length very cheap, and then I would finish
her at one of the great English boarding-schools. Yet if I can find a
good and cheap English one I may probably not send her abroad. Can
you and Mrs Temple advise me? My eldest son I am resolved shall go
to Eton this winter. I am to have only chambers in the Temple after
Christmas. I may perhaps come to you in autumn if Malone goes to
Ireland, so that the revising of Johnson's *Life* cannot proceed till winter.
I am much obliged to you for your prayer. I experience that piety
affords the only true comfort. My kindest love to you and yours. I am
forcing myself to be as busy as I can and think of going the Northern
Circuit.

Boswell to William Temple, 30 November 1789 [London]

My apology for not coming to you as I fully intended and wished
is really a sufficient one; for, the revision of my *Life of Johnson* by so
acute and knowing a critic as Mr Malone is of most essential consequence especially as he is *Johnsonianissimus*, and as he is to hasten to
Ireland as soon as his Shakspeare is fairly published, I must avail myself
of him *now*. His hospitality – and my other invitations – and particularly
my attendance at Lord Lonsdale's have lost us many evenings; but I
reckon that a third of the work is *settled*, so that I shall get to press very
soon. You cannot imagine what labour, what perplexity, what vexation
I have endured in arranging a prodigious multiplicity of materials, in
supplying omissions, in searching for papers buried in different
masses – and all this besides the exertion of composing and polishing.
Many a time have I thought of giving it up. However, though I shall
be uneasily sensible of its many deficiencies, it will certainly be to the
world a very valuable and peculiar volume of biography, full of literary
and characteristical anecdotes (which word by the way Johnson always
condemned as used in the sense that the French and we from them
use it, as signifying particulars) told with authenticity and in a lively
manner. Would that it were in the booksellers shops. Methinks if I had
this *magnum opus* launched, the public has not farther claim upon me;
for I have promised no more, and I may die in peace, or retire into
dull obscurity ... Such is the gloomy *ground* of my mind, that any
agreeable perceptions have an uncommon though but a momentary
brightness ... I walk about upon the earth with inward discontent,

though I may appear the most cheerful man you meet. I may have many *gratifications*, but the comfort of life is at an end.

Thursday 3 December 1789 [London]

Dined at Lord Lonsdale's with Governor [William] Penn, etc. Was allowed to be moderate in wine. Went home with Penn and had negus and a pipe cordially. In our way to his house, going up Bond Street in a hackney-coach, he talked of going Ambassador to America. I said, 'If you do, you must find a situation for me.' 'That I will,' said he; 'you shall be my Secretary.' 'Are you in earnest?' said I. 'Upon my honour, I am,' said he. 'Then,' said I, 'give me your hand,' which he did in a cordial manner. When at his house, I resumed this matter, and he told me that it would be a great advantage to him, that he would make the business very easy to me, and I should find myself very happy at Philadelphia. This was an opening for me into the New World.

NINE

Triumph and Despair
1790–1795

Early in 1790 Boswell completes his first draft of the Life, more than 400,000 words, and sets about revising it. He allows his journal to lapse for several months until April and is generally indolent and listless, suffering from renewed assaults of hypochondria. He flirts with several women, is worried to tears about money and considers re-marriage as a way out of these troubles, is anxious about his children, and generally suffers from loneliness. The girls seem too little respectful of him, while Sandy at Eton and James, his favourite, at Westminster School are also lonely and miss him. Sir Joshua Reynolds, Malone and John Courtenay raise his morale consistently, at innumerable dinner parties, but Lonsdale is still in the shadows chipping away at his self-respect.

1790

Boswell to Thomas Percy, 9 April 1790 [London]

... As to suppressing your Lordship's name when relating the very few anecdotes of Johnson with which you have favoured me, I will do anything to oblige your Lordship but that very thing. I owe to the authenticity of my work, to its respectability, and to the credit of my illustrious friend, to introduce as many names of eminent persons as I can. It is comparatively a very small portion which is sanctioned by that of your Lordship, and there is nothing even bordering on impropriety. Believe me, my Lord, you are not the only bishop in the number of great men with which my pages are graced. I am quite resolute as to this matter.

Thursday, 10 June 1790

I dined with Sir William Scott[1], by appointment, to sit upon my
record of the conversation between Johnson and him. Lady Scott,
whom I had seen several times, but always reserved, was today
exceedingly agreeable, in so much that I protested that I would take
her directly if Sir William would part with her. I asked if she had a
sister, and was informed she had one, Miss Fanny, four-and-twenty,
not so good a size as Lady Scott and not so domestic, but a Ranelagh
girl, as Sir William said; at the same time very good-humoured and
very religious, in so much that she reads select prayers and a sermon
every Sunday evening to her father's servants. 'Let me see her,' cried
I. 'This is the very woman that I should wish to have.' Lady Scott told
me that she had very lately refused a handsome young man. 'I am
happy to hear it,' said I. 'That is a proof what kind of man is agreeable
to her. I shall have a good chance.' In this manner we joked, I all the
while considering that a daughter of the ancient family of Bagnall of
Bagnall in Staffordshire, with £6,000 certain and to be probably a co-
heiress of estates to the value of £2,000 a year, was a most desirable
object. Lady Scott promised I should see her; but Sir William told me
that at this moment a young gentleman who would one day succeed
to a peerage was in suit of her, and I must wait the event. My scheme
was entirely convenience and ambition, being conscious that the loss
I had suffered would ever cloud my mind. But I thought that I might
take the chance of advantage, and being connected with Sir William
Scott might be of essential service to me.

Sunday 13 June 1790

My heart was sore for my son James, who complained of being
very unhappy at Westminster School. Poor little fellow, on the Sunday
when I first walked down with him to introduce him, he said to me,
'Is it not hard that what should be the most agreeable part of life is
made the most unhappy by being at school, and that to learn only the
dead languages?' I could not argue against this, but insisted on that kind
of education having formed the greatest men in this nation. He was
much cast down as we walked, but when we got to Prince's Street, he
said 'I find myself more composed.' Last Sunday, which was the day
on which he actually entered to the boarding-house, I was very

anxious. I made him kneel with me in the forenoon, and I prayed aloud for him, that as he was now about to enter on a new situation in life, GOD would be pleased to bless him and preserve him from the temptations to which he would be exposed. This day Veronica and he and I went to evening service about four o'clock: prayers and sermon in our parish church of Marylebone. My spirits were sadly depressed. I dined tête-a-tête with Malone and revised forty-six pages of my Life of Johnson.

[Lonsdale in London suddenly tells Boswell he wants him up at Carlisle. Painfully aware that Malone was about to depart for several months in Ireland and loath to lose any days of revision of the Life with him, Boswell prevaricates but writes to Lonsdale that he will honour his commitments this time but resign immediately afterwards. In the following entry he records their tempestuous quarrel on the day of their departure.]

Thursday 17 June 1790

Rose in very bad spirits. A little conversation with my dear friend Temple, and parted cordially. At nine, L.'s. No appearance. Waited almost two hours. Went home. All gone out. Returned. He at breakfast. Irritated at my going. Jackson with him. Before whom and Robinson his servant (when I represented how hard it was on me to go), he was in a fury, and said, 'You have some sinister motive.' 'How can your Lordship say so?' 'Because I know the man to whom I speak. I suppose you want to have a large fee.' 'Did your Lordship ever see anything in my conduct to make you think so?' 'You asked the Recordership of me. I did not wish you should be Recorder. But you were so earnest, I granted it. And now when duty is required, you would give it up. What have you done for your salary? I will advise the Corporation not to accept your resignation till you have attended the Midsummer Sessions as well as the election. I suppose you think we are fond of your company. You are mistaken. We don't care for it. I should have heard of no difficulties. It is your own concern. I suppose you thought I was to bring you into Parliament. I never had any such intention. It would do you harm to be in Parliament.' This was a full discovery. I had leave of absence for an hour; went to Malone, and told him. He advised me to go in apparent good humour and get away as soon as I could. It vexed me that I was dragged away from the printing of my *Life of Johnson*, and that perhaps Malone might be gone to Ireland before I could get back to London.

At L.'s again. Time was trifled away till the afternoon, I am not sure what hour. L. took me under the arm, and we walked by Grosvenor Square to Oxford Street, near Hanover Square, to get into his coach. As we walked, the bringing into Parliament was resumed, and he showed his poor opinion of me, saying I would get drunk and make a foolish speech. I talked too freely of my liberal and independent views, and of their inconsistency with being brought in by him unless special terms were granted. He was provoked. In the coach the same subject was unfortunately resumed, and I expressed myself, I do not recollect exactly how, but so as to raise his passion almost to madness, so that he used shocking words to me, saying, 'Take it as you will. I am ready to give you satisfaction.' 'My Lord,' said I, 'you have said enough.' I was in a stunned state of mind, but calm and determined. He went on with insult: 'You have kept low company all your life. What are you, Sir?' 'A gentleman, my Lord, a man of honour; and I hope to show myself such.' He brutally said, 'You will be settled when you have a bullet in your belly.' Jackson sat silent.

When we came to Barnet and entered the inn, I told him he had treated me very ill and very unjustly. He said, 'I will give you satisfaction now. I have pistols here.' 'If you please, my Lord; and I will be obliged to you for pistols.' 'What, Sir, against myself? Certainly not.' I went out and inquired if there was any regiment quartered there, thinking that I might get one of the officers to lend me pistols and be my second. There was none. I returned to him and said I would go back to London and find a friend, and let his Lordship know when we could meet. We had a cold dinner, during which he said it would seem strange to me when the friend I should bring would say that his words to me were warranted; that I was the aggressor, and ought to ask pardon; that I had attacked his honour. Looking on him really as a madman, and wishing upon principle never to have a duel if I could avoid it with credit, I protested that I had no such intention as he supposed; and then in order to give him an opportunity to have the matter adjusted, I asked his pardon for using expressions which his Lordship had imagined attacked his honour, but which I solemnly declared were not so meant by me. He then said he would not have used such words to me if he had not thought that my expressions were meant as he had supposed. Then we drank a glass of wine.

Captain Payne joined us and sat some time. After he was gone, and I was walking before the door of the inn, L. sent for me, and when I came, held out his hand and gave it me, saying, 'Boswell, forget all that is past.' Jackson said to me that the affair had been very well settled, and not a syllable about it should ever transpire. He said L. was interested in not mentioning it. After this we travelled on socially enough, but I was inwardly mortified to think that I had deceived myself so woefully as to my hopes from the GREAT LOWTHER, and that I was now obliged to submit to what was very disagreeable to me without any reward or hope of any good, but merely to get out of the scrape into which I had brought myself. We travelled all night, and on Friday lay at Doncaster.

Boswell to Edmond Malone, 30 June 1790 [Carlisle]

I do not think it is in the power of words to convey to you how miserable I have been since I left you ... You have had distress of mind. But your active spirit never failed within you. I have heard you say that you never sat listless by the fire. I have during these wretched days sat so, hours and hours. Everything that ever vexed me has returned. I feel myself a poor, forlorn being, with no permanent vigour of mind, no friend that can enable me to advance myself in life. A fortune sadly encumbered – children whom I can with difficulty support and of whom I am at a loss how to dispose with advantage and propriety – such is the general prospect. And for immediate feelings, added to ennui and self-upbraiding, I am again unfortunate enough to have one sore[2] of a certain nature contracted, I think, Monday fortnight, which alone gives me more pain and alarm than several which I had lately ...

How shocking is it to think that I was dragged away from my friend Temple, who came from Cornwall almost on purpose to see me and saw me so little – and was forced to interrupt my Life of Dr Johnson, the most important, perhaps now the only concern of any consequence that I ever shall have in this world. And what galls me and irritates me with impatience is the thought that I lose those hours which you could now have given me for revising my manuscript and that perhaps you may be gone before I get back to town. Even the fear of not being in London when at last your Shakspeare comes out is shocking. My dear friend! for GOD'S sake if you possibly can, let me have some consolation. The melancholy to which I am subject I know cannot be helped. But I beseech you try to alleviate such of my sufferings as can admit of soothing.

Monday 5 July 1790 [Carlisle]

What a wretched register is this! 'A lazar-house it seemed.' It is the journal of a diseased mind. I had passed a very uneasy night. The good cheer at Rickerby had been too much for my relaxed organs. I awaked in great concern about my son James, who I feared might be ruined at Westminster School. I called out piteously, 'O my poor son!' During all this time the loss of my valuable wife, who from my earliest consciousness had been my agreeable and confidential cousin and my cheerful comforter in all difficulties, was perpetually recurring upon my wounded spirit. I had eager vain stretchings of mind towards her. Alas, I could do nothing but lament. I thought that an earnest kind attention to her children would be the best exercise of my affection for her.

[When Boswell returned to London on 15 July, free at last of Lonsdale, Malone was still there and their work on the Life resumed, albeit interspersed with not a little socialising. He also had his hands full with Veronica and Euphemia and suffered from listlessness and a lack of overarching purpose except for what his sessions with Malone provided. But Malone left for Ireland in early December, after which he was on his own, working on a biography that seemed interminable and plagued with hypochrondria and money troubles.]

Friday 10 September 1790 [London]

Dined at home. How the rest of the day was passed I do not recollect. My life at present, though for some time my health and spirits have been wonderfully good, is surely as idly spent as can almost be imagined. I merely attend to the progress of my Life of Johnson, and that by no means with great assiduity, such as that which Malone employs on Shakspeare. I am losing for myself and children all the enjoyment of a fine place in the country. I am following no profession. I fear I am gradually losing any claim to preferment in the law in Scotland. But with the consciousness which I have of the nature of my own mind, I am sure that I am escaping innumerable hours of uneasiness which I should have were I in Scotland. I am in that great scene which I have ever contemplated with admiration, and in which there are continual openings for advantage.

[He keeps no journal between early September 1790 and February 1791.]

1791

Boswell to Edmond Malone, 29 January 1791 [London]

You will find this a most desponding and disagreeable letter, for which I ask your pardon. But your vigour of mind and warmth of heart make your friendship of such consequence that it is drawn upon like a bank. I have for some weeks had the most woeful return of melancholy, insomuch that I have not only had no relish of any thing, but a continual uneasiness and all the prospect before me for the rest of life has seemed gloomy and hopeless.

    ... The clear money on which I can reckon out of my estate is scarcely £900 a year. What can I do? My grave brother urges me to quit London, and live at my seat in the country; where he thinks that I might be able to save so as gradually to relieve myself. But, alas I should be *absolutely* miserable. In the mean time, such are my projects and sanguine expectations, that you know I purchased an estate which was given long ago to a younger son of our family, and came to be sold last autumn, and paid for it £2500—£1500 of which I borrow upon itself by a mortgage. But the remaining £1000 I cannot conceive a possibility of raising, but by the mode of annuity; which is, I believe, a very heavy disadvantage. I own it was improvident of me to make a clear purchase at a time I was sadly straitened; but if I had missed the opportunity, it never again would have occurred, and I should have been vexed to see an ancient appanage, a piece of, as it were, the flesh and blood of the family, in the hands of a stranger. And now that I have made the purchase, I should feel myself quite despicable should I give it up.

    In this situation, then, my dear Sir, would it not be wise in me to accept of 1000 guineas for my Life of Johnson, supposing the person who made the offer should now stand to it, which I fear may not be the case; for two volumes may be considered as a disadvantageous circumstance? Could I indeed raise £1000 upon the credit of the work, I should incline to *game*, as Sir Joshua says; because it *may* produce double the money, though Steevens kindly tells me that I have over-printed, and that the curiosity about Johnson is *now* only in our own circle. Pray decide for me; and if, as I suppose, you are for my taking the offer, inform me with whom I am to treat. In my present state of spirits, I am all timidity. Your absence has been a severe stroke to me. I am at present quite at a loss what to do. Last week they gave me six sheets. I have now before me in proof p. 456. Yet I have above 100 pages of my copy remaining; besides his *death*, which is yet to be written, and many insertions, were there room, as also seven-and-thirty letters, exclusive of twenty to Dr Brocklesby, most of which will furnish only extracts. I am advised to extract several of those to others, and leave out some; for my first volume makes only 516 pages and to have 600 in the second will seem awkward, besides increasing the expense considerably. The *counsellor*, indeed, has devised an ingenious way to thicken the first volume, by prefixing the index. I have now desired to have but one compositor. Indeed, I go sluggishly and comfortlessly about my work. As I pass your door I cast many a longing look.

Boswell to William Temple, 6 April 1791 [London]

I ... called on old [in his nineties] [Charles] Macklin the Comedian whom I found with a mind active and cheerful in his ninety second or third year. I could not but wonder while he related theatrical stories *sixty years old* ... Here sat I *forty years younger than him*, listless and desponding, and unable to rid my mind of a disagreeable sensation as if I had been sitting in *Edinburgh*. I really my dear Temple believe that as much pain may be suffered from *antipathies*, as from almost any cause. Would it not *torture* you to be again at Professor Hunter's eating *jeel*. The *possibility of a disturbed imagination* reducing me to the mode of existence in my youth frightens me. Alas! what *real advances* have I made *above* that state! How delusive is this low-spirited thought! – But indeed I much fear that to a speculating and very feeling mind all that life affords will at times appear of no effect. When I recall the infinite variety of scenes through which I have passed, in my moments of sound sensation, I am elated; but in moments of depression, I either forget them all, or they seem indifferent.

My Life of Johnson is at last drawing to a close. I am correcting the last sheet, and have only to write an Advertisement, to make out a note of Errata and to correct a second sheet of contents, one being done. I really hope to publish it on the 25 current. My old and most intimate friend may be sure that a copy will be sent to him. I am at present in such bad spirits, that I have every fear concerning it – that I may get no profit, nay may lose – that the public may be disappointed and think that I have done it Poorly – that I may make many enemies, and even have quarrels. – Yet perhaps the very reverse of all this may happen.

When my book is launched, I shall if I am alive and in tolerable health and spirits, have some furniture put into my chambers in the Temple, and force myself to sit there some hours every day, and to attend regularly in Westminster Hall. The chambers cost me £20 yearly, and I may reckon furniture and a lad to wait there occasionally £20 more. I doubt whether I shall get fees equal to the expence...

[There is a huge gap in the journal between 11 April 1791 and 16 August 1792. The Life of Johnson was published on 16 May 1791 in two quarto volumes. Seventeen hundred and fifty copies were printed, of which 800 sold in two weeks and almost all the rest by August 1792. Not surprisingly given the startling new style of biography Boswell had introduced into the literary world and the hostility toward Johnson nourished by many of the readers, the newspapers gave the work a mixed reception. With the additional information he harvested from the avalanche of letters he received, he soon began to work on a second edition that his printer Henry Baldwin began to print in April 1792.]

1792

Monday 3 September 1792 [St Gluvias, Cornwall] [Boswell has travelled to Cornwall to stay with William Temple.]

It rained heavier and more continued than any day I had yet seen in Cornwall ... Temple and I had recourse to one of the best modes of relief in rainy weather, which is to do something that occupies without straining or at all fatiguing the mind. We sorted according to years that large mass of letters of mine to him. Since our first correspondence in 1757. He was afterwards to arrange them according to their date. As I looked into several of them at different periods, I had curious sensations. However, amidst all the changes and varieties, and those pretty strong ones too, I could still trace enough of personal identity: warmth of heart and imagination, vanity and piety. My friend agreed with me that it was wonderful I had made myself the man I was, considering the extreme narrowness of my education; for he remembered me the most puritanical being, and the most timid in society; and now there was no man of more elevated ecclesiastical notions, more liberal views, and perhaps none so universally easy and of more address in social life. We laughed confidentially at my wonderful art of displaying extraordinary symptoms of learning and knowledge, when I had read so little in a regular way. Yet I had, as the French say, *feuilletté* a great many books, and had, like Johnson, the art of quickly seizing a general notion from perusing a small part.

[From October 1792 well into the new year, Boswell suffered from 'hypochondriac frost'.]

Sunday-11 November 1792 [London]

Had been troubled with disagreeable dreams. Could not force myself out of bed till it was too late, for morning service, and my children were in the same fault. I despised myself for having no order or proper authority in my house. I visited Malone and revised some additional Johnsoniana ... My son James and I then took a walk, and he and I and my two daughters went to church in the afternoon. Dined dully at home. Veronica drank tea at Mrs Paradise's, and Euphemia, James, and I at my brother David's. Wherein does this London life excel a life at Edinburgh or any other town? But I have accustomed myself to expect too exquisite a relish of existence. I received a just check this evening in a sentence of the fifth sermon *Left for Publication* by Dr Taylor, in which Dr Johnson observes that disquietude of mind often proceeds from our overrating our own abilities and forming too high expectations.[3] I this day began to drink a decoction of woods against the scurvy, of which I had for some time had appearances, and imagined that my bad spirits might be partly occasioned by it.

Saturday 24 November 1792

This was the day fixed by Mr Dilly for settling accounts with me and Mr Baldwin as to the quarto edition of my *Life of Dr Johnson*, etc. I was somewhat animated by the prospect, and walked pretty briskly to my worthy bookseller's, where I had a hearty breakfast, after which he produced to me the clear produce of the sale, exclusive of presents, amounting to £1,555.18.2. This was very flattering to me as an author. We proceeded to Baldwin's, where I cleared off a bond for £400 (part of the price of Knockroon[4] advanced to me by him and Mr Dilly) and a note of hand for £100 lent to me by himself. There was great satisfaction in thus paying principal and interest to two worthy friends who had assisted me with their credit. I then returned to Mr Dilly's, and after allowing for various sums which I owed him, there was a balance due to me of £608. I dined heartily at Baldwin's . . .

Friday 21 December 1792

I had been during all this fit of hypochondria miserably restless. I had some gratification, but a poor one, and that mixed with upbraidings, by lying long in the mornings in a kind of half sleepy stupefaction. When I came downstairs I was listless and fretful. I breakfasted without appetite, having as it were a bitter taste which communicated itself to everything. *Sincerum est nisi vas, etc*[5]. I often called on Malone, and found him fully occupied in historical and biographical researches, on which he was intent while I had absolutely no pursuit whatever. The delusive hope of perhaps getting into some practice at the bar was now dead, or at least torpid. The printing of my second edition of Dr Johnson's *Life* was the only thing I had to do. That was little, and was now nearly ended. I hurried into the streets and walked rapidly, shunning to meet people as much as I could, my perceptions being liable to such soreness from even looks and manner that I suffered acute pain on being accosted, and this was augmented by an unhappy imagination that it must appear how inefficient and troubled I was. Indeed Devaynes, my apothecary, said to me, 'You are not ill enough to stay at home, and yet you should not be going about.' I had scorbutic eruptions on different parts of my body, which fretted in the night, and I supposed that the humour which they indicated to be in my blood was one cause of my present indisposition.

1793

[On 17 July 1793 the second edition of the Life of Johnson was published, with a huge amount of new material and elaborate new explanatory notes.]

Advertisement to the Second Edition to The Life of Samuel Johnson, 1793

THAT I was anxious for the success of a Work which had employed much of my time and labour, I do not wish to conceal: but whatever doubts I at any time entertained, have been entirely removed by the very favourable reception with which it has been honoured. That reception has excited my best exertions to render my Book more perfect; and in this endeavour I have had the assistance not only of some of my particular friends, but of many other learned and ingenious men, by which I have been enabled to rectify some mistakes, and to enrich the Work with many valuable additions. These I have ordered to be printed separately in quarto, for the accommodation of the purchasers of the first edition. May I be permitted to say that the typography of both editions does honour to the press of Mr Henry Baldwin, now Master of the Worshipful Company of Stationers, whom I have long known as a worthy man and an obliging friend.

In the strangely mixed scenes of human existence, our feelings are often at once pleasing and painful. Of this truth, the progress of the present Work furnishes a striking instance. It was highly gratifying to me that my friend, Sir Joshua Reynolds, to whom it is inscribed, lived to peruse it, and to give the strongest testimony to its fidelity; but before a second edition, which he contributed to improve, could be finished, the world has been deprived of that most valuable man[6], a loss of which the regret will be deep, and lasting, and extensive, proportionate to the felicity which he diffused through a wide circle of admirers and friends.

In reflecting that the illustrious subject of this Work, by being more extensively and intimately known, however elevated before, has risen in the veneration and love of mankind, I feel a satisfaction beyond what fame can afford. We cannot, indeed, too much or too often admire his wonderful powers of mind, when we consider that the principal store of wit and wisdom which this Work contains, was not a particular selection from his general conversation, but was merely his occasional talk at such times as I had the good fortune to be in his company, and, without doubt, if his discourse at other periods had been collected with the same attention, the whole tenor of what he uttered would have been found equally excellent.

His strong, clear, and animated enforcement of religion, morality, loyalty, and subordination, while it delights and improves the wise and the good, will, I trust, prove an effectual antidote to that detestable sophistry which has been lately imported from France, under the false name of *Philosophy*, and with a malignant industry has been employed against the peace, good order, and happiness of society, in our free and prosperous country; but thanks be to GOD, without producing the pernicious effects which were hoped for by its propagators.

It seems to me, in my moments of self-complacency, that this extensive biographical work, however inferior in its nature, may in one respect be assimilated to the ODYSSEY. Amidst a thousand entertaining and instructive episodes the HERO is never long out of sight; for they are all in some degree connected with him; and HE, in the whole course of the History, is exhibited by the Authour for the best advantage of his readers...

Should there be any cold-blooded and morose mortals who really dislike this book, I will give them a story to apply. When the great *Duke of Marlborough*, accompanied by *Lord Cadogan*, was one day reconnoitering the army in Flanders, a heavy rain came on, and they both called for their cloaks. *Lord Cadogan*'s servant, a good humoured alert lad, brought his Lordship's in a minute. The Duke's servant, a lazy sulky dog, was so sluggish, that his Grace being wet to the skin, reproved him, and had for answer with a grunt, 'I came as fast as I could,' upon which the Duke calmly said, '*Cadogan*, I would not for a thousand pounds have that fellow's temper.'

There are some men, I believe, who have, or think they have, a very small share of vanity. Such may speak of their literary fame in a decorous style of diffidence. But I confess, that I am so formed by nature and by habit, that to restrain the effusion of delight, on having obtained such fame, to me would be truly painful. Why then should I suppress it? Why 'out of the abundance of the heart' should I not speak? Let me then mention with a warm, but no insolent exultation, that I have been regaled with spontaneous praise of my work by many and various persons eminent for their rank, learning, talents and accomplishments; much of which praise I have under their hands to be reposited in my archives at *Auchinleck*. An honourable and reverend friend speaking of the favourable reception of my volumes, even in the circles of fashion and elegance, said to me, 'you have made them all talk Johnson,' – 'Yes, I may add, I have *Johnsonised* the land' and I trust they will not only *talk*, but *think*, Johnson . . .

Monday 19 August 1793 [London]

Visited an old acquaintance in Queen Street; excellent. Dined at Baldwin's. Then went to Newgate to see the four men who had escaped from Botany Bay and assure them personally that I was doing all in my power for them[7]. I first called on Mr Kirby, the keeper, who kindly invited me to drink tea, which I did with his wife and niece and several other *ladies*. It was a curious thought that I was in *Newgate*; for the room was handsome and everything in good order as in the drawing-room of any good middle-rank family in any part of London. Mr Kirby did not partake with us, saying he did not drink tea above once in a month. He obligingly attended me into the gaol by the door from his house, which Akerman had built up for fear of the prisoners' breaking in, but he had opened. He invited me to eat beef with him on the 3 of September, the eve of St Bartholomew's Day, when the famous fair which goes by his name is proclaimed by the Lord Mayor, and he wrote a truly respectful note which he gave me to keep me in mind of it. I had frequently been in Newgate before, and had felt the crowding of the prisoners and their importunity for money very uneasy. But now when the commander-in-chief was with me, there was a wonderful difference. They were all uncovered [i.e. removed their hats], fell back on each side, and did not utter a word. It was so far pleasing that there was at present here nobody under sentence of death.

Tuesday 24, Wednesday 25, and Thursday 26 September 1793

I group these three days together because they were not distinguished from the general insipidity and gloom of my existence at this time, except that on Thursday I showed Temple Westminster School – where I had a dim perception of its celebrity as impressed on my early imagination – and brought my son James home to dinner. Temple was to leave me on Friday ... It vexed me exceedingly that both the last time when my old friend was with me, and now, my spirits were miserably bad, worse indeed now than then; and he observed to me that my temper was sadly changed for the worse, especially when I was at home with my daughters, at whom I was almost perpetually fretting. He saw that they did not treat me with the respect due to a parent. But he imputed this to the unsteadiness of my behaviour, as I sometimes was too free with them, and then attempted to keep them in too much restraint. I agreed with him in this, and also that they had good sense and good dispositions; but I maintained, and he admitted, that they ought not to go abroad so often, or to have company at my house in an evening without previously informing me and obtaining my approbation. He was so good as to speak to them; and it was settled that they should not go abroad in an evening or have company more than three days in each week and never on Sunday, it being however understood that their being at their uncle's should not be counted. It hurt me a good deal that they were at no pains to acquire the English pronunciation and tone, and were fond of associating with Scotch people who could do them no credit. I was indeed sensible that from the narrowness of my circumstances I could not maintain them in such a style as, according to the ways of the age, they could be much in fashionable life.

I was now not only disappointed in any views of ambition in the wide sphere of London, but from my having addicted myself almost entirely to English society, and my aversion to Scotch manners and contempt of provincial consequence being known, I had too much reason to apprehend that should I apply for the office of Lord of Session, I should not be able to obtain it. I was in truth in a woeful state of depression in every respect. The animating delusion that I might get practice in Westminster Hall had vanished; for I saw plainly that all my habits and appearances in public were, as Malone well observed, against me as a lawyer; and I was conscious that I had never applied seriously to English law, and could not bear the confinement and formal course of life which practice at the bar required. I yet shrunk from the thought of retiring to my seat in the country ... Thus my worthy friend and I speculated, while I considered that years were rolling on and age approaching ... I find it almost impossible *to take off an exact impression* of the state of my mind at this time.

1794

Thursday 13 February 1794

... I dined tête-à-tête with Malone very cordially. He talked like a practical philosopher against my being discontented with my lot in life; and when I showed him an exact view of my affairs, my income, deductions, and calculation of expense under different articles, from which it appeared that my fund for living was truly narrow, he did not think I had reason to complain, and observed that I was educating my children in the most laudable manner, and that ten dinners in a year to my friends would not make a difference of more than thirty pounds. At the same time he allowed that a few hundreds a year of addition would be most desirable for me. My constant cause of repining is having indulged hopes of attaining both to consequence and wealth, so as to raise my family to higher consideration; and finding no prospect of attaining my ambitious objects, I tried to soothe myself with the consideration of my fame as a writer, and that by the good management of my estate, and saving, I might in time pay my debts, in which case I should, besides raising at least one third the rent of what I inherited, add Dalblair £115, Willockshill £50, and Foardmouth £5–£170 yearly to the family estate[8] – Dalblair too being princely in extent, and should also give my second son the pretty little property of Knockroon. And supposing me to achieve only one half of these additions, I should be no unworthy Laird.

Boswell to Edmond Malone, 18 November 1794 [Auchinleck]

If I have been of consequence enough to you in my absence to make you think of me, you will possibly have wondered that you have not heard from me. The truth is that accursed constitutional disease of the spirits seised upon me in such a degree, that I could write of nothing but my own unhappiness; and I recollect my old friend Sir John Pringle censuring a witty but melancholy gentleman for troubling his friends with his complaints. 'He was (said Sir John) always resting his burden on his friends' shoulders.' Having a glimpse of cheerfulness, I on the first of this month sat down and wrote letters to you and Courtenay and expressed myself pretty heartily. So All Hail Malone and Courtenay, Courtenay and Malone All Hail! But upon reading those letters next day, I found they were wretched Lamentations. So I would not send them.

I have been uncommonly moderate in wine; so cannot blame myself. I have done some good to my estate, my tenants and the neighbourhood: But my existence has been not only negatively dull, but positively uneasy. I must do my daughters the justice to say, that they have conducted themselves very well. So it is myself alone that must answer....

How have you been? enviable man! ... Pray write to me. As the foolish virgins in the parable, said to the wise 'Give us of your oyl, for our lamp is gone out.' I have little more business to transact here. But why go to London? What have I to do there? I can see no prospect in life but a thick fog. Could I but recover those pleasing delusions which braced my nerves when I first entered Westminster Hall! In short could I have any object! – But I grow querulous. So, no more. My Dear Malone, in whatever state I am I never forget your kindness to me, and the innumerable moments of happiness which I owe to you, and I ever am with unalterable regard your obliged, affectionate, and faithful friend.

[On 12 April Boswell wrote the last entry in his full journal, doubtless concluding his life was no longer worth recording. We recall his remark when he began his London journal that he would not want to live any more than he could record. In his last few months his principal pleasure was in his family and narrowing circle of friends, especially in his son James, though to the end he remained frustrated about his daughters and discontented with his life, drifting with no fixed purpose. The following exchange of letters with James, while he was in Auchinleck for the second half of 1794, says it all.]

James Boswell, Jr to Boswell, 18 October 1794 [Westminster School, London]

Am sorry to find you writing about 'your dull and depressed spirits'. Pray, Sir, do not suffer yourself to be melancholy. Think not on your having missed preferment in London or any of these kind of things, the unreasonableness of which you yourself upon reflection must be sensible of if you consider that your manner of living has never been that of a man of business and that, in short, you have been entirely different in every respect from those who have been (in that line) more successful – they who have obtained places and pensions etc. have not the fame of having been the biographer of Johnson or the conscious exultation of a man of genius. They have not enjoyed your happy and convivial hours. They have not been known to Johnson, Voltaire, Rousseau, and Garrick, Goldsmith, etc., etc. They have not visited the patriots of Corsica. In short, would you rather than have enjoyed so many advantages have been a rich, though dull, plodding lawyer? You cannot expect to be both at the same time. Every situation in life has its advantages and disadvantages ... Let me then have in your next letter a declaration that you are now in excellent spirits.

Boswell to James Boswell Jr, 27 October 1794

My dear James, Last night I had the pleasure to receive a most sensible and animating letter from you concerning my depression of spirits and complaining of want of success in life; and truly, I must acknowledge that 'thou reasonest well'. For I am at all times satisfied that the circumstances in my lot which you enumerate are to me more valuable than any place or pension which I could have had without them. But unluckily I have all my life indulged fond hopes of raising myself, and of consequence my family, by obtaining some preferment which would be both honourable and profitable. In the common estimation of mankind a Lord of Session's place would have realised that hope. In mine, however, whose views were enlarged by being so much in England, any provincial appointment has long appeared beneath me. The manners of Edinburgh, too, disgusted me and, in short, LONDON has for these thirty years and upwards been the object of my wish as my scene of exertion. Much enjoyment have I had there, but as yet every ambitious aim has been disappointed. My constitutional melancholy is ever lurking about me, and perhaps I should impute to this the chief part of my unhappiness. The country does not at all suit me. I have no relish of its amusements or occupations. My temper is gloomy and irritable, and I am continually fretted by hearing of trespasses upon my woods and lands, and tenants falling behind in their rents. Add to this that my circumstances are so straitened that I am in a wretched state of uneasiness how to get my family supported, and at the same time pay the annuities and interest of debts which must be annually cleared. The expense of living here is much greater to me than in London. The wine and corn and hay consumed cost me half as much every week or more than all that is laid out in town; and then there must here be every day a dinner sufficient for a company, as we cannot be sure of being alone. I do not think I have had two comfortable days, putting together all the hours which should be reckoned so, since the 1st of July when I arrived here. Entertaining company is a weary labour to me, and when I pay visits I seem to myself to be fighting battles, yet I dread returning to London with your sisters, who distressed me so much there.

Boswell to James Boswell, Jr, 21 November 1794 [Auchinleck]

My dear James, Before me lies your admirable letter of the 10th, in which you write de consolatione like a true philosopher, who has observed human life and made just reflections. I will try to avoid repining. Yet at the same time I cannot be contented merely with literary fame and social enjoyments. I must still hope for some creditable employment, and perhaps I may yet attain it.

[At a meeting of the Club on 14 April, Boswell was suddenly taken ill. He died one month later.]

PART TWO

An Account of Corsica
The Journal of a Tour to that Island;
and Memoirs of Pasquale Paoli

Part I of the ACCOUNT is not included here, for it is a fairly routine and, on the whole, dull survey of the island's history, climate, geography and natural resources. In Part II, on the other hand, Boswell is unashamedly autobiographical. Indeed, much of the Account's dramatic impact when it was published in 1768 was owing to its refreshingly open self-portrayal. The public had scarcely ever encountered a piece of non-fiction like this in which the author revealed himself so candidly and recounted conversation with such vitality and dexterity. It was an immediate success, making Boswell famous overnight throughout Britain and the Continent. As Samuel Johnson wrote to him, 'Your History [Part I] is like other histories, but your Journal is in a very high degree curious and delightful. There is between the History and the Journal that difference which will always be found between notions borrowed from without and notions generated within ... You express images which operated strongly upon yourself, and you have impressed them with great force upon your readers. I know not whether I could name any narrative by which curiosity is better excited, or better gratified.'

Johnson might also have mentioned the theme of primitivism in the work, the same that appealed to both him and Boswell on their later journey to the Hebrides. Boswell's readers would also have been taken with his descriptions of the unexpected appearance of genteel and urbane civilisation in remote Corsica — the juxtaposition of the neo-classical and the Romantic that fascinated him in primitive environments.

His visit to Corsica and the writing up of his experiences there also crystallised his ambition for literary fame, although tragically this never exceeded his aspirations for social esteem and status. Writing, he discovered, could endow him with a protecting reputation, a screen, behind which he could take refuge. As he wrote in his Preface, 'A man who has been able to furnish a book which has been approved by the world, has established himself as a respectable character in distant society, without any danger of having that character lessened by the observation of his weaknesses. To preserve an uniform dignity among those who *see us every day, is hardly possible; and to aim at it, must put us under the fetters of perpetual restraint. The authour of an approved book may allow his natural disposition an easy play, and yet indulge the pride of superiour genius when he considers that by those who know him only as an authour, he never ceases to be respected.'*

Having resolved to pass some years abroad, for my instruction and entertainment, I conceived a design of visiting the island of Corsica. I wished for something more than just the common course of what is called the tour of Europe; and Corsica occurred to me as a place which no body else had seen, and where I should find what was to be seen no where else, a people actually fighting for liberty, and forming themselves from a poor inconsiderable oppressed nation, into a flourishing and independent state.

When I got into Switzerland, I went to see M. Rousseau. He was then living in romantic retirement, from whence, perhaps, it had been better for him never to have descended. While he was at a distance, his singular eloquence filled our minds with high ideas of the wild philosopher. When he came into the walks of men, we know alas! how much these ideas suffered.

He entertained me very courteously ... I had heard that M. Rousseau had some correspondence with the Corsicans, and had been desired to assist them in forming their laws. I told him my scheme of going to visit them, after I had completed my tour of Italy; and I insisted that he should give me a letter of introduction. He immediately agreed to do so, whenever I should acquaint him of my time of going thither; for he saw that my enthusiasm for the brave islanders was as warm as his own.

I accordingly wrote to him from Rome, in April 1765, that I had fixed the month of September for my Corsican expedition, and therefore begged of him to send me the letter of introduction, which if he refused, I should certainly go without it, and probably be hanged as a spy. So let him answer for the consequences.

The wild philosopher was a man of his word ... Furnished with these credentials, I was impatient to be with the illustrious chief[1]. The charms of sweet Siena detained me longer than they should have done. I required the hardy air of Corsica to brace me, after the delights of Tuscany.

I recollect with astonishment how little the real state of Corsica was

known, even by those who had good access to know it. An officer of
rank in the British navy, who had been in several ports of the island,
told me that I run the risk of my life in going among these barbarians;
for, that his surgeon's mate went ashore to take the diversion of
shooting, and every moment was alarmed by some of the natives, who
started from the bushes with loaded guns, and if he had not been
protected by Corsican guides, would have certainly blown out his
brains.

Nay at Leghorn, which is within a day's sailing of Corsica, and has
a constant intercourse with it, I found people who dissuaded me from
going thither because it might be dangerous.

I was, however, under no apprehension of going to Corsica, Count
Rivarola the Sardinian consul, who is himself a Corsican, assuring me
that the island was then in a very civilised state; and besides, that in
the rudest times no Corsican would ever attack a stranger. The Count
was so good as to give me most obliging letters to many people in
the island. I had now been in several foreign countries. I had found
that I was able to accommodate myself to my fellow creatures of
different languages and sentiments. I did not fear that it would be a
difficult task for me to make myself easy with the plain and generous
Corsicans.

The only danger I saw was that I might be taken by some of the
Barbary corsairs, and have a trial of slavery among the Turks at Algiers.
I spoke of it to Commodore Harrison, who commanded the British
squadron in the Mediterranean, and was then lying with his ship the
Centurion, in the bay of Leghorn. He assured me that if the Turks did
take me, they should not keep me long, but in order to prevent it he
was so good as to grant me a very ample and particular passport; and
as it could be of no use if I did not meet the corsairs, he said very
pleasantly when he gave it me, 'I hope, Sir, it shall be of no use to
you.'

Before I left Leghorn, I could observe that my tour was looked upon
by the Italian politicians in a very serious light, as if truly I had a
commission from my Court to negotiate a treaty with the Corsicans.
The more I disclaimed any such thing the more they persevered in
affirming it; and I was considered as a very close young man. I
therefore just allowed them to make a minister of me till time should
undeceive them.

I sailed from Leghorn in a Tuscan vessel which was going over to

Capo Corso for wine. I preferred this to a vessel going to Bastia because as I did not know how the French general was affected towards the Corsicans, I was afraid that he might not permit me to go forward to Paoli. I therefore resolved to land on the territories of the nation, and after I had been with the illustrious chief to pay my respects as to the French if I should find it safe.

Though from Leghorn to Corsica is usually but one day's sailing, there was so dead a calm that it took us two days. The first day was the most tedious. However, there were two or three Corsicans aboard, and one of them played on the *cetra*, which amused me a good deal. At sunset all the people in the ship sung the Ave Maria with great devotion and some melody. It was pleasing to enter into the spirit of their religion, and hear them offering up their evening orisons.

The second day we became better acquainted, and more lively and cheerful. The worthy Corsicans thought it was proper to give a moral lesson to a young traveller just come from Italy. They told me that in their country I should be treated with the greatest hospitality, but if I attempted to debauch any of their women I might expect instant death.

I employed myself several hours in rowing, which gave me great spirits. I relished fully my approach to the island, which had acquired an unusual grandeur in my imagination. As long as I can remember anything I have heard of 'the malcontents of Corsica, with Paoli at their head'. It was a curious thought that I was just going to see them.

About seven o'clock at night we landed safely in the harbour of Centuri ... The prospect of the mountains covered with vines and olives was extremely agreeable, and the odour of the myrtle and other aromatic shrubs and flowers that grew all around me was very refreshing. As I walked along, I often saw Corsican peasants come suddenly out from the covert; and as they were all armed, I saw how the frightened imagination of the surgeon's mate had raised up so many assassins. Even the man who carried my baggage was armed and, had I been timorous might have alarmed me. But he and I were very good company to each other. As it grew dusky, I repeated to myself these lines from a fine passage in Ariosto:

> E pur per selve oscure e calli obliqui
> Insieme van senza sospetto aversi.[2]

The next day, being Sunday, it rained very hard; and I must observe that the Corsicans with all their resolution are afraid of bad weather to a degree of effeminacy. I got indeed a droll but a just enough account of this from one of them: 'Sir,' said he, 'if you were as poor as a Corsican and had but one coat, so as that after being wet you could not put on dry clothes, you would be afraid too.' ...

The weather being now cleared up, I took leave of the worthy gentleman to whom I had been a guest ... I got a man with an ass to carry my baggage. But such a road I never saw. It was absolutely scrambling along the face of a rock overhanging the sea, upon a path sometimes not above a foot broad. I thought the ass rather retarded me, so I prevailed with the man to take my portmanteau and other things on his back ...

In writing this Journal, I shall not tire my readers with relating the occurrences of each particular day. It will be much more agreeable to them to have a free and continued account of what I saw or heard most worthy of observation.

For some time I had very curious travelling, mostly on foot, and attended by a couple of stout women who carried my baggage upon their heads. Every time that I prepared to set out from a village, I could not help laughing to see the good people eager to have my equipage in order and roaring out, 'The women, the women.'

I had full leisure and the best opportunities to observe everything in my progress through the island. I was lodged sometimes in private houses, sometimes in convents, being always well recommended from place to place. The first convent in which I lay was at Canari. It appeared a little odd at first. But I soon learnt to repair to my dormitory as naturally as if I had been a friar for seven years.

The convents were small, decent buildings, suited to the sober ideas of their pious inhabitants. The religious who devoutly endeavour to 'walk with God' are often treated with raillery by those whom pleasure or business prevents from thinking of future and more exalted objects. A little experience of the serenity and peace of mind to be found in convents would be of use to temper the fire of men of the world. ...

When I came to Murato, I had the pleasure of being made acquainted with Signor Barbaggi, who is married to the niece of Paoli. I found him to be a sensible, intelligent, well-bred man. The mint of Corsica was in his house. I got specimens of their different kinds of money in silver and copper; and was told that they hoped in a year or two to strike some gold coins. Signor Barbaggi's house was repairing, so I was lodged in the convent. But in the morning returned to breakfast and had chocolate, and at dinner we had no less than twelve well-dressed dishes, served on Dresden china, with a dessert, different sorts of wine, and a liqueur, all the produce of Corsica. Signor Barbaggi was frequently repeating to me that the Corsicans inhabited a rude, uncultivated country and that they lived like Spartans. I begged leave to ask him in what country he could show me greater luxury than I had seen in his house; and I said I should certainly tell wherever I went what tables the Corsicans kept, notwithstanding their pretensions to poverty and temperance. A good deal of pleasantry passed upon this. His lady was a genteel woman, and appeared to be agreeable though very reserved.

From Murato to Corte I travelled through a wild, mountainous, rocky country, diversified with some large valleys. I got little beasts for me and my servant, sometimes horses but oftener mules or asses. We had no bridles but cords fixed round their necks, with which we managed them as well as we could.

At Corte I waited upon the Supreme Council, to one of whom, Signor Boccheciampe, I had a letter from Signor Barbaggi. I was very politely received, and was conducted to the Franciscan convent, where I got the apartment of Paoli, who was then some days' journey beyond the mountains, holding a court of *sindacato* [circuit judges] at a village called Sollacarò...

These fathers have a good vineyard and an excellent garden. They have between thirty and forty beehives in long wooden cases or trunks of trees, with a covering of the bark of the cork tree. When they want honey they burn a little juniper-wood, the smoke of which makes the bees retire. They then take an iron instrument with a sharp-edged crook at one end of it and bring out the greatest part of the honeycomb, leaving only a little for the bees, who work the case full again. By taking the honey in this way they never kill a bee. They seemed much at their ease, living in peace and plenty. I often joked with them on the text which is applied to their order: 'Nihil *habentes et omnia possidentes.*' [3] . . .

I chose to stop a while at Corte to repose myself after my fatigues, and to see everything about the capital of Corsica. The morning after my arrival here, three French deserters desired to speak with me. The foolish fellows had taken it into their heads that I was come to raise recruits for Scotland, and so they begged to have the honour of going along with me; I suppose with intention to have the honour of running off from me as they had done from their own Regiments . . .

I went up to the Castle of Corte. The Commandant very civilly showed me every part of it. As I wished to see all things in Corsica, I desired to see even the unhappy criminals. There were then three in the Castle: a man for the murder of his wife, a married lady who had hired one of her servants to strangle a woman of whom she was jealous, and the servant who had actually perpetrated this barbarous action. They were brought out from their cells that I might talk with them. The murderer of his wife had a stupid, hardened appearance, and told me he did it at the instigation of the devil. The servant was a poor despicable wretch. He had at first accused his mistress but was afterwards prevailed with to deny his accusation, upon which he was put to the torture by having lighted matches held between his fingers. This made him return to what he had formerly said, so as to be a strong evidence against his mistress. His hands were so miserably scorched that he was a piteous object. I asked him why he had committed such a crime; he said, 'Because I was without under-standing.' The lady seemed of a bold and resolute spirit. She spoke to me with great firmness and denied her guilt, saying with a con-temptuous smile as she pointed to her servant, 'They can force that creature to say what they please.'

The hangman of Corsica was a great curiosity. Being held in the utmost detestation, he durst not live like another inhabitant of the island. He was obliged to take refuge in the Castle, and there he was kept in a little corner turret, where he had just room for a miserable bed and a little bit of fire to dress such victuals for himself as were sufficient to keep him alive; for nobody would have any intercourse with him, but all turned their backs upon him. I went up and looked at him. And a more dirty, rueful spectacle I never beheld. He seemed sensible of his situation and held down his head like an abhorred outcast.

It was a long time before they could get a hangman in Corsica, so that the punishment of the gallows was hardly known, all their criminals being shot. At last this creature whom I saw, who is a Sicilian, came with a message to Paoli. The General, who has a wonderful talent for physiognomy, on seeing the man said immediately to some of the people about him, 'Behold our hangman.' He gave orders to ask the man if he would accept of the office, and his answer was, 'My grandfather was a hangman, my father was a hangman. I have been a hangman myself and am willing to continue so.' He was therefore immediately put into office, and the ignominious death dispensed by his hands hath had more effect than twenty executions by firearms.

It is remarkable that no Corsican would upon any account consent to be a hangman. Not the greatest criminals, who might have had their lives upon that condition. Even the wretch who for a paltry hire had strangled a woman would rather submit to death than do the same action as the executioner of the law.

When I had seen everything about Corte, I prepared for my journey over the mountains, that I might be with Paoli ... I set out in very good order, having excellent mules and active, clever Corsican guides. My worthy fathers of the convent, who treated me in the kindest manner while I was their guest, would also give me some provisions for my journey, so they put up a gourd of their best wine and some delicious pomegranates. My Corsican guides appeared so hearty that I often got down and walked along with them, doing just what I saw them do. When we grew hungry we threw stones among the thick branches of the chestnut trees which overshadowed us, and in that manner we brought down a shower of chestnuts with which we filled our pockets, and went on eating them with great relish; and when this made us thirsty, we lay down by the side of the first brook, put our mouths to the stream and drank sufficiently. It was just being for a little while one of the prisca gens mortalium who ran about in the woods eating acorns and drinking water.

While I stopped to refresh my mules at a little village, the inhabitants came crowding about me as an ambassador going to their General. When they were informed of my country, a strong, black fellow among them said, 'English! they are barbarians; they don't believe in the great God.' I told him, 'Excuse me, Sir. We do believe in God, and in Jesus Christ too.' 'Um,' said he, 'and in the Pope?' 'No.' 'And why?' This was a puzzling question in these circumstances, for there was a great audience to the controversy. I thought I would try a method of my own, and very gravely replied, 'Because we are too far off.' A very new argument against the universal infallibility of the Pope. It took, however, for my opponent mused a while, and then said, 'Too far off! Why, Sicily is as far off as England. Yet in Sicily they believe in the Pope.' 'Oh,' said I, 'we are ten times farther off than Sicily.' 'Aha!'

said he, and seemed quite satisfied. In this manner I got off very well. I questioned whether any of the learned reasonings of our Protestant divines would have had so good an effect.

My journey over the mountains was very entertaining. I passed some immense ridges and vast woods. I was in great health and spirits, and fully able to enter into the ideas of the brave, rude men whom I found in all quarters.

At Bastélica, where there is a stately, spirited race of people, I had a large company to attend me in the convent. I liked to see their natural frankness and ease, for why should men be afraid of their own species? They just came in, making an easy bow, placed themselves round the room where I was sitting, rested themselves on their muskets, and immediately entered into conversation with me. They talked very feelingly of the miseries that their country had endured, and complained that they were still but in a state of poverty. I happened at that time to have an unusual flow of spirits, and as one who finds himself amongst utter strangers in a distant country has no timidity, I harangued the men of Bastélica with great fluency. I expatiated on the bravery of the Corsicans by which they had purchased liberty, the most valuable of all possessions, and rendered themselves glorious over all Europe. Their poverty, I told them, might be remedied by a proper cultivation of their island and by engaging a little in commerce. But I bid them remember that they were much happier in their present state than in a state of refinement and vice, and that therefore they should beware of luxury.

What I said had the good fortune to touch them, and several of them repeated the same sentiments much better than I could do. They all expressed their strong attachment to Paoli, and called out in one voice that they were all at his command. I could with pleasure have passed a long time here ...

When I at last came within sight of Sollacarò, where Paoli was, I could not help being under considerable anxiety. My ideas of him had been greatly heightened by the conversations I had held with all sorts of people in the island, they having represented him to me as something above humanity. I had the strongest desire to see so exalted a character, but I feared that I should be unable to give a proper account why I had presumed to trouble him with a visit, and that I should sink to nothing before him. I almost wished yet to go back without seeing him. These workings of sensibility employed my mind till I rode through the village and came up to the house where he was lodged.

Leaving my servant with my guides, I passed through the guards and was met by some of the General's people, who conducted me into an antechamber where were several gentlemen-in-waiting. Signor Boccheciampe had notified my arrival, and I was shown into Paoli's room. I found him alone, and was struck with his appearance. He is tall, strong, and well made; of a fair complexion, a sensible, free, and open countenance, and a manly and noble carriage. He was then in his fortieth year. He was dressed in green and gold. He used to wear the common Corsican habit, but on the arrival of the French he thought a little external elegance might be of use to make the government appear in a more respectable light.

He asked me what were my commands for him. I presented him a letter from Count Rivarola, and when he had read it I showed him my letter from Rousseau. He was polite but very reserved. I had stood in the presence of many a prince, but I never had such a trial as in the presence of Paoli. I have already said that he is a great physiognomist. In consequence of his being in continual danger from treachery and assassination, he has formed a habit of studiously observing every new face. For ten minutes we walked backwards and forwards through the room hardly saying a word, while he looked at me with a steadfast, keen, and penetrating eye, as if he searched my very soul.

This interview was for a while very severe upon me. I was much relieved when his reserve wore off and he began to speak more. I then ventured to address him with this compliment to the Corsicans: 'Sir, I am upon my travels, and have lately visited Rome. I am come from seeing the ruins of one brave and free people; I now see the rise of another.'

He received my compliment very graciously, but observed that the Corsicans had no chance of being like the Romans, a great conquering nation who should extend its empire over half the globe. Their situation, and the modern political systems, rendered this impossible. 'But,' said he, 'Corsica may be a very happy country.' He expressed a high admiration of M. Rousseau, whom Signor Buttafoco had invited to Corsica to aid the nation in forming its laws. It seems M. de Voltaire had reported, in his rallying manner, that the invitation was merely a trick which he had put upon Rousseau. Paoli told me that when he understood this, he himself wrote to Rousseau enforcing the invitation.

Of this affair I shall give a full account in an after part of my Journal.

Some of the nobles who attended him came into the room, and in a little we were told that dinner was served up. The General did me the honour to place me next him. He had a table of fifteen or sixteen covers, having always a good many of the principal men of the island with him. He had an Italian cook who had been long in France, but he chose to have a few plain substantial dishes, avoiding every kind of luxury and drinking no foreign wine.

I felt myself under some constraint in such a circle of heroes. The General talked a great deal on history and on literature. I soon perceived that he was a fine classical scholar, that his mind was enriched with a variety of knowledge, and that his conversation at meals was instructive and entertaining. Before dinner he had spoken French. He now spoke Italian, in which he is very eloquent.

We retired to another room to drink coffee. My timidity wore off. I no longer anxiously thought of myself; my whole attention was employed in listening to the illustrious commander of a nation.

He recommended me to the care of the Abbé Rostini, who had lived many years in France. Signor Colonna, the lord of the manor here, being from home, his house was assigned for me to live in. I was left by myself till near supper time, when I returned to the General, whose conversation improved upon me as did the society of those about him, with whom I gradually formed an acquaintance.

Every day I felt myself happier. Particular marks of attention were shown me as a subject of Great Britain, the report of which went over to Italy and confirmed the conjectures that I was really an envoy. In the morning I had my chocolate served up upon a silver salver adorned with the arms of Corsica. I dined and supped constantly with the General. I was visited by all the nobility, and whenever I chose to make a little tour I was attended by a party of guards. I begged of the General not to treat me with so much ceremony, but he insisted upon it.

One day when I rode out, I was mounted on Paoli's own horse with rich furniture of crimson velvet, with broad gold lace, and had my guards marching along with me. I allowed myself to indulge a momentary pride in this parade, as I was curious to experience what could really be the pleasure of state and distinction with which mankind are so strangely intoxicated. When I returned to the Continent after all this greatness, I used to joke with my acquaintance and tell them that

I could not bear to live with them, for they did not treat me with a proper respect.

My time passed here in the most agreeable manner. I enjoyed a sort of luxury of noble sentiment. Paoli became more affable with me. I made myself known to him. I forgot the great distance between us, and had every day some hours of private conversation with him.

From my first setting out on this tour, I wrote down every night what I had observed during the day, throwing together a great deal that I might afterwards make a selection at leisure.

Of these particulars, the most valuable to my readers, as well as to myself, must surely be the memoirs and remarkable sayings of Paoli, which I am proud to record.

Talking of the Corsican war, 'Sir,' said he, 'if the event prove happy, we shall be called great defenders of liberty. If the event shall prove unhappy, we shall be called unfortunate rebels.'

The French objected to him that the Corsican nation had no regular troops. 'We would not have them,' said Paoli. 'We should then have the bravery of this and the other regiment. At present every single man is as a regiment himself. Should the Corsicans be formed into regular troops, we should lose that personal bravery which has produced such actions among us as in another country would have rendered famous even a marshal.'

I asked him how he could possibly have a soul so superior to interest. 'It is not superior,' said he; 'my interest is to gain a name. I know well that he who does good to his country will gain that, and I expect it. Yet could I render this people happy, I would be content to be forgotten. I have an unspeakable pride. The approbation of my own heart is enough.'

He said he would have great pleasure in seeing the world and enjoying the society of the learned and the accomplished in every country. I asked him how with these dispositions he could bear to be confined to an island yet in a rude uncivilised state, and instead of participating Attic evenings, *noctes coenaeque Deum*,[4] be in a continual course of care and of danger. He replied in one line of Virgil: *Vincet amor patriae laudumque immensa cupido*.[5] This, uttered with the fine open Italian pronunciation, and the graceful dignity of his manner, was very noble. I wished to have a statue of him taken at that moment.

I asked him if he understood English. He immediately began and spoke it, which he did tolerably well. When at Naples, he had, known several Irish gentlemen who were officers in that service. Having a great facility in acquiring languages, he learnt English from them. But as he had been now ten years without ever speaking it, he spoke very slow. One could see that he was possessed of the words, but for want of what I may call mechanical practice he had a difficulty in expressing himself.

I was diverted with his English library. It consisted of some broken volumes of the *Spectator* and *Tatler*, Pope's *Essay on Man*, *Gulliver's Travels*, a *History of France* in old English, and Barclay's *Apology for the Quakers*. I promised to send him some English books...

He reasoned one day in the midst of his nobles whether the commander of a nation should be married or not. 'If he is married,' said he, 'there is a risk that he may be distracted by private affairs and swayed too much by a concern for his family. If he is unmarried, there is a risk that, not having the tender attachments of a wife and children, he may sacrifice all to his own ambition.' When I said he ought to marry and have a son to succeed him; 'Sir,' said he, 'what security can I have that my son will think and act as I do? What sort of a son had Cicero, and what had Marcus Aurelius?'

He said to me one day when we were alone, 'I never will marry, I have not the conjugal virtues. Nothing would tempt me to marry but a woman who should bring me an immense dowry with which I might assist my country.'

But he spoke much in praise of marriage, as an institution which the experience of ages had found to be the best calculated for the happiness of individuals and for the good of society. Had he been a private gentleman, he probably would have married, and I am sure would have made as good a husband and father as he does a supreme magistrate and a general. But his arduous and critical situation would not allow him to enjoy domestic felicity. He is wedded to his country, and the Corsicans are his children.

He often talked to me of marriage, told me licentious pleasures were delusive and transient, that I should never be truly happy till I was married, and that he hoped to have a letter from me soon after my return home, acquainting him that I had followed his advice and was convinced from experience that he was in the right. With such an engaging condescension did this great man behave to me. If I could but paint his manner, all my readers would be charmed with him ...

The *ambasciatore inglese*, as the good peasants and soldiers used to call me, became a great favourite among them. I got a Corsican dress made, in which I walked about with an air of true satisfaction. The General did me the honour to present me with his own pistols, made in the island, all of Corsican wood and iron and of excellent workmanship. I had every other accoutrement. I even got one of the shells which had often sounded the alarm to liberty. I preserve them all with great care.

The Corsican peasants and soldiers were quite free and easy with me. Numbers of them used to come and see me of a morning, and just go out and in as they pleased. I did everything in my power to make them fond of the British, and bid them hope for an alliance with us. They asked me a thousand questions about my country, all which I cheerfully answered as well as I could.

One day they would needs hear me play upon my German flute. To have told my honest natural visitants, 'Really, gentlemen, I play very ill,' and put on such airs as we do in our genteel companies, would have been highly ridiculous. I therefore immediately complied with their request. I gave them one or two Italian airs, and then some of our beautiful old Scots tunes: 'Gilderoy', 'The Lass of Patie's Mill', 'Corn rigs are bonny'. The pathetic simplicity and pastoral gaiety of the Scots music will always please those who have the genuine feelings of nature. The Corsicans were charmed with the specimens I gave them, though I may now say that they were very indifferently performed.

My good friends insisted also to have an English song from me. I endeavoured to please them in this too, and was very lucky in that which occurred to me. I sung them 'Hearts of oak are our ships, Hearts of oak are our men'.[6] I translated it into Italian for them, and never did I see men so delighted with a song as the Corsicans were with the Hearts of Oak. *Cuore di quercia*, cried they, *bravo Inglese*! It was quite a joyous riot. I fancied myself to be a recruiting sea officer. I fancied all my chorus of Corsicans aboard the British fleet.

Paoli talked very highly on preserving the independency of Corsica. 'We may,' said he, 'have foreign powers for our friends, but they must be friends at arm's length. We may make an alliance, but we will not submit ourselves to the dominion of the greatest nation in Europe. This people who have done so much for liberty would be hewn in pieces man by man rather than allow Corsica to be sunk into the territories of another country. Some years ago, when a false rumour was spread that I had a design to yield up Corsica to the Emperor, a Corsican came to me and addressed me in great agitation: "What! shall the blood of so many heroes, who have sacrificed their lives for the freedom of Corsica, serve only to tinge the purple of a foreign prince!" '

I mentioned to him the scheme of an alliance between Great Britain and Corsica. Paoli with politeness and dignity waived the subject by saying, 'The less assistance we have from allies, the greater our glory.' He seemed hurt by our treatment of his country. He mentioned the severe proclamation at the last peace, in which the brave islanders were called the rebels of Corsica. He said with a conscious pride and proper feeling, 'Rebels! I did not expect that from Great Britain.' . . .

This kind of conversation led me to tell him how much I had suffered from anxious speculations. With a mind naturally inclined to melancholy, and a keen desire of enquiry, I had intensely applied myself to metaphysical researches, and reasoned beyond my depth on such subjects as it is not given to man to know. I told him I had rendered my mind a *camera obscura*, that in the very heat of youth I felt the . . . *omnia vanitas*[7] of one who has exhausted all the sweets of his being and is weary with dull repetition. I told him that I had almost become for ever incapable of taking a part in active life.

'All this,' said Paoli, 'is melancholy. I have also studied metaphysics. I know the arguments for fate and free will, for the materiality and immateriality of the soul, and even the subtle arguments for and against the existence of matter. But let us leave these disputes to the idle. I hold always firm one great object. I never feel a moment of despondency.'

The contemplation of such a character really existing was of more service to me than all I had been able to draw from books, from conversation, or from the exertions of my own mind. I had often enough formed the idea of a man continually such as I could conceive in my best moments. But this idea appeared like the ideas we are taught in the schools to form of things which may exist, but do not: of seas of milk and ships of amber. But I saw my highest idea realised in Paoli. It was impossible for me, speculate as I pleased, to have a little opinion of human nature in him.

One morning I remember I came in upon him without ceremony while he was dressing. I was glad to have an opportunity of seeing him in those teasing moments when according to the Duc de La Rochefoucauld no man is a hero to his *valet de chambre*.[8] That lively nobleman, who has a malicious pleasure in endeavouring to divest human nature of its dignity by exhibiting partial views and exaggerating faults, would have owned that Paoli was every moment of his life a hero.

Paoli told me that from his earliest years he had in view the important station which he now holds, so that his sentiments must ever have been great. I asked him how one of such elevated thoughts could submit with any degree of patience to the unmeaning ceremonies and poor discourse of genteel society, which he certainly was obliged to do while an officer at Naples. 'Oh,' said he, 'I managed it very easily. I was known to be a singular man. I talked and joked and was merry, but I never sat down to play; I went and came as I pleased. The mirth I like is what is easy and unaffected. I cannot endure long the sayers of good things.'

How much superior is this great man's idea of agreeable conversation to that of professed wits, who are continually straining for smart remarks and lively repartees. They put themselves to much pain in order to please, and yet please less than if they would just appear as they naturally feel themselves. A company of professed wits has always appeared to me like a company of artificers employed in some very nice and difficult work which they are under a necessity of performing.

Though calm and fully master of himself, Paoli is animated with an extraordinary degree of vivacity. Except when indisposed or greatly fatigued, he never sits down but at meals. He is perpetually in motion, walking briskly backwards and forwards. Mr Samuel Johnson, whose comprehensive and vigorous understanding has by long observation attained to a perfect knowledge of human nature, when treating of biography has this reflection: 'There are many invisible circumstances which, whether we read as enquirers after natural or moral knowledge, whether we intend to enlarge our science or increase our virtue, are more important than public occurrences.' Thus Sallust, the great master of nature, has not forgotten in his account of Catiline to remark that 'his walk was now quick, and again slow, as an indication of a mind revolving something with violent commotion.'[9] Ever mindful of the wisdom of the Rambler, I have accustomed myself to mark the small peculiarities of character...

I gave Paoli the character of my revered friend Mr Samuel Johnson. I have often regretted that illustrious men, such as humanity produces a few times in the revolution of many ages, should not see each other;

and when such arise in the same age, though at the distance of half the globe, I have been astonished how they could forbear to meet.

'As steel sharpeneth steel, so doth a man the countenance of his Friend,' says the wise monarch. What an idea may we not form of an interview between such a scholar and philosopher as Mr Johnson and such a legislator and general as Paoli!

I repeated to Paoli several of Mr Johnson's sayings, so remarkable for strong sense and original humour ... I felt an elation of mind to see Paoli delighted with the sayings of Mr Johnson, and to hear him translate them with Italian energy to the Corsican heroes.

I repeated Mr Johnson's sayings as nearly as I could in his own peculiar forcible language, for which prejudiced or little critics have taken upon them to find fault with him. He is above making any answer to them, but I have found a sufficient answer in a general remark in one of his excellent papers: 'Difference of thoughts will produce difference of language. He that thinks with more extent than another will want words of larger meaning.'[10]

I hope to be pardoned for this digression, wherein I pay a just tribute of veneration and gratitude to one from whose writings and conversation I have received instructions of which I experience the value in every scene of my life...

Talking of various schemes of life fit for a man of spirit and education, I mentioned to him that of being a foreign minister. He said he thought it a very agreeable employment for a man of parts and address during some years of his life. 'In that situation,' said he, 'a man will insensibly attain to a greater knowledge of men and manners and a more perfect acquaintance with the politics of Europe. He will be promoted according to the returns which he makes to his Court. They must be accurate, distinct, without fire or ornament. He may subjoin his own opinion, but he must do it with great modesty. The ministry at home are proud.'...

Never was I so thoroughly sensible of my own defects as while I was in Corsica. I felt how small were my abilities and how little I knew...

The last day which I spent with Paoli appeared of inestimable value. I thought him more than usually great and amiable when I was upon the eve of parting from him. The night before my departure a little incident happened which showed him in a most agreeable light. When the servants were bringing in the dessert after supper, one of them chanced to let fall a plate of walnuts. Instead of flying into a passion at what the man could not help, Paoli said with a smile, 'No matter'; and, turning to me, 'It is a good sign for you, Sir ... It is a matrimonial omen; you must go home to your own country and marry some fine woman whom you really like. I shall rejoice to hear of it.' ... When I again asked Paoli if it was possible for me in any way to show him my great respect and attachment, he replied, 'Remember that I am your friend, and write to me.' I said I hoped that when he honoured me with a letter, he would write not only as a commander but as a philosopher and a man of letters. He took me by the hand and said, 'As a friend.' I dare not transcribe from my private notes the feelings which I had at this interview. I should perhaps appear too enthusiastic. I took leave of Paoli with regret and agitation, not without some hopes of seeing him again. From having known intimately so exalted a character, my sentiments of human nature were raised; while by a sort of contagion I felt an honest ardour to distinguish myself, and be useful as far as my situation and abilities would allow; and I was, for the rest of my life, set free from a slavish timidity in the presence of great men, for where shall I find a man greater than Paoli? ...

I was returning to Corte, but I varied my road a little from the way I had come, going more upon the low country and nearer the western shore. At Cauro I had a fine view of Ajaccio and its environs. My ague was some time of forming, so I had frequent intervals of ease, which I employed in observing whatever occurred ...

The General, out of his great politeness, would not allow me to travel without a couple of chosen guards to attend me in case of any accidents. I made them my companions to relieve the tediousness of my journey. One of them called Ambrosio was a strange iron-coloured, fearless creature. He had been much in war; careless of wounds, he was coolly intent on destroying the enemy. He told me, as a good anecdote, that having been so lucky as to get a view of two Genoese exactly in a line, he took his aim and shot them both through the head at once. He talked of this just as one would talk of shooting a couple of crows. I was sure I needed be under no apprehension; but I don't know how, I desired Ambrosio to march before me that I might see him.

I was upon my guard how I treated him. But as sickness frets one's temper, I sometimes forgot myself and called him 'block-head'; and once when he was at a loss which way to go, at a wild woody part of the country, I fell into a passion and called to him, 'I am amazed that so brave a man can be so stupid.' However, by afterwards calling him friend and speaking softly to him I soon made him forget my ill humour, and we proceeded as before. Paoli had also been so good as to make me a present of one of his dogs, a strong and fierce animal. But he was too old to take an attachment to me, and I lost him between Lyons and Paris. The General has promised me a young one to be a guard at Auchinleck.

At Bocognano I came upon the same road I had formerly travelled from Corte, where I arrived safe after all my fatigues. My good fathers of the Franciscan convent received me like an old acquaintance, and showed me a kind concern at my illness ...

On one of the days that my ague disturbed me least, I walked from the convent to Corte purposely to write a letter to Mr Samuel Johnson. I told my revered friend that, from a kind of superstition agreeable in a certain degree to him as well as to myself, I had during my travels written to him from *loca sollennia*, places in some measure sacred. That as I had written to him from the tomb of Melanchthon, sacred to learning and piety, I now wrote to him from the palace of Pascal Paoli, sacred to wisdom and liberty, knowing that, however his political principles may have been represented, he had always a generous zeal for the common rights of humanity. I gave him a sketch of the great things I had seen in Corsica, and promised him a more ample relation[11].

Mr Johnson was pleased with what I wrote here, for I received at Paris an answer from him which I keep as a valuable charter. 'When you return, you will return to an unaltered, and I hope unalterable, friend. All that you have to fear from me is the vexation of disappointing me. No man loves to frustrate expectations which have been formed in his favour; and the pleasure which I promise myself from your journals and remarks is so great that perhaps no degree of attention or discernment will be sufficient to afford it. Come home, however, and take your chance. I long to see you and to hear you, and hope that we shall not be so long separated again. Come home, and expect such a welcome as is due to him whom a wise and noble curiosity has led where perhaps no native of this country ever was before.'[12] ...

I quitted Corsica with reluctance when I thought of the illustrious Paoli. I wrote to him from Bastia informing him of my illness, which I said was owing to his having made me a man of so much consequence that, instead of putting me into a snug little room, he had lodged me in the magnificent old palace where the wind and rain entered.

His answer to my first letter is written with so much spirit that I begged his permission to publish it, which he granted in the genteelest manner, saying, 'I do not remember the contents of the letter, but I have such a confidence in Mr Boswell that I am sure he would not publish it if there was anything in it improper for public view; so he has my permission.' I am thus enabled to present my readers with an original letter from Paoli.

Patrimonio, 23 December 1765

Much esteemed Mr Boswell, I received the letter which you wrote to me from Bastia, and am much comforted by hearing that you are restored to perfect health. It is lucky for you that you fell into the hands of an able physician. When you shall again be seized with a disgust at improved and agreeable countries, and shall return to this ill-fated land, I will take care to have you lodged in warmer and better-finished apartments than those of the house of Colonna at Sollacarò. But you again should be satisfied not to travel when the weather and the season require one to keep within doors, and wait for a fair day. I expect with impatience the letter which you promised to write to me from Genoa, where I much suspect that the delicacy of the ladies will have obliged you to perform some days of quarantine for purifying you from every the least infection which you may have carried with you from the air of this country; and still more so, if you have taken the whim to show that suit of Corsican velvet and that bonnet of which the Corsicans will have the origin to be from the ancient helmets, whereas the Genoese say it was invented by those who rob on the highway in order to disguise themselves – as if during the Genoese government public robbers needed to fear punishment. I am sure, however, that you will have taken the proper method with these amiable and delicate persons, insinuating to them that the hearts of beauties are formed for compassion and not for disdain and tyranny, and so you will have been easily restored to their good graces.

... Wherever I am, your friendship will be present to my mind, and I shall be desirous to continue a correspondence with you...

PART THREE

The Hypochondriack

Beginning in October 1777, Boswell began publishing a series of monthly essays for the London Magazine, in which he had purchased a partnership interest, under the byline 'The Hypochondriack'. He kept writing them, without missing a month, until August 1783, by which time he had amassed a total of no fewer than seventy. Just before Dr Johnson's death he showed them to him. Johnson liked them and offered to make suggestions and revisions towards their publication as a book, though he died before he could do so and Boswell himself never got further to shepherding them into print than choosing forty or so for the volume.

The essays cover a wide range of subjects, about some of which he wrote more than one essay, including luxury, youth and age, love, marriage, executions, suicide, religion, penuriousness and wealth, dedications and diaries. Many are especially important because they are heavily autobiographical, such as four on hypochondria, four on drinking, three on living in the country, and three on death. One of Boswell's objectives in writing them, apart from his obsession with seeing himself in print, was that they focused and animated his mind during periods of depression. They made him sit down and write. Few of them have great depth, or are very original, but in the best of them he is a practical psychologist courageously probing the sources of his identity, confusion, happiness and unhappiness. Such originality as they have is linked to himself. As always in his writing, he is at his dramatic best when he is his own subject. In these essays, he is the only one on the stage, honestly and with frequent flashes of wit searching his own experience and society in an attempt to come to terms with himself. He knew he was risking exposing too much of himself to the public, that he might be accused of excessive egotism, but if he could achieve a 'transcript of the mind' in 'a hurry of spirits' it was worth the effort. The essays show him to be a man of our own times: spontaneous, openly curious, candid, humorous, immensely capable of self-judgment and self-analysis, and sensitive. They also illustrate his considerable skills in metaphor, simile, example and analogy, which bring down to earth his most abstract points.

No 5 (February 1778)
On Hypochondria

Why is it that all men who have excelled in philosophy, in politicks, in poetry, or in the arts, have been subject to melancholy? (Aristotle)

ARISTOTLE, whose profound investigation and variety of knowledge I always consider with wonder and reverence, appears to have admitted the opinion that melancholy is the concomitant of distinguished genius; and indeed he illustrates the opinion with much philosophical ability, and many remarks upon real life, as it fell under his own observation, selecting at the same time renowned characters of antiquity, to whom melancholy was said to be constitutional.

We *Hypochondriacks* may be glad to accept of this compliment from so great a master of human nature, and to console ourselves in the hour of gloomy distress, by thinking that our sufferings mark our superiority. I may use the expression *we Hypochondriacks*, when addressing myself to my atrabilious brethren in general, and not be afraid of giving offence; though I should not choose to do it to any particular person, as there might be some danger from irritable delicacy. Hypochondriacks themselves are not agreed that they have reason to be vain, or proud of their malady; and even if that were the case, it might not be quite safe to single one out. I remember hearing a late celebrated infidel tell that he was not at all pleased when the infidel wife of his friend, a poet of some eminence, addressed him in a company in London, 'we Deists.' – Speak for yourself, Madam, said he abruptly. And yet we are sure that Deists are exceedingly vain of their profession or way of thinking, or whatever they please to call it – for nothing but vanity could make them proclaim it to the world, when they are sure it can do no good to any body, and may do harm to many.

But whether from the diffidence which Hypochondria occasions, or from having closely studied numbers affected with that disease; I must, with all due respect to Aristotle, beg leave to doubt the proposition, that it is peculiarly to be found in men of remarkable excellence. And I think it is of importance that the proposition should not be believed – because I am certain that many who might have prevented the disease from coming to any height, had they checked its first appearances, have not only not resisted it, but have truly cherished it, from the erroneous flattering notion that they were making sure of the undoubted though painful characteristic of excellence, as young ladies submit without complaint to have their ears pierced that they may be decorated with brilliant ornaments.

Melancholy, or Hypochondria, like the fever or gout, or any other disease, is incident to all sorts of men, from the wisest to the most foolish. And I can assure my readers that I have found as dull and as coarse mortals; nay, as silly creatures as ever appeared upon earth, who had all the symptoms of it, and were as miserable from it as was compatible with their constitutions. For I do not dispute that men are miserable in a greater or lesser degree in proportion to their under-standing and sensibility. It is not every man who can be exquisitely miserable, any more than exquisitely happy. But the distemper indub-itably operates, though in different degrees, upon every species or constitution, as fire produces its effects, though in different degrees, upon every species of matter, however much or however little of a combustible nature.

Fire having been mentioned in the way of comparison with Hypo-chondria in one particular, I shall carry on the allusion somewhat farther, and observe, that as no wise man remains in supine negligence when he sees a fire break out and threaten destruction to his house, neither should he allow Hypochondria to gather strength, but should exert himself with all possible speed and activity to crush it in its beginning. As the first smoke from burning rouses activity to extinguish it; such should be the consequence upon the first rise of gloomy vapour in the mind. There is not the least doubt that Hypochondria, as well as fire, may be checked, if diligence, sufficiently early and sufficiently vigorous, be used. Indeed, in some very particular instances, the smoke and the melancholy are of such force as at once to incapacitate. But when a man cannot overcome them by himself, he must call in the aid of firemen or friends. Cheerful companions, by playing their pleasantry upon the mind, will soon dissipate the dreary clouds. Sensible, however, of human imperfection, I must acknowledge that as there are fires in the universe which all the power of the human race cannot extinguish, so there are excessive degrees of melancholy, which defy all our endeavours to remedy them, and which can be cured only by divine interposition. But as we should be careful not to think with the sluggard, that, 'there is a lion in the street'; we should

equally guard against imagining that there is a volcano within us, a
melancholy so dreadful that we can do nothing in opposition to it.
We should be particularly careful against resigning ourselves to the
mental distemper, when it vents itself in immoral acts, which a notion
of our being driven about as the Demoniacs were, makes us too ready
to excuse, and to deaden the voice of conscience upbraiding our
transgressions. The *Abbé Le Blanc*, in his Letters on the English Nation,
when treating of Hypochondria or vapours, makes a remark to this
purpose with much justice. He says, that people too often ascribe to
disease what is in reality vice.

Hypochondria affects us in an infinite variety of ways; for, a
disordered imagination teems with a boundless multiplicity of evils;
and the disorders of the body which I believe always attend the direful
disease, make such diversities of combination, that it is scarcely possible
to specify all the sufferings of a Hypochondriack.

Mr Green, in his poem entitled *The Spleen* [Matthew Green, *The Spleen*
(1737)], of which I have heard Mr Robert Dodsley boast as a capital
piece of the present age preserved in his collection, has enumerated
exceedingly well the effects of Hypochondria upon a mind of that
light structure which his seems to have been. Like one who describes
the stingings of thousands of insects but has not known the gnawings
of a wolf, or other such fierce animal, he brings together with truth
and vivacity the minute fretful pains which are generally suffered by
Hypochondriacks...

No 6 (March 1778)
On Hypochondria

The various numbers of its ills to tell,
To bulk excessive my discourse would swell. (Plautus)

NOTHING characterises a Hypochondriack more peculiarly than irre-
solution, or the want of power over his own mind. What that power
is by which the conscious spirit governs and directs the various mental
faculties, is, it must be confessed, utterly inexplicable as long as our

souls are enclosed in material frames. While a watch is shut up in its case, we cannot see how the operations of its curious machinery are carried on; and the operations of the mind may, I think, be very well assimilated to those of a watch, as that comparison probably suggests the justest conception of what we can only fancy. An eminent physician in Holland, entrusted at once with a medical chair in the university of Leyden, and with the health of the Prince of Orange, being asked what the soul was? paused, and then answered, 'C'est un ressort. It is a spring.' As the main-spring actuates the wheels and other component parts of a watch, so the soul actuates the faculties of the mind; and as the main-spring of a watch may either be broken altogether, or hurt in different degrees, we may justly talk from analogy in the same terms of the soul.

I am not unacquainted with the reasonings of materialists, that the whole man is composed of one substance. But whoever can really bring himself to believe, that the consciousness of power is an attribute of matter, is, I am pretty certain, not composed of the same substance that I am; for I have an immediate impression of that proposition being as impossible to be believed, as that my eyes are shut when I feel they are wide open, and perceive by them a number and diversity of objects. To reason or even fancy, concerning what we do not see, from what we have seen, is pleasing to the mind. And my similitude between a watch in its case, and the soul in its material frame, will, I persuade myself, be agreeable to all my readers, whose dispositions are mild, and who like better to be pleased with what they read, than to attack it. An ancient philosopher indeed, full of real or pretended honesty, declared it to be his wish that there were a window in his breast, that every body might see the integrity and purity of his thoughts. It would truly be very pretty and amusing if our bodies were transparent, so that we could see one another's sentiments and passions working as we see bees in a glass-hive.

This metaphysical piece of speculation has been produced by my feeling myself strangely averse to enter upon the fulfilment of the promise which I made in my last, to present my readers with some of my own particular observations of the effects of Hypochondria. To do it however, and that now, in this very paper, I am resolved; whether I shall do it well or ill; for I believe that firmly to reject all pleas of temporary inability, is the best way to acquire that best of all habits – a promptitude in execution.

One would at first wonder how a man should have any difficulty to tell what he himself has suffered. But the sufferings of a Hypochondriack, like the troubled dreams of a person in a fever, do not settle themselves with any permanent regularity in the memory. And indeed let any one try to express the most severe pains which he has endured, at any distance of time after they have ceased, and he will find his language quite inadequate; so that he must use those strong indefinite phrases which do not particularly specify any thing, convey any distinct meaning, or excite any lively perception.

Hypochondria sometimes brings on such an extreme degree of languor, that the patient has a reluctance to every species of exertion. The uneasiness occasioned by this state, is owing to a vivacity of imagination, presenting, at the same time, ideas of activity; so that a comparison is made between what is, and what should be. Languor, simply considered, is not uneasy; nor is any being unhappy by the privation of powers of which it has no notion. The snail nor the oyster is never dissatisfied for want of animation – but a being that has experienced activity is dejected in a quiescent state, after it has continued long enough to fill up the full measure of repose. To be therefore overpowered with languor, must make a man very unhappy; he is tantalised with a thousand ineffectual wishes which he cannot realise. For as Tantalus is fabled to have been tormented by the objects of his desire being ever in his near view, yet ever receding from his touch as he endeavoured to approach them, the languid Hypochondriack has the sad mortification of being disappointed of realising any wish, by the wretched defect of his own activity. While in that situation, time passes over him, only to be loaded with regrets. The important duties of life, the benevolent offices of friendship are neglected, though he is sensible that he shall upbraid himself for that neglect till he is glad to take shelter under the cover of disease. I indeed know an instance of a man[1] of excellence in understanding, fine taste, and nobleness of heart, who though admired in social intercourse, and distinguished in the highest public appearances, is subject occasionally to fits of languor; but he has a singular felicity of acquiescence in that state while it lasts, and although his friends are uneasy, he himself suffers no pain. He has, to be sure, an uncommon sweetness of disposition; and his rank and fortune place him above all dependence, while his friends depend upon him. So a cloud over the sun darkens those who are cheered by his light and heat; but the planet himself remains serene in celestial elevation. He reclines with a placid indolence, and philosophically exists without effort, smiling when his friends attempt to rouse him to activity, and telling them, 'I am content to be as I am.' So rare an instance as this is very pleasing to contemplate: for every sufferer is relieved by fancying that it is possible for him to be equally easy. We must, however, consider what is the usual distress of languid Hypochondria; its effects would be incredible were we not certain of them from experience. To pay a visit, or write a letter to a friend, does not surely require much activity; yet such small exertions have appeared so laborious to a Hypochondriack, that he has delayed from hour to hour, till friendship has grown cold for want of having its heat continued, for which repeated renewals, however slight, are necessary; or perhaps, till death has carried his friend beyond the reach of any tokens of his kindness, and then the regrets which pained him in the course of his neglect are accumulated, and press upon his mind with a weight of sorrow...

The uneasiness occasioned by languor is doubtless very great. But there is a worse state of Hypochondria, when the mind is so tender and sore that every thing frets it. When a man is in that state, he is not only harassed by the same pieces of business, which when in a sound state afford rather an agreeable exercise to his faculties: but even the company of those whom he loves and values is a burden to him, and affects him with irritation; unless indeed he has the comfort of a friend who will oppose him in nothing, nay will not trouble him with conversation but just as he appears to wish, watching him with soft attention, and as much as possible preserving an unison with him. In such a state, books, which have been well called silent friends, afford a kindly relief. Every man should then read what he likes best at the time. I have generally found the reading of lives do me most good, by withdrawing my attention from myself to others, and entertaining me in the most satisfactory manner with real incidents in the varied course of human existence. I look upon the *Biographia Britannica* with that kind of grateful regard with which one who has been recovered from painful indisposition by their medicinal springs beholds Bath, Bristol, or Tunbridge.

No 30 (March 1780)
On Drinking

'Drunkenness is a flattering devil, a sweet poison, a pleasant sin, which whosoever hath, hath not himself; which whosoever doth commit, doth not commit sin, but he himself is wholly sin.' (St Augustine, translated by Sir Walter Raleigh)

I promised many months ago to give my readers a paper upon drinking; and although I have not vanity enough to believe that there is much attentive expectation, I am now to fulfill my engagement.

Here again I am anxious to have it understood, that The Hypochondriack does not pretend to the wisdom and influence of a teacher. Did I consider myself as in that character, I should hardly venture to put any opinion or even any sentiment into these papers which has not been sanctified by great authority. But as I am only the companion of my readers, I have no scruple to write freely, as they will judge for themselves.

I do fairly acknowledge that I love drinking; that I have a constitutional inclination to indulge in fermented liquors, and that if it were not for the restraints of reason and religion I am afraid I should be as constant a votary of Bacchus as any man. To be sensible of this is a continual cause of fear, the uneasiness of which greatly counterbalances both the pleasure of occasional gratification and the pride of frequent successful resistance, and therefore it is certainly a misfortune to have such a constitution. My thoughts upon Drinking cannot be supposed to be quite uniform and fixed. Yet I flatter myself that as I have revolved the subject very often in my mind, and that too in very different states, I may bring together some particulars which will furnish a periodical essay sufficiently well.

The motto of this paper being a sentence of a saint, may perhaps be thought to portend a very rigid discourse. But they who think so will find themselves mistaken. And indeed I am rather apprehensive of erring upon the other side. As some of my readers may be curious to know where I have found so illustrious a translator of St Augustine as Sir Walter Raleigh, I shall tell them, that the sentence and its translation is in that great man's Instructions to his Son, in the chapter entitled, 'What inconveniences happen to such as delight in wine'; which begins thus:

'Take especial care that thou delight not in wine; for there never was any man that came to honour or preferment that loved it.' A proposition which many eminent characters both in ancient and modern times have proved not to be true. That lovers of wine have rarely been good members of society in the decent mediocrity of ordinary parts, is a juster remark. For men of superior talents have been able to rise high, notwithstanding the impediment of a vice which would have depressed feebler spirits.

It cannot be denied that by far the greatest part of mankind have in all ages been fond of drinking. Children and savages take fermented liquors with an eagerness which shows that the fondness is natural. And travellers have discovered that in countries where the art of making fermented liquors has not yet been discovered, there are other means of intoxication. Is not this a striking proof of the general unhappiness of the human race?

> O, mortal man! who livest here in toil,
> Do not complain of this thy hard estate;
> That like an emmet thou must ever moil
> Is a sad sentence of an ancient date.[2]

Does it not confirm the opinion of those who have thought and asserted that in this state of being man is restless and unhappy, and always willing to forget himself? Does it not proclaim the truth of what the gloomy but noble minded philosopher *Maupertuis* observes, that mankind are all agreed in this: '*de chercher des remèdes au mal de vivre* — to endeavour to find remedies for the pain of existence'?

An Hypochondriack is under peculiar temptations to participate freely of wine. For the impatience of his temper under his sufferings which are sometimes almost intolerable, urges him to fly to what will give him immediate relief. It has often occurred to me, that one must be obstinate to an extraordinary degree, who feeling himself in torment can resist taking what he is certain will procure him ease, or at least insensibility. To be sure we know that an excess in wine which alone can move a thick melancholy, will probably make us worse when its violent operation has ceased, so that it is in general better to bear the mental malady with firmness. Yet I am not sure but when the black distress has been of long continuance, it may be allowable to try by way of a desperate remedy, as poisons are sometimes given in medicine, what a joyous shock will produce. To have the mind fairly disengaged from its baneful foe, even for a little while, is of essential consequence. For it may then exert its latent vigour, and though hurt by its rough deliverer, be able to get the better of what pressed it down before in abject submission.

But we are not to consider the world as one immense hospital: and whenever we see a company with wine circulating amongst them, to think that they are patients swallowing a necessary potion. Drinking is in reality an occupation which employs a considerable portion of the time of many people; and to conduct it in the most rational and agreeable manner is one of the great arts of living. It is in vain for those who drink liberally to say that it is only for the sake of good company. Because it is very certain that if the wine were removed the company would soon break up, and it is plain that where wine is largely drunk there is less true social intercourse than in almost any other situation. Everyone is intent upon the main object. His faculties are absorbed in the growing sobriety, the progress of which becomes more rapid every round, and all are for the moment persuaded of the force of that riotous maxim which I believe has been seriously uttered, that 'Conversation spoils drinking.'

Were we so framed that it were possible by perpetual supplies of wine to keep ourselves for ever gay and happy, there could be no doubt that drinking would be the summum bonum, the chief good, to find out which philosophers have been so variously busied. We should then indeed produce in ourselves by the juice of the grape the effects which the seducing serpent pretended our first parents would feel by eating of the forbidden tree in the midst of the garden. We should 'be as gods knowing good and evil'; and such a wild imagination of felicity must have tilled the mind of Homer, when he thought of representing the gods of the Greeks as drinking in heaven, as he does in so high a strain of poetry, that one forgets the absurdity of the mythology ...

No 39 (December 1780)
On Hypochondria

THE Hypochondriack is himself at this moment in a state of very dismal depression, so that he cannot be supposed capable of instructing or entertaining his readers. But after keeping them company as a periodical essayist for three years, he considers them as his friends, and trusts that they will treat him with a kindly indulgence. He is encouraged by the compliments which an unknown reader at the London coffee-house has been pleased to pay him in this magazine for last month. He may hope that there are many such readers.

Instead of giving this month an essay published formerly, of which I have a few, that after a proper revision I intend to adopt into this series, I have a mind to try what I can write in so wretched a frame of mind; as there may perhaps be some of my unhappy brethren just as ill as myself, to whom it may be soothing to know that I now write at all.

While endeavouring to think of a subject, that passage in the Psalms, which I have prefixed as a motto to this paper, presented itself to my mind. 'In the multitude of my thoughts within me, thy comforts delight my soul.'

Language cannot better express uneasy perturbation of spirits than the Psalmist has here done. There is in the idea of multitude, disorder, fluctuation, and tumult; and whoever has experienced what I now suffer, must feel his situation justly and strongly described.

Let us select some of those thoughts, the multitude of which confounds and overwhelms the mind of a Hypochondriack.

His opinion of himself is low and desponding. His temporary dejection makes his faculties seem quite feeble. He imagines that every body thinks meanly of him. His fancy roves over the variety of characters whom he knows in the world, and except some very bad ones indeed, they seem all better than his own. He envies the condition of numbers, whom, when in a sound state of mind, he sees to be far inferior to him. He regrets his having ever attempted distinction and excellence in any way, because the effect of his former exertions now serves only to make his insignificance more vexing to him. Nor has he any prospect of more agreeable days when he looks forward. There is a cloud as far as he can perceive, and he supposes it will be charged with thicker vapour, the longer it continues.

He is distracted between indolence and shame. Every kind of labour is irksome to him. Yet he has not resolution to cease from his accustomed tasks. Though he reasons within himself that contempt is nothing, the habitual current of his feelings obliges him to shun being despised. He acts therefore like a slave, not animated by inclination but goaded by fear.

Every thing appears to him quite indifferent. He repeats from Hamlet,

> How weary, stale, flat, and unprofitable,
> To me seem all the uses of this world.

He begins actually to believe the strange theory, that nothing exists without the mind, because he is sensible, as he imagines, of a total change in all the objects of his contemplation. What formerly had engaging qualities has them no more. The world is one undistinguished wild.

His distempered fancy darts sudden livid glaring views athwart time and space. He cannot fix his attention upon any one thing, but has transient ideas of a thousand things; as one sees objects in the short intervals when the wind blows aside flame and smoke.

An extreme degree of irritability makes him liable to be hurt by every thing that approaches him in any respect. He is perpetually upon the fret; and though he is sensible that this renders him unmanly and pitiful he cannot help showing it; and his consciousness that it is observed, exasperates him so, that there is great danger of his being harsh in his behaviour to all around him.

He is either so weakly timid as to be afraid of every thing in which there is a possibility of danger, or he starts into the extremes of rashness and desperation. He ruminates upon all the evils that can happen to man, and wonders that he has ever had a moment's tranquillity, as he never was nor ever can be secure. The more he thinks the more miserable he grows...

Though his reason be entire enough, and he knows that his mind is sick, his gloomy imagination is so powerful that he cannot disentangle himself from its influence, and he is in effect persuaded that its hideous representations of life are true. In all other distresses there is the relief of hope. But it is the peculiar woe of melancholy, that hope hides itself in the dark cloud.

Could the Hypochondriack see any thing great or good or agreeable in the situation of others, he might by sympathy partake of their enjoyment. But his corrosive imagination destroys to his own view all that he contemplates. All that is illustrious in public life, all that is amiable and endearing in society, all that is elegant in science and in arts, affect him just with the same indifference, and even contempt, as the pursuits of children affect rational men. His fancied elevation and extent of thought prove his bane; for he is deprived of the aid which his mind might have from sound and firm understandings, as he admits of none such. Even his humanity towards the distressed is apt to be made of no avail. For as he cannot even have the idea of happiness, it appears to him immaterial whether they be relieved or not. Finding that his reason is not able to cope with his gloomy imagination, he doubts that he may have been under a delusion when it was cheerful; so that he does not even wish to be happy as formerly, since he cannot wish for what he apprehends is fallacious ...

While writing this paper, I have by some gracious influence been insensibly relieved from the distress under which I laboured when I began it. May the same happy change be experienced by any of my readers, in the like affliction, is my sincere prayer.

No 66 (March 1783)
On Diaries

It will be of great use to mark down every night, before going to sleep, what you have done during the day.

The ancient precept ... 'Know thyself', which by some is ascribed to Pythagoras, and by others is so venerated as to be supposed one of the sacred responses of the oracle at Delphos, cannot be so perfectly obeyed without the assistance of a register of one's life. For memory is so frail and variable, and so apt to be disturbed and confused by the perpetual succession of external objects and mental operations, that if our situation be not limited indeed, it is very necessary to have our thoughts and actions preserved in a mode not subject to change, if we would have a fair and distinct view of our character.

This consideration joined with 'the importance of a man to himself' has had some effect in all times. For we find that many people have written such registers, to which they have given the name of *Journals* or *Diaries*, from their being a record of each day in the course of life. 'The importance of a man to himself', simply considered, is not a subject of ridicule; for, in reality, a man is of more importance to himself than all other things or persons can be. The ridicule is, when self-importance is obtruded upon others to whom the private concerns of an individual are quite insignificant. A diary, therefore, which was much more common in the last age than in this, may be of valuable use to the person who writes it, and yet if brought forth to the public eye may expose him to contempt, unless in the estimation of the few who think much and minutely, and therefore know well of what little parts the principal extent of human existence is composed...

But it is a work of very great labour and difficulty to keep a journal of life, occupied in various pursuits, mingled with concomitant speculations and reflections, in so much, that I do not think it possible to do it unless one has a peculiar talent for Abridging. I have tried it in that way, when it has been my good fortune to live in a multiplicity of instructive and entertaining scenes, and I have thought my notes like portable soup, of which a little bit by being dissolved in water will make a good large dish; for their substance by being expanded in words would fill a volume. Sometimes it has occurred to me that a man should not live more than he can record, as a farmer should not have a larger crop than he can gather in. And I have regretted that there is no invention for getting an immediate and exact transcript of the mind, like that instrument by which a copy of a letter is at once taken off.

Perhaps it may not be for the advantage of every one to keep a diary. Should a man of great force of mind, impetuous in undertaking, and ardent in activity, examine himself frequently with nice attention, it might weaken and relax his powers, as taking it often to pieces will hurt the machinery of a watch. The important events and larger circumstances may be daily committed to writing. But he must not stop to examine the springs, or point out the detail, though these are what a philosopher would be most desirous to know...

... The chief objection against keeping a diary fairly registered, which [records] the state of our minds, and all the little occurrences by which we are intimately affected is the danger of its falling into the hands of other people, who may make use of it to our prejudice. An Hypochondriack is particularly prone to think of himself. Uneasiness directs his attention inwards. I have kept a diary for considerable portions of my life. And, in order to guard against detection of what I wished to be concealed, I once wrote parts of it in a character of my own invention, by way of a cypher, but having given over the practice for several years, I forgot my alphabet, so that all that is written in it must for ever remain as unintelligible to myself as to others. This was merely a loss. But a much worse circumstance happened. I left a large parcel of diary in Holland to be sent after me to Britain with other papers. It was fairly written out, and contained many things which I should be very sorry to have communicated except to my most intimate friends; the packages having been loosened, some of the other papers were chafed and spoiled with water, but the diary was missing. I was sadly vexed, and felt as if a part of my vitals had been separated from me, and all the consolation I received from [my] very good friend, to whom I wrote in the most earnest anxiety to make enquiry if it could be found any where, was, that he could discover no trace of it, though he had made diligent search in all the little houses, so trifling did it appear to him. I comfort myself with supposing that it has been totally destroyed in the carrying. For, indeed it is a strange disagreeable thought, that what may be properly enough called so much of one's mind should be in the possession of a stranger, or perhaps of an enemy. This should serve as a lesson not to write any thing in a diary, the discovery of which may do one essential hurt, unless the person who writes it carries his diary continually about with him . . .

If a diary be honestly and judiciously kept, it will not only be immediately useful to the person who keeps it, but will afford the most authentic materials for writing his life, which, if he is at all eminent, will always be an acceptable addition to literature; and in some instances it will give the most genuine view of many of the events and characters of the time. Diaries have been kept by persons of all ranks and denominations, and I fancy there is not one that will not in some degree interest an inquirer into human nature . . .

For my own part I have so long accustomed myself to write a diary, that when I omit it the day seems to be lost, though for the most part I put down nothing but immaterial facts which it can serve no purpose of any value to record. For instance, the diary of this day will be little more than that 'I sat quietly at home, and wrote The Hypochondriack, No LXVI, on diaries'.

No 68 (May 1783)
On Executions

... Of all public spectacles, that of a capital execution draws the greatest number of spectators. And I must confess that I myself am never absent from any of them. Nor can I accuse myself of being more hard hearted than other people. On the contrary, I am persuaded that nobody feels more sincerely for the distresses of his fellow-creatures than I do, or would do more to relieve them. When I first attended executions, I was shocked to the greatest degree. I was in a manner convulsed with pity and terror, and for several days, but especially nights after, I was in a very dismal situation. Still, however, I persisted in attending them, and by degrees my sensibility abated; so that I can now see one with great composure, and my mind is not afterwards haunted with frightful thoughts: though for a while a certain degree of gloom remains upon it. I can account for this curiosity in a philosophical manner, when I consider that death is the most awful object before every man, who ever directs his thoughts seriously towards futurity; and that it is very natural that we should be anxious to see people in that situation which affects us so much. It is true indeed that none of us, who go to see an execution, have any idea that we are to be executed and few of us need be under any apprehension whatever of meeting with that fate. But dying publicly at Tyburn, and dying privately in one's bed, are only different modes of the same thing. They are both death; they are both that wondrous, that alarming scene of quitting all that we have ever seen, heard, or known, and at once passing into a state of being totally unknown to us, and in which we cannot tell what may be our situation. Therefore it is that I feel an irresistible impulse to be present at every execution, as I there behold the various effects of the near approach of death, according to the various tempers of the unhappy sufferers, and by studying them I learn to quiet and fortify my own mind.[3]

PART FOUR

The Life of Samuel Johnson, LL.D.

From the moment it appeared on 16 May 1791, the Life of Johnson was a success, both critically and in the bookshops. In less than a year most of the 1,750 copies printed were sold and it became clear that a second edition was called for. Appearing in July 1793, 400 copies of the second edition were sold in one week. From the two editions Boswell made more than £2,500, a huge sum given the size of the contemporary market. From newspapers, friends and eminent acquaintances the praise rolled in, though some demurred and there was cavilling from political enemies and from readers who censured him, as they had earlier, for what they deemed his vain and irrelevant intrusions into the narrative, for casting himself in the role of Johnson's stooge in order to get the great man talking. Except from his own pen in his books on Corsica and the Hebrides, the public had never before seen this brand of personalised, anecdotal, conversational biography; and many did not know what to make of it. Others censured him for exposing Johnson's flaws, especially his personal eccentricities, sometimes grotesque manner, and alleged brutality. Boswell correctly anticipated being criticised with 'sneering jocularity' for including so much minute observation and particular talk and detail, such as describing Johnson's superstitiousness in counting the number of steps he took to pass through a doorway. But the praise vastly outweighed the criticism.

What Boswell did in his book was change the face of biography forever. For years he had been telling friends that his biography would be unprecedented, a storehouse of personal detail that would enrich future generations. He knew he was not writing a generalised character sketch of a public figure, as in classical biography, but an exploration of the landscape of his subject's mind. It would not be an 'ethical' biography; it would not set out to teach or moralise about human nature. Neither would this be a panegyric. Chronological events would be far less important than what Johnson 'privately wrote, and said, and thought'; it would be a portrait 'without reserve', honest, with shade as well as light.

Because Boswell is himself a major character in the work, it turns out to be an involuntary autobiography, a celebration of his own character and psyche, a canvas on which he could trace his own troubled, melancholic mind. Several reviewers roasted him for this, but much of the energy and vitality of the work is due precisely to his use of himself as a major theme. It is a significant reason why the book has maintained its preeminence in the art of biography. He shrugged off the criticism. Indeed, a good deal of the depth of feeling and understanding that informs the Life can be attributed to Boswell's deep suffering, his desolation and despair, after his wife died. Much of what he heard from Johnson or read in his writings and had previously assimilated as chiefly of biographical interest — fodder for his magnum opus — now he internalised and understood as never before. The Life is infinitely richer for it.

1763

Monday 16 May 1763

At last, on Monday the 16th May, when I was sitting in Mr Davies's back-parlour, after having drunk tea with him and Mrs Davies, Johnson unexpectedly came into the shop; and Mr Davies having perceived him through the glass-door in the room in which we were sitting, advancing towards us, — he announced his awful approach to me, somewhat in the manner of an actor in the part of Horatio, when he addresses Hamlet on the appearance of his father's ghost, 'Look, my Lord, it comes.' I found that I had a very perfect idea of Johnson's figure, from the portrait of him painted by Sir Joshua Reynolds soon after he had published his Dictionary, in the attitude of sitting in his easy chair in deep meditation, which was the first picture his friend did for him, which Sir Joshua very kindly presented to me, and from which an engraving has been made for this work. Mr Davies mentioned my name, and respectfully introduced me to him. I was much agitated; and recollecting his prejudice against the Scotch, of which I had heard much, I said to Davies, 'Don't tell where I come from.' — 'From Scotland,' cried Davies, roguishly. 'Mr Johnson,' (said I,) 'I do indeed come from Scotland, but I cannot help it.' I am willing to flatter myself that I meant this as light pleasantry to sooth and conciliate him, and not as an humiliating abasement at the expence of my country. But however that might be, this speech was somewhat unlucky; for with that quickness of wit for which he was so remarkable, he seized the expression 'come from Scotland', which I used in the sense of being of that country; and, as if I had said that I had come away from it, or left it, retorted, 'That, Sir, I find, is what a very great many of your countrymen cannot help.' This stroke stunned me a good deal; and when we had sat down, felt myself not a little embarrassed, and apprehensive of what might come next. He then addressed himself to Davies: 'What do you think of Garrick? He has refused me an order for the play for Miss Williams, because he knows the house will be full, and that an order would be worth three shillings.' Eager to take any opening to get into conversation with him, I ventured to say, 'O, Sir, I cannot think Mr Garrick would grudge such a trifle to you.' 'Sir,' (said he, with a stern look,) 'I have known David Garrick longer than you have done: and I know no right you have to talk to me on the subject.' Perhaps I deserved this check; for it was rather presumptuous in me, an entire stranger, to express any doubt of the justice of his animadversion upon his old acquaintance and pupil. I now felt myself much mortified, and began to think that the hope which I had long indulged of obtaining his acquaintance was blasted. And, in truth, had not my ardour been uncommonly strong, and my resolution uncommonly persevering, so rough a reception might have deterred me for ever from making any further attempts. Fortunately, however, I remained upon the field not wholly discomfited; and was soon rewarded by hearing some of his conversation . . .

Friday 1 July 1763

Let me here apologise for the imperfect manner in which I am obliged to exhibit Johnson's conversation at this period. In the early part of my acquaintance with him, I was so wrapped in admiration of his extraordinary colloquial talents, and so little accustomed to his peculiar mode of expression, that I found it extremely difficult to recollect and record his conversation with its genuine vigour and vivacity. In progress of time, when my mind was, as it were, *strongly impregnated with the Johnsonian æther*, I could, with much more facility and exactness, carry in my memory and commit to paper the exuberant variety of his wisdom and wit.

Thursday 21 July 1763

. . . He said, he would go to the Hebrides with me, when I returned from my travels, unless some very good companion should offer when

I was absent, which he did not think probable; adding, 'There are few people to whom I take so much to as you.' And when I talked of my leaving England[1], he said, with a very affectionate air, 'My dear Boswell, I should be very unhappy at parting, did I think we were not to meet again.' – I cannot too often remind my readers, that although such instances of his kindness are doubtless very flattering to me, yet I hope my recording them will be ascribed to a better motive than to vanity; for they afford unquestionable evidence of his tenderness and complacency, which some, while they were forced to acknowledge his great powers, have been so strenuous to deny.

[Johnson accompanied Boswell to Harwich from London to see him off for Utrecht.]

Friday 5 August 1763

Next day we got to Harwich to dinner; and my passage in the packet-boat to Helvoetsluys being secured, and my baggage put on board, we dined at our inn by ourselves. I happened to say it would be terrible if he should not find a speedy opportunity of returning to London, and be confined to so dull a place. JOHNSON. 'Don't, Sir, accustom yourself to use big words for little matters. It would *not* be *terrible*, though I *were* to be detained some time here.'...

We went and looked at the church, and having gone into it and walked up to the altar, Johnson, whose piety was constant and fervent, sent me to my knees, saying, 'Now that you are going to leave your native country, recommend yourself to the protection of your CREATOR and REDEEMER'...

My revered friend walked down with me to the beach, where we embraced and parted with tenderness, and engaged to correspondence by letters. I said, 'I hope, Sir, you will not forget me in my absence.' JOHNSON. 'Nay, Sir it is more likely you should forget me, than that I should forget you.' As the vessel put out to sea, I kept my eyes upon him for a considerable time, while he remained rolling his majestic frame in his usual manner: and at last I perceived him walk back into the town, and he disappeared.

1764

Spring 1764

He had another particularity, of which none of his friends ever ventured to ask an explanation. It appeared to me some superstitious habit, which he had contracted early, and from which he had never called upon his reason to disentangle him. This was his anxious care to go out or in at a door or passage, by a certain number of steps from a certain point, or at least so as that either his right or his left foot, (I am not certain which,) should constantly make the first actual movement when he came close to the door or passage. Thus I conjecture: for I have, upon innumerable occasions, observed him suddenly stop, and then seem to count his steps with a deep earnestness; and when he had neglected or gone wrong in this sort of magical movement, I have seen him go back again, put himself in a proper posture to begin the ceremony, and, having gone through it, break from his abstraction, walk briskly on, and join his companion. A strange instance of something of this nature, even when on horseback, happened when he was in the Isle of Sky. Sir Joshua Reynolds has observed him to go a good way about, rather than cross a particular alley in Leicester-fields; but this Sir Joshua imputed to his having had some disagreeable recollection associated with it.

That the most minute singularities which belonged to him, and made very observable parts of his appearance and manner, may not be omitted, it is requisite to mention, that while talking or even musing as he sat in his chair, he commonly held his head to one side towards his right shoulder, and shook it in a tremulous manner, moving his body backwards and forwards, and rubbing his left knee in the same direction, with the palm of his hand. In the intervals of articulating he made various sounds with his mouth, sometimes as if ruminating, or what is called chewing the cud, sometimes giving a half whistle, sometimes making his tongue play backwards from the roof of his mouth, as if clucking like a hen, and sometimes protruding it against his upper gums in front, as if pronouncing quickly under his breath, too, too, too: all this accompanied sometimes with a thoughtful look, but more frequently with a smile. Generally when he had concluded a period, in the course of a dispute, by which time he was a good deal exhausted by violence and vociferation, he used to blow out his breath like a Whale. This I suppose was a relief to his lungs; and seemed in him to be a contemptuous mode of expression, as if he had made the arguments of his opponent fly like chaff before the wind.

I am fully aware how very obvious an occasion I here give for the sneering jocularity of such as have no relish of an exact likeness; which, to render complete, he who draws it must not disdain the slightest strokes. But if witlings should be inclined to attack this account, let them have the candour to quote what I have offered in my defence.

1769

30 September 1769

On the 30 September we dined together at the Mitre...

Talking of a London life, he said, 'The happiness of London is not to be conceived but by those who have been in it. I will venture to say there is more learning and science within the circumference of ten miles from where we now sit than in all the rest of the kingdom.' BOSWELL. 'The only disadvantage is the great distance at which people live from one another.' JOHNSON. 'Yes, Sir, but that is occasioned by the largeness of it, which is the cause of all the other advantages.' BOSWELL. 'Sometimes I have been in the humour of wishing to retire to a desert.' JOHNSON. 'Sir, you have desert enough in Scotland.'

... We drank tea with Mrs Williams. I had last year had the pleasure of seeing Mrs Thrale[2] at Dr Johnson's for a short while in a morning, and had conversation enough with her to admire her talents and to show her that I was as Johnsonian as herself. Dr Johnson had probably been kind enough to speak well of me, for this evening he delivered me the following card from Mr Thrale and her, inviting me to Streatham.

On the 6 of October I complied with this obliging invitation, and found, at an elegant villa, six miles from town, every circumstance that can make society pleasing. Johnson, though quite at home, was yet looked up to with an awe, tempered by affection, and seemed to be equally the care of his host and hostess. I rejoiced at seeing him so happy.

He played off his wit against Scotland with a good humoured pleasantry, which gave me, though no bigot to national prejudices, an opportunity for a little contest with him. I having said that England was obliged to us for gardeners, almost all their good gardeners being Scotchmen. JOHNSON. 'Why, Sir, that is because gardening is much more necessary amongst you than with us, which makes so many of your people learn it. It is *all* gardening with you. Things which grow wild here must be cultivated with great care in Scotland. Pray now, (throwing himself back in his chair and laughing,) are you ever able to bring the *sloe* to perfection?'

I boasted that we had the honour of being the first to abolish the unhospitable, troublesome, and ungracious custom of giving vails to servants. JOHNSON. 'Sir, you abolished vails because you were too poor to be able to give them.' . . .

I know not from what spirit of contradiction he burst out into a violent declamation against the Corsicans, of whose heroism I talked in high terms: 'Sir,' (said he,) 'what is all this rout about the Corsicans? They have been at war with the Genoese for upwards of twenty years, and have never yet taken their fortified towns. They might have battered down the walls, and reduced them to powder in twenty years. They might have pulled the walls in pieces, and cracked the stones with their teeth in twenty years.' It was in vain to argue with him upon the want of artillery: he was not to be resisted for the moment.

On the evening of the 10 October, I presented Dr Johnson to General Paoli. I had greatly wished that two men, for whom I had the highest esteem, should meet. They met with a manly ease, mutually conscious of their own abilities, and of the abilities of each other. The General spoke Italian, and Dr Johnson English, and understood one another very well, with a little aid of interpretation from me, in which I compared myself to an isthmus which joins two great continents. Upon Johnson's approach, the General said, 'From what I have read of your works, Sir, and from what Mr Boswell has told me of you, I have long held you in great veneration.' . . .

Dr Johnson went home with me, and drank tea till late in the night. He said General Paoli had the loftiest port of any man he had ever seen. He denied that military men were always the best bred men. 'Perfect good breeding', he observed, 'consists in having no particular mark of any profession, but a general elegance of manners; whereas, in a military man you can commonly distinguish the brand of a soldier, l'homme d'épée.'

Monday 16 October 1769

He [Johnson] honoured me with his company at dinner on the 16 of October at my lodgings in Old Bond-street, with Sir Joshua Reynolds, Mr Garrick, Dr Goldsmith, Mr Murphy, Mr Bickerstaff and Mr Thomas Davies. Garrick played round him with a fond vivacity, taking hold of the breasts of his coat, and, looking up in his face with a lively archness, complimented him on the good health which he seemed then to enjoy; while the sage, shaking his head, beheld him with a gentle complacency. One of the company not being come at the appointed hour, I proposed, as usual upon such occasions, to order dinner to be served; adding, 'Ought six people to be kept waiting for one?' 'Why, yes,' (answered Johnson, with a delicate humanity,) 'if the one will suffer more by your sitting down, than the six will do by waiting.' Goldsmith, to divert the tedious minutes, strutted about bragging of his dress, and I believe was seriously vain of it, for his mind was wonderfully prone to such impressions. 'Come, come,' (said Garrick,) 'talk no more of that. You are perhaps, the worst – eh, eh!' – Goldsmith was eagerly attempting to interrupt him, when Garrick went on, laughing ironically, 'Nay, you will always look like a gentleman; but I am talking of being well or ill drest.' 'Well, let me tell you,' (said Goldsmith,) 'when my tailor brought home my bloom-coloured coat, he said, "Sir, I have a favour to beg of you. When anybody asks you who made your clothes, be pleased to mention John Filby, at the Harrow, in Water-Lane."' JOHNSON. 'Why, Sir, that was because he knew the strange colour would attract crowds to gaze at it, and thus they might hear of him, and see how well he could make a coat even of so absurd a colour.' ...

Mrs [Elizabeth] Montagu, a lady distinguished for having written an Essay on Shakspeare, being mentioned; – REYNOLDS. 'I think that essay does her honour.' JOHNSON. 'Yes, Sir; it does her honour, but it would do nobody else honour. I have, indeed, not read it all. But when I take up the end of a web, and find it packthread, I do not expect, by looking further, to find embroidery. Sir, I will venture to say, there is not one sentence of true criticism in her book.' GARRICK.

'But, Sir, surely it shows how much Voltaire has mistaken Shakspeare, which nobody else has done.' JOHNSON. 'Sir, nobody else has thought it worth while. And what merit is there in that? You may as well praise a schoolmaster for whipping a boy who has construed ill. No, Sir, there is no real criticism in it: none showing the beauty of thought, as formed on the workings of the human heart.' The admirers of this Essay may be offended at the slighting manner in which Johnson spoke of it; but let it be remembered, that he gave his honest opinion, unbiassed by any prejudice, or any proud jealousy of a woman intruding herself into the chair of criticism; for Sir Joshua Reynolds has told me, that when the Essay first came out, and it was not known who had written it, Johnson wondered how Sir Joshua could like it. At this time Sir Joshua himself had received no information concerning the authour, except being assured by one of our most eminent literati, that it was clear its authour did not know the Greek tragedies in the original. One day at Sir Joshua's table, when it was related that Mrs Montagu, in an excess of compliment to the authour of a modern tragedy, had exclaimed, 'I tremble for Shakspeare;' Johnson said, 'When Shakspeare has got _ for his rival, and Mrs Montagu for his defender, he is in a poor state indeed.'

Thursday 19 October 1769

... I passed the evening with him at his House...

I complained that he had not mentioned Garrick in his Preface to Shakspeare; and asked him if he did not admire him. JOHNSON. 'Yes, as "a poor player, who frets and struts his hour upon the stage"; – as a shadow.' BOSWELL. 'But has he not brought Shakspeare into notice?' JOHNSON. 'Sir, to allow that, would be to lampoon the age. Many of Shakspeare's plays are the worse for being acted: Macbeth, for instance.' BOSWELL. 'What, Sir, is nothing gained by decoration and action? Indeed, I do wish that you had mentioned Garrick.' JOHNSON. 'My dear Sir, had I mentioned him I must have mentioned many more: Mrs Pritchard, Mrs Cibber; – nay, and Mr Cibber too; he too altered Shakspeare.'...

Talking of our feeling for the distresses of others; – JOHNSON. 'Why, Sir, there is much noise made about it, but it is greatly exaggerated. No, Sir, we have a certain degree of feeling to prompt us to do good: more than that, Providence does not intend. It would be

misery to no purpose.' BOSWELL. 'But suppose now, Sir, that one of
your intimate friends were apprehended for an offence for which he
might be hanged.' JOHNSON. 'I should do what I could to bail him,
and give him any other assistance; but if he were once fairly hanged,
I should not Suffer.' BOSWELL. 'Would you eat your dinner that day,
Sir?' JOHNSON. 'Yes, Sir; and eat it as if he were eating it with me.
Why, there's Baretti[3], who is to be tried for his life tomorrow, friends
have risen up for him on every side; yet if he should be hanged, none
of them will eat a slice of plum-pudding the less. Sir, that sympathetic
feeling goes a very little way in depressing the mind.' . . .

BOSWELL. 'Foote has a great deal of humour?' JOHNSON. 'Yes,
Sir.' BOSWELL. 'He has a singular talent of exhibiting character.'
JOHNSON. 'Sir, it is not a talent; it is a vice; it is what others abstain
from. It is not comedy, which exhibits the character of a species, as
that of a miser gathered from many misers: it is farce, which exhibits
individuals.' BOSWELL. 'Did not he think of exhibiting you, Sir?'
JOHNSON. 'Sir, fear restrained him; he knew I would have broken
his bones. I would have saved him the trouble of cutting off a leg; I
would not have left him a leg to cut off.'[4] BOSWELL. 'Pray, Sir, is
not Foote an infidel?' JOHNSON. 'I do not know Sir that fellow is an
infidel; but if he be an infidel, he is an infidel as a dog is an infidel;
that is to say, he has never thought upon the subject.' BOSWELL. 'I
suppose, Sir, he has thought superficially, and seized the first notions
which occurred to his mind. JOHNSON. 'Why then, Sir, still he is
like a dog that snatches the piece next him. Did you never observe
that dogs have not the power of comparing? A dog will take a small
bit of meat as readily as a large, when both are before him.'

Thursday 26 October 1769

I know not how so whimsical a thought came into my mind, but I
asked, 'If Sir, you were shut up in a castle and a new-born child with
you, what would you do?' JOHNSON. 'Why, Sir. I should not much
like my company.' BOSWELL. 'But would you take the trouble of
rearing it?' He seemed, as may well be supposed, unwilling to pursue
the subject: but upon my persevering in my question, replied, 'Why
yes, Sir, I would; but I must have all conveniences. If I had no garden,
I would make a shed on the roof, and take it there for fresh air. I
should feed it, and wash it much, and with warm water to please it,

not with cold water to give it pain.' BOSWELL. 'But, Sir, does not heat relax?' JOHNSON. 'Sir, you are not to imagine the water is to be very hot. I would not coddle the child. No, Sir, the hardy method of treating children does no good. I'll take you five children from London, who shall cuff five Highland children. Sir, a man bred in London will carry a burden, or run, or wrestle, as well as a man brought up in the hardiest manner in the country.' BOSWELL. 'Good living, I suppose, makes the Londoners strong.' JOHNSON. 'Why, Sir, I don't know that it does. Our chairmen from Ireland, who are as strong men as any, have been brought up upon potatoes. Quantity makes up for quality.' BOSWELL. 'Would you teach this child that I have furnished you with any thing?' JOHNSON. 'No. I should not be apt to teach it.' BOSWELL. 'Would not you have a pleasure in teaching it?' JOHNSON. 'No. Sir, I should not have a pleasure in teaching it.' BOSWELL. 'Have you not a pleasure in teaching men? – There I have you. You have the same pleasure in teaching men, that I should have in teaching children.' JOHNSON. 'Why, something about that.'...

When we were alone, I introduced the subject of death, and endeavoured to maintain that the fear of it might be got over. I told him that David Hume said to me, he was no more uneasy to think he should not be after this life, than that he had not been before he began to exist. JOHNSON. 'Sir, if he really thinks so, his perceptions are disturbed; he is mad: if he does not think so, he lies. He may tell you, he holds his finger in the flame of a candle without feeling pain; would you believe him? When he dies, he at least gives up all he has.' BOSWELL. 'Foote, Sir, told me, that when he was very ill he was not afraid to die.' JOHNSON. 'It is not true, Sir. Hold a pistol to Foote's breast, or to Hume's breast, and threaten to kill them, and you'll see how they behave.' BOSWELL. 'But may we not fortify our minds for the approach of death?' – Here I am sensible I was in the wrong, to bring before his view what he ever looked upon with horrour; for although when in a celestial frame, in his 'Vanity of Human Wishes', he has supposed death to be 'kind Nature's signal for retreat', from this state of being to 'a happier seat', his thoughts upon this awful change were in general full of dismal apprehensions. His mind resembled the vast amphitheatre, the Coliseum at Rome. In the centre stood his judgement, which, like a mighty gladiator, combated those apprehensions that, like the wild beasts of the Arena, were all around in cells, ready to be let out upon him. After a conflict, he drove them back into their dens; but not killing them, they were still assailing him. To my question, whether we might not fortify our minds for the approach of death, he answered, in a passion, 'No, Sir, let it alone. It matters not how a man dies, but how he lives. The act of dying is not of importance, it lasts so short a time.' He added, (with an earnest look,) 'A man knows it must be so, and submits. It will do him no good to whine.'

I attempted to continue the conversation. He was so provoked, that he said, 'Give us no more of this'; and was thrown into such a state of agitation, that he expressed himself in a way that alarmed and distressed me; showed an impatience that I should leave him, and when I was going away, called to me sternly, 'Don't let us meet tomorrow.'

I went home exceedingly uneasy. All the harsh observations which I had ever heard made upon his character, crowded into my mind; and I seemed to myself like the man who had put his head into the lion's mouth a great many times with perfect safety, but at last had it bit off.

Next morning I sent him a note, stating, that I might have been in the wrong, but it was not intentionally; he was therefore, I could not help thinking, too severe upon me. That notwithstanding our agreement not to meet that day, I would call on him in my way to the city, and stay five minutes by my watch. 'You are,' (said I,) 'in my mind, since last night, surrounded with cloud and storm. Let me have a glimpse of sunshine, and go about my affairs in serenity and cheerfulness.'...

Upon entering his study, I was glad that he was not alone, which would have made our meeting more awkward...

I whispered him, 'Well, Sir, you are now in good humour.' JOHNSON. 'Yes Sir.' I was going to leave him, and had got as far as the staircase. He stopped me, and smiling, said, 'Get you gone in'; a curious mode of inviting me to stay, which I accordingly did for some time longer. This little incidental quarrel and reconciliation, which, perhaps, I may be thought to have detailed too minutely, must be esteemed as one of many proofs which his friends had, that though he might be charged with bad humour at times, he was always a good-natured man; and I have heard Sir Joshua Reynolds, a nice and delicate observer of manners, particularly remark, that when upon any occasion Johnson had been rough to any person in company, he took the first opportunity of reconciliation, by drinking to him, or addressing his discourse to him; but if he found his dignified indirect overtures sullenly neglected, he was quite indifferent, and considered himself as having done all that he ought to do, and the other as now in the wrong.

1773

Tuesday 27 April 1773

He said, 'Goldsmith should not be for ever attempting to shine in conversation: he has not temper for it, he is so much mortified when he fails. Sir, a game of jokes is composed partly of skill, partly of chance. A man may be beat at times by one who has not the tenth part of his wit. Now Goldsmith's putting himself against another, is like a man laying a hundred to one who cannot spare the hundred. It is not worth a man's while. A man should not lay a hundred to one, unless he can easily spare it, though he has a hundred chances for him: he can get but a guinea, and he may lose a hundred. Goldsmith is in this state. When he contends, if he gets the better, it is a very little addition to a man of his literary reputation: if he does not get the better, he is miserably vexed.'

Johnson's own superlative power of wit set him above any risk of such uneasiness. Garrick had remarked to me of him, a few days before, 'Rabelais and all other wits are nothing compared with him. You may be diverted by them; but Johnson gives you a forcible hug, and shakes laughter out of you, whether you will or no.'

Goldsmith, however, was often very fortunate in his witty contests, even when he entered the lists with Johnson himself. Sir Joshua Reynolds was in company with them one day, when Goldsmith said, that he thought he could write a good fable, mentioned the simplicity which that kind of composition requires, and observed, that in most fables the animals introduced seldom talk in character. 'For instance,' (said he,) 'the fable of the little fishes, who saw birds fly over their heads, and envying them, petitioned Jupiter to be changed into birds. The skill' (continued he,) 'consists in making them talk like little fishes.' While he indulged himself in this fanciful reverie, he observed Johnson shaking his sides, and laughing. Upon which he smartly proceeded, 'Why, Dr Johnson, this is not so easy as you seem to think; for if you were to make little fishes talk, they would talk like WHALES.'

Friday 7 May 1773

Goldsmith's incessant desire of being conspicuous in company, was the occasion of his sometimes appearing to such disadvantage as one should hardly have supposed possible in a man of his genius. When his literary reputation had risen deservedly high, and his society was much courted, he became very jealous of the extraordinary attention which was every where paid to Johnson. One evening, in a circle of wits, he found fault with me for talking of Johnson as entitled to the honour of unquestionable superiority. 'Sir,' (said he,) 'you are for making a monarchy of what should be a republic.'

He was still more mortified, when talking in a company with fluent vivacity, and, as he flattered himself, to the admiration of all who were present; a German who sat next him, and perceived Johnson rolling himself, as if about to speak, suddenly stopped him, saying, 'Stay, stay, – Toctor Shonson is going to say something.' This was, no doubt, very provoking, especially to one so irritable as Goldsmith, who frequently mentioned it with strong expressions of indignation.

Monday 10 May 1773

... as I was to set out on my return to Scotland next morning, I was desirous to see as much of Dr Johnson as I could. But I first called on Goldsmith to take leave of him. The jealousy and envy which, though possessed of many most amiable qualities, he frankly avowed, broke out violently at this interview. Upon another occasion, when Goldsmith confessed himself to be of an envious disposition, I contended with Johnson that we ought not to be angry with him, he was so candid in owning it. 'Nay, Sir,' (said Johnson,) 'we must be angry that a man has such a superabundance of an odious quality, that he cannot keep it within his own breast, but it boils over.' In my opinion, however, Goldsmith had not more of it than other people have, but only talked of it freely.

He now seemed very angry that Johnson was going to be a traveller; said, 'he would be a dead weight for me to carry, and that I should never be able to lug him along through the Highlands and Hebrides.'

Nor would he patiently allow me to enlarge upon Johnson's wonderful abilities; but exclaimed, 'Is he like Burke, who winds into a subject like a serpent?' 'But,' (said I,) 'Johnson is the Hercules who strangled serpents in his cradle.' ...

I have known him at times exceedingly diverted at what seemed to others a very small sport. He now laughed immoderately, without any reason that we could perceive, at our friend's [Sir Robert Chambers] making his will; called him the testator, and added, 'I dare say, he thinks he has done a mighty thing. He won't stay till he gets home to his seat in the country, to produce this wonderful deed: he'll call up the landlord of the first inn on the road; and, after a suitable preface upon mortality and the uncertainty of life, will tell him that he should not delay making his will; and here, Sir, will he say, is my will, which I have just made, with the assistance of one of the ablest lawyers in the kingdom; and he will read it to him (laughing all the time). He believes he has made this will; but he did not make it: you, Chambers, made it for him. I trust you have had more conscience than to make him say, "being of sound understanding"; ha, ha, ha! I hope he has left me a legacy. I'd have his will turned into verse, like a ballad.'

In this playful manner did he run on, exulting in his own pleasantry, which certainly was not such as might be expected from the authour of 'The Rambler' but which is here preserved, that my readers may be acquainted even with the slightest occasional characteristics of so eminent a man.

Mr Chambers did not by any means relish this jocularity ... and seemed impatient till he got rid of us. Johnson could not stop his merriment, but continued it all the way till we got without the Temple-gate. He then burst into such a fit of laughter, that he appeared to be almost in a convulsion; and, in order to support himself, laid hold of one of the posts at the side of the foot pavement, and sent forth peals so loud, that in the silence of the night his voice seemed to resound from Temple-bar to Fleet-ditch.

This most ludicrous exhibition of the awful, melancholy, and venerable Johnson, happened well to counteract the feelings of sadness which I used to experience when parting with him for a considerable time. I accompanied him to his door, where he gave me his blessing.

1776

[Boswell has accompanied Johnson on a visit to Oxford.]

Thursday 21 March 1776 [Oxfordshire]

We dined at an excellent inn at Chapel-house, where he expatiated on the felicity of England in its taverns and inns, and triumphed over the French for not having, in any perfection, the tavern life. 'There is no private house,' (said he,) 'in which people can enjoy themselves so well, as at a capital tavern. Let there be ever so great plenty of good things, ever so much grandeur, ever so much elegance, ever so much desire that every body should be easy; in the nature of things it cannot be: there must always be some degree of care and anxiety. The master of the house is anxious to entertain his guests; the guests are anxious to be agreeable to him: and no man, but a very impudent dog indeed, can as freely command what is in another man's house, as if it were his own. Whereas, at a tavern, there is a general freedom from anxiety. You are sure you are welcome: and the more noise you make, the more trouble you give, the more good things you call for, the welcomer you are. No servants will attend you with the alacrity which waiters do, who are incited by the prospect of an immediate reward in proportion as they please. No, Sir; there is nothing which has yet been contrived by man, by which so much happiness is produced as by a good tavern or inn.'

[From Oxford they made their way to Lichfield, Johnson's birthplace.]

Saturday 23 March 1776

... I saw here, for the first time, oat ale; and oat cakes not hard as in Scotland, but soft like a Yorkshire cake, were served at breakfast. It was pleasant to me to find, that 'Oats', the 'food of horses', were so much used as the food of the people in Dr Johnson's own town. He expatiated in praise of Lichfield and its inhabitants, who, he said, were the 'most sober, decent people in England, the genteelest in proportion to their wealth, and spoke the purest English'. I doubted as to the last article of this eulogy: for they had several provincial sounds; as, there, pronounced like *fear*, instead of like *fair*; *once* pronounced *woonse*, instead of *wunse*, or *wonse*. Johnson himself never got entirely free of those provincial accents. Garrick sometimes used to take him off, squeezing a lemon into a punch-bowl, with uncouth gesticulations, looking round the company, and calling out, 'Who's for poonsh?'

Very little business appeared to be going forward in Lichfield. I found however two strange manufactures for so inland a place, sail-cloth and streamers for ships; and I observed them making some saddle-cloths, and dressing sheepskins: but upon the whole, the busy hand of industry seemed to be quite slackened. 'Surely, Sir,' (said I,) 'you are an idle set of people.' 'Sir,' (said Johnson,) 'we are a city of philosophers: we work with our heads, and make the boobies of Birmingham work for us with their hands.'

Friday 12 April 1776 [London]

We discussed the question whether drinking improved conversation and benevolence. Sir Joshua maintained it did. JOHNSON. 'No, Sir: before dinner men meet with great inequality of understanding; and those who are conscious of their inferiority, have the modesty not to talk. When they have drunk wine, every man feels himself happy, and loses that modesty, and grows impudent and vociferous: but he is not improved; he is only not sensible of his defects.' Sir Joshua said the Doctor was talking of the effects of excess in wine; but that a moderate glass enlivened the mind, by giving a proper circulation to the blood. 'I am' (said he,) 'in very good spirits when I get up in the morning. By dinner-time I am exhausted; wine puts me in the same state as when I got up; and I am sure that moderate drinking makes people talk better.' JOHNSON. 'No, Sir; wine gives not light, gay, ideal hilarity; but tumultuous, noisy, clamorous merriment. I have heard none of those drunken, – nay, drunken is a coarse word, – none of those *vinous* flights.' SIR JOSHUA. 'Because you have sat by, quite sober, and felt an envy of the happiness of those who were drinking.' JOHNSON. 'Perhaps, contempt. – And, Sir, it is not necessary to be drunk one's self, to relish the wit of drunkenness. Do we not judge of the drunken wit of the dialogue between Iago and Cassio, the most excellent in its kind, when we are quite sober? Wit is wit, by whatever means it is produced; and, if good, will appear so at all times. I admit that the spirits are raised by drinking, as by the common participation of any pleasure: cock-fighting, or bear-baiting, will raise the spirits of a company, as drinking does, though surely they will not improve conversation. I also admit, that there are some sluggish men who are improved by drinking; as there are fruits which are not good till they are rotten. There are such men, but they are medlars. I indeed allow that there have been a very few men of talents who were improved by drinking; but I maintain that I am right as to the effects of drinking in general...'

I observed, that wine did some people harm, by inflaming, confusing, and irritating their minds; but that the experience of mankind had declared in favour of moderate drinking. JOHNSON. 'Sir, I do not say it is wrong to produce self-complacency by drinking; I only deny that it improves the mind. When I drank wine, I scorned to drink it when in company. I have drunk many a bottle by myself; in the first place, because I had need of it to raise my spirits; in the second place, because I would have nobody to witness its effects upon me.'

May 1776

I am now to record a very curious incident in Dr Johnson's life, which fell under my own observation ... and which I am persuaded will, with the liberal-minded, be much to his credit.

My desire of being acquainted with celebrated men of every description, had made me, much about the same time, obtain an introduction to Dr Samuel Johnson and to John Wilkes, Esq. Two men more different could perhaps not be selected out of all mankind. They had even attacked one another with some asperity in their writings; yet I lived in habits of friendship with both. I could fully relish the excellence of each; for I have ever delighted in that intellectual chemistry, which can separate good qualities from evil in the same person.

Sir John Pringle, 'mine own friend and my Father's friend,' between whom and Dr Johnson I in vain wished to establish an acquaintance, as I respected and lived in intimacy with both of them, observed to me once, very ingeniously, 'It is not in friendship as in mathematics, where two things, each equal to a third, are equal between themselves. You agree with Johnson as a middle quality, and you agree with me as a middle quality; but Johnson and I should not agree.' Sir John was not sufficiently flexible; so I desisted; knowing, indeed, that the repulsion was equally strong on the part of Johnson; who, I know not from what cause, unless his being a Scotchman, had formed a very erroneous opinion of Sir John. But I conceived an irresistible wish, if possible, to bring Dr Johnson and Mr Wilkes together. How to manage it, was a nice and difficult matter.

My worthy booksellers and friends, Messieurs Dilly in the Poultry, at whose hospitable and well-covered table I have seen a greater number of literary men, than at any other, except that of Sir Joshua Reynolds, had invited me to meet Mr Wilkes and some more gentlemen on Wednesday, May 15. 'Pray' (said I,) 'let us have Dr Johnson.' – 'What, with Mr Wilkes? not for the world (said Mr Edward Dilly) Dr Johnson would never forgive me.' – 'Come,' (said I,) 'if you'll let me negotiate for you, I will be answerable that all shall go well.' DILLY. 'Nay, if you will take it upon you, I am sure I shall be very happy to see them both here.'

Notwithstanding the high veneration which I entertained for Dr Johnson, I was sensible that he was sometimes a little actuated by the spirit of contradiction, and by means of that I hoped I should gain my point. I was persuaded that if I had come upon him with a direct proposal, 'Sir, will you dine in company with Jack Wilkes?' he would have flown into a passion, and would probably have answered, 'Dine with Jack Wilkes, Sir! I'd as soon dine with Jack Ketch.' I therefore, while we were sitting quietly by ourselves at his house in an evening, took occasion to open my plan thus: – 'Mr Dilly, Sir, sends his respectful compliments to you, and would be happy if you would do him the honour to dine with him on Wednesday next along with me, as I must soon go to Scotland.' JOHNSON. 'Sir, I am obliged to Mr Dilly, I will wait upon him –' BOSWELL. 'Provided, Sir, I suppose, that the company which he is to have, is agreeable to you.' JOHNSON. 'What do you mean, Sir? What do you take me for? Do you think I am so ignorant of the world, as to imagine that I am to prescribe to a gentleman what company he is to have at his table?' BOSWELL. 'I beg your pardon, Sir, for wishing to prevent you from meeting people whom you might not like. Perhaps he may have some of what he calls his *patriotic friends* with him.' JOHNSON. 'Well, Sir, and what then? What care I for his *patriotic friends*? Poh!' BOSWELL. 'I should not be surprised to find Jack Wilkes there.' JOHNSON, 'And if Jack Wilkes should be there, what is that to me, Sir? My dear friend, let us have no more of this. I am sorry to be angry with you; but really it is treating me strangely to talk to me as if I could not meet any company whatever, occasionally.' BOSWELL. 'Pray forgive me, Sir: I meant well. But you shall meet whoever comes, for me.' Thus I secured him, and told Dilly that he would find him very well pleased to be one of his guests on the day appointed.

Upon the much-expected Wednesday, I called on him about half an hour before dinner, as I often did when we were to dine out together, to see that he was ready in time, and to accompany him. I found him buffeting his books, as upon a former occasion, covered with dust, and making no preparation for going abroad. 'How is this, Sir?' (said I.) 'Don't you recollect that you are to dine at Mr Dilly's?' JOHNSON. 'Sir, I did not think of going to Dilly's: it went out of my head. I have ordered dinner at home with Mrs Williams.' BOSWELL. 'But, my dear Sir, you know you were engaged to Mr Dilly, and I told him so. He will expect you, and will be much disappointed if you don't come.' JOHNSON. 'You must talk to Mrs Williams about this.'

Here was a sad dilemma. I feared that what I was so confident I had secured would yet be frustrated. He had accustomed himself to show Mrs Williams such a degree of humane attention, as frequently imposed some restraint upon him; and I knew that if she should be obstinate, he would not stir. I hastened down stairs to the blind lady's room, and told her I was in great uneasiness, for Dr Johnson had engaged to me to dine this day at Mr Dilly's, but that he had told me he had forgotten his engagement, and had ordered dinner at home. 'Yes, Sir, (said she, pretty peevishly,) Dr Johnson is to dine at home.' – 'Madam,' (said I,) 'his respect for you is such, that I know he will not leave you unless you absolutely desire it. But as you have so much of his company, I hope you will be good enough to forego it for a day; as Mr Dilly is a very worthy man, has frequently had agreeable parties at his house for Dr Johnson, and will be vexed if the Doctor neglects him today. And then, Madam, be pleased to consider my situation; I carried the message, and I assured Mr Dilly that Dr Johnson was to come, and no doubt he has made a dinner, and invited a company, and boasted of the honour he expected to have. I shall be quite disgraced if the Doctor is not there.' She gradually softened to my solicitations, which were certainly as earnest as most entreaties to ladies upon any occasion and was graciously pleased to empower me to tell Dr Johnson, 'That all things considered, she thought he should certainly go.' I flew back to him still in dust, and careless of what should be the event, indifferent in his choice to go or stay I; but as soon as I had announced to him Mrs Williams's consent, he roared, 'Frank, a clean shirt,' and was very soon dressed. When I had him fairly seated in a hackney-coach with me, I exulted as much as a fortune-hunter who has got an heiress into a post-chaise with him to set out for Gretna-Green.

When we entered Mr Dilly's drawing room, he found himself in the midst of a company he did not know. I kept myself snug and silent, watching how he would conduct himself. I observed him whispering to Mr Dilly, 'Who is that gentleman, Sir?' – 'Mr Arthur Lee.' – JOHNSON. 'Too, too, too,' (under his breath,) which was one of his habitual mutterings. Mr Arthur Lee could not but be very obnoxious to Johnson, for he was not only a patriot but an American. He was afterwards minister from the United States at the court of Madrid. 'And who is the gentleman in lace?' – 'Mr Wilkes, Sir.' This information confounded him still more; he had some difficulty to restrain himself, and taking up a book, sat down upon a window-seat and read, or at least kept his eye upon it intently for some time, till he composed himself. His feelings, I dare say, were awkward enough. But he no doubt recollected his having rated me for supposing that he could be at all disconcerted by any company, and he, therefore, resolutely set himself to behave quite as an easy man of the world, who could adapt himself at once to the disposition and manners of those whom he might chance to meet.

The cheering sound of 'Dinner is upon the table,' dissolved his reverie, and we all sat down without any symptom of ill humour ... Mr Wilkes placed himself next to Dr Johnson, and behaved to him with so much attention and politeness, that he gained upon him insensibly. No man eat more heartily than Johnson, or loved better what was nice and delicate. Mr Wilkes was very assiduous in helping him to some fine veal. 'Pray give me leave, Sir: – It is better here – A little of the brown – Some fat, Sir – A little of the stuffing – Some gravy – Let me have the pleasure of giving you some butter – Allow me to recommend a squeeze of this Orange; – or the lemon, perhaps, may have more zest.' – 'Sir, Sir, I am obliged to you, Sir!' cried Johnson, bowing, and turning his head to him with a look for some time of 'surly virtue', but, in a short while, of complacency ... [*Wilkes then makes a pejorative remark about Garrick.*]

I knew that Johnson would let nobody attack Garrick but himself, as Garrick once said to me, and I had heard him praise his liberality; so to bring out his commendation of his celebrated pupil, I said, loudly, 'I have heard Garrick is liberal.' JOHNSON. 'Yes, Sir, I know that Garrick has given away more money than any man in England that I am acquainted with, and that not from ostentatious views. Garrick was very poor when he began life; so when he came to have money, he probably was very unskillful in giving away, and saved when he should not. But Garrick began to be liberal as soon as he could; and I am of opinion, the reputation of avarice which he has had, has been very lucky for him, and prevented his having many enemies. You despise a man for avarice, but do not hate him. Garrick might have been much better attacked for living with more splendour than is suitable to a player: if they had had the wit to have assaulted him in that quarter, they might have galled him more. But they have kept clamouring about his avarice, which has rescued him from much obloquy and envy.' ...

Mr Arthur Lee mentioned some Scotch who had taken possession of a barren part of America, and wondered why they should choose it. JOHNSON. 'Why, Sir, all barrenness is comparative. The *Scotch* would not know it to be barren.' BOSWELL. 'Come, come, he is flattering the English. You have now been in Scotland, Sir, and say if you did not see meat and drink enough there.' JOHNSON. 'Why yes, Sir; meat and drink enough to give the inhabitants sufficient strength to run away from home.' All these quick and lively sallies were said sportively, quite in jest, and with a smile, which showed that he meant only wit. Upon this topic he and Mr Wilkes could perfectly assimilate; here was a bond of union between them, and I was conscious that as both of them had visited Caledonia, both were fully satisfied of the strange narrow ignorance of those who imagine that it is a land of famine. But they amused themselves with persevering in the old jokes. When I claimed a superiority for Scotland over England in one respect, that no man can be arrested there for a debt merely because another swears it against him; but there must first be the judgement of a court of law ascertaining its justice; and that a seizure of the person, before judgement is obtained, can take place only, if his creditor should swear that he is about to fly from the country, or, as it is technically expressed, is in *meditatione fugæ*. WILKES. 'That, I should think, may be safely sworn of all the Scotch nation.' JOHNSON. (to Mr

Wilkes) 'You must know, Sir, I lately took my friend Boswell and showed him genuine civilised life in an English provincial town. I turned him loose at Lichfield, my native city, that he might see for once real civility: for you know he lives among savages in Scotland, and among rakes in London.' WILKES. 'Except when he is with grave, sober, decent people like you and me.' JOHNSON. (smiling) 'And we ashamed of him.'...

This record, though by no means so perfect as I could wish, will serve to give a notion of a very curious interview, which was not only pleasing at the time, but had the agreeable and benignant effect of reconciling any animosity, and sweetening any acidity, which in the various bustle of political contest, had been produced in the minds of two men, who though widely different, had so many things in common – classical learning, modern literature, wit, and humour, and ready repartee – that it would have been much to be regretted if they had been for ever at a distance from each other.

Mr Burke gave me much credit for this successful *negotiation*; and pleasantly said, that 'there was nothing to equal it in the whole history of the *Corps Diplomatique.*'

1777

Tuesday 16 September 1777

I mentioned to Dr Johnson that David Hume's persisting in his infidelity, when he was dying, shocked me much. JOHNSON. 'Why should it shock you, Sir? Hume owned he had never read the New Testament with attention. Here then was a man, who had been at no pains to inquire into the truth of religion, and had continually turned his mind the other way. It was not to be expected that the prospect of death would alter his way of thinking, unless GOD should send an angel to set him right.' I said, I had reason to believe that the thought of annihilation gave Hume no pain. JOHNSON. 'It was not so, Sir. He had a vanity in being thought easy. It is more probable that he should assume an appearance of ease, than that so very improbable a thing should be, as a man not afraid of going (as, in spite of his delusive theory, he cannot be sure but he may go,) into an unknown state, and not being uneasy at leaving all he knew. And you are to consider, that upon his own principle of annihilation he had no motive to speak the truth.' The horrour of death which I had always observed in Dr Johnson, appeared strong tonight. I ventured to tell him, that I had been, for moments in my life, not afraid of death; therefore I could suppose another man in that state of mind for a considerable space of time. He said 'he never had a moment in which death was not terrible to him' ...

Even the powerful mind of Johnson seemed foiled by futurity. But I thought, that the gloom of uncertainty in solemn religious speculation, being mingled with hope, was yet more consolatory than the emptiness of infidelity. A man can live in thick air, but perishes in an exhausted receiver.

Sunday 21 September 1777

... When we had done with criticism, we walked over to [Samuel] Richardson's, the authour of 'Clarissa', and I wondered to find Richardson displeased that I 'did not treat Cibber with more respect'. 'Now, Sir, to talk of respect for a player!' (smiling disdainfully). BOSWELL. 'There, Sir, you are always heretical: you never will allow merit to a player.' JOHNSON. 'Merit, Sir! what merit? Do you respect a rope-dancer, or a ballad-singer?' BOSWELL. 'No, Sir: but we respect a great player, as a man who can conceive lofty sentiments, and can express them gracefully.' JOHNSON. 'What, Sir, a fellow who claps a hump on his back, and a lump on his leg, and cries "I am Richard the Third"? Nay, Sir, a ballad-singer is a higher man, for he does two things; he repeats and he sings: there is both recitation and music in his performance: the player only recites.' BOSWELL. 'My dear Sir! you may turn anything into ridicule. I allow, that a player of farce is not entitled to respect; he does a little thing: but he who can represent exalted characters, and touch the noblest passions, has very respectable powers; and mankind have agreed in admiring great talents for the stage. We must consider, too, that a great player does what very few are capable to do: his art is a very rare faculty. Who can repeat Hamlet's soliloquy, "To be, or not to be," as Garrick does it?' JOHNSON. 'Any body may. Jemmy, there (a boy about eight years old, who was in the room), will do it as well in a week.' BOSWELL. 'No, no, Sir: and as a proof of the merit of great acting, and of the value which mankind set upon it, Garrick has got a hundred thousand pounds.' JOHNSON. 'Is getting a hundred thousand pounds a proof of excellence? That has been done by a scoundrel commissary.'

This was most fallacious reasoning. I was sure, for once, that I had the best side of the argument.

1778

Tuesday 7 April 1778

... BOSWELL. 'I think, Sir, you once said to me, that not to drink wine was a great deduction from life.' JOHNSON. 'It is a diminution of pleasure, to be sure; but I do not say a diminution of happiness. There is more happiness in being rational.' BOSWELL. 'But if we could have pleasure always, should not we be happy? The greatest part of men would compound for pleasure.' JOHNSON. 'Supposing we could have pleasure always, an intellectual man would not compound for it. The greatest part of men would compound, because the greatest part of men are gross.' BOSWELL. 'I allow there may be greater pleasure than from wine. I have had more pleasure from your conversation. I have indeed; I assure you I have.' JOHNSON. 'When we talk of pleasure, we mean sensual pleasure. When a man says, he had pleasure with a woman, he does not mean conversation, but something of a very different nature. Philosophers tell you, that pleasure is contrary to happiness. Gross men prefer animal pleasure. So there are men who have preferred living among savages. Now what a wretch must he be, who is content with such conversation as can be had among savages! You may remember an officer at Fort Augustus, who had served in America, told us of a woman whom they were obliged to bind, in order to get her back from savage life.' BOSWELL. 'She must have been an animal, a beast.' JOHNSON. 'Sir, she was a speaking cat.'

I mentioned to him that I had become very weary in a company where I heard not a single intellectual sentence, except that 'a man who had been settled ten years in Minorca was become a much inferiour man to what he was in London, because a man's mind grows narrow in a narrow place.' JOHNSON. 'A man's mind grows narrow in a narrow place, whose mind is enlarged only because he has lived in a large place: but what is got by books and thinking is preserved in a narrow place as well as in a large place. A man cannot know modes of life as well in Minorca as in London; but he may study mathematics as well in Minorca.' BOSWELL. 'I don't know, Sir: if you had remained ten years in the Isle of Col, you would not have been the man that you now are.' JOHNSON. 'Yes, Sir, if I had been there from fifteen to twenty-five; but not if from twenty-five to thirty-five.' BOSWELL. 'I own, Sir, the spirits which I have in London make me do every thing with more readiness and vigour. I can talk twice as much in London as any where else.'

Saturday 2 May 1778

On Saturday, May 2, I dined with him at Sir Joshua Reynolds's, where there was a very large company, and a great deal of conversation; but owing to some circumstance which I cannot now recollect, I have no record of any part of it, except that there were several people there by no means of the Johnsonian school; so that less attention was paid to him than usual, which put him out of humour; and upon some imaginary offence from me, he attacked me with such rudeness, that I was vexed and angry, because it gave those persons an opportunity of enlarging upon his supposed ferocity, and ill treatment of his best friends. I was so much hurt, and had my pride so much roused, that I kept away from him for a week; and, perhaps, might have kept away much longer, nay, gone to Scotland without seeing him again, had not we fortunately met and been reconciled. To such unhappy chances are human friendships liable.

Friday 8 May 1778

On Friday, May 8, I dined with him at Mr Langton's. I was reserved and silent, which I suppose he perceived, and might recollect the cause. After dinner, when Mr Langton was called out of the room, and we were by ourselves, he drew his chair near to mine, and said, in a tone of conciliating courtesy, 'Well, how have you done?' BOSWELL. 'Sir, you have made me very uneasy by your behaviour to me when we were last at Sir Joshua Reynolds's. You know, my dear Sir, no man has a greater respect and affection for you, or would sooner go to the end of the world to serve you. Now to treat me so –.' He insisted that I had interrupted him, which I assured him was not the case; and proceeded – 'But why treat me so before people who neither love you nor me?' JOHNSON. 'Well, I am sorry for it. I'll make it up to you twenty different ways, as you please.' BOSWELL. 'I said today to Sir Joshua, when he observed that you tossed me sometimes – I don't care how often, or how high he tosses me, when only friends are present, for then I fall upon soft ground: but I do not like falling on stones, which is the case when enemies are present. – I think this a pretty good image, Sir.' JOHNSON. 'Sir, it is one of the happiest I have ever heard.'

The truth is, there was no venom in the wounds which he inflicted at any time, unless they were irritated by some malignant infusion by other hands. We were instantly as cordial again as ever, and joined in hearty laugh at some ludicrous but innocent peculiarities of one of our friends. BOSWELL. 'Do you think, Sir, it is always culpable to laugh at a man to his face?' JOHNSON. 'Why, Sir, that depends upon the man and the thing. If it is a slight man, and a slight thing, you may; for you take nothing valuable from him.'

Tuesday 12 May 1778

On Tuesday, May 12, I waited on the Earl of Marchmont, to know if his Lordship would favour Dr Johnson with information concerning Pope, whose Life he was about to write.[5] Johnson had not flattered himself with the hopes of receiving any civility from this nobleman; for he said to me, when I mentioned Lord Marchmont as one who could tell him a great deal about Pope, 'Sir, he will tell me nothing.' I had the honour of being known to his Lordship, and applied to him of myself, without being commissioned by Johnson. His Lordship behaved in the most polite and obliging manner, promised to tell all he recollected about Pope, and was so very courteous as to say, 'Tell Dr Johnson I have a great respect for him, and am ready to show it in any way I can. I am to be in the city tomorrow, and will call at his house as I return.' His Lordship however asked, 'Will he write the Lives of the Poets impartially? He was the first that brought Whig and Tory into a Dictionary. And what do you think of his definition of Excise? Do you know the history of his aversion to the word *transpire*?' Then taking down the folio Dictionary, he showed it with this censure on its secondary sense: 'To escape from secrecy to notice; a sense lately innovated from France, without necessity.' 'The truth was, Lord Bolingbroke, who left the Jacobites, first used it; therefore, it was to be condemned. He should have shown what word would do for it, if it was unnecessary.' I afterwards put the question to Johnson: 'Why, Sir,' (said he,) 'get abroad.' BOSWELL. 'That, Sir, is using two words.' JOHNSON. 'Sir, there is no end of this. You may as well insist to have a word for old age.' BOSWELL. 'Well, Sir, *Senectus*.' JOHNSON. 'Nay, Sir, to insist always that there should be one word to express a thing in English because there is one in another language, is to change the language.'

I availed myself of this opportunity to hear from his Lordship many particulars both of Pope and Lord Bolingbroke which I have in writing. I proposed to Lord Marchmont that he should revise Johnson's Life of Pope: 'So' (said his Lordship,) 'you would put me in a dangerous situation. You know he knocked down Osborne the bookseller.'

Elated with the success of my spontaneous exertion to procure material and respectable aid to Johnson for his very favourite work, 'The Lives of the Poets', I hastened down to Mr Thrale's at Streatham, where he now was, that I might insure his being at home next day;

and after dinner, when I thought he would receive the good news in the best humour, I announced it eagerly: 'I have been at work for you today, Sir. I have been with Lord Marchmont. He bade me tell you he has a great respect for you, and will call on you tomorrow at one o'clock, and communicate all he knows about Pope.' – Here I paused, in full expectation that he would be pleased with this intelligence, would praise my active merit, and would be alert to embrace such an offer from a nobleman. But whether I had shown an over-exultation, which provoked his spleen; or whether he was seized with a suspicion that I had obtruded him on Lord Marchmont, and had humbled him too much; or whether there was any thing more than an unlucky fit of ill-humour, I know not; but, to my surprise, the result was, – JOHNSON. 'I shall not be in town tomorrow. I don't care to know about Pope.' MRS THRALE: (surprised as I was, and a little angry.) 'I suppose, Sir, Mr Boswell thought, that as you are to write Pope's Life, you would wish to know about him.' JOHNSON. 'Wish! why yes. If it rained knowledge I'd hold out my hand; but I would not give myself the trouble to go in quest of it.' There was no arguing with him at the moment. Some time afterwards he said, 'Lord Marchmont will call on me, and then I shall call on Lord Marchmont.' Mr Thrale was uneasy at his unaccountable caprice; and told me, that if I did not take care to bring about a meeting between Lord Marchmont and him, it would never take place, which would be a great pity. I sent a card to his Lordship, to be left at Johnson's house, acquainting him, that Dr Johnson could not be in town next day, but would do himself the honour of waiting on him at another time. – I give this account fairly, as a specimen of that unhappy temper with which this great and good man had occasionally to struggle, from something morbid in his constitution. Let the most censorious of my readers suppose himself to have a violent fit of the tooth-ache, or to have received a severe stroke on the shin-bone, and when in such a state to be asked a question; and if he has any candour, he will not be surprised at the answers which Johnson sometimes gave in moments of irritation, which, let me assure them, is exquisitely painful. But it must not be erroneously supposed that he was, in the smallest degree, careless concerning any work which he undertook, or that he was generally thus peevish. It will be seen, that in the following year he had a very agreeable interview with Lord Marchmont, at his Lordship's house;

and this very afternoon he soon forgot any fretfulness, and fell into conversation as usual.

1781

Friday 20 April 1781

On Friday, April 20, I spent with him one of the happiest days that I remember to have enjoyed in the whole course of my life. Mrs Garrick, whose grief for the loss of her husband was, I believe, as sincere as wounded affection and admiration could produce, had this day, for the first time since his death, a select party of his friends to dine with her. The company was Miss Hannah More, who lived with her, and whom she called her Chaplain; Mrs Boscawen, Mrs Elizabeth Carter, Sir Joshua Reynolds, Dr Burney, Dr Johnson, and myself. We found ourselves very elegantly entertained at her house in the Adelphi, where I have passed many a pleasing hour with him 'who gladdened life'...

Somebody said the life of a mere literary man could not be very entertaining. JOHNSON. 'But it certainly may. This is a remark which has been made, and repeated, without justice; why should the life of a literary man be less entertaining than the life of any other man? Are there not as interesting varieties in such a life? As a literary life it may be very entertaining.' BOSWELL. 'But it must be better surely, when it is diversified with a little active variety – such as his having gone to Jamaica; – or – his having gone to the Hebrides.' Johnson was not displeased at this...

He and I walked away together; we stopped a little while by the rails of the Adelphi, looking on the Thames, and I said to him with some emotion that I was now thinking of two friends we had lost, who once lived in the buildings behind us, Beauclerk and Garrick. 'Ay, Sir,' (said he, tenderly,) 'and two such friends as cannot be supplied.'

1783

Friday 21 March 1783

He repeated to me his verses on Mr Levett[6], with an emotion which gave them full effect; and then he was pleased to say, 'You must be as much with me as you can. You have done me good. You cannot think how much better I am since you came in.'

He sent a message to acquaint Mrs Thrale that I was arrived. I had not seen her since her husband's death. She soon appeared, and favoured me with an invitation to stay to dinner, which I accepted. There was no other company but herself and three of her daughters, Dr Johnson, and I. She too said, she was very glad I was come, for she was going to Bath, and should have been sorry to leave Dr Johnson before I came. This seemed to be attentive and kind; and I who had not been informed of any change, imagined all to be as well as formerly. He was little inclined to talk at dinner, and went to sleep after it; but when he joined us in the drawing-room, he seemed revived, and was again himself.

Talking of conversation, he said, 'There must, in the first place, be knowledge, there must be materials; – in the second place, there must be a command of words; – in the third place, there must be imagination, to place things in such views as they are not commonly seen in; – and in the fourth place, there must be presence of mind, and a resolution that is not to be overcome by failures; this last is an essential requisite; for want of it many people do not excel in conversation. Now I want it: I throw up the game upon losing a trick.' I wondered to hear him talk thus of himself, and said, 'I don't know, Sir, how this may be; but I am sure you beat other people's cards out of their hands.' I doubt whether he heard this remark. While he went on talking triumphantly, I was fixed in admiration, and said to Mrs Thrale, 'O, for short-hand to take this down!' 'You'll carry it all in your head,' (said she;) 'a long head is as good as short-hand.' . . .

After musing for some time, he said, 'I wonder how I should have any enemies; for I do harm to nobody.' BOSWELL. 'In the first place, Sir, you will be pleased to recollect, that you set out with attacking the Scotch; so you got a whole nation for your enemies.' JOHNSON. 'Why, I own, that by my definition of *oats* I meant to vex them.'[7]

BOSWELL. 'Pray, Sir, can you trace the cause of your antipathy to the Scotch.' JOHNSON. 'I can not, Sir.' BOSWELL. 'Old Mr Sheridan says, it was because they sold Charles the First. JOHNSON. 'Then, Sir, old Mr Sheridan has found out a very good reason.'

[No date, 1783]

Johnson's love of little children, which he discovered upon all occasions, calling them 'pretty dears', and giving them sweetmeats, was an undoubted proof of the real humanity and gentleness of his disposition.

Nor would it be just ... to omit the fondness which he showed for animals which he had taken under his protection. I never shall forget the indulgence with which he treated Hodge, his cat: for whom he himself used to go out and buy oysters, lest the servants having that trouble should take a dislike to the poor creature. I am, unluckily, one of those who have an antipathy to a cat, so that I am uneasy when in the room with one; and I own, I frequently suffered a good deal from the presence of this same Hodge. I recollect him one day scrambling up Dr Johnson's breast, apparently with much satisfaction, while my friend smiling and half-whistling, rubbed down his back, and pulled him by the tail; and when I observed he was a fine cat, saying, 'why yes, Sir, but I have had cats whom I liked better than this;' and then as if perceiving Hodge to be out of countenance, adding, 'but he is a very fine cat, a very fine cat indeed.'

This reminds me of the ludicrous account which he gave Mr Langton, of the despicable state of a young gentleman of good family. 'Sir, when I heard of him last, he was running about town shooting cats.' And then in a sort of kindly reverie, he bethought himself of his own favourite cat, and said, 'But Hodge shan't be shot; no, no, Hodge shall not be shot.'

December 1783

In the end of this year he was seized with a spasmodic asthma of such violence, that he was confined to the house in great pain, being sometimes obliged to sit all night in his chair, a recumbent posture being so hurtful to his respiration, that he could not endure lying in bed; and there came upon him at the same time that oppressive and fatal disease, a dropsy. It was a very severe winter, which probably aggravated his complaints; and the solitude in which Mr Levett and Mrs Williams had left him, rendered his life very gloomy. Mrs Desmoulins, who still lived, was herself so very ill, that she could contribute very little to his relief. He, however, had none of that unsocial shyness which we commonly see in people afflicted with sickness. He did not hide his head from the world, in solitary abstraction; he did not deny himself to the visits of his friends and acquaintances; but at all times, when he was not overcome by sleep, was ready for conversation as in his best days.

1784

Wednesday 5 May 1784

On Wednesday, 5 May, I arrived in London, and next morning had the pleasure to find Dr Johnson greatly recovered...

One morning afterwards, when I found him alone, he communicated to me, with solemn earnestness, a very remarkable circumstance which had happened in the course of his illness when he was much distressed by the dropsy. He had shut himself up, and employed a day in particular exercises of religion, – fasting, humiliation, and prayer. On a sudden he obtained extraordinary relief, for which he looked up to Heaven with grateful devotion. He made no direct inference from this fact; but from his manner of telling it, I could perceive that it appeared to him as something more than an incident in the common course of events. For my own part, I have no difficulty to avow that cast of thinking, which by many modern pretenders to wisdom, is called superstitious. But here I think even men of dry rationality may believe, that there was an intermediate interposition of divine Providence, and that 'the fervent prayer of this righteous man' availed.

Wednesday 19 May 1784

He charged Mr Langton with what he thought want of judgment upon an interesting occasion. 'When I was ill,' (said he,) 'I desired he would tell me sincerely in what he thought my life was faulty. Sir, he brought me a sheet of paper, on which he had written down several texts of Scripture, recommending Christian charity. And when I questioned him what occasion I had given for such an animadversion, all that he could say amounted to this, – that I sometimes contradicted people in conversation. Now what harm does it do to any man to be contradicted?' BOSWELL. 'I suppose he meant the manner of doing it; roughly, – and harshly.' JOHNSON. 'And who is the worse for that?' BOSWELL. 'It hurts people of weak nerves.' JOHNSON. 'I know no such weak-nerved people.' Mr Burke, to whom I related this conference, said, 'It is well, if when a man comes to die he has nothing heavier upon his conscience than having been a little rough in conversation.'

11 June 1784 [Oxford]

... I had the resolution to ask Johnson whether he thought that the roughness of his manner had been an advantage or not, and if he would not have done more good if he had been more gentle. I proceeded to answer myself thus: 'Perhaps it has been of advantage, as it has given weight to what you said: you could not, perhaps, have talked with such authority without it.' JOHNSON. 'No, Sir; I have done more good as I am. Obscenity and Impiety have always been repressed in my company.' BOSWELL. 'True, Sir; and that is more than can be said of every Bishop. Greater liberties have been taken in the presence of a Bishop, though a very good man, from his being milder, and therefore not commanding such awe. Yet, Sir, many people who might have been benefited by your conversation, have been frightened away. A worthy friend of ours [Langton] has told me, that he has often been afraid to talk to you.' JOHNSON. 'Sir, he need not have been afraid, if he had any thing rational to say. If he had not, it was better he did not talk.'

30 June 1784

I accompanied him in Sir Joshua Reynolds's coach, to the entry of Bolt-court. He asked me whether I would not go with him to his house; I declined it, from an apprehension that my spirits would sink. We bade adieu to each other affectionately in the carriage. When he had got down upon the foot-pavement, he called out, 'Fare you well;'

and without looking back, sprung away with a kind of pathetic briskness, if I may use that expression, which seemed to indicate a struggle to conceal uneasiness, and impressed me with a foreboding of our long, long separation...

Soon after this time Dr Johnson had the mortification of being informed by Mrs Thrale, that 'what she supposed he never believed', was true; namely, that she was actually going to marry Signor Piozzi, an Italian music-master. He endeavoured to prevent it; but in vain. If she would publish the whole of the correspondence that passed between Dr Johnson and her on the subject, we should have a full view of his real sentiments. As it is, our judgment must be biassed by that characteristic specimen which Sir John Hawkins has given us: 'Poor Thrale! I thought that either her virtue or her vice would have restrained her from such a marriage. She is now become a subject for her enemies to exult over; and for her friends, if she has any left, to forget, or pity.'

It must be admitted that Johnson derived a considerable portion of happiness from the comforts and elegancies which he enjoyed in Mr Thrale's family; but Mrs Thrale assures us he was indebted for these to her husband alone, who certainly respected him sincerely...

Alas! How different is this from the declarations which I have heard Mrs Thrale make in his life-time, without a single murmur against any peculiarities, or against any one circumstance which attended their intimacy.

Wednesday 3 November 1784

I unfortunately was so much indisposed during a considerable part of the year, that it was not, or at least I thought it was not, in my power to write to my illustrious friend as formerly, or without expressing such complaints as offended him. Having conjured him not to do me the injustice of charging me with affectation, I was with much regret long silent. His last letter to me then came, and affected me very tenderly:

DEAR SIR,

I HAVE this summer sometimes amended, and sometimes relapsed, but, upon the whole, have lost ground very much. My legs are extremely weak, and my breath very short, and the water is now encreasing upon me. In this uncomfortable state your letters used to relieve; what is the reason that I have them no longer? Are you sick, or are you sullen? Whatever be the reason, if it be less than necessity, drive it away; and of the short life that we have, make the best use for yourself and for your friends. * * * * * *. I am sometimes afraid that your omission to write has some real cause, and shall be glad to know that you are not sick, and that nothing ill has befallen dear Mrs Boswell, or any of your family. Lichfield, 3 November 1784. SAM JOHNSON

Yet it was not a little painful to me to find, that in a paragraph of this letter, which I have omitted, he still persevered in arraigning me as before, which was strange in him who had so much experience of what I suffered. I, however, wrote to him two as kind letters as I could; the last of which came too late to be read by him, for his illness encreased more rapidly upon him than I had apprehended; but I had the consolation of being informed that he spoke of me on his death-bed, with affection, and I look forward with humble hope of renewing our friendship in a better world.

I now relieve the readers of this Work from any farther personal notice of its authour who if he should be thought to have obtruded himself too much upon their attention, requests them to consider the peculiar plan of his biographical undertaking. Soon after Johnson's return to the metropolis, both the asthma and dropsy became more violent and distressful ... Still his love of literature did not fail.

December 1784

I trust, I shall not be accused of affectation, when I declare, that I find myself unable to express all that I felt upon the loss of such a 'Guide, Philosopher, and Friend'. I shall, therefore, not say one word of my own, but adopt those of an eminent friend, which he uttered with an abrupt felicity, superior to all studied compositions: − 'He has made a chasm, which not only nothing can fill up, but which nothing has a tendency to fill up. − Johnson is dead. − Let us go to the next best: − there is nobody; − no man can be said to put you in mind of Johnson.'

Notes

Introduction

1 On the Reid episode, see Gordon Turnbull, 'Boswell and Sympathy: the Trial and Execution of John Reid', in *New Light on Boswell*, ed. Greg Clingham (1991) pp. 104–15.

One: Beginning the Journal 1762–1763 (pp. 3–56)

1 William McQuhae, the tutor in Lord Auchinleck's household who tutored Boswell and his brothers John and David, and confidential friend, greatly encouraged and supported him; and John Johnston (of Grange), who was a dear Edinburgh university friend and a fellow hypochondriac. Boswell wrote the entire London journal with the idea that Johnston would read it, sending it to him through the post in weekly parcels, together with a letter. Boswell always knew Johnston as 'Grange', the name of his family seat.

2 Boswell very likely had an affair with Heron's wife, Jean, daughter of Lord Kames, while he stayed for several days at Kirroughtrie.

3 Lord Kames and Boswell had left Kirroughtrie together and were making their way to Kames, Kames' seat.

4 Thomas David, the younger of Boswell's two brothers.

5 Andrew Erskine, twenty-two, like Boswell a melancholic, but unlike Boswell a good poet later admired by Robert Burns, was an enthusiast of Scottish poetry. He and Boswell became collaborators in 1763 when they audaciously published their frequently nonsensical correspondence with each other. They were good but not especially intimate friends.

6 Alexander Boswell, Lord Auchinleck, an Advocate and a respected judge, as well as a classical scholar, was not a good father to his three sons, especially James, his eldest. He shared little of James's literary interests and was disdainful of his passion to mingle with the famous (chiefly literary) figures of his day. Lady Auchinleck, completely dominated by her husband, was a devout Presbyterian, though loving and gentle. In her way, her religious influence was as blighting to James as his father's chilling impatience and dogmatism.

7 West Digges was a leading actor in the Edinburgh theatre who became something of a gallant and an elegant idol for Boswell.

8 Alexander Montgomerie, Tenth Earl of Eglinton, thirty-nine at this time and an indolent bachelor, was a rake and accomplished sportsman. He was a close friend of the Duke of York, the King's brother, and intimate with John Stuart, the Third Earl of Bute, Prime Minister and a Scotsman whom the English loved to hate. When Boswell ran away to London in the spring of 1760 to escape the

oppressiveness of his father's strict hand, he was at his father's request rescued by Eglinton from a flirtation with Catholicism and the shabby London world in which he had landed. But Eglinton achieved this by introducing Boswell thoroughly into his libertine world of 'the great, the gay, and the ingenious'. It was in a sense an indoctrination from which Boswell never recovered. Boswell was now hoping that Eglinton would help him get into the Guards.

9 Both the young Duke of York and Eglinton were angry at Boswell for having indiscreetly dedicated to them his doggerel poem, *The Cub at New-Market*, that grew out of some hobnobbing he did the previous year with these men.

10 Boswell had decided that the patronage of the Duchess of Northumberland was an effectual way to obtain the Commission in the Guards he hungered for. She invited him to the occasional social gathering and did take up the matter with people of influence, but his lack of money and father's probable opposition behind his back set the seal on his failure.

11 Boswell travelled to London with an introduction to Charles Douglas, Tenth Duke of Queensberry, in his hand, hoping for his help in securing a commission in the Guards. The Duchess, Lady Catherine Hyde, was one of the most famous women of her day, friend of poets and dramatists the likes of Alexander Pope, William Congreve and John Gay. Lieutenant-General Archibald Douglas was a relative of Queensberry's, to whom Boswell had been referred.

12 The Commander-in-Chief in Great Britain and Colonel of the First Foot Guards.

13 An actress named Mrs Anne Lewis, who acted at Covent Garden.

14 After giving two guineas to Louisa and paying for a pair of lace ruffles, Boswell had almost run through the £25 his father let him have every six weeks. Until his next payment, he had to economise strictly, which included a regimen of bread and cheese.

15 They had agreed to a week's moratorium on seeing each other.

16 This is one of the early signs during this period in London of Boswell's recurring hypochondria or melancholia.

17 Boswell's father had just finished building a Palladian mansion at Auchinleck to replace the old 'castle' in which Boswell grew up and which for the rest of his life he nostalgically romanticised as part of his family history.

18 George Dempster, a genial Edinburgh friend who is thirty at this point, was a Scots lawyer who with his independent wealth became a Member of Parliament. He and Boswell always remained good friends.

19 The most celebrated actor in the eighteenth century, Garrick was one of Boswell's early heroes. Like Johnson, with whom he travelled up to London in 1737, Garrick was a native of Lichfield. He was elected to The Club in 1773.

20 The former Eva Maria Violetti.

21 *The Cub at New-Market: A Tale*, 1762.

22 He had talked himself temporarily into abandoning the Guards scheme and retreating to a legal career in Edinburgh.

23 Boswell met William Temple when they were students at Edinburgh University. Temple's fortunes had been wrecked when his father went deeply into debt and

he was obliged to go into the Church. For the rest of their lives he and Boswell were the most intimate of friends and wrote to each other voluminously. Temple, Johnston and McQuhae were the only friends to whom Boswell was willing to show his journal in the early years.

24 John Wilkes was a thirty-five-year-old political firebrand who had fallen foul of the government by publishing an essay (no 45) in his periodical *The North Briton* in which he suggested that the King had countenanced a Government lie about the recent Peace. Urbane and charming, and totally unpredictable, he became something of a hero of the masses and at times a role-model for Boswell. They became good friends.

25 Macheath is the gallant, libertine hero-highwayman in John Gay's *The Beggar's Opera*, Boswell's favourite play. Boswell habitually tried to imagine himself as Macheath.

26 From *The Beggar's Opera*.

27 In the *Life of Johnson*, Boswell recalled, 'In progress of time, when my mind was, as it were, *strongly impregnated with the Johnsonian æther*, I could with much more facility and exactness carry in my memory and commit to paper the exuberant variety of his wisdom and wit' (1 July 1763).

28 Robert Levet was, in Johnson's words, 'an excellent practiser' of medicine whom Johnson took off the streets and made a member of his household. Johnson wrote one of his most moving poems about Levet.

29 With his plans for the Guards having come to nothing, Boswell by this time had agreed with his father that if he were allowed to study law at Utrecht for a year, to be followed by a tour of several months through Germany and Switzerland – his father was against a visit to Italy – he would return to Edinburgh and settle down to practise law as an Advocate.

Two: Travels 1763–1766 (pp. 57–123)

1 The Rev Robert Brown, British Agent in Utrecht, minister of the English Presbyterian Church; Belle de Zuylen, better known in these pages as Zélide.

2 The translations of the French themes are taken from the Yale edition, *Boswell in Holland*.

3 Boswell's method of journalising has changed. In London he wrote mostly from memory whereas increasingly now he writes memoranda to himself of the previous day's events, later turning them into journal entries.

4 She was forty-three.

5 Almost certainly Jean Home, the daughter of Henry Home, Lord Kames, the eminent author and judge.

6 Whom Rousseau had asked to take Boswell under his wing.

7 John Wilkes was prudently cooling his heels in Italy as he definitely was not the Government's favourite politician.

8 Horace, *Odes*, III. xxvi. 2.

9 Because the roads were bad and there was the danger of bandits along the coastal route to France, Boswell decided to sail instead.

10 Paoli gave this dog, named Jachone, as a goodbye present to Boswell, thus providing some of the more bathetic moments in these earlier stages of his return.

11 Boswell later crossed out passages describing his persecution of the dog.

12 Boswell was suffering from an ingrown toenail aggravated by his trek through Corsica in boots that were too small for him.

13 These were notices that Boswell himself had placed in the papers.

14 Pitt resigned on 5 October 1761 because his Cabinet had not backed his decision to declare war against Spain.

Three: Settling Down 1766–1769 (pp. 124–153)

1 A spa about a day's journey from Auchinleck in Dumfriesshire.

2 Mrs Dodds, probably the wife or daughter of some small Scottish laird, was separated from her abusive husband who was then living with another woman. She was clearly a woman of ill-breeding.

3 Temple had taken his orders in the church and accepted a small living in Mamhead, Devon.

4 Shortly after Boswell wrote this letter, he broke off the affair.

5 Elizabeth Diana Bosville, the beautiful daughter of his friend Godfrey Bosville in Yorkshire, with whom Boswell developed a very close friendship. She eventually married Sir Alexander Macdonald of Skye, who re-enters the picture unflatteringly when Boswell visits Skye with Dr Johnson in 1773.

6 Catherine Blair.

7 Soon after this Catherine Blair decided to marry someone else, the news of which Boswell took in his stride.

8 This child by Mrs Dodds is Boswell's second illegitimate offspring. The first was a son, Charles, with Peggy Doig in Edinburgh, born soon after Boswell's arrival in London in 1762. It died.

9 An advocate is a barrister who appears in court; an agent is a 'writer' or solicitor who manages cases but does not appear in court.

10 Holy Trinity Church, Shakespeare's burial place, where Arne's oratorio, Judith, was being performed.

Four: Early Marriage Years 1770–1774 (pp. 154–199)

1 The public gallows in Edinburgh were in the Grassmarket at the foot of the West Bow.

2 This could be the lingering malaria which he contracted in Corsica and for which he had taken treatment over the years.

3 His father's attitude towards his marriage being what it was, Margaret never accompanied Boswell on his visits to Auchinleck.

4 Idler, No 49.

5 Hastie, a Scottish schoolmaster, was removed from his job for caning his pupils too severely. The Court of Session restored him, but the teacher's enemies

appealed the case to the House of Lords. Boswell, who was his counsel in Edinburgh, was in London to plead on his behalf before the House of Lords.

6 General James Edward Oglethorpe, the founder of the colony of Georgia in 1732. Boswell had known and liked him since 1768.

7 He was writing from memory when composing the *Life of Johnson*, perhaps fifteen years after the event.

8 Boswell had avoided Wilkes in 1768 and 1769. Wilkes had spent some time in gaol again but since been elected Alderman of London and now Sheriff of the city.

9 Hester Lynch Thrale was one of Johnson's closest confidantes. She kept her own collection of Johnson anecdotes and conversation, and eventually published them in her *Anecdotes of the Late Samuel Johnson* (1786) that, with its inaccuracies and distortions, infuriated Boswell and other Johnsonians. It was also good enough to frustrate Boswell. By the time of the Hebridean tour, she had already become formidable competition for him in Johnson's affections.

10 Beauclerk was the great-grandson of Charles II and Nell Gwyn – in Boswell's words, 'a man of wit, literature and fashion in distinguished degree'.

11 The scholarly, tall, sober Bennet Langton was one of 'the young dogs of this age' whom Johnson loved. He and Boswell became very close.

12 Made famous, of course, by the witches in *Macbeth*.

13 Johnson had reluctantly accepted the suggestion that Philip Stanhope, Fourth Earl of Chesterfield, be approached to be the patron of the *Dictionary*, but Chesterfield did little or nothing to help during the years Johnson struggled to complete the massive project.

14 Boswell's Bohemian servant.

15 They were on their way to Armadale, to be guests of Sir Alexander and Lady Macdonald. She was the former Elizabeth Diana Bosville, a beauty, whom Boswell briefly had considered marrying. Even in London he had found her fairly untalkative; and after living in Skye apparently she became even more so.

16 Boswell's whole account of their reception by Sir Alexander and Lady Macdonald is extremely negative. He deleted much of it for the first edition of the *Tour* but what was left still enraged Macdonald and impelled him eventually to write what Boswell construed as a challenge to a duel. The duel was avoided but the perceived threat caused Boswell many a sleepless night.

17 Boswell heavily inked out the rest of this paragraph.

18 Donald Maclean, Laird of Coll, whom Boswell called 'young Coll'; they had just met him at Talisker. Coll invited them to his island where later Boswell and Johnson, stranded by poor weather, spent more days than they bargained for.

19 Maclean, chief of the clan, at whose house they stayed on Inchkenneth.

20 'The venerable seat of ancient sanctity', where St Columba in 563 founded a monastery, a base for the eventual conversion to Christianity of all of Scotland.

21 From Thomas Parnell's 'Hymn to Contentment'.

22 Samuel Ogden, *Sermons on Prayer*.

23 Pringle had strongly liberal religious views.

24 *Journey to the Western Isles* (1775).

25 Johnson published his *Journey* in January 1775. In his first paragraph, Johnson praised Boswell's companionship, 'whose acuteness would help my inquiry, and whose gaiety of conversation and civility of manners are sufficient to counteract the inconveniencies of travel'.

26 John Reid had several years earlier been acquitted of sheep-stealing, with Boswell's help, but now he was before the Court again, once more accused of stealing sheep. Boswell threw himself with excessive zeal into defending Reid. He lost but won deserved praise for his efforts. His reckless post-trial efforts, however, to save Reid from execution ended up alienating a number of the judges and generally damaging his reputation as an Advocate.

27 Another sheep-stealer executed in the Grassmarket a year earlier.

Five: Boswellian Extremes 1775–1778 (pp. 200–234)

1 Thomas Percy was famous for his *Reliques of English Poetry* (1765). He became Bishop of Dromore in 1782.

2 Margaret Stuart ('Peggie' Cunynghame), wife of Lt. Col. James Archibald Stuart, the Earl of Bute's second son. She was a good friend of Margaret Boswell's and became Boswell's confidante during his long visits to London over the years.

3 On a visit to Temple in Devon in the spring, Boswell had ceremoniously sworn under a yew tree that he would moderate his intake of alcohol.

4 Boswell's third child and first son, Alexander, was born on 9 October.

5 Boswell had recently begun to use Greek letters and other symbols as a shorthand to conceal meaning in his entries, chiefly but not exclusively from Margaret.

6 Although he could ill afford it, Boswell had purchased this estate in 1767.

7 This was Boswell's first meeting with the well-known poetess Anna Seward – 'the swan of Lichfield'.

8 From this point on Margaret's tuberculosis continues to worsen.

9 Effie was his second daughter and Sandy his eldest son Alexander.

10 Boswell's frail second son, David, was born on 15 November 1776.

11 Johnson well knew that Mrs Catherine Macaulay disliked him for, as she thought, insulting her Whiggishness.

Six: In the Middle of Life's Journey 1779–1782 (pp. 235–259)

1 By dining in the Temple commons a prescribed number of days in each of twelve terms, Boswell planned to qualify for the London bar as a barrister. He did not finish his twelve terms until 9 February 1786.

2 For some time Boswell has been in great pain from an inflamed toe.

3 Boswell feared that as his father was no longer making an appearance on the High Court of Justiciary owing to ill health, people were less inclined to call on him for his legal services.

4 For family and financial reasons, Boswell grudgingly decided against his

springtime visit to London. Ever since deciding this early in the year, he suffered from stronger than usual attacks of hypochondria.

5 Lady Auchinleck, with whom Boswell was carrying on constant warfare and whom he deprecatingly called the 'noverca', is on the receiving end of a great deal of hostility in the journal. He was convinced that she was trying to drive his father away from him.

6 Boswell's middle brother, John, suffered acutely from mental illness for much of his life. One of the more tender themes in Boswell's life is how he cared for his brother and attempted to make life bearable for him, although John proved to be a cross that the whole family had to bear.

7 David Boswell had recently returned after twelve years in Valencia.

8 'Ah, how all that reminds me that I no longer am anything.'

9 It is not possible to say to what sexual diversion Boswell refers as someone has ripped out two pages of the journal for 18 February.

10 John Stobie, clerk to Lord Auchinleck, a little man whose officiousness and dourness Boswell despised.

Seven: Lairdship and Literature 1782–1785 (pp. 260–283)

1 A biography of Kames was one of Boswell's long-term literary projects. This is the first of a series of interviews he had with Kames just before his death.

2 Fanny Burney's novel.

3 Boswell had 'tasted her delicate lips'.

4 In 1777 Boswell had agreed with his fellow proprietors of the London Magazine to write a series of monthly essays for the magazine. He wrote seventy.

5 The old site of the castle, which teemed with sacred associations of family and country for Boswell.

6 Logie remains unidentified.

7 Boswell's Letter to the People of Scotland on the State of the Nation had been published the previous December, 'to endeavour to rouse a spirit for property and the Constitution in opposition to the East India Bill' (Journal, Friday 26 December). It was well received, even eliciting a letter of praise from William Pitt.

8 Passion Week.

9 Johnson did burn them.

10 His Hypochondriack essays.

11 The Tour to the Hebrides was published on Saturday 1 October 1785.

12 Boswell had spent seven months in London.

Eight: Johnsonianissimus 1786–1789 (pp. 284–311)

1 Lord Thurlow.

2 Hester Lynch [Thrale] Piozzi had just published her Anecdotes of the Late Samuel Johnson, LL.D. Malone thought it was 'entertaining' but both he and Boswell were scandalised by its distortions of the truth.

3 Boswell had included in his Tour to the Hebrides Hester Thrale's remark that she

could not get through Elizabeth Montagu's *Essay on Shakespeare*. In this entry the reader may wish to consult the corresponding notes in Peter S. Baker, *et al.*, *The Correspondence of James Boswell with David Garrick, Edmund Burke, and Edmond Malone* (New Haven, 1986).

4 The dark house Boswell had let for himself and his family.

5 Because of anti-semitism in Valencia, where he lived for twelve years, David had taken to calling himself Thomas David, hence T. D.

6 A village south of London popular among Gypsies.

7 Garforth, Satterthwaite and Lowther, MPs, also were under Lonsdale's thumb and shared Boswell's misgivings about their dependence on the 'Great Man'.

8 The founder of Pennsylvania who later offered to employ Boswell as his Secretary if he became Ambassador to America.

9 Lonsdale's seat, just south of Penrith.

10 Member of the Carlisle Common Council.

11 Percy's *Reliques of Ancient English Poetry* was published in three volumes in 1765, the same year he was elected to The Club. He was measured and objective, and very concerned about his own reputation and what Boswell might say about him in the *Life of Johnson*. His relations with Boswell cooled after publication.

Nine: Triumph and Despair 1790–1795 (pp. 312–330)

1 Scott was a good friend of Johnson's and one of his executors.

2 By going 'three times' in a day to a 'stranger' for sex, he had contracted another attack of gonorrhoea.

3 *The Yale Edition of the Works of Samuel Johnson*, xiv, pp. 57–58.

4 Boswell had recklessly gone into debt in October 1790 by purchasing Knockroon, an estate once part of Auchinleck, as patrimony for his son James. He paid more than it was worth in order to restore it to his family's estate.

5 'Unless the vessel is clean, whatever you put in turns sour' (Horace, *Epistles*, I, ii. 54, translated by H. R. Fairclough, Loeb ed.).

6 Sir Joshua Reynolds died on 23 February 1792.

7 In 1792 Boswell had taken up the sensational case of the four men and one woman, Mary Broad, the wife of one of the men, who had escaped from Botany Bay, Australia, after a ten-week journey of 3,000 miles to Timor in a small boat with one sail and six oars. In Timor, however, they were handed over to the authorities and brought back to England where they stood trial. Their case was the talk of the town, Boswell attempting to influence the authorities to be lenient towards them. Perhaps as a result, Mary Broad was pardoned. The four men remained in Newgate, though they too were released in October 1793.

8 Properties near Auchinleck.

An Account of Corsica (pp. 333–352)

1 Pasquale Paoli, the Corsican patriot and leader in the island's struggle for independence.

2 'Together through dark woods and winding ways / They walk, nor on their hearts suspicion preys' (*Orlando Furioso*, i. 22).

3 'Having nothing, and yet possessing all things' (II Corinthians 6.10).

4 'The nights and banquets of the gods' (Horace, *Satires*, II. vi. 65).

5 'The love of country will prevail, and the overwhelming desire for praise' (*Aeneid*, vi. 823).

6 David Garrick wrote the words of this song, and William Boyce the music.

7 'All is vanity'.

8 Boswell got this wrong: La Rochefoucauld's *Maxims* do not contain this statement.

9 *Rambler*, no. 60.

10 *Idler*, no. 70.

11 This account has not survived.

12 Boswell quoted the entire letter in the *Life of Johnson* under 14 January 1766.

The Hypochondriack (pp. 355–371)

1 Probably Bennet Langton, fellow member of The Club.

2 Boswell's rendering of the opening lines of James Thomson's *Castle of Indolence*.

3 Boswell copied out the above passage from an article for the *Publick Advertiser* on 25 April 1768.

The Life of Samuel Johnson, LL.D. (pp. 375–411)

1 Boswell was about to set off on his travels to Holland, Germany, Switzerland, Italy, Corsica and France.

2 Hester Thrale, wife of the brewer Henry Thrale, became Boswell's chief rival as a recorder and publisher of Johnson's conversation. They owned a large house in Streatham where they welcomed Johnson and other literati for twenty years. Johnson even had his own room there.

3 Giuseppe Baretti was an Italian man of letters who lived in London. He was a member of Johnson's circle and for a time lived in the Thrale household at Streatham tutoring the children. Boswell, who had met him in Venice in 1765, disliked him. Baretti was presently on trial for stabbing a bully on the street who one night attacked him.

4 Samuel Foote, the playwright, who had lost a leg.

5 The eminent Scot Hugh Hume, Third Earl of Marchmont, was almost legendary in Boswell's mind because of his close friendship with Alexander Pope and his political fame as Tory leader of the Opposition during Robert Walpole's administration as Prime Minister. Boswell regarded this lengthy interview with Marchmont as a memorable *coup*. In it he suggested that Marchmont might be of use to Dr Johnson who was then writing his 'Life of Pope'.

6 Robert Levet, an indigent surgeon, was a member of Johnson's household.

7 Johnson's definition of oats was, 'A grain, which in England is generally given to horses, but in Scotland supports the people'.

The Yale Editions of the
Private Papers of James Boswell

Research Editions

Catalogue

Catalogue of the Papers of James Boswell at Yale University, by Marion S. Pottle, Claude Colleer Abbott and Frederick A. Pottle, 3 Vols. (Edinburgh: Edinburgh University Press; New Haven: Yale University Press, 1993).

Correspondence

VOLUME 1 *The Correspondence of James Boswell and John Johnston of Grange*, edited by Ralph S. Walker (London: Heinemann; New York: McGraw Hill, 1966).

VOLUME 2 *The Correspondence and Other Papers of James Boswell Relating to the Making of the "Life of Johnson*,*"* edited by Marshall Waingrow (London: Heinemann; New York: McGraw Hill, 1969; 2nd edition, corrected and enlarged, Edinburgh: Edinburgh University Press; New Haven: Yale University Press, 2001).

VOLUME 3 *The Correspondence of James Boswell with Certain Members of the Club*, edited by Charles N. Fifer (London: Heinemann; New York: McGraw Hill, 1976).

VOLUME 4 *The Correspondence of James Boswell with David Garrick, Edmund Burke, and Edmond Malone*, edited by Peter S. Baker, Thomas W. Copeland, George M. Kahrl, Rachel McClellan, and James Osborn with the assistance of Robert Mankin and Mark Wollaeger (London: Heinemann; New York: McGraw Hill, 1986).

VOLUME 5 *The General Correspondence of James Boswell 1766–1769*, Vol. 1: 1766–1767, edited by Richard C. Cole with Peter S. Baker and Rachel McClellan, and with the assistance of James J. Caudle (Edinburgh: Edinburgh University Press; New Haven: Yale University Press, 1993).

VOLUME 6 *The Correspondence of James Boswell and William Johnson Temple, 1756–1795*, Vol. 1: 1756–1777, edited by Thomas Crawford (Edinburgh: Edinburgh University Press; New Haven: Yale University Press, 1997).

VOLUME 7 *The General Correspondence of James Boswell 1766–1769*, Vol. 2: 1768–1769, edited by Richard C. Cole, with Peter S. Baker and Rachel McClellan, and with the assistance of James J. Caudle (Edinburgh: Edinburgh University Press; New Haven: Yale University Press, 1997).

VOLUME 8 *The Correspondence of James Boswell with James Bruce and Andrew Gibb, Overseers of the Auchinleck Estate*, edited by Nellie Pottle Hankins and John Strawhorn (Edinburgh: Edinburgh University Press; New Haven: Yale University Press, 1998).

Life of Johnson

Volume 1 *Boswell's Life of Johnson: An Edition of the Original Manuscript, in Four Volumes*, Vol. 1: 1709–1765, edited by Marshall Waingrow (Edinburgh: Edinburgh University Press; New Haven: Yale University Press, 1994).

Volume 2 *Boswell's Life of Johnson: An Edition of the Original Manuscript, in Four Volumes*, Vol. 2: 1766–1776, edited by Bruce Redford, with Elizabeth Goldring (Edinburgh: Edinburgh University Press; New Haven: Yale University Press, 1998).

Trade Editions

Boswell's London Journal 1762–1763 edited by Frederick A. Pottle (New York: McGraw Hill; London: Heinemann 1950, 1963; Edinburgh: Edinburgh University Press 1991; New Haven: Yale University Press 1992).

Boswell in Holland, 1763–1764 edited by Frederick A. Pottle (New York: McGraw Hill; London: Heinemann 1952).

Portraits, by Sir Joshua Reynolds, edited by Frederick W. Hilles (New York: McGraw Hill; London: Heinemann 1952).

Boswell on the Grand Tour: Germany and Swithzerland, 1764, edited by Frederick A. Pottle (New York: McGraw Hill; London: Heinemann 1953).

Boswell on the Grand Tour: Italy, Corsica, and France, 1765–1766, edited by Frank Brady and Frederick A. Pottle (New York: McGraw Hill; London: Heinemann 1955).

Boswell in Search of a Wife, 1766–1769, edited by Frank Brady and Frederick A. Pottle (New York: McGraw Hill; London: Heinemann 1956).

Boswell for the Defence, 1769–1774, edited by William K. Wimsatt, Jr and Frederick A. Pottle (New York: McGraw Hill; London: Heinemann 1959).

Boswell's Journal of a Tour to the Hebrides with Samuel Johnson, LL.D., 1773, edited by Frederick A. Pottle and Charles H. Bennett (New York: McGraw Hill; London: Heinemann 1961).

Boswell: The Ominous Years, 1774–1776, edited by Charles Ryskamp and Frederick A. Pottle (New York: McGraw Hill; London: Heinemann 1963).

Boswell in Extremes, 1776–1778, edited by Charles McC. Weis and Frederick A. Pottle (New York: McGraw Hill; London: Heinemann 1970).

Boswell, Laird of Auchinleck, 1778–1782, edited by Joseph W. Reed and Frederick A. Pottle (New York: McGraw Hill; London: Heinemann 1977; Edinburgh: Edinburgh University Press; New Haven: Yale University Press 1993).

Boswell: The Applause of the Jury, 1782–1785, edited by Irma S. Lustig and Frederick A. Pottle (New York: McGraw Hill; London: Heinemann 1981).

Boswell: The English Experiment 1785–1789, edited by Irma S. Lustig and Frederick A. Pottle (New York: McGraw Hill 1986).

Boswell: The Great Biographer 1789–1795, edited by Marlies K. Danziger and Frank Brady (New York: McGraw Hill 1989).